ALTAR, CROSS, AND COMMUNITY

ALTAR, CROSS, AND COMMUNITY

BY

W. F. LOFTHOUSE, M.A.

Tutor in Old Testament Languages and Literature and in Philosophy, Handsworth College.
Author of 'Ethics and Atonement.'

WIPF & STOCK · Eugene, Oregon

Wipf and Stock Publishers
199 W 8th Ave, Suite 3
Eugene, OR 97401

Altar, Cross, and Community
By Lofthouse, W. F.
Copyright©1921 Methodist Publishing - Epworth Press
ISBN 13: 978-1-5326-3171-9
Publication date 4/25/2017
Previously published by Epworth Press, 1921

CVI OLIM
HVIVS OPVSCVLI
INITIA PLACVERVNT
EI NON OMNINO ABREPTAE
CONFECTVM PLACEAT

PREFACE

SOME years ago, in a volume called *Ethics and Atonement*, I endeavoured to show that the object of the Atonement was ethical; that is, that it was to enable us, in Biblical language, to 'do righteousness,' and that such righteousness was not fulfilled simply by actions of a certain kind, but by the maintenance of certain personal relations. In a second book, *Ethics and the Family*, I argued that the type of the society in which these relations are adequately maintained is to be found in the family, the society of husband and wife, parents and children, brothers and sisters; and I urged that the universal existence of the family, though in diverse forms, showed that these relations are in the true sense of the word natural to mankind.

In these lectures I take up what has long seemed to me a subject connected with both these claims. The rite of sacrifice is almost as widespread as the institution of the family, and I have here given reasons for holding that just as the family, at its best, furnishes the type of moral intercourse between persons, in the same way sacrifice, rightly understood, furnishes the type of the reconciliation by which these relations are made possible; a reconciliation which is the same in principle when both parties are human and when one is divine.

The book does not claim to be a treatise on the Atonement. At most, it considers an aspect of the doctrine which no treatise on the Atonement can afford to neglect; the less so because, through the whole history of Christian theology, sacrifice and atonement, the altar and the cross, have been so closely linked together.

The object of the founder of these lectures was a discussion of some vital religious truth which should be of special use to candidates for ordination in the Wesleyan Methodist Church; and although, owing to the business of the Wesleyan Conference, few candidates are now able to hear the lectures, I have ventured to keep in view the needs, as I understand them, of those for whom the foundation was originally designed, alike in my selection of references and the extent of the familiarity with the vaious topics here treated which I have assumed. My most daring hope would be that those who carry to the community the message of reconciliation, without which no community can live a worthy or tolerable life, should find in these pages some words which will illumine their heavenly vocation.

I express my warm thanks to my friends, the Rev. W. F. Howard, M.A., B.D., who has read through the MS. and given me valuable suggestions ; the Rev. C. H. Rose, B.A., who has gone through the proofs ; and the Rev. A. B. Bateman, who has compiled the indices.

HANDSWORTH COLLEGE,
June, 1921.

CONTENTS

CHAP.		PAGE
I.	CULT AND SPIRIT	11
II.	THE CHILDHOOD OF SACRIFICE	32
III.	INDIA AND GREECE	58
IV.	THE MYSTERIES	81
V.	THE HEBREW SACRIFICES	95
VI.	THE REACTION AGAINST SACRIFICE	125
VII.	JESUS	154
VIII.	THE BEGINNINGS OF THEOLOGY	183
IX.	THE SACRIFICIAL DEATH OF CHRIST	210
X.	THE EUCHARIST AND THE MASS	244
XI.	FAITH AND FORGIVENESS	264
XII.	SACRIFICE AND RECONCILIATION	286
	NOTE ON PRIESTHOOD	307

ALTAR, CROSS, AND COMMUNITY

I

CULT AND SPIRIT

ONE of the striking features of the intellectual life of to-day is its interest in comparative religion. At the moment when ethnic customs and religious practices and beliefs are dying out, touched by the desolating hand of what passes for civilization, we commence to attend to what will soon have passed beyond the reach of all investigation. Two generations ago, when the process of decay and degradation had already begun, this interest was unknown. The pioneers of commerce, searching for new markets in virgin lands, or new commodities in markets grown old, thought of the natives only as so much material to be exploited, or, where intractable, destroyed. To the religious world 'the heathen in his blindness' was simply a strange being out of whose mind error was to be cleansed as quickly as possible to make room for saving truth. Weird and gruesome tales of savage life were repeated; every one read or thought himself familiar with Robinson Crusoe and his simple islanders who used to ascend the top of their mountain and say 'Oh' to their unknown deity at its summit; and the early missionaries, among the most heroic of mortals, returned from their fields and told of cannibal practices, hairbreadth escapes, and unintelligible customs happily disappearing before the grave and sensible manners of middle-class England. That there could be any value, scientific or practical, in the customs themselves was wholly unsuspected. The few works that appeared on what would now be called ethnology were, save by a very few, unread.

The change came with the application of the conception of evolution to human life and history. Darwin bade the physiologist consider the ape, or rather the ape-like ancestor of man; but the study of human institutions and beliefs soon showed itself at once more fascinating, more productive, and more workable to the majority of intelligent people. Herbert Spencer, whose work, it must not be forgotten, was parallel to Darwin's rather than dependent on it, led the way with the new science, if science it could be called, of sociology. Ten years later, in 1870, as far as Englishmen were concerned, E. B. Tylor put the new studies, so to speak, on their feet with his work on Anthropology.

Tylor's interest was encyclopaedic. He paid as much attention to the development of bows and arrows, and of looms and cooking utensils, as to the gradual changes of human ideas about kings and gods, and the effect of these changes on the outward face of society. But the notion of the unity of the race, its development at once continuous and almost infinitely various, and the importance of every stage in that development, gained ground with surprising rapidity, until two insistent questions came very widely to be put: Can we understand the higher without a careful study of the lower? and, Is the higher, as we call it, anything else than simply the later? Can it claim any reverence which we deny to the earlier?

It is easy to see how startling the answers to such questions might be directly they were applied to religion. Such an application was first made, in this country, by Sir J. G. Frazer, in his epoch-making work, *The Golden Bough*. Appearing in 1890, in a modest couple of volumes, expanded in subsequent editions to more than a dozen, it used a mass of hitherto neglected material in order to trace, in the religions of every continent and almost of every country and community, the efficacy of the practice of killing and eating the god, and the magical nature and origin of rites supposed to be religious. The immense labours of the veteran anthropologist in the intervening thirty years, and the unflagging industry of a host of travellers and investigators whose accounts of uncivilized and semi-civilized tribes are piling up material faster than it can be examined and arranged, have exercised a profound influence on that world which is neither scientific nor religious, but believes that science and religion, though moving along different lines, can never be wholly sundered.

CULT AND SPIRIT

Religion would seem to stand on much firmer ground now that it is seen to occupy a universal and commanding position in human life. Christianity, however, might appear to have less cause for gratitude, when a parallel or a prototype of the Eucharist itself is found in some repulsive rite practised by naked savages in the Australian bush.

For all the massiveness of Frazer's work, his conclusions have never been regarded as beyond the reach of criticism. The territory of religious anthropology knows no despots, and though the existent material is now enough to stock a capacious library, a student who has not had the advantage of devoting to it the whole of a long life need not fear, with due caution and what the Greeks would call $αἰδώς$, to enter these solemn 'woods of Westermain.' An honoured and lamented predecessor of mine in this lectureship, though he had made a European reputation by contributions of permanent value to another subject, felt himself fully justified in devoting to these questions a portion of his already overcrowded hours. He, indeed, had the genius to make out of a $πάρεργον$ what others could with difficulty accomplish through the leisure of specialized study. To such genius I can lay no claim. I can only admire it from afar. But no more than others whose work is similar to mine can I avoid consideration of the larger problems involved in the study of the Old Testament, or an attempt to share with others whatever guidance I may believe myself to have found.

Frazer's early work fixed attention on sacrifice. That sacrifice, it is true, was not the killing of a victim to offer to the god, but the killing of the god himself. Whether this curious rite was the origin of all sacrifice, and therefore, perhaps, of all ceremonial approach of man to God, cannot be said to be established, but it has given fresh emphasis to the fact that in all religion—that is, in all non-Christian religion—sacrifice is central; it is not a single rite, one of many; it is as central as it is practically universal, gathering around it taboos, methods of securing holiness, priestly powers and limitations, magical practices, and the bonds of mystical confraternities. It is found in every country and every faith. It links the most distant peoples together with strange similarities in the rites it imposes—North American Indians and classical Greeks, Kaffirs and Hebrews, primitive corn-spirit worshippers and European peasants. It is as universal in Hinduism to-day as in the Brahmanism—in many respects so different—from which Hinduism sprang, alike in the stately temples of Benares and in the outcaste villages of the Deccan. Even in Buddhism, as now practised, in spite of the negative attitude of its founder, sacrifices of a kind are regularly offered, however subordinate the rôle they fill.

For nearly two thousand years the Jews, banished from the home and centre of their religion, have offered no sacrifices; but their ancient law is unchanged. At every celebration of the Passover the pious Jew whispers, 'Next year at Jerusalem'; and if the recent settlement of Palestine should have the consequences hoped for by every Zionist, the sacrifices at the Holy Place may be restored within the experience of the present generation. Islam, borrowing so many of its beliefs from the religions which it cursed, naturally took no account of the sacrifices which had long since passed away; heathen offerings and heathen beliefs it professed to repudiate altogether; but the ceremonial at Mecca during the services conducted by or on behalf of the pilgrims there culminates on the 'Day of Sacrifice,' as it is called, when the pilgrim places his victim—a sheep or camel or some other animal—facing the Kaaba, and pierces its throat with the cry 'God is great.'[1]

Evidently a ceremony so universal must have answered a deep-seated need. It meets us wherever we turn. In some form or other it is always there already. It must have sprung up spontaneously. Individual rites of sacrifice may be watched coming into recognition; sacrifice itself never. It is not due to any teacher or group of teachers. Teachers have suggested, controlled, and developed its rites; they have also, as we shall see, protested against it in vigorous and uncompromising language. It persists, like the family, through all the changes and shocks of history. If anything could have killed it, it would have been killed long ago. Whatever the stage of tribal or racial development, whatever the conception of the god,

[1] S. M. Zwemer, *Arabia, the Cradle of Islam*, ch. iii. Other rites are familiar to students of Islam which preserve sacrificial ideas that are purely pagan.

CULT AND SPIRIT

celestial, demoniac, or diabolical, whatever the place filled by religion in the life of the community, the altar and the offering will be found hard by the shrine.

What is the need which is thus met? It must be real and permanent, even though often dimly felt; and it would appear that the consciousness of a need so widespread and strong must have been something more than dim. Hitherto students of comparative religion have been more interested in cataloguing the different kinds of sacrificial rite than in asking what caused the rite to come into existence at all. Full justice has been done to the extraordinary minuteness and, as we can hardly help feeling it, the amazing capriciousness of the ritual acts; and it has often been deemed sufficient, at the end, to explain them as so many gifts or bribes or magical performances. Whether such simplicity as this can possibly be held to correspond to the diversity of the acts which have resulted from it we shall have to inquire later. Meanwhile sacrifice, as we have said, is there; it has given, and still gives, something to the vast majority of mankind which they can get in no other way, and which they will not do without.

To-day, however, among the more civilized and, as we call them, Christian nations of the West, the need is apparently no longer felt. In Europe, North America, Australia, and wherever the white races have expelled the coloured, sacrifice is no more. The Christian builds no altar and brings no victim. Where the influence of Western society is dominant, as in the mongrel life of South Africa, even apart from the missionaries, sacrifice begins to disappear. Among the Moslems also, wherever Islam is more than a veneer, it is quite subordinate, save on one great day in the Moslem year; and we can hardly deny that the Moslem performance is a survival of the old Arabian paganism, like the veneration of the rude black stone built into the wall of the Kaaba itself.

Is, then, the need no longer felt, or has it been supplied in some other way? Is it related to certain states of society which Christianity and Islam have left behind, or have those two religions their own way of circumventing it? And what shall we say of Judaism? Have the Jews lost by its absence in the centuries that have passed since the destruction of the Temple, or have they found some

16 ALTAR, CROSS, AND COMMUNITY

substitute for it in the life that was forced on them by their oppressors?

We must not forget, however, that there is really no such clear line to be drawn between sacrifice and non-sacrifice. If there were, it would be hard to decide on which side of the line to place Christianity; for though Christianity has abolished the practice, it has preserved the conception. At the centre alike of its theology and its popular religious ideas is the cross, and the great act upon the cross is spoken of as the world's sacrifice; Christ is the sacrificial victim for the sins of the world. The Christian is taught that he comes to God thereby, just as the pagan or Jew learns that he comes to God by the blood of bulls or goats. The Christian's hope of salvation rests in the blood shed in that sacrifice, and the spot around which his holiest memories of worship gather he has almost in every age called an altar. If the rite has ceased, the Christian has done his best to perpetuate it in his thought. To all save the more spiritual, a doctrine apart from its embodiment in some rite is cold and lifeless. Pagan sacrifice involves for the most part but little doctrine; the rite is everything; and in many instances the rite exercises an immense emotional appeal on the spectators. For the Christian Church that appeal has been found in the Mass, the central act of worship for both Latin and Greek faiths. Indeed, it is not too much to say that sacrifice has been much more prominent in Christianity than in many forms of heathenism; for while, in the latter, sacrifice is often but one means of approach to God, though the most important, in Catholic, as opposed at least to Protestant Christianity, it is central for all life and redemption; and for the same reason it is actually more prominent in Christianity than in Judaism.

Yet a certain fundamental difference between Christianity and all other religions remains. It has often been said by theologians that in Christianity the sacrifices, as types, are fulfilled, and rendered needless. The ancient sacrifices, at least of the Jews, were held to point forward, like the prophecies, to Christ. But, on reflection, this seems to imply the strange view that all the world was given something imperfect in order that, at a given moment, the perfect might be recognized. But even apart from the doubtful value of giving to one age the less worthy in order

CULT AND SPIRIT

that another might receive the more worthy when it was offered, it may be replied that the possession of the imperfect does not lead to the recognition of the perfect. It may be that, when the new wine is presented to a man, he remarks that the old is better. The most that can be said is that the knowledge and practice of the sacrificial rites prepared men for teaching about Christ's death which otherwise would have been unintelligible to them. The sacrifices were not provided as a proof of Christianity; they were a *preparatio evangelica*.

Even such a fulfilment as this, however, is not easy to express in terms either of history or experience. Wherever Christ is accepted, the need for the pagan sacrifices disappears or is satisfied in a new way. The Jews, however, to whom in the Mosaic Law were given the clearest ' types,' recognize no fulfilment of them in the cross. Nor, again, is the teaching to which these ' types ' were said to point, and by which they were superseded, at all clear. That Christ died for our sins is universally believed; how His death affected our sins or ourselves has never been stated with authority or precision. It is a commonplace with regard to religious rites in general that the rite itself is one and important; the explanations of it are various and felt to be comparatively unimportant. The worshipper may even be told that it does not matter what he believes or thinks so long as he performs the correct ritual. Traces of this attitude of mind can be found in the discipline of the Christian Church. Complaints are often heard that orthodoxy lays an impossible burden on men's reasons or consciences. Those who make these complaints forget how many matters the Church has left undecided. This is particularly true as regards the doctrine of the cross. Particular religious communities have emphasized, and even regarded as all-important, some one explanation; but this cannot be said of the Church as a whole. In what did the sacrificial character of the death of Christ consist? To propitiate God? To show God's love? To pay the necessary price of sin? To set an example of renunciation to mankind? And, in any case, how did it take away sin?

This diversity of views, however, only shows for Christianity what the divergence of sacrificial ritual proves for religion as a whole. There is something within it all which answers some deep-seated need. Men cannot give up the thing. They cannot get away from religion, nor, in religion, from sacrifice. The Christian cannot get away from the cross, however greatly it perplexes him. In the perpetuation of all religious belief and practice the prestige of orthodoxy doubtless counts for a great deal. So does that religious conservatism which is familiar among pagans and Christians alike. All habits tend to fix themselves, most of all habits which are so rich in valued associations as those of religion. But this does not explain everything. Habits must serve a useful end, or nature, in her love of economy, will eliminate them in the long run. To discover the end of sacrifice would lead us a long way to the centre of religion. We see the altar; who is the unknown God who first commanded its erection? We see the rite; what mysterious longings prompted its elaboration?

But we must not overstate the case. To many people sacrifice, so far from being the centre of religion, is a stumbling-block. As we shall see later, it has been, in the history of religious thought, the object of a whole series of resolute attacks. Even if these have been in the main unsuccessful, they are significant. At the present day it must be confessed that to large numbers sacrificial teaching makes no appeal at all. They feel the attraction of the life and figure of Christ, but they find in any sacrificial interpretation of His life only a paganism to be got rid of or lamented. Was it, they ask, that God might be appeased? That is the negation of religion. Was it that the innocent might suffer for the guilty? That is immoral. The evangelical 'plan of salvation' strikes them as cumbrous and artificial. Why is it not enough that we should simply do right, and serve God and our own day and generation? Many keen workers in the cause of social welfare go farther and blame the churches, more especially the evangelicals, for actual selfishness. The character of many popular hymns lends weight to the accusation. They assume, and even urge, a concentration of interest on the saving of one's own soul which, to the careful reader of the Gospels, is the reverse of Christ like. The story of the Good Samaritan, the discourse on

CULT AND SPIRIT

the Last Judgement, and even the Parable of the Prodigal Son, seem to cry out against the scheme; and many sincere Christians would feel relieved if it could be set aside altogether.

Certainly the impression conveyed by a comparison between the activities of the Church and the world in which they are carried on is unfortunate. We have to reckon with vast tracts of heathenism, possibly more appalling in Europe than elsewhere, commercial strife, industrial misery, the exploitation of foreign markets and backward peoples, vice, and irreligion. In face of all this, to argue about a mediatorial sacrifice, or the piacular value of the Atonement, seems worse than a waste of time. What does any view about the rationale of sacrifice matter when the world is calling out for the salvation of men from the worst of evils? Nor is it a valid reply that without orthodoxy there can be no achievement of salvation, since the orthodox are for the most part not much nearer to accomplishing this salvation than others, and, some would add, no more in earnest about it.

This impatience with sacrificial teaching must not force us to the conclusion that sacrifice itself is a hoary error, to be swept away with all speed. Even those who do not regard religion as central in humanity can hardly maintain this. For the service of man must mean the supply of man's needs, especially of those secular needs which he has sought to fulfil through sacrifice. We cannot think of sacrifices as artificial 'types,' given to man for his temporary satisfaction or as a source of curiosity or expectation. The variety and the common characteristics of sacrifice make this impossible. The actual means to this satisfaction we may regard as a delusion. It is difficult not to do so if we think of the ugliness and superstition and cruelty of many pagan rites. But unless we are to regard the whole human race, and the Christian Church as well, as involved in a vast error, we must respect the search for the end, and criticize or appraise, in the light of the teachings of Christ, the manner in which the search has been carried out.

For this task the methods of the theologian are not enough. Re-grouping of proof-texts will do no more than it has already done.[1] Nor is there more hope from the criticism of existing theological theories. All the revelations of God which we possess have come through man's thoughts about Him. We cannot be sure about any authentic revelation till we have examined the medium in which it has reached us. This is true even of the words of Christ in the Gospels. At the beginning of every inquiry lies the question, ' What have men thought of God, and what has led them so to think ? '

What, then, we must ask, is the object of sacrifice ? Most will answer, atonement. This is true of the Jewish and the Christian world, and of paganism also. But atonement is a word obscured by a thousand interpretations. How do we know that the Hebrew word so translated is identical in meaning with the Greek word used by Paul ? Did Paul himself know what was meant by the Hebrew lawgiver ? But since, when we use the word, we are thinking of Paul rather than of the Hebrew codes, much will be gained if we employ a better translation of Paul's Greek, and for ' atonement ' substitute ' reconciliation.' In the intercourse of ordinary and familiar life reconciliation means putting ' at one ' two parties who have been sundered. In religion, as in the special language of sacrifice, those two parties are man and God. Reconciliation implies the existence of a breach, however that breach arose. There can be no peace or contentment till the breach is healed. Human analogies readily throng to the mind. They are furnished by every dispute in the industrial or political world of which we read in the daily papers. But they must be used with caution, since, in the sphere of religion, only that kind of breach can be thought of in which one party is entirely blameless, and eager for the breach to be healed. How else can we think of God ? Yet in other religions, and even in Christian theology, God has often been thought of otherwise, as if He needed to be persuaded, argued, or even bribed into

---

[1] If we are to pay attention to modern critical discussions, proof-texts will do still less for us in the future. Rashdall's *Idea of the Atonement in Christian Theology*, for example, suggests that as little is left to us to-day in the way of authoritative New Testament statement as Schmiedel seemed to have left us twenty years ago. But those who shrink from the method must not be satisfied with saying that they disapprove of its results they must show that the method itself is unsound.

CULT AND SPIRIT

reconciliation. It is no light task to distinguish between God as He is and men's ideas of God. It is not easy to remember that our own ideas of God may easily misrepresent what God really is.

It will therefore follow that the methods adopted for healing the breach will be relative to men's conceptions of God's attitude to the breach. But the breach is there, and it is to be healed, for the pagan as for the Christian. There is really only one alternative to this view, and that is that sacrifice is something given up, or paid, to the god, to receive a *quid pro quo*—favour, prosperity, a definite gift, or forgiveness for sin. It matters little here whether sacrifice is regarded as a gift or a payment. Sacrifice indeed may be, and often is, conceived as a gift, just as it has often been conceived as a payment or a bribe. But this is not necessary, nor is it original. The etymology of the word, if stress may be laid on this, points in the same direction. It suggests the act of making something sacred or holy. It will follow from this that there is little ground for regarding sacrifice as something given up or surrendered. Our modern use of the term, as when we say that we let something go 'at a sacrifice,' or that we are giving 'to the point of sacrifice,' is inevitably misleading and has nothing to recommend it.

Apart from all this, indeed, the notion of giving up, or even of giving, is alien to the present-day conception of religion. How should a man pay, or bribe, God? And where is the need, if God's goodwill is assured and constant? With the great words of Micah[1] in our mind, we are apt to lay emphasis on good deeds, service to mankind, doing right. Protestantism, while opposing Catholic 'works' in the interest of Paulinism, has kept all this, though somewhat irregularly, to the front. 'As in heaven, so on earth.' We find the proof of the superiority of Christianity to other religions in its works of mercy, its determination to build the kingdom of heaven on earth. We point to our hospitals, our philanthropies, our reforms. And if, beside them, slums and brothels still exist, it is the task of religion to clear these monstrosities away. The world owes an enormous debt to this conception of religion; if the 'plan of salvation' has been left behind for a 'crusade,' most

[1] vi. 8.

people would feel the substitution to be all to the good. But to exchange the idea of a gift for that of service has meant, in practice, the neglect or rejection of sacrifice.

Protestantism has forgotten another thing, equally familiar to Roman Catholic devotion and to more recent psychological investigations, and not unknown in the older world of paganism—the 'sick soul.' When the soul is 'sick' it is useless to command it to 'do' or 'serve.' It 'lies helpless at the pool.' We must not confine this experience to the 'conviction of sin,' produced so widely during the evangelical revival of the eighteenth century. The formulae of the 'mystery religions,' which were attracting their multitudes while the infant Christian communities were beginning to make themselves felt in the bewildered pagan world, show how common was the burden of moral and spiritual asthenia, and how eagerly release from it was sought in any promising quarter. 'The cult of Asclepius became diffused in every direction, and the god received the two highly significant titles of "saviour" and "warm friend of man." In fact, healing came to be one of the chief desiderata of sin-sick souls. And in these cases, as is natural, it is often difficult to distinguish between disease of body and disease of soul.'[1] To confine your demand to 'good works' is to leave half the humanity around you untouched.

And good works are none too common, even where they have been regarded as of primary importance. In Protestant England the chief impulse to them has come from the evangelicals—Wesley, the 'Clapham Sect,' Wilberforce, Lord Shaftesbury—the very section of the Church which laid most emphasis on the atoning sacrifice. These men were, indeed, often one-sided in the actual reforms they championed,[2] but who is not? If the 'saints' were deaf to the cries of unorganized and exploited labour at home, few other ears were open. And the modern reaction against all theories of reconciliation or atonement cannot be said to be producing a much larger amount of practical service. The impulse which has turned men from the older doctrinal positions appears now to be leading them past 'works'

[1] H. A. A. Kennedy, *Vital Forces of the Early Church*, ch. x.

[2] See Hammond, *The Town Labourer*, ch. xi., 'The Conscience of the Rich.'

CULT AND SPIRIT

altogether to Christian Science or Theosophy, and to be helping to clear the way for the new paganism which frankly seeks its own pleasure or advantage and scouts the idea that a man is his brother's keeper.

The life of definite service for mankind, indeed, is now independent of the influence of any Church. It is found in them all, yet in all of them its exponents are in the minority. It is seldom referred to officially in the churches, and as seldom organized.[1] It is generally treated as the special interest of the few, the only notable exceptions being the Quaker community and the Salvation Army. Unwearied and heroic social service is performed outside the membership of all the churches; and there is a general complaint that enthusiasm for it always means less enthusiasm for what is known as 'church work,' or for general church fellowship. The reason is that between the service of man and the life of the Church there is a distinct gulf, which comparatively few have seriously tried to bridge. Hence such service lacks the great inspiration given by Catholicism, Calvinism, and Evangelicalism in the past. We may criticize those systems as narrow, but they faced enormous obstacles and a deadweight of neglect and opposition with a vigour and success which we cannot forgo, yet cannot secure. And they were all based on reconciliation.

It may be that such reconciliation between man and God will not again become the absorbing interest it has been; but one thing is increasingly clear—the necessity for reconciliation between man and man. Neo-paganism has already been mentioned. A more deadly foe to society is selfishness, not least so because we are coming to regard it as half justifiable. The industrial and political worlds are full of struggling groups and 'interests.' Each wants to secure and acquire. 'And why not?' The universal troubling of the waters in the past war has greatly strengthened this attitude. Apart from the actual sternness of the teaching of misery and death, the war has shown us all—individuals, nations, communities, interests—that nothing is to be had without demanding it, and that almost anything

---

[1] Methodists will not need to be reminded of the stress laid in Wesley's *Rules of Society* upon practical Christianity; but the general neglect into which this stress has fallen, even in official pronouncements on church membership, is significant.

may be had if the demand is sufficiently strong and threatening. We may personally sympathize with the demands of one or other party, or both, but the whole procedure means strife and hatred, which menace private safety and public stability and even our common civilization. It is not enough to secure minimum wages or old age pensions, or enormous business profits or immense reserves of capital, or industrial legislation that would once have been scoffed at as grandmotherly. Daring experiments in all these directions have been made in the last twenty years, and how much are we farther on?

There is no minimum of money or of comfort which we can expect to satisfy either others or ourselves. There is no ' datum-line ' of material or moral well-being at which ' good works ' can aim. A starving man asks simply for bread, but when he has got it he will want to alter the conditions which allowed starvation, and to reckon with those who profited from such conditions, or tolerated them. To help the defeated in the battle for life means that the battle is ever renewed. The real foe is not misery, but jealousy and hate. How can we reconcile the opponents? We need a science of reconciliation. Even higher than the commendation bestowed on the Good Samaritan is the blessing of the peacemaker.

If the outlines of such a science could be drawn, what would be its scope? Would it lay down laws for the healing of breaches between man and man, or between man and God also? Some, perhaps, would hardly take such a question seriously. There can be no analogy, they would say, between the one kind of breach and the other, because God is wholly different from man in His relation to any kind of breach. This difference may, however, be overstated. In many cases of a breach between man and man one of the parties is, like God, wronged, and eager to set the matter right. We may think of Hosea or Imogen, of the father of a prodigal, or of a deserted wife. The wrongdoer is then in much the same case, whether he has sinned against man or God. If both parties are selfishly estranged the case is more difficult; but even there the difference is perhaps chiefly one of degree rather than kind. The reconciler has to inspire both parties, instead of only one, with the desire for the right course of action in order to

CULT AND SPIRIT

'make it up.' The problem of the breach where God, not man, is the injured party, paradox as it sounds, is really easier, since God is eager for the reconciliation, and (at least in the Christian representation) takes every possible step to secure it. If the second problem—of the breach between man and man—is to be attacked, it will only be solved by starting with the first, and going on as far as possible. We must know how to be reconciled to God before we can understand reconciliation with our brother.

We are thus brought back to the study of sacrifice. Our immediate task must be to study reconciliation between man and God; our hope, to arrive at a formula for the process of reconciliation between man and man. There is indeed a sense in which the former is impossible without the latter. If we think rightly of God, we cannot be at peace with Him when we are at enmity with man. Jesus has emphasized the same thing. 'So if you remember, even when you are offering your gift at the altar, that your brother has any grievance against you, leave your gift at the very altar and go away; first be reconciled to your brother, then come back and offer your gift.'[1] That is to say, reconciliation to God cannot be attempted before the willingness to be reconciled to man is there; the latter is even one of the conditions of the former; but it was none the less the former which Jesus was emphasizing, and with which we must begin. We need not conclude from this that there can be no peace on earth till all are Christians. Human reconciliation is possible without a conscious reconciliation to God, or a knowledge of the principles of reconciliation. Recovery from disease may precede medical knowledge and the existence of even 'necessary' hygienic conditions. But if we would understand the meaning of reconciliation between man and man we must study the relations of man and God.

Some will perhaps ask, 'Why drag in ethnic sacrifices? Is not the New Testament enough?' And it may be plausibly argued that in paganism reconciliation is the opposite of what it is in Christianity, since in Christianity God is eager to be reconciled to man, while in paganism man is endeavouring to reconcile God to himself. But

[1] Matt. v. 23, 24.

the sacrifice which is central to Christianity, whether it is thought of as offered by man or on behalf of man, involves some action of man to God, as distinctly as do the sacrifices of paganism. And the ethnic offerings are more than 'types.' The New Testament points back to the rites of Judaism, and Jewish sacrifices are not to be thought of save as closely akin to ethnic. In other words, those who first interpreted the death of Christ as a sacrifice (and they are, for Christians, the highest authorities) linked it, though doubtless unconsciously, with the whole religious development of man. They were passing from Calvary to Mount Moriah, and from Mount Moriah to the stone circle. They found at Calvary the desire, not of the Jews merely, but of all nations.

Others again will ask, ' Why delay over the New Testament? It is only an interpretation. Keep to anthropology and the ethnic rites.' But to draw the line at either the higher or the lower ritual is unphilosophical. All ethnologists admit the importance of the questions, ' Why was this done? ' and ' Why did men value this? ' When the persons involved try to tell us why they valued it, as Christians have done, why should we neglect them? We may find a guide there to other values. Further, in any institution which exhibits evolution (as all institutions do), the beginning of the process does not really explain the end, nor the end the beginning. Each throws light on the other. When we can actually get at neither, we must get as near as possible. Calvary, to any one who would understand its universal appeal, can as little do without the stone circle as the stone circle can do without Calvary. The student of religion will reverence both as impressive phenomena. The Christian will reverence the sacred stones because of his adoration for the cross.

In all the higher religions, devotional act and devotional thought develop together. The ritual expands; the reasons for the ritual, as given by scholars and theologians, grow more profound. In Christianity, however, the great sacrificial act is not, and cannot be, repeated. But Christianity has been more than its contemplation and the attempt to give reasons for it. The Eucharist is repeated, and repeated as a sacrament, or even a sacrifice. In the prevailing rites of the Eucharist there are many resemblances to the ethnic sacrifices—the celebrant, the special place, the prayers of access, gifts, a common consumption of food, and the social or communal character of the celebration. If there is no actual *mactatio*, or slaughter of the victim, there is a definite concentration of thought on its death. The emotional effect is the same in kind, though sometimes weaker, sometimes stronger, in degree. There is not the exciting effect of the sight of the spurting blood, the sudden collapse of the stricken animal; but the impression created by an elaborate Mass—the solemn and dim-lit building, the silent crowds, the subtle music, the bells, the vestments, the incense-laden air, the *hoc est corpus*, and the actual wafer and chalice—may be greater than any that could be experienced in a shrine in the recesses of a jungle, or the underground celebration of an Oriental mystery.[1]

The majority of Catholics have tended to emphasize this, as if they recognized its kinship with the ethnic; and they were influenced by classical and Teutonic traditions in the development of the eucharistic ritual. Protestantism has shrunk from this elaboration of the Christian ceremonial; whatever its doctrines of the Lord's Supper, it has confined the rites to the simplest elements, though, save in rare instances, its sects have never dropped the service altogether. It has, indeed, refused to follow Zwingli in regarding the Supper as only a memorial. It has almost universally concentrated the attention of the worshippers on the sacrifice of Christ and the ritual act. If it has come to no general agreement as to the precise character of the sacred meal, it is assured that as the sacrifice of Christ has effected reconciliation between man and God, the Supper perpetuates its validity, and the worshipper appropriates its benefits.

The Eucharist points to another element in ethnic sacrifices hitherto unmentioned—the communal feast. Students of the Old Testament are familiar with the distinction between the 'whole burnt-offering,' where the victim was entirely consumed, and the 'peace-offering,' where a part of it was eaten by the offerer, his friends, and the officiating priest. The same distinction is to be observed in many ethnic religions. But it would be a mistake to

[1] See Cumont, *Les Mystères de Mithra*, p. 167 (2nd edition, 1913).

press the difference. Both kinds of sacrifice centred in an offering to the divine power; and the ritual of this offering, with the Hebrews as with others, was practically the same in both instances. But is there not a difference in idea? Apparently there is, if we go back to the most primitive instances of the communal feast, or what are often considered to be such. There the sacred 'totem' animal, which takes the place of the god, is himself eaten by the worshippers.[1] And the classes of sacrifice in which man offers a victim to the god, and the god offers himself as a victim to man, would seem to be wholly distinct. But, as we shall see below, the significant thing in both is the same—the entrance of the worshippers into the closest attainable relations with the god, although the means by which this entrance is effected may differ according to the demands of the differing circumstances which call for the rite. Eating together has always been regarded, in religion as in general social life, as a sign of unity and good fellowship. For those who have been foes it is a sign of reconciliation. For persons who had previously been at variance, to hear Mass together was to proclaim that they had become friends. And it can hardly be accidental that the rite which symbolized or consummated the reconciliation of God with His worshippers should have also become the symbol of the reconciliation, or the union, of the worshippers with one another.

Thus the Eucharist, as a constant and vital institution of the Christian Church, supplies the looked-for link between reconciliation to God and reconciliation to man. It fixes attention on both, and uses each to strengthen the other. It implies that they naturally go together.[2] This conception is far in advance of ordinary Christian practice. For the most part Christianity, while it has recognized the two great commandments, has persisted in keeping them apart, not really believing that the second is 'like unto' the first. It has been willing to credit men with love to

[1] See E. Durkheim, *Les Formes Élémentaires de la Vie Religieuse* (1912), pp. 465 ff., where the author points out that if the worshippers need the periodic renewal of the vigour of the divinity, the divinity needs the sacrifice that alone makes this renewal possible.

[2] We may compare the words of the Anglican service, 'Ye that do truly and earnestly repent you of your sins, and are in love and charity with your neighbours.'

CULT AND SPIRIT

God when they have clearly been full of hatred and envy to their neighbours, and it has seldom attempted to analyse what is implied either by love to God or to men.[1] The definite teaching of the early Church on this point, like every other doctrine, cannot be preserved by a symbol, even by one so expressive and august as the Eucharist. But it follows distinctly from the Christian view of reconciliation; and if our exposition of that view is to be complete we shall have to do justice, before we have concluded our task, to the double aspect of that majestic process.

We have now arrived at the point where we can see the course before us. We must begin with the more primitive sacrifices, or what may be considered to be such, and disentangle as far as we can the definite ideas and impulses which are woven into their bizarre and complex designs. We shall then study the more developed systems of India, important because of their special elaboration, and of Greece, equally important because of the significance of Greece for all subsequent Western culture. We cannot pass in review the systems which have characterized all the typical stages of religion; but if we can trace, in the sacred places of India and Greece, the ideas which we have already found in the rude practices of the jungle and the bush, we may be fairly certain that they would not be wanting to a more ambitious and exhaustive survey. We shall then turn to the Old Testament, which touches the religious institutions of paganism at every point, alike in its imitations and its avoidances of current and familiar pagan practices and its underlying kinship of ideas, but which, under a criticism more drastic than is found elsewhere, steadily develops to a level no paganism has ever attained. That criticism must itself be examined; and, from its appearance in India and Greece as well as in Israel, we shall have to observe that sacrifice, if universal as a means of reconciliation with heaven, has produced the most vigorous reactions against itself in the very quarters where it had most influence.

This naturally leads to a consideration of the teaching on the subject set forth by Jesus, who carries on the protest against sacrifice, and yet whose death has been the source of the most elaborate doctrine of sacrifice ever given to the

Cf. 1 John iv. 20 f

world. This doctrine we shall have to trace rapidly from its beginnings in apostolic times to its development in the great Catholic and Protestant theologians. We shall find it, in details, almost as varied as the different sacrificial rites themselves, but we shall attempt to extract from its various forms the principles of reconciliation, if they can be found there, so far as they have been recognized or implied. And a Christian student at all events need not apologize if he proposes to test the value of these doctrines by their conformity to the conception of reconciliation he has found in the words of Jesus.

With a very brief discussion of the subject of Priesthood, which is too closely connected with the general practice of sacrifice and of the steady development of Christian institutions to be passed over in silence, we must estimate the results of our study for the problems of reconciliation—religious, social, and political—which face us to-day. This last stage of our journey is the least trodden of any, but it ought surely to be felt as the most important. Most treatises on the Atonement end before they have reached the point where they would be really valuable. They achieve some explanation of the rationale of the salvation of the soul, and even of the race, through the cross and death of Christ. But a man does not need, and cannot use, such a rationale for the saving of his soul, and, however clearly it may have been shown that Christ's death avails for the race, the race is as much in need as ever of being saved from the thousand ills that afflict it and have afflicted it from time immemorial. We are thus forced to ask whether a treatise on the Atonement which does no more than most treatises have attempted in the past has ever rendered any service to the two main ends of the gospel—the turning of the individual to Christ, and the redemption of society from the tyranny of hate and lust and greed to the liberty of the sons of God. Unless we can apply the law of the Atonement, as we may call it, to the concrete problems of society, our wisdom at its best is mere foolishness.

Such an inquiry demands more than theology by itself can give. It must call in the aid, not only of ethnology, but of psychology. Both theologians and ethnologists have suffered from the absence of psychological imagination.

CULT AND SPIRIT

We cannot blame theology if, criticizing the various theories to which she has given birth, she maintains the studious aloofness of an abstract science. But she must recognize that, in so doing, she cannot satisfy souls which know the yearnings, the hopes and the despairs of the search for God, or heal a society heaving in the throes of volcanic convulsions. And all workers in the field of ethnology, whether as observers or collators, deserve our gratitude for noting the externals of the rites of forest or bush or prairie, as a musician might jot down the notes of a negro slave-song, without a hint of the hope or terror or bewilderment of the savage in the moonlit clearing or the slave in the mud swamp. But the first requisite in dealing with men, whether to influence them or only to understand, is to know their needs and aims and instincts, and to sympathize with every passing but often tyrannous mood. If philosophy begins with wonder, sympathy is the source of any useful and fruitful psychology, and hence of any real knowledge of the profound laws which are manifested in human action. If, then, reconciliation lies at the centre of the Church's preaching—at the heart of the 'good news' with which the Church has been entrusted—it will be necessary to understand both the laws according to which that reconciliation acts, and the need which it has to fulfil. Should the study in the following pages assist this understanding, it will be enough.

II

THE CHILDHOOD OF SACRIFICE

THE student of the institution of sacrifice is met on the threshold of his task by two serious difficulties. The first arises from the bewildering variety of the material that is flung at his feet. He finds himself dealing with different stages of civilization and culture and differing physical conditions. The objects sacrificed vary as much as the motives and aims of the sacrificers, the supposed character of the gods to whom the sacrifice is brought, and the ritual with which it is offered on the altar—if there is, indeed, an altar at all. What is there in common between the Veddah and the Mexican, the Bushman and the Chinese, the Dahomeyan and the ancient Roman? Any collection of facts grows speedily unmanageable; generalization on the data appears impossible.

The student's plight, however, is not hopeless. He will not have proceeded far in his work of collection before he finds certain common elements, alike in actual rites and in the ideas that seem to lie beneath them. He finds, for example, much the same conception of the semi-physical relation of the god to his worshippers among the North American Indians as among the Australians; the same practice of choosing a place for sacrifice among the Vedic Hindus as among the early Romans. Such instances of similarity, even where no connexion seems possible, meet the anthropologist constantly. He finds them in language, fairy tales, marriage customs; he finds them so often that he will even suspect that some mysterious tendencies to uniformity have led the human race, in spite of all differences of surroundings and attainment, along the same path. These similarities are nowhere more noticeable than in religion. If it were possible to trace these growths to the same seed, or to detect any common elements in the various

THE CHILDHOOD OF SACRIFICE 33

soils from which they have sprung, our first difficulty would be surmounted.

There is a second, arising from what may be called the invention of the explanatory myth. For most sacrificial practices the sacrificer has a reason. This reason, as students agree, will nearly always be wrong. The intellect is always trying to rationalize instinct. The result is often specious but unreliable. Such scepticism of the myth, indeed, applies to religions and social customs alike, modern as well as ancient. In the actual order of events, practice comes first; myth, or theory, if we may use a more respectable term, comes second. What we really want to discover is the reason, or the mode of reasoning, that gave rise to the practice in the first instance. Some reason there must have been, but it would soon be forgotten. By the side of the correct and traditional action it mattered little. Questions, however, could not be prevented. Children, young and grown-up, have always wanted to ask, Why do we do this? Some answer is necessary, even though the truth may seem unattainable, or only unadvisable, as when children to-day ask inconvenient questions about the birth of a pet animal or a baby brother. Such was the origin of the stories of Persephone, Iphigenia, or the Capitoline geese. Among the Hebrews, the rites of circumcision and the Passover sacrifice would seem to have been considerably older than the events which were subsequently narrated to account for them.[1]

To-day the mythical explanations are studied in connexion with the rites as effects rather than causes, though it is recognized that the story may point out some element in the rite which existing accounts of the rite have omitted. But how are we to get back to the forgotten hope or fear? Here we are assisted by the very diversity of the rites in question, when we can help it out by some imaginative consideration of the elementary needs of mankind in the jungle, the mountain, or the bush. We must, however, learn to ask a question which is the reverse of that which has to be put by every scientific historian or investigator of past events. The latter, whether he is examining the descriptions of Herodotus or Livy, an eighteenth-century

[1] See, for other examples, A. Lang, *Custom and Myth*.

34 ALTAR, CROSS, AND COMMUNITY

broadsheet, a mediaeval chronicler, or a Semitic tradition, must ask, What sort of occurrence would have led to the statement or tradition before me? We have to ask, What sort of idea or belief would have led to the type of act narrated or witnessed?

Of one error we must beware, namely, that we can detect the primitive. 'If we can work back to the sacrificial ideas of primitive peoples,' it is argued, 'we shall be able to watch the institution of sacrifice at its birth.' The same hope has been entertained by the searchers for the origin of religion. Various races have been studied of late with praiseworthy attention and self-abnegation, under the impression that they exhibit, or that they can enable us to approach, the primitive type of man. The type has been looked for among the Australians, the Veddahs of Ceylon, the Todas of the Nilgiris, the Andaman Islanders, and many others.[1] If only the destructive advance of civilization had not forestalled us, we might have had the advantage of examining a race which, physically at least, seems much nearer to the anthropoid—the Bushman. But no race carries the word 'primitive' written on its face or across its social life. It is true that we can find savages who know nothing of the institutions and implements that most human beings possess; yet they may, none the less, have risen from a still lower level. Thus the Australians possess a knowledge of woodcraft and a complicated system of marriage relationships and groups which suggest a very lengthy process of acquisition. Or races and tribes may well have fallen in the scale of human attainment. What they actually possess, startling as it often is, may be the remains of some larger equipment. For instance, a race that could produce the Bushman drawings—achievements which are marked by a feeling for animal life that a modern artist might envy—can hardly be at the beginning of its development; and it is remarkable that these drawings find a close parallel in the pictures of the caves of Aurignac, produced in the later palaeolithic age, some twenty thousand years ago.[2]

---

[1] See, for examples, the works of Spencer and Gillen, Seligman, Rivers.

[2] See the reproductions in Bleek, *Specimens of Bushman Folklore* (1911), and Hoernes, *Urgeschichte der bildenden Kunst in Europa*, 2nd edition, 1915.

THE CHILDHOOD OF SACRIFICE 35

Most savage races neither go up nor down; they are stationary till some change arises in their environment and conditions of life; then they may leap forward, as did the Greeks, or fall into degradation, like the North American Indians, the Peruvians, the Polynesians, or the Kaffirs of the modern South African towns. The same characteristics will appear in the customs or beliefs of the highest and lowest races; the solemn driving away of the scapegoat, for instance, was practised by the Greeks and Hebrews, and may be witnessed among the Dravidian Badagas to-day; the inspection of the liver of a sacrificial animal was carried out before important operations by Babylonian kings, generals of the Roman Republic, and prehistoric Etruscans, as it is carried out to-day in the jungles of Borneo.[1] To use the term 'primitive' really begs the question. The truth is that accepted modes of satisfying needs or avoiding dangers have a remarkable survival value; so have the needs themselves. The reluctance of Nicias, a cultured Athenian 'Tory of the old school,' of high military rank, to move against the enemy on an unlucky day, reminds one of the Bantu wife who will not pronounce the syllables that form part of the name of her husband. The universality of what we carelessly call superstition, however, has this advantage. The 'primitive' may have passed away and be irrecoverable, but we can see and study what is almost as primitive as anything we can desire in what is before our own eyes.[2]

Anthropologists in general have followed one or other of two possible methods—the extensive or the intensive. The best example of the first is Frazer, who takes some practice or institution, such as circumcision, avoidance of the wife's mother, killing and eating the god, or boiling the kid in its mother's milk, and traces it all over the world, with pages of examples, often taken indiscriminately from

---

[1] cf. Ezek. xxi. 21. Other references are given in W. W. Fowler, *Roman Essays and Interpretations*. A diagram of the significant portion of the liver of a pig will be found in Hose and McDougall, *Pagan Tribes of Borneo*, vol. ii.

[2] Cf. Thucydides, vii. 50, Plutarch, *Nicias*, 23, 24, and Molema, *The Bantu*, p. 139. The 'superstitious man' of Theophrastus' *Characters* (c. 320 B.C.) would be at home in Bond Street and in many an out-of-the-way English village to-day.

every continent.[1] Such a method proves clearly enough how similar are the most diverse peoples, but does nothing to explain why the practice in question is present here and absent there, and in any case takes it out of its surroundings. For example, the Kaffirs and the Todas, being both of them pastoral people, keep their women very carefully away from their cattle. But in view of the other wide differences between them, can we assume that the reason, if we could discover one, would be the same in both races?

The second method is certainly more attractive. There is no breathless hurrying over continents; we are allowed to take up our residence in one tribe and get to know it with some degree of intimacy. In this way W. H. R. Rivers has studied the Todas, H. A. Junod the Thongas, A. B. Ellis the natives of the lower Congo region, and W. Crooke the Indians of the North-west Provinces.[2] The drawback is that so large is the field that unwearied industry can explore but a small part of it. Safe generalization seems as far off as ever. For science, however, the minute, as such, does not exist. The value of instances lies, not in their number, but their selection and treatment. *Ex pede Herculem.* It is probable that the best results are obtained from the intensive study of a few well-chosen peoples by trained and sympathetic observers. But neither method can surmount the two difficulties mentioned above. The bewildering diversity of customs and beliefs is neglected by the intensive method, and the extensive pants vainly in pursuit. For the 'primitive,' neither method can yield any criterion.

Both methods, too, have suffered from the absence of psychology. The extensive method can have little time for psychological considerations. The intensive has so many details to record that reasons and motives are often pushed aside. It may be replied that this is inevitable. How can we tell the reasons for an action? It is hard enough to divine the reasons of men of our own race and neighbourhood; harder when we are dealing with the

[1] His method is seen in a striking and, it may be, a perilous form, in *Folklore in the Old Testament.* Compare also Westermarck's writings, e.g. *The History of Human Marriage* and *The Development of Moral Ideas.*

[2] Some idea of the number of these studies can be gathered from the bibliographical references of any of Frazer's books.

THE CHILDHOOD OF SACRIFICE 37

inhabitant of that strange country, the world of a child ; and when we have to do with savages, interpretative psychology breaks down. Yet the savage is not a hopeless riddle. If he were, we could neither sympathize with him nor understand him. But sympathy, when linked with imagination, is a cause as well as an effect of successful interpretation. Without imagination there could be no psychology at all.

Nor is the task, when resolutely faced, so distressingly hard. An enormous gulf, indeed, seems to stretch between white and black, as wide as that which separated Jew and Gentile in the Middle Ages.[1] Yet, as Shakespeare was brave enough to say, there are abundant points in common —simple pleasures and pains, hunger, sleep, family affection, social excitement, conditions of bodily ease, the fear of the dark and the unknown, self-assertion and self-abasement, and the reactions to tyranny and loyalty. The primary instincts and emotions are the most powerful with us as with them.[2] They bind the human race together. Divergences in conduct meet us on all sides ; but these exist between different civilized people, and not between civilized and savage only. They can be explained by circumstances, physical and social environment, knowledge, customs and convictions, each of which has a history that can sooner or later be traced. Life means the attempt to gain what are fundamentally the same satisfactions amidst our differing conditions. The desire for food is one and the same thing in the Australian bush and in Melbourne and Sydney, however different the acts in which it issues. The desire for sexual pleasure is one ; but in the bush it issues in the corroboree or the opportunities of the tribal festival; in the city it issues in the dancing-hall or the brothel. Self-assertion and ambition are equally potent in an American Indian Reservation and in Lombard Street ; and men are everywhere ridden by fear, whether its objects are demons and outlawry or bankruptcy and unemployment. But, if once we recognize the change of circumstance and training, we can see the similarity of the springs of conduct ; we can understand, for instance, why the English labourer

---

[1] For the educated negro's view of this gulf cf. Du Bois, *The Souls of Black Folk*.
[2] See McDougall, *Social Psychology*, ch. iii.

thinks of a horseshoe when the Chinese peasant thinks of a rag on a neighbouring tree. The first requisite for interpreting our fellow men is to realize that they are as rational as we are. What we call irrationality is simply the recognition of things which we do not recognize, or vice versa. Even animals can be understood if we can learn to enter the animals' limited world. The civilized man is as irrational to savages as they are to him.

To apply this to our special task, the study of sacrifice. At first sight we do not seem to have gained much. We are still left with a discordant mass of rites and conceptions—gift, tribute, bribe, thank-offering, propitiation, sign of fellowship, and so on.[1] Can we reduce these to a common origin, such as the slaughter of the god, or the totemistic meal? The high authority of Frazer and Robertson Smith has induced a widespread view that sacrifice began in some purpose of which the special values attached to these two performances formed, as it were, the two moments.[2] But even if proof of this were possible, there would be no need to elaborate it here. The historical origin of sacrifice, if we could discover it, would tell us as little as the historical origin of religion itself. Our quest is psychological rather than historical. We want to arrive at the sense of need which led to the offering of sacrificial gifts or the payment of sacrificial tributes or bribes. Any attempt to mark off stages in the development of the rites must end by recognizing that the stages are logical rather than chronological. They are dependent on physical and psychical environment. And behind all such stages, as far as we can distinguish them, whether in simple or complex societies, there appear to lie certain simple desires —to keep off dangerous and attract and strengthen friendly powers ; to get rid of what would keep the friendly powers at a distance ; and to secure some sort of communion with them. That is to say, if we imagine human

[1] Compare, for example, the catalogue of the different kinds of sacrifice given, *sub voce*, in the *Encyclopaedia Britannica* (N. W. Thomas), the *Encyclopaedia Biblica* (G. F. Moore), Hastings' *Dictionary of the Bible* (W. P. Paterson), and the recent German encyclopaedia, *Religion in Geschichte und Gegenwart* (Gressmann).

[2] The 'communion' meal of the Australian totem-group has lent considerable support to the view of Robertson Smith, while modifying it in certain particulars. See the works of Spencer and Gillen, Howitt, Roth, and Durkheim, *op. cit.*, pp. 480 ff.

THE CHILDHOOD OF SACRIFICE 39

beings, as we know them, placed in a hostile and mysterious world, with their familiar wants, social feelings, hopes, and belief in the unseen, this is what they would attempt to accomplish. And with the hardening and elaboration of ritual, universally to be observed in religion, the development and differentiation of rites can be understood.

All this requires some explanation. 'Belief,' we say, 'in the unseen.' What kind of unseen? All men, we are told, believe in a god. This is, of course, not the same thing as to say that they believe in God. In what kind of god do they believe? The most superficial acquaintance with comparative religion makes it clear that these gods are very different from the God of Christianity. There is no innate conception of God. Sometimes the belief is in a diffused and awful divine energy called 'Mana' by the Polynesians, or 'Orenda' by some North American Indian tribes, and most of the gods men actually worship are formed after the likeness of the powers, human or non-human, that most deeply impress the worshippers.[1] The Kaffir's god will have the attributes of a tribal chief, just as Anselm's god reminds us of a magnificent feudal lord, and the early Hebrew's god makes us think of a glorified sheikh. Even the Australian's Daramulun or Baiamee suggests one of the wise old men whom his horde unhesitatingly obeys, with the addition of some undefined power, like the power that he feels behind the world in which he lives. If we would reconstruct the actual beliefs of men about their gods, we must put aside our modern religious conceptions of omnipotence, omniscience, and the like, with their long theological history. Low religious ideas, even in communities which seem in other respects more advanced, occur along with low or unco-ordinated social organization. In the forces which govern his life and demand his allegiance the savage, equally with his descendant, sees beings like those whom he knows.

Thus the world in which early man has to carry on his affairs is mysterious; but mystery does not play so large a part in it as we, with our scientific explanations of things, might have expected. The mental life of savages, like that of all other men, is dominated by their interests. We

[1] Compare Xenophanes' quaint but acute suggestion of the lion-shaped gods that lions would worship; also Ps. l. 21.

are interested in what we feel we need for the furtherance of our life and its satisfactions. And to our interests, understood in this sense, our attention is practically shut up. In a world where conditions are simple and strenuous, needs and interests, like the impulses which drive men to their satisfaction, will be simple and direct. The fundamental human needs in every age are food, mating or family life, shelter, and protection or security, and, when these are attained, some degree of comfort. And in a world whose most conspicuous elements are wild beasts, diseases, famine, storm, and hostile men, these needs have to be satisfied somehow, and the host of dangers to life and limb guarded against. Of the real nature of these dangers early man has small idea. For the most part he personalizes them, as a child, tossing feverishly through the night, will think of his pain as if it were some one beneath the bed-clothes with him. Possibly neolithic man imagined the sabre-toothed tiger to possess qualities as 'human' as those of the cave-men living on the other side of his hills. Certainly the modern savage, his descendant, finds a human or quasi-human being behind both plague and tempest. And, with that vague idea, he does not trouble to speculate farther as to its character or even its personality (the word would be unintelligible to him); what he is interested in is how to keep on good terms with it, or render it unable to hurt him.[1]

Again, the savage, like all other human beings, lives in a society; and this society includes, not only his friends and enemies, human and animal, but, in all save the most elementary stages, his tribal chief or chiefs, and his gods. What his friends may be expected to do he knows pretty well; and if they do anything else, he takes the first opportunity of admonishing them. The chief is more mysterious. He is, in fact, almost as much of a god as a man. He is a part of the tribe, of course, and he can be relied upon for protection and leadership; but he must be treated with courtesy and caution, and he can only be approached if certain rules are observed, the infringement of any one of which may be visited with terrible penalties, from the chief himself or from the powers

[1] Is this a less or more advanced idea than the belief of the sailor that if he carries a certain kind of caul with him to sea he can laugh at a cyclone?

THE CHILDHOOD OF SACRIFICE 41

at his back. And as for the gods, how can he think of them but as exalted tribal chiefs? His only interest in them is keeping on good terms with them and securing their help. Naturally, therefore, he is guided by his experience of what is demanded by the chiefs. He must not approach them empty-handed; but whether we call his offering a gift, a tribute, a payment, or a bribe, makes little difference; he has not arrived at the stage when any differentiation is possible. He may even think of it as he would think of a charm, a love-philtre, or a 'sending,' which may be successful if the right words have been muttered over it, and the 'doctor' from whom he got it was sufficiently honest and skilful. He knows, too, that the correct formulae of salutation must be used and the rules observed, or the interview, when he has the opportunity or the courage to secure it, will end in disaster. And if he can never be sure of the mood in which he will find the chief, how can he be sure that, for all his precautions, the gods will be any more kindly?

The gods, too, like the chiefs, are tribal; they will, therefore, be most naturally approached for tribal or common needs—a tribal hunt, a fishing expedition, the safety of the herds, the fertility of the crops, the vigour of the seed-corn, success in war, freedom from disease. And since these things concern the whole tribe, the proper person to lead the approach is the chief, who, as being in some measure a god himself, is far more likely to be successful and avoid mistakes. It is not easy for us to place ourselves at the side of the savage as he prepares for the sacrifice by which this approach is made. We must use our imagination if we would understand the empire of the sacrifice over the deeper and more fundamental emotions of mankind. Let us figure some African tribal village in dire trouble. The crops are failing, the gardens are parched, the rains will not come.[1] Or some mysterious

---

[1] Since the first need of man is food, the connexion between food and religion, as soon as the agricultural stage of culture has been entered, will be clear enough. Hence, for example, the importance of the corn-spirit in early ritual (see Mannhardt, W., *Wald- u. Feldkulte* (2nd ed.), i. pp. 603 ff.). The first hymn which Western religion has given us is the prayer of the Arval Brothers for good harvests: *Enos lases juvate*, &c. The practice is paralleled in the D'Entrecasteaux Islands, east of New Guinea, where professional singers invoke the spirits of the growing vegetation at the planting (Jenness and Ballantyne, *Northern D'Entrecasteaux*, 1920).

pestilence has appeared, and old and young are at the gates of death. Uneasy memories of broken customs and licence unchecked are stirred by the distress. Early man lives near to the brink of calamity. He has no reserves. The passion, too, which breaks customary rules and brings down the anger of divine powers is sternly but often unsuccessfully held in bondage. And now the health and prosperity which heaven is wont to give are gone. How can the path be opened again for these gifts? How can man once more find his way to God? There is a way—the appointed way of offering and sacrifice. The hour is fixed. The little community performs its traditional lustrations, and undergoes the traditional abstinences. When all are assembled on the sacred spot the priest or the chief brings the offering —the goat or the fowl or the ox—utters the prescribed word, performs the fatal act, and sends the creature as the messenger—their representative, their forerunner—into the presence of the god; while the eager, hard-pressed crowd around him, their bodies, it may be, racked by suffering, as their minds by suspense, follow tensely every detail, hoping that the barrier between the god and his worshippers will fall before the sacred victim, and that, once fallen, it will not arise again to block their way to safety and communion.

Such an account would do no serious injustice even to the earlier sacrifices of the Chosen People. It is only necessary to remember that sacrifices were periodical as well as occasional, and that they served the purposes of prevention or, as we might say, insurance, as well as of cure. The barrier might rise simply through lapse of time, or the necessary vigour of the divinity might gradually decay,[1] and any formal approach to the god, called for by joy as well as sorrow, or demanded by the return of the sacred season, would naturally be preceded by an act of sacrifice. And when all the men were going off on a hunting expedition, on whose success depended the existence of the whole village, or when they were starting on the war-path, about to enter strange localities and come into conflict with the gods as well as the men of hostile tribes, whence none of them might ever return, we can imagine the fears of

---

[1] See ch. i., p. 28, note.

THE CHILDHOOD OF SACRIFICE 43

those who stayed behind, and of those who marched forth.[1]

From the midst of such desires sacrifice would seem to take its rise. It is communal rather than individual. When all act, hunt, and trek together, and no one decides anything for himself, no one thinks of going alone to a god. This is not because the individual is too unimportant to attract the notice of the god, but because he is conscious of no need, in which the god could be expected to take an interest, which is not shared by others. To say this, it may be argued, is to assign a utilitarian origin to religion, or at least to sacrifice. But the utilitarian is not the egoistic. Each man does his part in securing the needs of the whole group from the god. He has not yet learnt the difference between selfishness and unselfishness. Both, in their simpler forms, are quite possible for him. But religion is a way of supplying needs through the unseen powers. Even Christianity claims to secure the fulfilment of man's greatest need; and its popular presentations have often forgotten the needs of society in the stress they have laid on individual salvation. Not so the savage. He cannot conceive of any salvation which is not the salvation of his society. But to say that religion meets human needs is not a reproach, but a credential. The real weakness of religion shows itself when it is thought of, not as deliverance from danger or as the supply of need—as 'good news,' that is—but as an arbitrary system of duties which must be performed if disastrous consequences are not to follow.

So envisaged, sacrifice seems to point to the gift or, as we may call it, the bribe. To offer a gift or a payment to a superior, either a chief or a god, when we want something from him, seems natural enough. That it is often so regarded is indubitable. But there are several serious difficulties in the way of supposing that this is the universal, or even the original, idea of sacrifice. In the first place, as Wundt,[2] among others, has pointed out, sacrifice takes us back to an age when private property was as yet unknown,

---

[1] This will perhaps help to explain the special ceremonies and abstinences of the primitive warrior, hinted at in 1 Sam. xxi. 4 f. There is little of the Western bravery of 'facing fearful odds' in the savage. Even the 'warlike' Fijians and Masai would never face a danger that they could avoid.

[2] See his *Elements of Folk-Psychology* (tr. Schaub), pp. 240, 432 f.

and could not therefore be transferred. When everything is shared, gifts are impossible. You cannot make a present of an ox to a chief when the ox is already as much his as yours.[1] To this two replies may be made. First, the sacrifice may be offered to the god as the common property of the clan. But in that property the god himself shares; he can as little receive a gift as can the chief. But could not some article be given to him which the individual does not share with others, such as an ornament or a weapon? In these things we have the rudiments of personal, as opposed to real, property. The answer is that such articles are never given in sacrifice originally; and though later on, when the idea of property has been fully developed, property may be transferred to the gods, sacrifice as an institution antedates such a period, and remains distinct from the votive offering.

Secondly, why should gifts be confined to certain classes of objects, while others are rigidly forbidden, and confined to classes, moreover, which do not always include the objects most valuable either to men or, presumably, to the god? The American Indian, for instance, offers a little tobacco, or solemnly blows its smoke towards the unseen; the Thonga ejects some saliva with a word of dedication. And if we rule these out (though there is no real ground for doing so) as abnormal, we have still to explain why the list of objects which the god desires, or will consent to receive, is so small.

Further, the chief objects in those lists are animals, but only animals of certain species; here, too, the gods have their likes and dislikes. These animals have to be slaughtered; and the methods of their slaughter and the disposal of their bodies are as carefully prescribed as their species. Now, why should the sacrifice be killed? It is commonly assumed that to kill the animal is the only way to transfer it from the human to the divine sphere; that because the god is unseen, the animal he receives must be dead. But this is surely not self-evident. Why should not the animal have been simply kept apart for the use of the god or his servants, the chiefs or the priests? And why should the slaughter be always accompanied by certain ritual acts or words, without which the whole performance

[1] Cf. Ps. l. 10.

THE CHILDHOOD OF SACRIFICE 45

would be a failure? It is true that the gods are sometimes thought of as themselves desiring the sacrifice, as in the famous passage in one of the Babylonian accounts of the flood[1]; but in most cases the chief anxiety of the offerer, it must be confessed, is lest the offering should be refused. If the gods desire gifts, it is strange that they seem so unwilling to take them when they have the chance.

Again, the sacrifice is often followed by a meal made of the victim; that is, the animal is not so much given as shared. It may indeed be said that the spirit or soul of the animal is given to the god, while its body, for which the god could have no use, is thus pleasantly and conveniently kept from being wasted. But this overlooks the fact that the meal is itself part of the ceremonial, and that the god and the worshippers are thought of as sharing a common table. To ask a person to dinner is not the same thing as to present him with a testimonial; and if the chief importance was attached to the gift, to turn the sacrifice into a common meal, where the god was only one of the participants, seems a curious way of emphasizing it.

It is equally difficult to think of the offerings as payments or bribes. The price must have, in any transaction, some proportion to the value of the goods purchased; but this proportion is rarely, if ever, thought of in the case of sacrifice. The offering is assigned, whatever the worth of the boon desired. This definite limitation is as unreasonable and self-destructive in the case of a payment as a bribe; and, while many gods are undoubtedly conceived of as possibly malign and certainly dangerous powers, not to be approached save at command, and as likely to send disaster as well as blessing, the general relations between worshippers and their gods are very different from those of a suitor and a corrupt judge. Bribery would at best explain some rather exceptional forms of religious action.

A common view is that sacrifices are means to expiation. Man has sinned; the god is angry; and that anger must be

[1] When Ut-napishtim, the Babylonian Noah, offered the first sacrifice after the waters had abated, ' the gods smelt the savour, the gods gathered like flies over the sacrifice. When at last the lady of the gods drew near, she said, Let the gods come to the sacrifice ' (Gilgamesh Epic, tab. xi., col. iii.; it may be read in Rogers, *Cuneiform Parallels to the Old Testament*, p. 99). Cf. Gen. viii. 21.

appeased by an offering. The theory is certainly plausible, for a serious worshipper, coming to his god, could scarcely fail to think of his sins and to dread some divine reaction against them; and conceptions of godhead, even in the more developed religions, are not so high that we can rule out from them the readiness to be mollified, even with blood. The human desire to glut one's sense of power by the sight of another's suffering can easily pass into the belief that the god must see some agony or bloodshed before he will be propitiated. But this theory, too, would only explain some sacrifices, not all. In the majority of sacrifices the god is thought of as favourably disposed to his worshippers—as being of one kin with them; the sacrificial festival is a time of joyous intercourse between god and men; and the fact that the victim is constantly shared—the god having his part, as the honoured chief or guest, and the worshippers theirs—makes the idea of expiation a psychological impossibility. We must not explain the whole of sacrifice from its evolution, or perversion, among dark or cruel races, or in periods of fear and despair. In many sacrifices the attitude of the worshippers is not one of unwillingness but of eager generosity; in many instances the object offered is so common that it could never be considered a sacrifice in our colloquial sense; in others, as at various harvest festivals, it is offered just at the period when it is not rare, but plentiful.

Shut out from these accounts of sacrifice, what explanation shall we find? None but what is, after all, the simplest—that sacrifice is a means of getting into communion with the god, so that his gifts may be received without any barrier to stop them. The god is in heaven, wherever heaven may be supposed to be; and, however well disposed, he is a being of secret and uncanny powers, dangerous to approach. 'See God and die,'[1] as the old Hebrews said; and man, in his rough-and-tumble life of violence and passion and carelessness and sin, cannot of himself, without special measures and precautions, come where the blessings of heaven might be his. Moreover, the primitive objects of desire are really more than material possessions, even such important possessions as food. They are rather the means to these possessions—life, with all it implies

[1] Cf. Gen. xxxii. 30; Isa. vi. 5.

THE CHILDHOOD OF SACRIFICE 47

of strength, effectiveness, and wellbeing; and the goodwill and kindly disposition of the deity. Life is one, whether animal or vegetable, human or divine; and it can be preserved or extended, and its subtle power or 'mana' acquired in larger measure, by the appropriate acts. Similarly, the goodwill of the deity, which as experience shows can be but too readily lost, can also be regained in certain ways which older generations have handed down. So, if life is brought to the god, he will bring life to the community, and the community will possess, for its various needs, the resources (if we may use very modern language) of all the might of the unseen powers of heaven. Life can be conferred upon him, or awakened within him, by different means. He may be invited to a feast, or a ritual and imitative dance may be performed to affect him; to the savage, a solemn dance or action-song always has great symbolical or, as the psychologist would say, suggestive value. But since life is one, in the god and among his fellow tribesmen, it is natural to think of it as specially rich in the chief; hence the best way of bringing new life to the god may easily appear to lie in the offering of the chief. The chief is indeed himself a kind of god. Or, if the society is too early to have developed special chiefs, some priest or warrior may be chosen for this purpose. But strong reasons would soon be felt for modifying this practice. No society could afford to kill off its most valuable members, especially if the original purpose for so doing were forgotten. Why not offer some other life—perhaps a child, more particularly the first-born—in whom vigour might be supposed to be pre-eminent; or some person whom the lot, as the exponent of the will of the god himself, might point out? Perhaps a slave would do, the more so if he were previously treated like an honoured member of the community.[1] In any case, to shed the blood of a member of the community is a serious thing, not to be contemplated save on special occasions, and with special protective rites; and the savage mind—a strange mixture, as always, of conservatism and utilitarianism—argues that the offering of an

[1] Cf. Verg. *Aen.* ii. 118 ff., 'Animaque litanda . . . quem poscat Apollo.' It is clearly impossible to decide upon any chronological order in the development of ideas about sacrifice, human and animal. A careful discussion of human sacrifice will be found in Westermarck, *Origin and Development of Moral Ideas*, vol. i., ch. **xix**.

animal will effect the same end. The animal will have to be chosen with care ; it will generally itself be a sort of member of the community, domestic, not wild, and the rites will be as solemn and elaborate. The result confidently expected is the same. Obviously sacrifice, so understood, is more than gift or bribe. It is an attempt to get into touch with the god, to open or reopen relations with him. The worshipper cannot yet say, ' Nothing in my hands I bring,' although what he does bring is not thought of as a payment. But he is actuated by something more than the wish for a gift in return. His wish is for the influence, the presence, we might almost say the spirit, of his god in the daily life of his tribe ; and it is the life itself which he offers, and not the commercial value or preciousness attributed to it, that counts in his approach.

It may seem irreverent to use such language as this of howling barbarians, whose rites are as bizarre as their gods are cruel or stupid or careless.[1] But the gods are *numina praesentia* ; they do not dwell apart on an Olympus or in an Epicurean paradise. They do not even bestow good things. They bestow themselves. It is their presence in the midst of the host or the congregation, as the Hebrews would say, that is desired. For there is a bond of kinship between them and their worshippers. They cannot cast off their own people. They can be ' entreated,' or even forced, to become willing to communicate themselves. If we prefer to follow the view of the origin of sacrifice which implies that the divine power was conceived of as being liable to wear out, so that it had to be reinforced or reinvigorated by the life of a kindred human being or animal, the feeling of kinship with the god, which the sacrifice makes real and available, is equally clear.

We are dealing, in fact, with the germ of the idea of fellowship. It is the production or restoration of fellowship which is accomplished by the sacrifice. Even when the emotional effect of the rite is heightened by reckless and cruel slaughter, or attenuated to the offering of a few vegetables or cakes with no public ceremonial at all, the wish for fellowship stands out. This characteristic is responsible for every advance in religion. When the sacrifice is no more than an attempt to bring some boon

[1] Cf. the sacrifice to Baal on Mount Carmel (1 Kings xviii.).

THE CHILDHOOD OF SACRIFICE 49

from powerful but unwilling hands, religion stands still or falls back. A gift remains a gift—something handed over by the stronger to the weaker, the richer to the poorer ; and the man or the society which wants a gift will always be tempted to make sure of it by offering something for it, changing the personal expression of fellowship or dependence into a commercial transaction. The idea that the god can be paid or bribed has degraded religion in every age. But when once the need is felt to be, not for something that the god can hand over, but for the god himself, religion can move forward. That movement is all the more definite when the need is felt to be mutual, and when the sacrifice, establishing connexion between the two parties, leads to the satisfaction of the god's need for his human kinsfolk as well as theirs for him.

As the conception of the god grows in the community, the conception of the significance of union with him will grow too, until something like real spirituality is reached. Indeed, we are startled from time to time by the depth of religious feeling in sheer paganism. Doubtless it is all ' interested.' But could it be anything else ? Is religion, even in Christianity, disinterested ? All depends on what our interests are understood to be. If they centre on the practice of the presence of God, however crudely envisaged, they will be capable of being gradually purified and exalted till we ' seek the things that are above.'

The foregoing argument may not appear convincing to every reader. Few arguments outside the sphere of mathematics and exact measurement ever do. And when we are dealing with a subject so many-sided and complex as religion, we can hope neither for necessary deductions nor complete enumeration of instances. The best arguments are but tentative generalizations from a few particulars. The keenest investigator can only hope that he has not left out any relevant considerations. But our task is easier than some of those presented to us by the study of comparative religion. We have but to provide a link between the things which, in sacrificing, a man wishes for, and what he does. We do not need to discuss the origins or the definitions of religion. It does not matter for our purpose whether the first man was equipped with any religious notions at all, nor whether those earliest notions of his were inspired by fear or hope or love. We have simply to take him as we find him when he offers sacrifice. At this stage he obviously believes in gods, and in gods who are at all events capable of being brought into some sort of friendly relation with him. If, then, we put man's wishes at their lowest—for food and shelter, clothing and security, for him and his group—we have to ask what it is, in his opinion, that makes sacrifice likely to lead to their fulfilment.

To that question, we believe, we have supplied an answer. He will get what he wants, he thinks, by coming into some more or less close relation to his god; and this relation will be gained by the offering of some life, or substitute for a life, in a prescribed and solemn way. It is life which makes life available. But it will be convenient at this point to give some typical examples, drawn from different parts of the world and different periods of history, so that this view may be tested. If there is any common element in these examples, the differences between them will only increase its significance.

Let us first take the Saracens described by Nilus in the fourth century A.D., a type which certainly carries us back to a stage far anterior to the rise of Christianity or even Judaism. The tribe is assembled for the camel sacrifice. 'The camel chosen as the victim is bound upon a rude altar of stones piled together, and when the leader of the band has thrice led the worshippers round the altar in solemn procession, accompanied by chants, he inflicts the first blow while the last words of the hymn are still upon the lips of the congregation, and in all haste drinks of the blood that gushes forth. Forthwith the whole company fall on the victim with their swords, hacking off pieces of the quivering flesh and devouring them raw with such wild haste that in the short interval between the rise of the day star, which marked the hour for the service to begin, and the disappearance of its rays before the rising sun, the entire camel, body and bones, skin, blood, and entrails, is wholly devoured.'[1]

Let us now turn to West Africa. In some part of the street of most villages is built a low hut, sometimes not

---

[1] W. Robertson Smith, *Religion of the Semites* (2nd ed.), p. 338.

THE CHILDHOOD OF SACRIFICE 51

larger than a dog-kennel, in which charms are hung.[1] In this hut, among some tribes, is placed a rudely carved idol, generally a female. If the chief is ill, or a pestilence has begun to ravage the village, or a superior hostile force is approaching, a goat will be brought, its throat cut, and the blood will be allowed to fall to the ground at the door of the hut, while the body of the goat is laid there also. On happier occasions food is placed before the hut, and if there is sufficient, a village feast will be made, and every one will join in consuming the food, sharing it, so to speak, with the deity.

A very full account of the sacrifices of a Bantu tribe, in Portuguese South-east Africa, is given by Junod. The sequence of acts is as follows: when some need is felt, or a calamity feared, or the rains have failed, the divining bones are first consulted, as to the recipient and the details of the sacrifice; the eldest male member of the family comes forward to preside over the performance; the victims are then brought by those who have been designated, or who have volunteered to provide them. The actual killing of the animals is performed by the nephews of the president on the mother's side—a relic of the matriarchate which is very widespread; at each thrust of the assegai and cry of the victim, the crowd utters loud shouts of joy—the sacrifice is being accepted; the carcase is then cut open, parts of it are set aside for the gods, as well as the half-digested grass found in the intestines, always in these rites looked upon as the most important element. A portion of this grass, which is called ' psanyi,' is then mixed with the blood of the animal, and the president puts the stuff into his mouth and ejects it along with some saliva; this is understood to be the means of consecrating the offering or actually sending it into the presence of the god. The sacrificial festival appears to end in something of disorder; the nephews ' steal the offering and run away, followed by the throng, who throw pellets of "psanyi" at them. They eat the portion of the gods.' It must also be noticed that the sacrifice is regularly accompanied by prayers for specific or general blessings.[2]

[1] Nassau, *Fetishism in West Africa*, p. 92.
[2] H. A. Junod, *Life of a South African Tribe*, vol. ii., pp. 383 ff.; and cf. H. Merker, *Die Masai*, p. 199, for a clear example of some kind of sacrifice being regarded as necessary with prayer.

An interesting contrast to this procedure of the Thongas is offered by the rites at one of the large Japanese temples at Ise. The first requirement is a special ceremony of purification, by which all accidental defilement is cleared away. The priests then form a line between the place where the offerings are arranged and the altar, and pass the offerings down from one to the other, setting them finally on a series of small tables. While this is being done music is performed. When it is over, a formula of prayer is recited, succeeded by ceremonial dances, performed by men and subsequently by women, in the temple court.[1] The offerings are not wholly of food; they include silk, and a branch of the sacred Sakaki tree, with certain specified ornaments. What is edible is afterwards eaten by the priests; formerly, it is said, the people used to join in the feast.[2]

In the ancient Roman religion, the offerings were common articles of food, portioned out with true Roman frugality.[3]

---

[1] The following account of a sacrifice witnessed in Borneo by two careful and competent observers furnishes an interesting illustration to the above (Hose and McDougall, *Pagan Tribes of Borneo*, vol. ii., pp. 52 ff.). First, Tama Bulan, the officiating chief, a man of considerable personal influence among his tribesmen, washes himself with water and pigs' blood (pigs, though ordinarily treated with no reverence, are indispensable at sacrifices). After this preliminary purification, three men of the upper class take their seat beneath a leaf-shelter to look for omens, the most propitious omen being three hawks to the right, one to the left, and one circling above them. Next, fowls and pigs are brought for sacrifice, and two great poles of timber are set up before the long house, rudely carved into a likeness intended to represent Bali Penyang, the supreme deity, to act as altars. Tama Bulan officiates before the first, and his nephew, who had been one of the omen seekers, in a precisely similar manner before the other. He begins by sprinkling water on the image with a frayed stick, and rapidly prays. Three fowls are taken, one after another, their heads pinched off (as in the Hebrew rite), and their blood is sprinkled on the image. The throat of a pig is then gashed, and its blood also is flung on the image and on the other men and on Tama Bulan, while all join in the prayers. Meanwhile, four boys in the house are beating drums, to drown all sounds of evil omen. Then another pig and fowl are killed, and their carcases are fixed to the top of poles set upright. Another pig is brought to Tama Bulan, and while he prods it, as if to secure its attention, he gives it a message for the gods. Its throat is then cut, and Tama Bulan dilutes its blood with water and scatters it over the bystanders, still muttering his prayers. He does the same with the blood of the fowl, and then, his part done, he goes off to wash himself. The frayed stick is placed, as if sacred, under the rafter of the house.

[2] Moore, *History of Religions*, i., p. 193.

[3] Cf. Hor. *Od.*, i. 34: ' Parcus deorum cultor et infrequens.' Horace is not quite just to his countrymen here; *parcus* the Roman might be in his worship; if so, it was not necessarily because he was stingy, but because

THE CHILDHOOD OF SACRIFICE 53

The place of the offering was, as in India, some specially chosen spot, where the sods were cut to denote its sanctity[1]; and with veiled head the housekeeper or the priest, duly purified beforehand, brings the food, animal or vegetable, which is to avert the wrath of those mysterious beings, the gods, and to ensure their favour to his crops or his stock.

In all these cases sacrifice is clearly the act of the community or group. This may be larger or smaller—the size does not matter—but the group is generally the political or social unit, the tribe or clan, or the family. The representative, who takes the leading part in the rite, is naturally either the chief, or the father or eldest member of the group, or the priest, the 'specialist' in divine things, who may be counted on to preserve the tradition and avoid mistakes. The object desired is one which the whole group will share. This may be the getting rid of 'sin' or the guilt of some act of disobedience that has caused the outraged gods to withhold the simple needs of their suppliants; or success in hunting and fishing or battle, the growth of the crops, and favourable seasons; or the assurance that the god, with his potent influence, is in their midst. This divine presence, indeed, is what is really asked for in the majority of cases; the rites themselves suggest that what they are felt to point to is something more than a material blessing; while the god, living and active in their midst, is the source of everything that can be needed.[2]

Again, the examples we have passed in review prove that the offering is more than a gift. A great deal more attention is paid to its ceremonial condition and its treatment than to its marketable value. This would be unintelligible if the gods were thought of as grasping or avaricious chiefs. It is plainly something in

the gods did not ask for more than these simple gifts. *Infrequens* he certainly was not. Every occasion of his working life called for worship, as every event that he could wish for therein was presided over by some deity.

[1] *Templum*, temple, is derived from *temno*, to cut, and was first of all the sacred spot of ground, carefully marked, on which offerings might be made, or the space of sky marked off in which to observe omens in the flight of birds. The same is true of the Greek τέμενος.

[2] Compare the joy of the Hebrews when the ark was brought into their camp before the Philistines (1 Sam. iv. 5, ff.).

the worshipper himself that they mainly desire. And that something, that reverence or punctilious obedience, is manifested by the worshipper in order to secure a corresponding attitude in the god. Even when the offering becomes a periodic or daily one, of food or some other requisite for life, the mode of offering it demands the same care. If it were a case of payment, how should we explain the fact that the offering is often so palpably out of all quantitative relation to the result expected ? As we force our way to these ancient or secluded altars we are really watching the attempts of the untutored soul to get into touch with his god ; we might almost say to 'get right with' him. This is equally true if the sacrifice is offered with the joyful shoutings of confident kinship with the tribal god, or with the shuddering desire to propitiate him, or to banish from the midst something that has caused him to avert his face. What is important is the relation that has to be maintained on both sides. As a member of the tribal society, or at least in a definite position in regard to it, the god has certain functions to discharge for its benefit, which can be looked for unless something has gone wrong, or he has grown weak, and which he will no more forget than the chief will forget his duties and responsibilities. The tribesmen, too, have their definite functions towards him : to keep the tribal marriage laws, to respect the decisions of the elders, to avoid forbidden foods and places, and so on ; if these are broken, the proper relations between the two parties are broken also ; anything may then happen, unless those relations are restored.

We have purposely emphasized the material character of the results of this communion to show that the communion itself is much more than merely material. But we must not suppose that the results themselves are material and nothing more. The indwelling of the god is not always desired simply for what is craved for by the body. The god is often loved, if we may judge from the expressions quoted, not only as a giver, but as a friend. It would not generally occur to the savage—it did not to the ancient Hebrew—to make a distinction between these two characters. Possibly at the first stage of worship a man desires the presence of the gods for what he can get from

THE CHILDHOOD OF SACRIFICE 55

them. But there gradually develops a sense of mutual affection, which is not concerned with gifts that can be measured or weighed, as a child may rejoice in the coming of his father, even if the father has brought no present with him save his own delightful companionship.

If this is forgotten, religion will become indistinct from magic, and will speedily disappear. An influential school of anthropologists defines magic as the performance of certain rites to gain ends of one's own, as opposed to the ends of the community. This will explain why magic has always been frowned on by the community's representatives and laws. Wizards, when not elevated into officials by the tribe, and so won over to the tribal service, have always been set under a ban.[1] By others it is thought of as the use of certain means, more or less occult, to influence impersonal nature in contrast to the personal gods. The employment of a term like 'personal,' when we are dealing with any one but a philosopher, is far from safe. What does the untutored shepherd or hunter know of personality? Yet there is a difference, according as the object is thought of as bestowed by a power whom the suppliant has rendered propitious, or as automatically forced and driven into the hands of the man who can pronounce certain mysterious words or possesses some particular amulet or charm. Magic has been called the mother of science; what is the difference, to the uninstructed mind, between the amulet and the lightning rod, between spell and prayer, or between a common charm like rain-making and such a sacrifice as the offering of the Thonga 'psanyi' for a good harvest? The difference is not in what is done, but in what is expected. Is this regarded as a boon to be obtained, or a presence to be secured? A boon is much more definite than a divine presence; and magic is always much more definite than religion. But only in the presence which is required by religion is there life and progress.

The first definition of magic also raises difficulties. Religion asks for what the community desires. But why can it not also, like magic, represent the individual? Does it only consecrate what our modern psychologists call the Herd-complex, and leave the Ego-complex

[1] Cf. Exod. xxii. 18 ; 1 Sam. xxviii. 7 ff.

to neglect or anathema?[1] The answer is that the individual will not be likely to dissociate himself from the community at all unless his wishes are definitely anti-social; and then he can expect no sympathy from the communal gods, or from the community itself. Religion is communal, and it rests on an ordered relation between gods and men. And sacrifice, although it does not pretend to cover the whole field of religious feeling or practice, is also communal, and the maintenance of that ordered communal relation without which religion expires is its end.[2]

To urge this is not so daring as it may seem. There is no need to contend that these two elements, personality and community, are embodied in every sacrifice; or that ideas of gift or bribe, which we have refused to recognize as essential to sacrifice, are never present in the mind of the worshipper. Could the preceding paragraph be translated into the language of some child of the jungle or the bush, he would indeed be surprised. But what moves us most powerfully is not always that of which we are most conscious. And what can lie behind sacrifice, as we observe it, save these two conceptions— a person to be approached, and a society to approach him? Others come in to modify or overlay them—the very ideas, perhaps, which we have repudiated. But these obstacles only cause temporary deflections of the main stream. Such motives have appeared constantly, and they appear still, even in Christianity. But is Christianity for that reason

---

[1] See A. G. Tansley, *The New Psychology*, pp. 206 ff.

[2] See p. 41. Psychologically, magic, in spite of frequent assertions to the contrary, is as distinct from science as from religion. The savage possesses a rudimentary science of his own, which has nothing to do with magic. He stores up his own experience, and the experience of his friends. He discovers, for instance, reasoning ' from particulars to particulars,' that the use of certain herbs delivers him from certain pains or diseases. There is no mystery about the proceeding. He can pick the herbs and apply them for himself. But when these fail he will turn to the ' specialist' who has dealings with a world which he himself, with no special powers of initiation, cannot hope to enter. On the other hand, Durkheim, *op. cit.*, suggests that without religion there could have been no magic, since, if men had not known the orderly though mysterious world of the tribal divinities, they would never have suspected the occult world of the magician. Further, while the idea of magic is everywhere, its forms are constantly changing. Magic has no institutions, no cult. A useful list of references is given by Marett, art. ' Magic,' in Hastings' *Encyclopaedia of Religion and Ethics*.

THE CHILDHOOD OF SACRIFICE 57

a system of bribery or of commercial dealings with heaven?

Sacrifice is far wider than the varying rites and practices of Christianity; it is found where morality, in our sense, is unknown, where the life of man is 'nasty, brutish, short,' where ignorance and cruelty are appalling, and where what we call virtue would be regarded as disloyalty or insanity. Yet, in all his gropings and hardships, his terror at the unknown or his savagery to foes and even friends, his callousness to the sufferings of the weak, and his dark and turbulent passions, man has made the discovery, in the midst of his blindness, of these two great principles on which society and religion would both seem to rest, and he has never wholly lost them. Throughout all his feeling after God he has held to the great rite that has embodied these ideas, even though he has all but forgotten the ideas themselves. The course of his religious life, like a narrow path through the jungle, winding aimlessly till apparently it is near to dying out altogether, is explained when we, with our knowledge of all that religion means or ought to mean to us, can thus detect the latent convictions of the trembling and baffled pilgrims who long since blazed the trail and kept open the track.

III

INDIA AND GREECE

To study the records of primitive sacrifice, with their bewildering and repulsive details, is to be tempted to the conclusion that the savage 'disquiets himself in vain'; and we should expect that with larger experience and greater control over environment the cumbrous and repellent proceedings would be quietly dropped. That would be to ignore their remarkable 'survival value.' Nothing would seem more obvious than that the hunter should discover success to be based on better tracking and weapons, or the warrior on better tactics and missiles, and that both would therefore pay more attention to thought and plans and less to prayers and offerings. The hunter does not, indeed, despise tracking, even when he prays to the bear to become his victim; and the warrior does not despise tactics, however careful he may be to keep up his war-dances and his war-path taboos.[1] But no accumulating experience shakes his belief that he needs something more than this. Success in life is not a mere matter of human skill and implements. And there are large departments of life in which skill and implements will avail nothing, as for example, birth, sickness, love, and perils from demons. Hence sacrifice is not a mark of either indolence or self-distrust. To some it may result from the desire to take no risks or lose nothing for want of asking. To others, and perhaps to most, at certain times and in certain moods, it is the recognition that life is a partnership with the unseen.

Such a partnership may be purely utilitarian; but it may also lead to important consequences for good or evil. If the unseen world is peopled by lust or greed, cunning or caprice, a corresponding servility or cunning will be implanted in the human partners. If the gods are felt to be,

[1] See C. H. Tout, *British North America*, and H. Merker, *Die Masai*, for examples.

INDIA AND GREECE

even imperfectly, pure, righteous, and benignant, the desires and impulses of earth will be modified and exalted by the moral superiority and insistent demands of heaven. Even apart from this, the persistence of sacrifice is evidence for a certain 'nostalgia' for the unseen, whether it is thought to be useful or not. Man is restless till he is in touch with God. The sense of that partnership could hardly have survived if it were merely utilitarian. It has been too seldom justified by success. But in the human breast is something which no failure or disappointment can shake—the longing to be at one with the unseen, and even (we can hardly reject the phrase) to be a fellow worker with God.

Thus, as civilization grows, and with it man's control over nature, the richness and solemnity of sacrifice grows also. The most elaborate rituals are found in those pre-Christian societies where political and social and even industrial organization had reached the highest levels, in China and Babylon, Mexico and Egypt. We need not deny that the political value of religious institutions was well understood in antiquity, and that if religious systems had not existed it would at least have been thought advisable by some advanced minds to invent them, supposing that such a proceeding were conceivable. But these considerations do not explain why the indirect method of sacrifices should have been employed by the rulers when they could have reached their end so much more directly and shortly; or why sacrifices were perpetuated in a hundred shapes which had nothing to do with the desire with which every ruler has to reckon, for *panem et circenses*.

The vigour with which sacrifices have maintained themselves in the higher civilizations can best be studied in the rites of ancient India and Greece. We possess more details and a much larger literature of the former than of any other systems, such as those of Mesopotamia and Egypt; and although the sacrifices of Greece have passed away like those of Babylon and Thebes, the atmosphere of Greece is intelligible and modern to us. We are at home in Athens and Ephesus as we can never be on the Nile or the Euphrates. The Indian ritual, as we find it in the Vedas and Brāhmanas, is now no more; but the descendants of the men who assisted at the Aswamedhas of thirty centuries ago are performing ceremonies which developed from them in a continuous succession, and the impulses and convictions that lie behind the ancient and modern worships are fundamentally the same.

A further advantage in choosing these two types of worship is that while they lead us back, like most of the institutions of Greece and India, to a common source now buried in the dim past, they exhibit striking contrasts. The sacrificial ritual of Greece was predominantly communal and periodic. Indian religious practice is not communal, nor, in the sense of the Greeks, periodic. The great Indian festivals, or 'melas,' of to-day are held at stated seasons, and the enormous crowd of pilgrims, often gathered from all parts of the country, assists at the solemn procession of the god, but each person performs his 'puja' for himself. Even in Vedic times no sacrifice was ever offered by a whole community.[1] The worshipper, with whatever expert advice he could secure, chose his own time for the offering, and the priests whom he employed carried it out for his own benefit, just as the Brahmans do to-day. Another difference is that in India, as in Palestine, there was less diversity than in Greece. The priestly caste was more influential, and so was able to introduce a regularity and uniformity impossible for the priests in the multitudinous city states of Greece, where, indeed, their position was often as much political as religious. The result is that while the Greek practices baffle us by their variety, and still more by the myths (always likely to mislead) which are attached at least to the more familiar sacrifices, they are for the most part much nearer to the primitive. Indian religion in Vedic times was the cultus of a body of aristocrats who kept themselves and their rites almost morbidly distinct from the mass of the population they had conquered. The Greeks, with their ready hospitality to ideas, and their willing recognition of the ἐπιχώριοι θεοί, cheerfully preserved what they found in their new homes side by side with what they brought with them from the north.

The Indian sacrifices, like all others, are a development

---

[1] This does not, however, really conflict with what was said at the end of ch. ii. The rites were prescribed by the authority recognized by society, and performed for objects of avowed social utility.

INDIA AND GREECE

of the simple and natural desire to satisfy human needs with the aid of heaven. But in the rites, as we can study them in the sacrificial manuals, the separate needs are wholly subordinated to the general desire to gain the favour of the gods, and even this desire is almost buried by the accumulated details of the rites themselves, the immense importance of carrying out each one with absolute correctness, and the caution that is necessary when a mortal enters into personal dealings with a god. The whole process, indeed, suggests a twofold aspect. The worshipper is drawn to it; he cannot refuse it; the gods themselves demand it of him; he cannot expect their favour if he denies it; they themselves, without it, will lack the food they need in order to perform their own proper functions. On the other hand, to pass through the portals into the divine world, so to speak, is to lay oneself open to the action of invisible and all but incalculable powers, so potent for evil as well as for good that one might be forgiven for preferring not to face the labour of due preparation, the expense of worthy performance, and the perils of a single false step. For, once the sacrifice is begun, it must be continued to the end, in spite of any weariness or mischance; as if one set in motion a powerful machine, which might catch the operator in its terrible limbs, and could at best be watched and guided till it had come to rest.

The sacrifices were not all of equal importance. The divine functions which were to be aroused were not all equally potent, and the preparations therefore did not always make the same demands. But some preparations were always necessary, and chief among these was fasting. Most races have discovered the value of fasting in securing religious emotion or susceptibility. Australian and North American Indian lads, for example, always fasted before initiation, and before the adventure of finding their totem or guardian spirit, or of receiving the supernatural powers of the magician. Fasting was a well-known preparation for the greater religious services among the Jews; and the importance laid on fasting communion in Catholic Christianity, though it has often borne a materialistic interpretation—the desire that no ordinary food should mingle with the consecrated wafer in the body of the recipient—certainly points back to the psychological effect of abstinence.

But in some cases, and more particularly before the great Soma offering, fasting is but a small part of the preparations. The worshipper, who is thus to come into the closest contact with the gods, and to perform an act which affects and takes place in the divine world, must himself be, as it were, a god. He is to be carefully purified; hair is to be removed, nails to be clipped. He is clothed in new linen garments. He dwells apart in a special hut. He has to keep his hands closed, as if he were an embryo just being born into a new world. This may last for months, until he has got rid of his old self altogether.[1]

For the sacrifice itself, considerations of time and place are essential. As in Babylon and Rome, certain days and seasons are dangerous, as then the demons are free, or at least less restricted; while the new and the half moon seem naturally to suggest a propitious moment. The Hindus, like the ancient Greeks and Romans, and some of the earlier Semites, had no temples or localities possessing a permanent sanctity. The sacrifice was offered in the open, the actual spot being decided on by the aid of the priests.[2] Within this is a more carefully marked piece of ground, the 'vedi,' where the actual immolation is to take place. Special care is needed also that the fire should be pure. The Romans could bring fire from the flame, never extinguished, on the sacred hearth; the Hindus always produced a new fire by friction; for to the Hindus the fire, Agni, is itself a god, with his three bodies, terrestrial (the domestic fire), atmospheric (light), and celestial (the sun). And three corresponding fires are needed—the householder's fire, which, unlike the rest, is lit from the hearth; the sacrificial fire, which will consume the offerings; and the southern fire, as it was called, to keep off the demons

---

[1] See Hubert et Mauss, *Mélanges d'Histoire des Religions*, 1909, pp. 24 ff. They also describe the preparations for lesser sacrifices, where the worshipper is not 'divinized,' but only consecrated. They also refer to the rites which secure the fitness of the high-priest for the ceremonies of the Day of Atonement as given in *Yoma*, ch. ii., and to the opening of the Satapatha Brāhmana: 'the worshipper rinses his mouth; until this is done, he is not in a condition to sacrifice. Water is pure. He becomes pure in the inward parts. He passes from the world of men to that of the gods' (*Sacred Books of the East*, ed. F. Max Müller, vol. xii., p. 4; for the caution needed, cf. p. 9).

[2] Unlike *templum* and τέμενος, the Semitic 'beth' or 'house' implies a continuous residence.

INDIA AND GREECE 63

who would fain pollute the whole performance. No one god is usually approached, but a group of gods, or perhaps all the gods, are invited to the feast. Here are priests reciting ancient prayers or new ones composed for the occasion. Here is the private chaplain of the worshipper, ready to prevent any ritual mistake which would neutralize the value of the offering. Another priest spreads the mats for the gods to sit on.

Then the important moment approaches. The animal to be slaughtered enters the divine world, taking the worshipper with him, or, as we may put it, it brings the divine world into the midst of the human. It has been already examined and certified as without blemish, like the Hebrew victim; it is itself purified or bathed in water; its pardon is asked and its gracious willingness to be offered up. It would appear that the animal itself is a possibly dangerous object, and so must be placated, for sacrifice lets loose the spirit of the victim, which must therefore be rendered propitious. The priest then draws near with a special formula. He alone is specially in touch with the divine, and can safely handle the divine victim.[1] The animal is made to drink water, and anointed with butter and other libations. A torch symbolizing Agni is carried round it three times. The animal is then strangled or suffocated, if possible without being allowed to make a sound, while the spectators turn their backs upon the violent action. It is then divided into parts. The blood and the offal are for the demons; certain parts are solemnly carried to the altar for the gods; certain others are taken into the priest's hands, divine fertility is invoked over them, and they are then eaten, part by the priest, part by the sacrificer; the remainder can then be enjoyed by priest and laymen.[2] It only remains to secure the transition back to the normal world. Some of the implements used are burnt or otherwise destroyed; the remains of the carcase are disposed of; the persons involved purify themselves with lustrations as the sacrificer, turning to the fire, says, ' O Agni, I have made my vow; I have become a man once

[1] Cf. Hubert et Mauss, *op. cit.*, pp. 42, 45.

[2] Hubert and Mauss point out that the ritual for vegetable sacrifices is identical in its important elements. In the case of the Soma offering, only vegetables are used.

more. I descend from the world of the gods to the world of men.' In the case of the Soma offering the order of the lustral baths seems to show the actual reversal of the process of consecration.[1]

It is clear that we are dealing here with no elementary rite. Every detail of this complicated and leisurely proceeding has obviously been thought out. The whole ritual implies the existence of an influential priesthood and a religiously-minded laity. To attempt to find any close link between this sacrifice and the primitive offerings made by the distant ancestors of these Aryan chieftains, or the pre-Moslem Arab sheikhs, or the leaders of savage tribes and clans, would seem as futile as to look for one and the same religious conception in High Mass at St. Peter's and the simple thanksgivings of the Didache or the Epistle of Clement. But when the procedure is analysed, two very striking facts are manifest; the various elements are all of them found in other cults, Semitic, Greek, and Roman, developed and primitive; and the purpose which shines through their elaborate rites, and has time to reveal itself in their slow progress, reveals an unexpected rationality in the more fragmentary and hurried rites of other cults.

In the first place the purifications, the solemn choice of the holy place, the reverent address to the selected beast itself, the insistence on a rigidly prescribed method of taking its life, the special care at the moment of its slaughter, the manipulation of the blood, the meticulous exactness in the distribution of the parts of the body, and the solemn close or finale of the whole ceremony, are not to be thought of as so many priestly inventions, presumably intended to enhance the honour of the priestly caste. They are the expressions of a widely diffused conviction as to the significance and office of sacrifice, which is not so much obscured as clarified by the extension of the ritual. And a closer examination will show that the full ritual of the Vedas, which has just been summarized, instead of adding extraneous and artificial elements to what was originally simple and naïve, merely emphasizes, by a number of minor precautions, what was in the rite of the sacrifice from the beginning. The Vedic sacrifice may be considered, not as the evolution of sacrifice, but its type.

[1] *Sat. Brāhmana* (*ed. cit.*), pp. 272 f.

INDIA AND GREECE 65

And secondly, in the Vedic ritual, the underlying purpose cannot be mistaken. We may not assert that the purpose was present to every one who took part in it, or that the object of the rite, in the minds of those who shaped it, was identical with the hopes of the individual offerer. Hinduism has gone beyond most religions in dissociating the external practice, on which it insists, from the opinions entertained about it, to which it attaches no importance. The language of the Vedic hymns often suggests nothing more than barter. The gods want food and Soma, the worshippers want crops and cattle.[1] But why the special attention to the purity of the offerer, the position, not of one priest only, but of a whole body of clergy, the fear of some ritual error, and the number of things to be attended to after the animal has been killed and therefore presumably handed over to the gods, its recipients? Such details would be more than useless—they would be absurd—if the purpose were simply to transfer a valuable object from one owner, either a king or a simple farmer, to another, a tribal deity. The whole sacrifice is a means to secure a solemn and safe meeting, in an equally solemn place, between God and man. Each party is understood to be naturally averse from encountering the other, man because of the mysterious holiness of God, God because of the weakness and 'profaneness' of man. All the arrangements are made with a view to overcoming the grounds of this aversion, or, to repeat our already familiar expression, to breaking down the existing barrier; and these arrangements centre in the actual presentation of the animal.

In modern India the ritual of sacrifice is very different. No animal is killed in the orthodox Brahman sacrifices; it is even necessary to compensate on occasion the person who lights the sacrificial fire and who may therefore incur the guilt of destroying some insect life.[2] The gods are still summoned to the sacrifice, and the symbol of each is given its proper place; but the value of the sacrifice chiefly depends on the number of Brahmans invited and entertained, the number of mantras or sacred formulae repeated

[1] Cf. Hubert et Mauss, *op. cit.*, pp. 126 ff.
[2] The rites of Kali, however, involve the killing of animals still; and the Hindu doctrine of harmlessness (*ahimsa*) has left the aboriginal cults untouched.

E

by them, and the amount of ghee or clarified butter emptied over the fire. The great sacrifices are not performed of necessity at stated times, but every exalted and religious person is expected to acquire the merit of performing one or more of them at least once in a lifetime. The expense may amount to hundreds of pounds. Regular ceremonies also mark the transitions from one state of life to another—birth, marriage, death, and the like. These *rites de passage* generally take place on a spot in the house or courtyard marked off by the astrologer. The worship of the temples, which has no parallel in Vedic times, consists mainly in the tendance of the idol, its washing, dressing, feeding, or the ceremonies connected with its being taken out in procession or put to rest.[1]

When brought into relation with the Vedic rites, we can partly see how these fantastic and very often purely commercial practices have arisen. At the same time the older and simpler sacrifices become intelligible. We have already seen that they cannot be explained simply as gifts or bribes or expiations. Even if the worshipper of to-day, as undoubtedly happens constantly, thinks of them in no other way, no one explanation will fit all the sacrifices or account for certain elements which constantly appear. But let us regard them, like the Vedic rite, as the means for securing a meeting between man and God, and we begin to understand them. Naturally, the purposes which that meeting is intended to accomplish will differ in different instances. The particular business the worshipper may have with his god will vary—the request for a favour, the striking of a bargain, the confession of a fault, or the pleasant and satisfying sense of contiguity and renewed goodwill. What the sacrifice accomplishes is the possibility of coming into contact at all. When we understand this, we can see why it has been possible to divide sacrifices into so many classes, and why, in spite of all this diversity, sacrifices exhibit such noteworthy similarities, both at the most diverse levels of culture and among the most widely sundered races.

[1] The fullest account of present-day Hindu ritual is to be found in *The Rites of the Twice-born*, by Mrs. Sinclair Stevenson, 1920; see also *Int. Rev. Missions*, Oct. 1920, pp. 588 ff.

INDIA AND GREECE 67

But it will probably be felt that our conclusion is too wide for the facts hitherto collected. Can it really be asserted that man's attitude to the unseen powers and his dealings with them are fundamentally the same—that is, that religion is at bottom one, at the court of Aryan chiefs and in the kraals and wigwams of nomad savages? To join together or reconcile man and God by the intermediation of a quasi-divine victim may have been the conception of sacrifice handed down in a school of Hindu priests, and it may be possible to interpret some pagan rites in these terms. Can we suppose that all sacrifices are not only capable of this interpretation, but that they are incapable of any other?

Such a question calls for the examination of all present and past forms of sacrifice, a task which no investigator will ever complete or attempt. If it could be carried through, we may be permitted to doubt whether any one formula would express the bewildering mass of instances to hand. But if, the more closely we examine the main types, we seem to see more clearly a number of diverging practices which yet point to a single conception as their origin, we shall be inclined to admit that man, who testifies to the unity of his race in so many ways—in his myths and folk-tales, his social organization and his psychic life—is united in the deepest part of him, his religious beliefs and hopes. We now turn, therefore, to the sacrifices of ancient Greece, not in the hope of detecting, as we have detected in India, a dominant and centralized practice; but in order to ask whether, in the diversity of the practices which the Greeks preserved all through the ages of their most advanced civilization, we can discover any hidden bond or link to unite them, and others with them.

As is natural where primitive and developed, savage and civilized, are so closely intermingled, the problem of the origins of Greek religion has been keenly debated of late. The time-honoured hypothesis that the Hellenic culture was superimposed on that of an earlier or Pelasgic race is very doubtful. The evidence rather points to a firmly seated mass of religious beliefs in the various races inhabiting the Mediterranean basin, from Spain to Syria, distinct alike from India and Babylon on the one hand and the

Northern tribes on the other.[1] In the eastern half of this area a large influence was exerted by the Cretan civilization through most of the second millennium B.C.[2] Influence was also inevitably exerted by Egyptian culture, but not, it would seem—at least to any large extent—by Egyptian religion, either in south-eastern Europe or western Asia.[3] Into this area came the Hellenes, from the north, bringing with them their own deities, as the Aryans invaded India, bringing with them their Vedic gods. Unlike the Aryans, the Greeks made little attempt to keep either themselves or their religion separate; and although, thanks to Homer and the powerful traditions of both literature and art, later ages identified Greek religion with the worship of the 'Olympians,' the rites and the objects of Greek worship, popular and official, expressed beliefs and hopes which are rarely explicit in the Homeric poems.[4] To the student of origins, Homeric religion is at once late and artificial.

This does not mean, however, that we can afford to despise the assistance of Homer, least of all in reconstructing Greek ritual. The evidence we possess for that ritual, in inscriptions and on vases, is enormous, and is still growing; but it is only when we fall back on the descriptions of Homer that we can fit the puzzling fragments into a picture at all clear and informing. It is convenient, therefore, to preface any account of Greek sacrifices by the ritual of a typical offering, as it can be gathered, with the help of our wider evidence, from the Homeric poems themselves. When the group of worshippers was assembled, and the animal was in readiness, holy water was brought forward for

[1] See L. R. Farnell, *Greece and Babylon*, ch. xiii., for instances where Greece and Israel agree with one another as against Babylonian religion, the conclusion suggested being that religious similarity is a matter of geographical contiguity as well as, and perhaps more than, racial affinities, real or supposed.

[2] See, for striking examples, A. J. Evans, *Mycenean Tree and Pillar Cult*, 1901.

[3] Foucart, however, in *Les Mystères d'Eleusis*, sees much Egyptian influence on the Eleusinian cult. This, though improbable, is not necessarily inconsistent with what is said above.

[4] All this has been very vigorously stated in Miss Jane Harrison's *Prolegomena to the Study of Greek Religion*, 1903. The sharp distinction which she there draws between Olympian and chthonic deities must not be overstated. There is much in common between the two; Olympians could be regarded as θεοὶ ἀποτρόπαιοι or vice versa; and it does not follow that because Homer and others preferred to regard the Olympians as cheerful and gracious they were universally so regarded.

INDIA AND GREECE

purification, and the worshippers took stalks of barley in their hands, apparently from off the altar, and held them up. The leader of the rite called on the god to whom the sacrifice was being offered, and, lifting his hands, uttered the prayer for the special blessing desired.[1] At the same moment the barley stalks were thrown forward, possibly to convey the sanctity of the altar from which they had been removed to the victim.[2] The frontal hair of the animal was then cut off by the leader. This completed the initial part of the sacrifice. Next, the victim was killed. The general custom was to fell the creature with an axe and then to draw its head back and cut its throat. If it was destined for the gods of the underworld, however, its head was held so as to point downwards; and if the animal was sufficiently small—a pig or a goat—it was held up so that its blood would drop down on the altar. The women present raised the ritual cry while this was being done, and certain pieces of flesh were then cut off, wrapped in fat, and placed on the altar.[3] Meanwhile, libations were poured; portions of the entrails were handed to the worshippers, to be solemnly tasted, after which the remainder of the body was cut up to form the material of the feast with which the rite was completed. Later on, garlands, as signs of purity,[4] were placed on the heads of the offerers and the victim; incense was kindled, and a burning torch was quenched in a bowl of the water which had been used to sprinkle the victim and the altar, and the altar was sprinkled with sacrificial blood.[5]

---

[1] See, for example, Hom. *Iliad*, i. 446 ff., xix. 254 ff.; *Od.*, xiv. 419 ff.

[2] See a paper by L. R. Farnell on 'Communion in Greek Religion,' *Hibb Journ.*, ii., pp. 313 ff.

[3] Compare the place of fat in the ritual of the Hebrew altar, p. 104.

[4] Eur., *Her. Furens*, 677.

[5] For full accounts of Greek ritual see Stengel, P., *Opfergebräuche der Griechen*, 1910. It is significant that there is no mention of the ritual use of blood in Homer. There the gods like blood as little as men. But the sacredness of blood and its connexion with life are prominent in Greek ritual, as also in that of the Hebrews (see p. 117), and representations of altars on vases often have red blood-streaks to mark them. In sacrifices to chthonic or earth deities, blood took the place of the wine offered in libations to the gods of the upper air. There was a large diversity in the animals sacrificed. Over Patroclus, Achilles killed sheep and cattle, four horses and two dogs, as well as twelve Trojan youths (*Il.*, xxiii. 166 ff.). Aphrodite loathed the pig, but welcomed the hare; the pig was, however, connected with Demeter's rites. Wild animals were seldom offered, save to Artemis. Horses and asses were offered to the earth gods. In Homer horses were offered to the winds, or as a precaution against floods.

The ritual is not so elaborate as that of the Vedas, but the resemblance is unmistakable. The emphasis on the sanctity of the altar and the victim, and the care taken by the worshippers that they should be joined ceremonially to the animal, and the animal to the god, suggest ' the intention to sanctify the animal and fill it with the divine spirit ; and as the altar was the centre to which that spirit was attracted, the aim would be effected by establishing a *rapport* between the deity represented by the altar and the victim.'[1] We must be careful not to go too far in expounding the religious ideas of the worshippers. In Greece, as in India, opinions mattered little as long as the practice was correct.[2] But the practice grew out of certain ideas ; and, as far as we can see, these ideas, in their simpler forms, both in Greece and India, are curiously alike. The victim is brought to the holy place, the spot where the gods are, so to speak, at home. It is itself at home there ; and by its slaughter—that is, its intimate association with the gods— men and gods, connected each with the animal on the altar, are linked up to one another.

Thus the essential features of sacrifice as we have so far observed them reappear in the typical Greek offering. But, since Homer is far from exhausting Greek religious practice, we must turn to the rites in which the Homeric aristocrats took no interest, or, as it might be more correct to say, which they had not yet had time to assimilate. And here we are on much more difficult ground, for most of the notices of these rites in literature are fragmentary or unsympathetic ; the poets, the philosophers, and even the orators, were the very men who held such performances to be far beneath their level of culture ; as for the antiquarians, like Pausanias, their observation was industrious, but their knowledge was imperfect and their conclusions often precarious. The aesthetic sense of the Greeks prevented any attempt to represent them faithfully. The vase-painters reproduced certain details, always modifying them in accordance with their artistic feelings, but the greater sculptors, and the tragedians, confined themselves almost entirely to the Olympians.

[1] L. R. Farnell, art. ' Sacrifice (Greek),' *E.R.E.*
[2] A remark of T. R. Glover's in *Jesus in the Experience of Men* (p. 63) is equally true of India and Greece : ' Sacrificial language was used by all, understood by none.'

INDIA AND GREECE

The only reliable conclusions, therefore, are those we can draw from the comparison of the largest possible number of instances. From these it would appear that at the bottom of at any rate a great deal of Greek religion lay the desire of the primitive agriculturalist for good crops. And, indeed, it is only in our modern urbanized life, with corn from every country in the world able to find its way to our shores, that anxiety for the next harvest ceases to be pressing. In a poor country like Greece the state of the crops was as interesting to the countrymen of Pericles or Demosthenes as it could have been to the subjects of Cecrops. Thus the ancient 'fertility sacrifices' could never grow antiquated, though the precise reason for their ritual might have been long forgotten. The early farmers were conscious of a *numen*—a divinity in the soil. They might plough the fields and scatter the seed, but a higher power made it grow, or, if neglected or weakened by lack of tendance, let it rot. And when it had grown, and the crop was ready for cutting, it was charged with divinity, and the subtle essence had to be both rendered harmless to those who, with sickle and knife, invaded its holiness, and continued in vigour for the crops of the next season. Further, the crops were the concern of the whole village community, or of the tribal family. The celebrations, therefore, had a communal character, and as city life developed from the earlier agricultural settlement, the sacrifices were still more definitely the expression of group life, belonging either to the city as a whole or to some recognized and permanent department of it.

All this is borne out by the fact that the official civic sacrifices were constantly connected with the agricultural seasons, harvest or seed-time. In many cases they involved ritual dances, whose object undoubtedly was, like that of similar dances in all parts of the world, to stimulate the reproductive power of the corn, or of the spirit that dwelt within it. The ceremonial killing of the animal, which is not necessarily more religious than the dance and song which accompanies it, is obviously the act by which the whole community puts itself in the right relation to the unseen powers on whose goodwill its very life depends.

If we ask why the life of a creature should be taken in order that these relations may be maintained or repaired, a hint may be obtained from a remarkable and often-quoted rite which, by its very absurdity—or what seems so to us—reveals the beliefs which prompted it. The Buphonia was held in Athens in the middle of the summer, just when the threshing was ended. Barley and wheat cakes were laid on the altar of Zeus Polieus, the Zeus of the community, and oxen were driven round the altar. As soon as one of them began to eat the cakes, this action was regarded as a sign that he was the appointed victim. He was felled, and his throat cut. The holders of the axe and the knife immediately flung away their weapons and fled.[1] The bystanders, unable or unwilling to catch them, turned upon the axe and knife, which were then solemnly brought to trial, and, in the absence of the human agents, judged guilty and condemned to be thrown into the sea. Meanwhile the carcase was flayed, and the meat used as material for the communal feast which followed; but the hide of the ox was stuffed with straw, sewn up, set on its feet, yoked to a plough, and treated as if it had been safely brought back to life.[2]

Here there is something much more than the mere killing of an animal in honour of a god, or as an attempt to secure his favour. It is not, however, in this instance the manipulation of the blood or the disposal of the carcase which is of special importance, but the character of the victim. By virtue of his contact with the altar he becomes holy, and this in a double sense; his life, charged with spiritual potency, can be made available as 'spiritual' food for the community, who thus 'have communion with the altar' and the god. But, as he is thus united with the god, his death is a sacrilegious outrage, needing to be both punished and annulled. It may be that the victim was itself regarded as actually divine, and that the rite thus represented the slaughter of a god, who, by voluntarily approaching the altar, marked himself out for death.

[1] For the flight of the two men as murderers compare the title of the Roman festival, 'Poplifugia,' which apparently refers to the flight of the bystanders from the scene of the crime of the victim's death. The festival of the 'Regifugium' may point to the same practice, the *rex* being the officiating priest; cf. the title *rex sacrificulus*. See W. Warde Fowler, *Roman Festivals of the Period of the Republic*, 1899.

[2] The account is given in Pausanias i. 24, 25. It can be found summed up in Miss Harrison, *op. cit.*, or in L. R. Farnell, art. 'Sacrifice (Greek),' *E.R.E.*

INDIA AND GREECE

The rite, thus interpreted, has been illustrated by a similar rite carried out at Magnesia, where the finest available bullock was chosen, led in procession through the town at seed-time, and, when he had made some conventional sign that he accepted his destiny, kept for a month, and then, after another procession and prayer, killed and eaten. He was then himself regarded as Zeus Sosipolis, the preserver of the city.[1] This recalls instances where a human being, often a slave or a criminal, was treated for a set interval with every indulgence, and then sacrificed. Whether the human being, as a sacrifice, came first, and the animal was a substitute for it in a milder age, is doubtful.[2] The facts certainly do not suggest that human, as distinct from animal, sacrifice was original, and we need not suppose that much interest was taken in the nature of the divinity of the victim, human or animal, if this was believed in at all. More important, for our purpose, is the fact that the victim was charged with divine qualities, whose benefit he could hand on to the worshipper, and that this belief had got so firm a hold on men in highly civilized communities that on the strength of it they were willing to act what must have seemed to uninstructed strangers a rather ridiculous stage-play.[3]

The same desire to ensure fertility and prosperity by ceremonial union with the god through the sacrifice is plain in many of the festivals of Italy. At the famous Latin Festival, which lasted on till the third century A.D., and was attended by the magistrates of all the Latin cities, on pain of expulsion from the League, the Roman consul had to make an offering of milk, and the other magistrates brought sheep and cheeses. The consul then sacrificed a white unyoked heifer, on which the full company had to feed. The ceremony was followed by a general festivity; but the actual rite was so important that if any error were made, the whole had to be repeated. A similar ceremony

---

[1] Kern, *Die Inschriften von Magnesia*, Berlin, 1900, quoted by Farnell, *op. cit.*

[2] Cf. Gen. xxii., and see p. 47.

[3] The persistence of primitive ideas and practices was shown on Christmas Day, 1916, when the Metropolitan of Athens solemnly excommunicated a bull's head, representing the body of Venizelos, and cast a stone at it. Each member of the crowd then flung another stone and a curse with it Ελληνες ἀεὶ παῖδες, as the Egyptian priests said to Herodotus.

was performed at Iguvium for the Latin stock inhabiting the plain below the town. The rustic festival of the Parilia, to take an example at the opposite end of the social scale, served a like purpose for the safety of the sheep. In April, when lambing time was well over, the shepherds used to decorate the fold, purify the sheep, and drive them through a consecrating or cathartic fire, which they also leapt through themselves, and shared with Pales the offerings they had brought, praying at the same time for their flocks and for forgiveness for any evil unwittingly committed.[1]

In the Roman religion the gods were notoriously lacking in character. They had their functions very carefully marked off, but they could hardly be called persons. They were like so many centres of specialized 'mana.'[2] And if we can rid ourselves of the influence of the Olympian tradition, we shall have to admit that the same thing is to a large extent true of the Greek divinities. The name and history matter little. The function is everything. If the performance was correct, the unseen forces, as if acting according to some dimly discerned law of nature, would do their work, whether they were known as gods or chthonic powers or heroes and dead ancestors. The performances differ like the myths which were invented to account for them; the principle is the same. Zeus Polieus and the 'Eniautos daimon' of Miss Jane Harrison can be approached with the same confidence. 'And this,' some would say, 'reduces the whole thing to magic.' On the contrary, it is possible to see, in this reliance on an unseen power who can be trusted to respond to reverent worship and earnest invocation, at least the feeling after the adoration of a righteous God, who is in reality one and supreme.[3] The God who gives us rain and fruitful seasons, filling our

---

[1] See W.W. Fowler, *op. cit.*, pp. 81 f., 95 ff., 227. In the last instance it would appear that contact with the god was obtained directly through the fire, the offerings being a further inducement to the divine spirit to be present. At another rustic festival, which lasted on into historical times, the Compitalia, sacrifices were originally offered to the Lares or spirits of the fields, at the spots where the paths on the farm crossed one another.

[2] Cf. ch. ii. p. 39.

[3] Greek and Roman paganism did not persecute. How could it, when it was wedded to the maxim '*Cujus civitas, ejus deus*,' and when its gods were so slightly differentiated from one another, even in name? The Christians were persecuted by the state, not by the priests.

INDIA AND GREECE

hearts with food and gladness, had not left Himself without witness.

The readers of Matthew Arnold's *Culture and Anarchy*, with its insistence on the sunny character of Hellenic worship, used to feel a shock at the discovery that the dark sense of guilt and fear was as deeply embedded in the Greeks as in the Semites. A plague, an untoward circumstance, or some continued misfortune, would fill a community with the conviction that some evil had been committed, perhaps quite unintentionally, but leaving a pollution which could only be made to bring its malevolent action to an end through some ceremony of riddance. Sometimes a specialist in such matters would be sent for, like Epimenides from Crete; or application for instruction would be made to an oracle; or strolling prophets and sorcerers would be engaged, to prescribe sacrifices and charms, all ending with a pleasant meal, at not too great an expense.[1] But the wise Greek did not always wait for emergencies. There are many instances of periodical purification. At Athens, in the Thargelia, for example, which were held about the beginning of June, two persons were made to run the gauntlet in the streets, and then flung outside the city or put to death, as if loaded with the misdeeds of the population.[2] These human scapegoats were known as φαρμακοί, from φάρμακον, a drug or medicine, or as καθάρματα, off-scourings. This proceeding, however, can hardly be called a sacrifice. There is no attempt to get into touch with a god; the intention is simply to get rid of the evil or guilt, regarded as so much polluted substance or dirt, as completely and expeditiously as possible. As such it appears in almost all societies.[3] It is often, indeed, joined to a true sacrifice, as in the rite of the Jewish Day of Atonement; but the function of the sacrifice in that case is different, namely, to reopen relations with the deity after the pollution which prevented them has been thus purged away.

We must not judge these time-honoured rites by our

[1] Plato, *Rep.*, ii. 364.
[2] Aristoph., *Ran.*, 733; cf. also Aristoph., *Pl.*, 454. In Basden, *The Ibos of Nigeria*, 1920, an account is given of a practice of selecting a criminal, tying him to a tree, or half burying him in the ground, and transferring to his head, by a solemn laying on of hands, all the 'sins' of the community, and then loading him with insults and leaving him to die a horrible death.
[3] Cf. Frazer, *The Scapegoat*, pp. 31 ff.

standards. With their solemn sequence of familiar yet impressive acts, the prestige and high authority of the state behind them, the presence of a crowd of like-minded people, as at a national function, and the belief that in some way they and all who watched them were conferring a real though dimly understood benefit on the state and linking the human to the divine, they would be capable of arousing deep, and in the quite true sense of the word religious emotions, perhaps considerably deeper than what is experienced by many a Christian at an ordinary ' morning service.' Such emotions would be quite independent of the needs which the sacrifices were originally intended to supply. But in regard to certain other needs and emotions, such sacrifices would be useless—the mystical longing for actual union with the divine and the assurance of escape from the limitations and evils of this finite and mortal life. Man does not live by bread alone. And there grew up in course of time on Hellenic soil a number of expedients for supplying him with more spiritual food. Prominent among these was the cult of Dionysus, originally like Apollo a non-Hellenic god, who reached Greece from Thrace by way of Thessaly and Boeotia. His devotees, like the Thyiads at Apollo's sanctuary at Delphi, ranged over the mountains at night, sometimes in mid-winter, and strange and terrible stories were told about their eating raw and even human flesh. Their dances were ' mysteries '—that is, kept secret from all but the initiated—and the frenzy with which their repellent yet fascinating rites were carried out, and the rage with which they were supposed to fling themselves on critics and opponents, has found expression in the wild and magnificent poetry of Euripides' *Bacchae*. Observers plainly did not understand the rites, nor probably did the initiates themselves; but they appear to have resulted from religious ' archaising '; to be a throwback, as it were, to the original impulse of sacrifice before it had been tamed and civilized. The bands of devotees who rushed madly over the snowy hillsides under the moon, where no profane eye was allowed to gaze on them, are like the initiates in some savage totem group or confraternity, removed from the ordinary ways of the tribe and prepared by long and exhausting vigils to enter into relations with their guardian spirit; to be, in fact, possessed by him. The

INDIA AND GREECE

raw meat which they devour is the flesh of an animal which is identified with the god himself. Dionysus is identical with the bull which is sacrificed to him; and, like the sacrifice, he dies and comes to life again. And through their union with the godhead the worshippers know that they escape from death and gain immortality.

Salvation and sanctification here were through a sacrifice which is really the deity's bestowal of himself ; and the results might have been strange if such an impulse had survived in its essentials until Christianity had invaded the Hellenic world. But its manifestations were too bizarre and erratic to receive anything but frowns from established authority. Its place was taken by other and non-Hellenic cults, in which its archaic idea of sacrifice was less prominent. A more ordered and controlled, and at the same time in reality a more daring attempt to reach the same end, is found in the Eleusinian mysteries. Like the Dionysiac rites, these were confined to the initiates; unlike them, they were organized and carried through under the protection of the Athenian state. The officials could only be selected from one or other of two families; the state recognized and even enforced the due celebration of the festivals. There were two each year; the lesser, in spring, held in Athens itself, and the greater, in autumn, at Eleusis, some ten miles distant. The state was ready to punish in the severest fashion any violation of the rules and prohibitions of the rite, especially the rule of secrecy, and sacrifices for the wellbeing of the city and its inhabitants were a regular part of the proceedings.

Although the rule of secrecy was absolute, and, as far as we know, never broken, its application was narrow, and much of the celebration was of necessity quite public. On the 14th of Boedromion, about October 1, the sacred objects were brought from Eleusis to Athens; on the 15th the initiates gathered, and on the 16th they were purified and went 'into retreat.' After two days' interval for an intercalary festival of Asclepius called the Epidauria, the sacred objects were carried back in procession to Eleusis on the 19th and 20th. The initiating ceremonies then took place. These began with a sacrifice to the two goddesses who presided over the festival, Demeter and Kore, and the initiates announced their fitness to watch the spectacles that were to follow by repeating the words ' I have fasted, I have drunk the *kukeon* (a consecrated mixture of meal and water), I have taken [the objects] in the chest, and after taking them I have replaced them in the basket and from the basket into the chest.'[1] The ceremony implied by these words is generally held to point to some sort of mystical union with the goddesses, after which the initiates were shown a representation in which they were supposed to travel to the world of the dead, and then enter the Elysian fields. At the same time, definite instruction was given to them by the hierophant, or master of the mysteries, which assured them that through this union they would themselves reach a blessed immortality.

This concluded the first stage of the mysteries, which was known as the μύησις, or initiation proper. But there was a second, the ἐπόπτεια, or vision, to which the initiate was allowed to proceed after the interval of at least a year. As the second was not, like the first, essential to salvation, many were satisfied without it. But its effect, emotional and even intellectual, would seem to have been greater. It consisted, as far as can be gathered from our naturally scattered and fragmentary information, of two sets of dramatic representations; the former, the death and mutilation of Dionysus, followed by the restoration of his body, and, in addition to this, the solemn exhibition of a blade of wheat; the latter, the union between Zeus and Demeter—the 'hierogamos,' or sacred marriage—which was supposed to take place in secret, while the initiates waited outside, until the hierophant announced that an infant, Brimos, had been born.[2] The position of Dionysus by the side of the two goddesses at the second initiation is gathered

---

[1] Jevons, *Introduction to the Study of Religion*, ch. xxiv., suggests the belief in some form of transubstantiation here. Farnell (*loc. cit.*) doubts this; but there may well have been involved a deep religious experience in eating what was regarded as in some way connected with the divine being. The Greek initiates were not mediaeval theologians, and we need not suppose that they troubled themselves about the difference between eating the god and entering into the spirit of the god by means of the consecrated food and drink.

[2] See Foucart, *Mystères d'Eleusis*, esp. chs. xv., xvi., xviii., xx. What little explicit information is given us as to the actual things kept secret is obtained chiefly from Clem. Alex., *Protrepticus*, pp. 13-19 (Ed. Potts), and Hippolytus, v. 1. A vivid but less detailed account of the Eleusinian mysteries will be found in Loisy, *Les Mystères Païens et le Mystère Chrétien* pp. 51-84.

INDIA AND GREECE

from a number of inscriptions; and Foucart derives it from the Egyptian teaching about Osiris, himself a vegetation deity, who is killed at each harvest and then brought to life again.

It is equally easy to see in these services nothing but the action of capricious and even obscene superstition, and to detect similarities to the Christian teaching and faith. That the Eleusinia influenced the practices and beliefs of early Christianity is highly improbable, although Percy Gardner has suggested that Paul's acquaintance with them during his stay at Corinth led to his organization of the Lord's Supper.[1] Farnell, who recognizes the importance of the Orphic tenets of divine birth, death, and resurrection in the Hellenic world, doubts their presence at Eleusis. He prefers to see, instead of any direct influence, a 'parallel between the great Attic mysteries and the Christianity that silenced them.' And this he finds, 'not in their vital concepts, but generally in the religious temper of mind they evoked, and specially in the ideal of a *Madre dolorosa* and in their hopes of posthumous salvation, and on the ritualistic side in the ideas associated with baptism, purification, and sacrifice, and in the organization of the ceremonial.'[2]

Certainly the mysteries gathered round them sincere and penetrating religious feeling, and that there should be similarities where religion is real and earnest is not surprising. That a faith which for many centuries enjoyed the respect of many of the noblest Greek minds was rooted in superstition, or worse, cannot be seriously maintained. The union with the god whose death and return to life were symbolized by the stalk of wheat, the offspring of the seed that had fallen into the ground and died, assured the worshipper that he, too, was an heir of salvation, and that death had no more dominion over him. The episode of the sacred marriage told him that the powers of nature on which all human life depended were constantly renewed, and that, since to him a son had been given, seed-time and harvest would not fail. In a world where ecclesiasticism and politics together had laid their cold hand on the traditional, and to him unmeaning, cults of his city, the

---

[1] See below, p. 199, and Clemen, *Primitive Christianity and its non-Jewish Sources*, Eng. Trans., pp. 186 ff.

[2] *Hibb. Journ.*, ii. 403.

effect of such a personal and intimate assurance of what he most needed to know must have been overwhelming.

It is significant that in the mysteries of Eleusis, as in those of Samothrace and Crete, sacrifice plays a comparatively unimportant part. But what was said of the Dionysiac celebration can be applied to Eleusis. The instructions and 'mystery plays' of Eleusis appealed directly to the impulses which have found a less direct satisfaction in sacrifice—the longing to draw near to God, to be ' at one with ' Him, to be assured of that state of body and mind in which His favours can be counted on. True, the mysteries speak of deliverance and escape, not of forgiveness; and, as far as we know, the moral element in the instruction given was very slight. But apart from this difference (and it cannot well be over-emphasized) between the offers made by the mysteries and the gifts of Christianity, we can venture to say that the hierophants of Eleusis, like the preachers of Jerusalem and Antioch, held out the sure and certain hope of reconciliation and resurrection. It is only when we appreciate the likenesses between the offers of the two faiths that we can understand their differences, and the reason why, when the one has decayed and passed away for ever, the other still lives.[1]

---

[1] See Verrall, *The Bacchants of Euripides*, 1910, for a suggestive account of the ' faith ' and ' experience ' of the (Dionysiac) mysteries as described in the Bacchae (pp. 159 f.) : ' It is a spirit which appeals chiefly to simple folk ; it is more congenial to women than to men, though a man possessed by it may gain, especially over and through women, an almost unlimited influence. It is rapidly infectious. . . . Of certain virtues it is specially productive, as of courage, both to suffer and to act. It bestows upon the faithful an exquisite happiness, a supreme sense of harmony and joy.'

IV

THE MYSTERIES

THE mysteries of Eleusis described in the last chapter were one of the links which bound the vigorous paganism of republican Greece to the age of dying and dead beliefs which preceded the triumph of Christianity. When we pass from the fifth or fourth century B.C. to the first years of the Roman Empire we are sensible of an enormous change. The old independent states of Greece and Italy which made the political history of their time so crowded and so futile have passed away. They are now mere municipalities. In their place has come, not a nation or a group of nations, but a world-state. The populations of this state have not only learnt to share the same citizenship, and to acquiesce in a world where, politically, there was neither Jew nor Greek, barbarian nor Scythian; they have intermingled.[1] Trade and slavery have settled hosts of Orientals in Greece and Italy. Roman merchants have made themselves at home in the harbours of every country; and Roman soldiers have been settled, in camps and demobilization colonies, on the borders of German forests and Asiatic deserts. In this new cosmopolitan atmosphere the old civic religions could not breathe. Endowed with no aggressive missionary impulse, they could not hold their own ground. And when interest ceased in the fortunes of the city, faith in the city gods could no longer triumph over the absurdities of their rites. So long as Athens stood for everything they hoped and admired and believed, in this life and the next, the city fathers could solemnly sit in judgement on the axe that had felled the sacred bull. When Athens became one city among many, though still the fairest, the proceeding was childish. The philosophers regarded the ceremonies which the state functionaries still performed as an English professor might regard the

[1] ' Syrus in Tiberim defluxit Orontes ' (*Juv.*, iii. 62).

miracle of S. Januarius at Naples or the worship at a holy spring in Macedonia on the festival of the Transfiguration. Simple men and women felt that their ritual was neither better nor worse than a score of others; and the new and comprehensive state turned their minds to the thought of an equally comprehensive religion, if it could be found.

The old faiths were doomed, but the sacrifices did not die out. Custom, tradition, and the separation of ritual from belief and theory prevented this. And the heart of man was unchanged. It still demanded what, for a time, sacrifice alone seemed able to give. But the demand was met in a different way, and from a different source. With the decay of the old faiths came the rise of the mystery religions. In the first three centuries of the empire, and in some quarters for two or three centuries earlier, the mystery religions took the place of the older paganism in the Mediterranean world. Until recently their existence was hardly suspected; even now the study of them moves through great stretches of ignorance. But many inscriptions have recently come to light; numbers of references in ancient authors have been detected and brought together; and it is possible to see something of the real religious impulse and enthusiasm which carried them up and down the Roman world, and something of the rituals and, if we may use the term, the creeds which won them their devotees. The centuries of their wider expansion and influence were the centuries when Christianity was learning its strength. Likenesses, real or supposed, between them and Christianity lie on the surface; interaction and rivalry between them were inevitable, and compels as much attention to the mysteries from the Christian theologian as from the student of religion in general. An observer of the third century might have been forgiven if he had supposed that the mystery religions and Christianity were really making the same promises to devout humanity, and that in the struggle between them for existence the mysteries would even be victorious.

Our own business, however, is not with the mysteries in general, but with the light they can throw on the place of sacrifice in religion. It would seem at first that these new religions, as they poured in from the East, pushed sacrifice into as subordinate a position as did the similar, though quite distinct, mysteries at Eleusis. They emphasized the very things that the civic cults cared nothing for—individual devotion, the communication of authoritative teaching, and the enthusiastic acceptance of a new way of life. Their temples were far more like Christian churches than were the shrines of an Athena Polias or a Zeus Sosipolis. They were designed for the worship of a congregation and the more or less dramatic representation of the death of the god; like the Christian churches which now began to appear in town and country, they were halls, or basilicae, rather than wide and open courts, with relatively tiny shrines. None the less, they touched the older cults more closely than was often suspected. They all centred in a divine death which was in some sort a sacrifice, and which, as it led to his rising again, brought eagerly desired blessings to the worshippers and to society. And it was through participation in that death that the worshipper came into a close and intimate personal relation with the god, and could receive all that the god had to give. If we accept the theory—advocated in one form or another by scholars so independent as Frazer, Farnell, and Miss Harrison—that sacrifices, at least in many instances, originated in the representation of the death of the god, and that the god was thus also the victim, the resemblance between the mysteries and the cults they superseded becomes the closer. It does not fall to us, however, to discuss this view, since it cannot in any case go back to the origins of sacrifice, when the belief in a widely diffused superhuman power was only crystallizing into belief in a definite goddess or god; and it certainly was not present in the minds of Hindus or of most Greeks in historical times.

There was, indeed, a distinct family likeness between the various mysteries. They remind one of the Christian sects, holding the same broad and fundamental beliefs with the same passionate conviction, yet each pursuing its own way with its own priesthood and services, as if it alone held the keys of knowledge and salvation. Cybele and Attis, mother and son, came to Europe from Asia Minor. Cybele was perhaps identical with Ma-Bellona. Other deities were Anahita and Sabazius. From the Egypt of the Ptolemies came Isis, with her husband Osiris or Serapis, and her son

Horus. From Syria came the Syrian goddess, possibly the source of Baal, Melkart, and the other originally female Semitic deities, who, after they had changed their sex, lived on by the side of the females in whom they had originated.[1] From Persia, with its powerful and attractive Mazdean faith, came Mithra, who travelled even more widely than Isis, and threatened for a time to dispute the empire of the Roman world with Christ. All these religions, except the last, rested on the myth of the violent death of the god, lamented and then brought to life by the goddess, his mother or his wife; all go back to a definite connexion with the life of the corn or the vine, destroyed and then returning in new strength; and all transfer this victory over death to the victory of the initiate, vouchsafed by the grace of the goddess, after due fastings and abstinences and more or less wild excitement, over all the weaknesses and limitations of mortality. The cults appear to have made a powerful appeal, both by their higher and their baser features. The excitement, rising at times to positive frenzy, as in the self-mutilation in the recruits for the priesthood of Cybele, reminds us of the religious manias of the Middle Ages or a negro revival,[2] and it would be intensified by the strong sexual element involved in the myths and much of the ritual. The finer minds were drawn to the offer of illumination, the insistence on purity, and the deliverance from the fear of death.[3] Few would be insensible to the fascination of a secret doctrine, and a ceremony which, like the Freemasonry of later times, made those who had taken part in it brothers of one another, and overcame the isolation which all men dread, and which the older cults had ceased to counteract. And with this social bond with other human beings was cemented an intimate bond with the godhead itself. The mysteries knew no distinction of race or of class, and so appealed to the sentiment of a common humanity, which seems to have been potent everywhere under the earlier empire; and the cults, though at first liable to authoritative displeasure and

[1] See G. A. Barton, *Semitic Origins*, 1902.
[2] See Davenport, *Primitive Traits in Religious Revivals*.
[3] Cf. Heb. ii. 15; *Lucr.* ii. 55: 'Sic nos in luce timemus Interdum nihilo quae sunt metuenda magis, quam Quae pueri in tenebris pavitant'; and Verg., *Georg.*, ii. 490 ff.: 'Felix qui potuit rerum cognoscere causas, Atque metus omnes et inexorabile fatum Subjecit pedibus.'

THE MYSTERIES 85

proscription, brought into the West the Oriental reverence for the divinity of the monarch, and were for that reason vigorously supported by several of the later emperors, and regarded as commendable and even fashionable.

An interesting parallel for their rapid spread can be found in the success of Islam, both in India and Africa. The convert to Islam finds himself the equal of every Moslem, in his own and other countries; he is treated with new respect by European officials; he is conscious of being lifted above the superstitions of paganism; and he becomes a member of a powerful organization which does not make uncomfortably severe demands on his conduct, while it assures him of consideration and support in this world and of paradise in the next. Yet we must not be too hard either on the mysteries or on Islam. Too many other religious movements have gained by the worldly advantages they had to offer. But no religious movement has depended on this fortunate and generally evanescent circumstance for its real success. There are nobler things in Islam than the probability of social advancement for its convert. It has sometimes ' paid ' to be a Christian, but the Christianity of Francis of Assisi and John Wesley knows nothing of payment in such coin as this. And the mysteries would have flourished if there had been no Elagabalus to exploit them.

A detailed account of one of these ' varieties of religious experience' is given by Apuleius at the close of his *Metamorphoses*. The hero of the story, Lucius, after various adventures, some of which border on the obscene, is changed into an ass, and he seeks long and fruitlessly to get rid of the repulsive disguise. At last he is led by a dream to look for help from the priests of Isis, by whom he will be delivered from his burden. He is then to be initiated, and to remain through life a devoted servant of the goddess, his deliverer. Isis herself describes how this deliverance will start from the eating of a rose, which a priest will give him as he watches a procession; and she adds: ' Remember that the rest of your life will belong to me till your latest breath; you will live your life in bliss and glory under my protection; when, at its close, you descend to the grave, there also you will find that my favour crowns your worship. And if you honour me with constant and exact devotion, I myself will lengthen your life beyond its allotted span.' She reveals herself as the deity who is worshipped under all known divine names; and she lays on him the obligation of absolute chastity and self-control. We might almost be listening to the address of the Virgin to some budding Catholic saint. 'The *Metamorphoses*, where the author has sown lewdness with full hands, culminates in a vision of purity and piety.'[1] Restored to his human shape, Lucius takes up his abode in a cell in the temple of the goddess, until it shall please her to ordain his initiation. He fasts and attends all the services of the temple. At last the day arrives. After instruction by the priest whom the goddess has chosen for the ceremony he is immersed in a purificatory bath, and is bidden to fast for another ten days. Then he is taken into the temple with other initiates, clothed in a new robe, and led into the secret chambers, where he touches, as he says, the frontier of death, is carried across all the elements, sees the sun shining at midnight, and approaches the gods both of the underworld and of heaven. He is thus brought back from death to life like a true Osiris, and next morning he is the centre of a ceremony which appears to mean nothing less than a kind of apotheosis. A year later, while in Rome, he is bidden to undergo a second initiation, and, after that, a third. But no hint is given of further revelations, such as would lead us to recall the 'vision' which followed the 'initiation' at Eleusis; and one cannot but share his fleeting suspicion that the priests were not averse to making money out of the devotion of the pious laity. But Apuleius, who certainly was not inventing his incidents, and is careful throughout not to divulge what would be held sacred from the uninitiated, says enough to show that, with all the baser elements that may have enabled a cult to retain popularity in that corrupted world, union with an exalted divinity in purity of heart and newness of life was the prize sought after, and sometimes obtained.[2]

---

[1] Loisy, *Les Mystères Païens et le Mystère Chrétien*, p. 145.

[2] Apul. *Met.*, xi. The earlier sections of this remarkable book must not blind us to the religious feeling implied towards the end. There are a good many references in Greek literature to the moral effect of the mysteries on their adherents. Diodorus, for instance, asserts that the mystae of Samothrace became more just and pious through initiation. We must beware of giving a Christian content to words like 'purification' and

THE MYSTERIES 87

On the religion of Mithra we have fuller information, though unfortunately information with many gaps. The inscriptions and reliefs which bring us into direct touch with its followers have been found widely spread over the Roman Empire, and the remains of Mithraea, or places where the worship of Mithra was celebrated, are as numerous. Into the Greek world the cult never penetrated, perhaps because the ground had been occupied before its advance from the East began, and because the special type of converts it attracted were not to be found there. Where Christianity was strongest Mithraism was weakest. But it was everywhere in Italy and Western Gaul; on the Danube and in central Europe; all down the Rhine frontier, and even in Britain, especially along Hadrian's wall. The majority of the remains, as well as the sites where they have been discovered, show clearly that Mithra won his most conspicuous conquests in the army, and specially in its more distant forces[1]; but groups of Orientals, both freemen and slaves, seem to have founded their faith wherever, in earlier centuries, the simpler Italian religion had flourished.

Mithraism is a descendant of the old Iranian religion, with its two rival powers of Ormuzd and Ahriman. Originally allied very closely in its sacrificial religion to the Vedic system, this ancient Persian faith laid great stress, as Herodotus noticed, on morality and truth-telling.[2] Its dualism led to the growth of eschatological beliefs in the final triumph of good over evil; and a definitely spiritual element was introduced by the great reformer Zarathustra, who, however, did not permanently affect the popular faith to any large extent. From its native home it spread to Babylon, and then westwards to Syria, receiving a deposit from every place it visited. The cosmogony of Babylon coloured its myths; the passionate rites of Syria, and, later, of Cilicia, lent a dark intensity to its more secret practices; and the Hellenistic

---

holiness.' And there is no thought of redeeming love in the mysteries. But they do point to a distinct spiritual elevation. Cf., however, P. Gardner, *Religious Experience of St. Paul*, p. 87.

[1] See the map of the Roman Empire in F. Cumont, *Textes et Monuments*, vol. i., 1899, marking all the places where Mithraea and Mithraic monuments have been discovered.

[2] Hdt. i. 136.

schools, and the mysteries of Isis, in their several ways, taught it the value of the offer of illumination. Hence it lent its appeal to almost every class in the motley world in which it was now at home. The Stoic philosopher himself, when he entered a shrine, would be reminded of his own picture of the universe.

Just as, in the Egyptian mysteries, Isis overshadowed the older object of worship, Osiris, the newer Iranian faith rested, not in Ormuzd, but in a subordinate figure, Mithra, a hero half cosmogonic, half cultural. After a life of varied activities on earth, Mithra had entered heaven, and thence presided over the destinies of his worshippers, a human deity who touched men's hearts as the exalted Ormuzd could never do, and who, as the typical warrior, found a host of admirers in the Roman legions in Europe and Asia.[1] The faith, however, was in many respects as conservative as it was hospitable. Its rites preserved something of the original savagery of the mountain and the forest; its sanctuaries were known as *spelaea*, or caves, and were either underground, or constructed below the level of the earth. When the worshipper descended into the dimly lit hall, he found rows of seats for clergy and laity, strange statues of symbolical figures, of which Time, with a lion's head, was the most prominent. The initiates were divided into seven grades, consisting of crows, occults, soldiers, lions, Persians, sun-runners (*heliodromi*), and fathers. Each of these appears to have been entered by its proper ceremonies, and entailed definite vows. The affairs of the various congregations were administered by carefully chosen functionaries, organized on the model of the Roman municipalities. It is noteworthy that the sexual element is entirely absent. Women were never admitted to the worship, and stress was laid, as in other mysteries, but apparently with more success, on continence and self-control.

The most prominent object in the shrines, like the representation of the crucifixion in Christian churches after the third century, was Mithra's slaughter of the bull. The type of the group was traditional. The hero, in tunic and Phrygian cap, has one knee on the fallen creature. He is

---

[1] In the later Roman Empire the army and a definite religious faith were not the incompatible things they have since been supposed to be.

THE MYSTERIES 89

forcing its head back and cutting its throat. A dog leaps up at its side, while a scorpion and a serpent endeavour to consume the liquids which flow from its dying body. From the bull's tail grow stalks of wheat. At either side is a youth holding a torch; and around the group are generally placed cosmological figures of the sun, the four winds, and time, or episodes in the life of Mithra. The story told that Mithra had been commanded by the sun to slay the bull; this he did after much labour, and from its body came the life-giving juices which then fertilized the earth, and which the emissaries of evil in vain tried to consume. It would seem that, as in the stories of Osiris and Dionysus, the bull is really the source of life—a sort of double of Mithra himself, or at any rate a friend and not a foe to the hero and to humanity. His death, thus equivalent to the death of Mithra, is the source of all life. Mithraism in its turn leads us back to the idea of a great sacrifice offered for the benefit of mankind, and of a secular progress from death to life which is the explanation of the riddle of the universe.

We can hardly avoid a smile when we think of the war-scarred veterans of the Roman legions, fresh from some fierce conflict with Picts or Teutons, crowding into their underground shrines and bowing before grotesque shapes representing time and the changing courses of the sun. But every religion offers more than any one worshipper can take. Possibly the common soldier thought no more of the cosmogony of his faith than most adherents of Christian Science think of the metaphysical problems raised by Mrs. Eddy's views about evil. But his heart leaped forth at the spectacle of the invincible hero, friend and ally of the glorious sun, into whose inner circle he might eventually enter. The military hierarchy of officials appealed to him, and when the sacramental feasts were held, to the honour and in the presence of the god, he was well content to serve at first as a crow or a Persian, in the hope of becoming a lion, or even a father, later on.[1] When the

---

[1] A bas-relief from Konjica, representing a Mithraic communion and many other Mithraic scenes, will be found in Cumont, *Mystères de Mithra*, p. 164. Justin, *Apol.*, i. 66, urges that the demons taught the use of the bread and cup to the sectaries of Mithra, in parody of the Christian Eucharist. For the communion feast in the Eleusinia see p. 78; for the

ceremonial wine at these banquets, like the Persian Haoma or the Vedic Soma, gave him physical strength, wisdom, and courage to face the powers of evil, and the promise of a blessed immortality, he might well rejoice in his faith. But we must not minimize the influence even of cosmogony. Knowledge of the structure of the universe is necessary to those who would reach the seventh heaven[1]; and in a 'liturgy,' or manual of directions, for the Mithraic initiate, which appears to go back to the end of the second century A.D., it has been suggested that we have the statement of a religious law of thought which exemplifies itself in all the more widely diffused cults; it begins with the semi-physical approach to god and its sacramental completion; it proceeds to the spiritual union in affection and love; adoption as a child of the god; the new birth, and the ascent of the soul through the universe to the god.[2]

It will already have become plain that, in spite of the difference in name, the various mystery cults were all closely connected. Reitzenstein's treatment of the Hellenistic mystery religions implies that they were really one, animated by the same ideal of γνῶσις, or knowledge. This knowledge, however, is not to be thought of as intellectual theory; it is rather a personal communion with God. It is religious and not philosophical. The mystery (the Greek word can be used either for the actual process of initiation or the knowledge conferred thereby) is the means whereby this knowledge is attained, and, as a result, the godhead[3] enters his devotees, expelling their old personality and making them complete or spiritual. If the Hellenistic religions could lead to this 'unio mystica,' it may be asked, what more was left for Christianity to do?

Attis mysteries cf. the formula quoted by Firmicus Maternus, *De errore prof. rell.*, 'I have eaten from the drum, and drunk out of the cymbal, and become an initiate of Attis.' A. Dieterich, *Eine Mithrasliturgie*, 2nd edition, 1910, gives a list of all known remains (18) of ancient liturgies, pp. 213 ff.

[1] Compare the 'Weltbild' which underlies Dante's *Divina Commedia*.

[2] Dieterich, *op. cit.*, pp. 95 ff.

[3] Πνεῦμα, or spirit, is also often used to express the essence or true being of the deity. Both conceptions throw a suggestive light on Pauline terminology. See Reitzenstein, *Hellenist. Mysterienreligionen*, esp. pp. 135–185.

THE MYSTERIES

It has often been suggested that these religions were the source whence Christianity drew some of its most characteristic teaching, as well as the order of its most sacred service. But it must not be supposed that the borrowing was all on one side. We know little of these religions and their phrases and formulae before the second century A.D., and not much more of them until two centuries later still. By that time the Christian Church was highly organized, and had a system, an apologetic, and a polemic of its own, directed both to the more learned and the populace. It had shown a power of expansion and a missionary zeal, both in the East and the West, which must have been the envy of the priests of Isis and Attis; it had withstood the most savage persecutions, and thus had gained a reputation for martyr courage which the mysteries never attempted to reproduce; it had established a tradition of morality which the devotees of Isis, for all their lip-service, never contemplated.[1] Its ecclesiastical organization bound the various communities together into a body whose fighting force could be concentrated at any one point; and its traditions were not shadowy tales of barbarian grossness which were only tolerable because, as myths, they could be treated, like Homer, with the utmost freedom; they were securely based on memoirs, written by eye-witnesses, of one who had lived and died and risen again in the very world and in the very age in which His followers dared to find in a crucified provincial the Saviour of the world. The Christians, with the Old and New Testaments in their hands, and all the Jewish hatred of the devils whom the pagans worshipped, had little need to sit at the feet of Mazdean or Mandean teachers.[2] But the leaders of the mystery religions would have been either more or less than human if they had not taken advantage of the hints ' for

---

[1] See Dieterich and Reitzenstein, *opp. citt.* Anrich, *Das antitke Mysterienwesen*, and Cumont, *Les Religions Orientales*, are more cautious. Vigorous criticism will be found in Clemen, *Primitive Christianity and its Non-Jewish Sources*, and Kennedy, *St. Paul and the Mystery Religions*. In none of these works, however, is there an adequate study of the effect of the mystery religions on the Christianity of the post-apostolic ages, or of the counter-effects of Christianity upon them.

[2] How impossible, for example, to imagine that a Christian could have written the first ten books of Apuleius' *Metamorphoses*.

the construction of sheep-folds' which even a superficial knowledge of Christianity would give.[1]

We must return, however, to the relation of the mysteries to sacrifice. From the sacrifices considered in the last chapter the mysteries have carried us far. The sacrifices were to obtain some material or tangible good; the mysteries to satisfy a longing of the soul. The sacrifices bound together the men of a family or city; the mysteries united men of the most diverse classes and races. The sacrifices repeated the slaughter of the victims season after season, year after year; no one sacrifice ever made another unnecessary; the mysteries went back to a sacrifice in the distant past, which thereafter needed but to be symbolized or recalled. The sacrifices offered the animal to the god; the mysteries celebrated the offering of the god himself to some higher god, or to humanity. The mysteries seem nearer to the ideals of mysticism than to the system of sacrifice. They lift the worshipper out of himself; they purge his vision and purify his soul; he becomes a spectator of reality; one can almost apply the well-known phrases of the mediaeval mystics to the aims of the Mithraic priests. But there is a difference. The mystic proper will have no intermediaries between himself and God; his access must be immediate. And the body and its senses are useless. Nothing must be in action except the mind and the soul. Not so the mystery religions. Each has its objects to be seen, its dramatic performances to be watched, its sacred food to be eaten, its journey from dark to light to be completed, and the death of its god to be re-enacted.

In some cases, as in the Attis mystery, the actual slaughter of the divine animal is repeated, and the initiates enter into the spirit of the god by being 'baptized' in the blood that spurts from the veins of the immolated bull. But for the most part the sacrifices, while they could not be altogether expelled from the rites of the mysteries, were interpreted in a mystical sense. 'Prayers,'

[1] Apparently most of the Gentile knowledge of Christianity was superficial. In the magic texts hitherto examined many reminiscences of Judaism occur, but none of Christianity, except in one passage, where Jesus is called the god of the Hebrews (Dieterich, *op. cit.*, p. 45). We are reminded of the famous phrase of the Roman historian: 'Judaeos, impulsore Chresto, assidue tumultuantes,' &c. But our knowledge of the popular literature, which till the last few years was almost unsuspected, is too small even yet to justify any confident assertions.

THE MYSTERIES 93

says an old author, 'without sacrifices are only words ; with sacrifices they are words with souls. The word gives energy to life, and life gives soul to the word.'[1] If, therefore, they carry us away from genuine mysticism, which has no place for sacrifice or mediation at all, these religions also lead us far beyond the sphere of the older civic sacrifices. They do not simply enable men, by the due manipulation of a victim's blood, to receive certain external boons which heaven might otherwise withhold. They offer union with the godhead, a deep sense of brotherhood with man, and the profoundly satisfying consciousness of purity and the seeds of immortality. But in doing this they revive, though perhaps quite unconsciously, the ideas which dominated the practice of sacrifice in its earliest stages, and were forgotten as civilization and culture advanced. For originally the god himself died in order to live again in his fellow tribesmen ; and their approach to him was not that of suppliants for a definite and material favour, but for his entrance into themselves. The difference was that in the early stages of religion, as later in less savage times, the sacrifice was periodic. The divine power might decay unless a renewed death reinvigorated it. In the mysteries, physical death sank in importance behind the spiritual and sacramental approach ; and while, in the early ages, the boon expected was the vague though precious influx of some divine 'mana,' or fertilizing and semi-magical power, in the mysteries it was knowledge, victory, illumination, friendship with the god. Thus, too, the mysteries preserved what we have so far felt to be central in all sacrifice—the idea of reconciliation. They needed, like their predecessors, no succession of sacrificial victims to bring their adherents into touch with their deity. The deity himself, by his explanation of the story of his death, had revealed the manner in which this *rapport* could be gained. All that was needed was the right attitude on the part of the worshipper, and the moment chosen by the god. For the god was himself the mediator, the sacrifice,

---

[1] Sallust, 16, ap. Reitzenstein, *op. cit.*, p. 182. For a fuller account of this Sallust, who was a friend and tutor of the Emperor Julian, see Murray, *Four Stages in Greek Religion*, p. 173. 'To approach God,' he continues, 'we need a medium and a mediator. The medium between life and life must needs be life. We find this in the sacred animal.' Sacrifices were finally forbidden by Theodosius in 391 A.D.

through which his worshippers brought to him their devotion of pure lips and thoughts and prayer. To study the mysteries is to be reminded at one moment of the degradation of pagan worship as Paul expressed it in his letter to Rome, at another of its exaltation as Paul described it in his speech at Athens.[1]

[1] 'There was much in these religions which rendered them preparatory to the gospel. The idea of redemption, of mystical union, of new birth, was in them. They satisfied for some, and intensified for others, the yearning after purity which the gospel fully met. Gentile converts brought something with them into Christian worship from their native mysteries, partly enriching, if often corrupting thereby, the sobriety of the Church. St. Paul . . . did not reject the offering. . . . What there seems no reason to suppose is that he believed himself mystically one with Christ because pagans or pagan converts put the idea into his head' (A. Nairne, *The Faith of the New Testament*, p. 97

V

THE HEBREW SACRIFICES

WE have now traced the practice of sacrifice over a large and varied area of religious thought and attainment. Beginning with the simpler forms of the rite, among less developed peoples, we found two characteristics more or less definitely prominent in them all. In spite of the wide diversity of actual performances and of conceptions about the deity, the offering is regularly regarded as one in which the whole community shares, and its object is to bring that community into right, and even intimate, relations with its god. In fact, the feeling of intimacy is generally more noticeable in the simpler cults. Only as the cults expand does it give way to awe. We then turned to watch the development of sacrifice in two highly cultured races. With the early Hindus we found an amazing expansion, until the rite seemed to shake itself entirely free from its proper relation to its end or object, and grow according to some inner law of its own being. Among the Greeks there were seen constant survivals of the earlier and relatively savage ideas. While the Hindus expanded the rite in order to preserve untainted its original efficacy, the Greeks were satisfied simply to continue the traditional usages. Their intellectual interest, instead of devoting itself to the elaboration of the rites, left them, like so many erratic boulders, gaunt but irremovable, in the midst of their unwearied philosophic and social criticism.

The Hindus furnish the supreme example of the tendency inherent in all rites to gather accretions round them, for aesthetic, emotional, and even utilitarian reasons[1]; it was necessary for the rite to be at once orderly and impressive, and to be safe from any danger of losing its efficacy through ignorance or inadvertence. Man could be sure of coming into touch with heaven, but only by following with the

---

[1] Cf. W. H. Frere, *Principles of Religious Ceremonial*, pp. 71 ff., for the tendencies to elaboration seen in the Christian ritual.

utmost precaution the way which heaven had appointed. The central idea of the Hindu cultus was thus reconciliation. Other elements entered in; notably fear of the results of an unworthy or uninstructed approach, and that consciousness of holiness or freedom from ritual uncleanness or impurity which may be the source of a profound satisfaction. The offerings or gifts were often very valuable in themselves; the holocaust of a hundred horses, or Aswamedha, could have been no light thing, even for a powerful monarch; but the solemnity of the ritual itself is proof enough that to the Hindus, as to worshippers in a much earlier stage of religious thought—for example, to the aboriginal tribes whom the Hindus looked down on, even then, with undisguised contempt—the point of importance was not the worth of the gift, but its manipulation so as to secure that it would lead the way into communion with the god who received it.[1]

The Greeks were not religious in the same fashion as the Hindus. Their religion was dominated by their political or civic sense. Their sacrifices were the means of keeping the gods friendly to the state, as their laws were the means of keeping the citizens of the state friendly to one another. The religion of the Greeks, as of the Romans, was primarily a 'polis-religion'; and even the family sacrifices were rites performed by definite social groups. The solemn act of entrance into satisfactory relations with the deity was one in which the individual took part only as he was a member of the sacrificing community. And in the later ages of Greek religion, when the 'polis' system had broken down under the new political conditions of Alexander's successors and the Roman Empire, the Greek cities still maintained the worship of their specific gods[2]; and the newer Oriental cults, which permitted no limitations of political citizenship, simply formed new groups in which the sense of membership was quite as strong as in the old city state, and, when the cults involved sacrifice, the sacrifice was still entirely communal.

---

[1] Most of the aboriginal rites noticed by Indian travellers are 'riddance ceremonies,' designed to drive away harmful powers; but this does not apply to the various birth, marriage, and death rites; and even when the worshipper simply asks the god to let him alone, he must reach some sort of common ground with him.

[2] Cf. Acts xiv. 13; xix. 23 ff.

THE HEBREW SACRIFICES

We now approach the sacrifices of the Old Testament, which to most English readers are far more familiar, and, because of their influence on the writers of the New Testament and on the religious world in which Jesus Himself grew up, more important. These sacrifices have often been regarded as forming a class to themselves, marked off from all ethnic rites by a peculiar sanctity, a kind of prophetic witness to the truths of Christianity still to be revealed. But the Old Testament system constantly reminds us of the characteristics already observed in the practices of the jungle and the bush, as well as of India and Greece. It recalls to us still oftener its own specific background of Semitic beliefs. In the Arabian tribe the conception of kinship was, and still is, specially strong and well formed. It involved the belief, not only that all the kinsmen shared the same blood, but that the tribal god shared it too; and that the life of the whole community, in which the men were as necessary to the god as the god was necessary to the men,[1] rested in this mystic and sacred blood. This belief led Robertson Smith, in his account of Semitic sacrifices, to lay special stress on them as tribal and totemistic meals, in which the god was actually devoured by the worshippers to perpetuate his divine activity in their midst. It also influenced much of Frazer's earlier work.

Most students of the subject now recognize that too much importance was formerly attached to totemism as an element in Semitic religion. Totemism, which is by no means clearly to be detected save in Australia and among the North American Indians, was invoked to explain what could, without difficulty, be accounted for in other ways. But sacrifice as a means of renewing the bond between the god and his fellow tribesmen is quite plain in Semitic cults; and it becomes conspicuous as the Old Testament is studied. In the Old Testament, indeed, we have a development of sacrifice from rites that differ little from those of Arab tribes[2]—the nearest representatives to-day of the Bedouin stage of Hebrew life before the tribes entered Canaan—to

---

[1] See E. Durkheim, *Les Formes Élémentaires de la Vie Religieuse*, pp. 486 ff.

[2] Ancient Arabian sacrifices, however, did not include actual burning on the altar; see Wellhausen, *Reste Arabischen Heidenthums*, 2nd edition, pp. 114 ff.

a ritual as leisured and majestic, and, we may add, artificial, as that of India itself. And at the Hebrew altar the old lives on beside the new, so that a rite, like the rite for the Day of Atonement, can combine elements whose first appearance we can date with some degree of certainty with others which take us back to an immemorial antiquity. The Old Testament is a manual for the historical study of sacrifice and sacrificial religion, and it implies the idea which seems to be implied in all early sacrifice—the re-establishment of certain more or less definite relations between the deity and his human dependents or kinsmen.

The difficulties, however, in the way of using the Old Testament for this purpose are formidable. All our knowledge of Hebrew sacrifice comes from the Hebrew writings, biblical and post-biblical.[1] And our materials in the Bible itself are to be found in the references to sacrifice in the historical sections, in the addresses of the prophets and the allusions in the poetical compositions collected in the book of the Psalms, and far more fully in the various codes of ritual preserved in the Pentateuch. Of these, the historical books were obviously written long after many of the events they relate. The descriptions of religious ceremonial in the books of Chronicles are certainly influenced by the practice of the period when those books were written; and the same is probably true, to a less degree, of the books of Kings. On the other hand, the prophets present us with contemporary material of the highest value and importance; the sacrifices of which the prophets spoke were going on before their eyes. But their references are coloured by their own strong polemical views. Convinced as they were that sacrifices were altogether useless for the purpose of any approach to God, they were more concerned to emphasize this futility than to hand on details of what they could not but despise. The references to be found in the Psalms are very valuable as expressing the actual place of the ceremonies in the religious experiences of the writers, but they are most of them tantalizingly allusive and brief; it may be that their very brevity is significant.

The actual codes as we have them in the Pentateuch are highly instructive. They are, in the first place, easily

[1] Such as the *Yoma*, or tractate on the Day of Atonement.

THE HEBREW SACRIFICES 99

distinguishable from one another, and can be dated with much confidence. But only in the latest, or Priests' Code, have we anything approaching what might be called a rubric for the practice of the altar; from a comparison between it and the earlier documents we can only conclude that in earlier times the details were too well known to be considered worth writing down, or that details were not prescribed at all, but left to the officiant. These codes, however, were all of them compilations, not the promulgations of new laws; it follows, therefore, that even in the latest code we may meet elements that belong to a quite early age, and that we shall look in vain, in any one of the codes, for a definite and homogeneous presentation of any sacrificial theory. It is only an inattentive reading, which shrinks from the labour of comparing passage with passage, or else a determination to maintain a certain view at the cost of ingenious but highly improbable harmonization, that refuses to recognize the existence of these independent bodies of law. As we shall have to refer now to one and now to another, and as an appreciation of their distinctive qualities throws much light, in spite of inevitable uncertainties, on the development of sacrificial practices among the Hebrews, a brief sketch of their history will be of use.

The earliest code is known as the Book of the Covenant.[1] It is inserted in what is denoted the Elohist document, the product of a school of religious leaders and writers in the northern half of Palestine which reflects the traditions and aspirations of Ephraim, for long periods the leading tribe among the Hebrews. Before it was combined with other writings to form the Pentateuch, this document existed as a continuous though partial history of Hebrew origins; and while making use of many older traditions, oral and probably written, it was not actually completed till after the establishment of the monarchy.[2] How much older the code

[1] It is contained in Exodus xxi. 1 to xxiii. 19.
[2] Most students are inclined to place it between Jeroboam I and Ahab, and a little later than the parallel Judaean document. It must certainly be earlier than Elijah. The present writer is not convinced that it was later than the division of the kingdom; but since, like so many other Hebrew historical writings, it is only the setting down of what in substance had been handed on for many generations, the exact moment of its compilation and 'publication' is of little importance. See Proksch, *Das Nordhebräische Sagenbuch*, 1906.

100 ALTAR, CROSS, AND COMMUNITY

is than the document which has preserved it for us it is impossible to say. We can only go by internal evidence, which points to a period after the Hebrews had settled down as small farmers in Palestine, but before there had been time for them to make any great advances in economic or political organization. The code is mainly civil rather than ritual; but the references to religious rites correspond to what we can learn of them from other notices of the earlier cults. Connected with it are two decalogues, or arrangements of brief legal principles in groups of ten.[1] These certainly go back to an earlier age, although in some of their clauses they have been considerably expanded.[2]

Next in order of time comes the code found in the centre of the book of Deuteronomy (chh. xii.–xxvi.). The distinguishing mark of this code is the stress which it lays on the law of a single central sanctuary. This was certainly unsuspected at the time of Elijah, and it must be later than the composition of the Elohist document. Ritual laws take a much more prominent place than in the Book of the Covenant, and running through the whole of its legislation there is a humanitarian tone which marks a distinct moral and spiritual advance beyond the rough and even wild justice of its predecessor. In all probability it was written in the reign of Manasseh, and extends the principles of the abortive reformation carried out by Hezekiah; it was found lying in an obscure corner during the restoration of the Temple under Josiah, and it gave the immediate impulse to the great movement of the centralization of religion which he accomplished.[3] A smaller group of laws, arranged in no precise order, but all of them emphasizing 'holiness,' as a quality both of the people and the land, is found in the second half of the Book of Leviticus. Like

---

[1] Exod. **xx.** 1-17, and Exod. **xxxiv.** 17-26. See Kent, C. F., *Israel's Laws and Legal Precedents*, pp. 16-20.

[2] R. H. Kennett, *Deuteronomy and the Decalogue*, 1920, has recently elaborated his view that this code dates from a period after the fall of Samaria, and is an effort to 'Israelize the alien population,' p. 11. This, however, involves very serious difficulties.

[3] See 2 Kings xxii., xxiii.; reference may also be made to Driver's *Deuteronomy* (Int. Crit. Comm.) and McCurdy, *History, Prophecy, and the Monuments*, Bk. ix., chh. ii. and iii.). A further account, with special reference to the arguments of one of the chief opponents of this view, will be found in an earlier lecture in this series—J. W. Moulton's *Witness of Israel*, pp. 120 ff.).

THE HEBREW SACRIFICES

Deuteronomy, it breathes strong humanitarian sympathies, but it pays more attention to ceremonial prohibitions and restrictions[1] than to the description of correct ritual. The striking resemblances it contains to Ezekiel's sketch of the ideal procedure of the Temple suggest that it should be dated during his period, the earlier part of the sixth century, one or two generations later than the promulgation of Deuteronomy.

The most elaborate legislation is that known as the Priests' Code, found in the latter part of Exodus, the earlier half of Leviticus, and large sections of Numbers. This code implies that Israel is now a church rather than a state; the basis of society is religious rather than political. The priests form a hierarchy, and have definite revenues allotted to them; the various kinds of sacrifices are carefully distinguished from one another, and the ritual of each is at last given in detail. The fact that in the time of Ezra and Nehemiah its provisions had to be enforced as part of the law of Moses, while many of them were at the same time evidently unfamiliar to the majority of the Jews, suggests that this code had been worked up by Ezra and his circle in Babylon, and brought by him to be promulgated in Palestine when the opportunity arose, as it actually did about 445 B.C.

What is commonly spoken of as the 'law of Moses' is thus a combination of four successive editions of the law, recognized by the Hebrews as originated, in the first instance, by their national legislator. It is clear that the study of any rite must take account of the code in which it is mentioned. There is much overlapping, for the successive codes were not written to supplement their predecessors, but to present a more or less full account of the important elements in the praxis as their authors conceived it. As a general rule the codes grow more elaborate with time; but, remembering how strongly conservative all ritual tends to be, constantly modifying, but very rarely inventing, we must be prepared to find, even in the latest code, elements which may actually be older than the earliest.

With the codes as a whole we have here nothing to do.

[1] As, for example, the social disabilities, or 'taboos,' of the priests, and the definition of forbidden kinds of food.

We confine ourselves to their statements about sacrifice and their use of sacrificial terminology. And although there are naturally many divergences in the four codes, the same general ideas are to be found in them all. That is to say, at all periods of their development the Hebrew sacrifices can be distinguished from those of any other people. There are no breaks in their history. If, however, we desire information on the origin of Hebrew sacrifice, the codes give us no assistance at all. Like the historical portions of the Pentateuch, they assume sacrifice as a recognized religious institution, which we can at best observe at various stages of its growth. We do not know to what extent the Hebrew practice before the entrance into Canaan differed from that which we find in the codes. The description of the tabernacle and of the establishment of the priesthood in Exodus is certainly coloured by later ideas.[1] It expresses, under the guise of a narrative of the desert wanderings, the conceptions which shaped the rubric of the post-exilic Temple.

The codes themselves, then, tell us nothing about the reasons for the practices they lay down; at most they refer to the historical occasions, real or supposed, which they commemorate. But the second and third throw a good deal of light on the attitude of at least the more spiritual of the worshippers, by their 'parenetic' references to Jehovah's will and character; and the fourth code is full of sacrificial terms—'make atonement,' 'sin,' 'forgiveness,' 'a sweet savour unto Jehovah,' and the like. But they do not explain these terms, and, indeed, their use rather adds to the problem than clears it up. Further, the Hebrew rites tended to undergo Canaanite influence. This would be but natural when Hebrew and Canaanite were living side by side, and even using the same sanctuaries; and it is clear from the denunciations of the prophets. Some of these syncretistic practices are also condemned in the codes; others are silently rejected; but they illustrate the lack of any authoritative ritual and the various and heterogeneous influences which modified the development of the institution.

It is none the less possible to draw a picture of the Hebrew sacrifice, whether we think of it as offered in the

[1] See, for instance, Driver's *Exodus*, in *C.B.S.*, on Exod. xxxv.

THE HEBREW SACRIFICES 103

Temple, with its elaborate and costly furniture, or on some hill-top, beneath one or more conspicuous trees, with its heap of uncut stones serving as the altar, its row of pillars or sacred stones placed there from time immemorial, and its sacred pole. In each instance the worshipper brings his victim to the altar, where the priest is waiting for him. He lays his hands upon the animal's head, and announces aloud the reason for which it is offered. He then kills the animal, and the priest performs the prescribed rites with the blood, while all or part of the animal is burnt on the altar. Or perhaps it is a spring morning in the earlier period of Israel's history, when the barley harvest has just begun, and the whole village comes up to the high place. The first sheaf of the harvest is solemnly brought to the altar, and moved backwards and forwards before it by the priest ; unleavened cakes are there, ready to be eaten. The victim—a sheep or a goat—is brought up, and its throat cut by a representative of the village ; the priest catches the blood in a bowl and dashes it on the altar, or on one of the stones ; he then takes out the fat of the inwards and burns it upon the altar, while the rest of the flesh is boiled and eaten by the worshippers, with the priest in their midst, to the accompaniment of much merriment and good cheer. Centuries after such celebrations as these, when the local shrines had disappeared, and in the great open Temple court at Jerusalem, where the altar was still of unhewn stones, the priests, presiding over the worshippers' slaughter of their victims, still sprinkled the blood and burnt the fat, pouring the libations of wine and burning the incense (a necessary procedure in a hot climate where there was much blood and offal about) with every aid to solemnity and awe, yet preserving the same essential features as when their ancestors officiated on some hill-top with its pillar and pole beneath the trees.[1]

Sacrifices in ancient Israel were thus both communal and personal. Their character, however, was predominantly

[1] The excavations at Gezer and elsewhere have enabled us to see the exact structure of the high places, as they were used by Canaanites and Hebrews. But certain features of the arrangements of these spots—for example, the so-called cup marks—suggest either that we do not yet know every part of the ritual, or that the Hebrews dropped certain elements which figured in the Canaanite ceremonial. See R. A. S. Macalister, *The Excavation of Gezer*, 3 vols, 1912, and Vincent, *Canaan d'après l'Exploration récente*, 1907.

social. They were the natural accompaniment of festivals, for the family, the clan, or the whole nation, as well as of great occasions like the breaking out of war or the gaining of a victory, and they were offered by the leader, the king, or the head of the family group. The priest was not always needed; but as time went on he became increasingly important. He was at first felt to be necessary because, as a man specially in touch with the god, he could approach him with relative impunity, and could see that in the whole performance there was no dangerous breach of the traditional ritual.[1] But his special character made it advisable for him to take the most important part of the ceremony himself—the manipulation of the blood and the fat. He could be relied on to do all that the lay worshipper could not be sure of doing; and his experience could be relied on to recognize and avoid any uncleanness or ritual impropriety.

Even in early times there were two distinct kinds of sacrifice—the peace-offering, as it is called in our translation, and the whole burnt-offering. The first was a communal sacrifice pure and simple, when the group not only provided the victim, but enjoyed its consumption. Since an animal was never slaughtered in those early times without being offered to the god,[2] the feast was often doubtless a more important element in the mind of the worshippers than the sacrifice. In the peace-offering, as described in Leviticus, each party to the transaction had his appointed share of the victim. To Jehovah went the blood and the fat; the blood was 'taboo' to human beings, and the fat was regarded as a special delicacy, to be reserved for the chief personage at the banquet. To the priest went the breast and shoulder; the lay host and guests took the rest. This division between

---

[1] Compare the relief of Micah when he found that he could get a Levite for his priest instead of being left to his own devices in his religious activities (Judges xvii. 13). Cf. Hdt. i. 132: 'The Persians do not offer sacrifices without the presence of a magian,' or priest.

[2] This was also true of the heathen Arabs. In Hebrew one and the same word, 'zebach,' means to kill an animal and offer a sacrifice. In the early days no one ate meat except on the occasion of a sacrifice. To use a phrase of Professor Burkitt's (*J.T.S.*, Oct., 1920, p. 65), every one habitually connected worship with the ritual of the slaughter-house and the dinner-table. The coming of the change is marked in Deut. xii. 15.

THE HEBREW SACRIFICES 105

priest and laymen may not have been original, but some understanding as to what the priest could claim evidently existed from early times.[1] The whole burnt offering (the Hebrew name for it means an 'ascent'), when the entire victim 'went up' in fire on the altar like Elijah's sacrifice on Mount Carmel, was thought to be more solemn, and in early times was reserved for comparatively rare occasions, though the later legislation, in its characteristic desire to increase the solemnity and awe of the cultus, exalted it above the peace-offering. The offerings were the same in both; the difference between them is simply one of the method and kind of reconciliation desired or felt to be needed. In the peace-offering the deity is invited into the friendliest sort of intimacy with the worshippers; in the latter the bond between them is not simply to be renewed or emphasized; it has either been broken by some fault on the side of the worshippers, or it must be assured, beyond the possibility of risk, in view of some coming danger. In either case sacrifice is simply the means for tightening the link between the two parties.

Another thing may safely be said about Israelite ritual, and it is perhaps the most important of all. In the course of its development it underwent assimilation to the rites already existing in Canaan. This is clear from our actual knowledge of the high places where sacrifices were offered; from the inscriptions of the Northern Semites, Phoenicians, and others, which show a remarkable similarity to the Hebrew cultus; and from the confusion to be observed in the Israelite mind behind Jehovah and Baal.[2] To an outsider, watching a Canaanite and an Israelite act of worship, it would be difficult to detect much difference between the two. In this respect the prophets seem to have been like the outsider. They roundly condemned Israelite sacrifices as they would have condemned those of the pagans. The former were as perilously steeped in ostentation and vice and false ideas of the deity as the latter. But to the sympathetic student of popular religious

---

[1] Cf. 1 Sam. ii. 13 ff.
[2] See, for example, G. A. Cooke, *North Semitic Inscriptions*, 1903, pp. 2, 32, &c., and cases in the Old Testament where Baal, the Canaanite name for the local deities, is obviously used of Jehovah, e.g. 1 Chron. viii. 33, 2 Sam. iv. 4, &c. (when for Bosheth Baal should be read), and Hos. ii. 16.

ideas in the Old Testament, Baal is properly a local fertility god, worshipped naturally at agricultural festivals, first-fruits, harvest, and ingathering. If there were any ethical elements in that worship, they are unknown to us; provision, however, was made in the cult for the satisfaction of the most licentious passions,[1] while human sacrifices, at great emergencies or important undertakings, were clearly recognized.

All these practices, as is well known, can be paralleled in Israel; and it is easy to understand how the Hebrew peasant, living in much closer contact with the Canaanite than with the higher spirits to be found at the religious centres of his own people, came to confuse the 'Baal,' or master, whom his neighbours worshipped in such attractive and impressive ways, with the god of his fathers. But to the instructed Israelite, even before the advent of the 'writing' prophets, Jehovah is different from Baal, and from all heathen deities, because, as we may express it, He has a character. Like the gods of the nations, He has certain likes and dislikes; unlike them, the things He likes are not gifts that can be put into His hands, so to speak, nor are His dislikes affronts and refusals to bring tribute; but certain attitudes of mind, which result in conduct and a way of life. He hates acts of 'folly in Israel'—acts which revolt the moral sense of the nation—and the arrogance and greed of 'sons of Belial'; and He is the protector of the poor and friendless and the upholder of the traditional rights of the common man.[2]

The lot of the plain man in Israel was at all times a hard one. Compelled in most parts of the country to toil hard to wrest a living from the earth, in earlier periods forced to defend his little holding against both raids and organized invasions, and under the monarchy oppressed by taxation or exploited by the money-lender, and as uncertain as the average Oriental to-day of justice when he appealed to the law if his hands were empty, he learnt, as no one else did,

---

[1] Possibly these had some religious significance in stimulating the divine energy of reproduction by a kind of sympathetic magic. But passion has often shown itself capable of making out of religion a justification or an excuse.

[2] Cf. 2 Sam. xiv. and the story of Naboth, 1 Kings xxi.; also Pss. cxlvi. lxxii., &c.

THE HEBREW SACRIFICES 107

to look to Jehovah for the justice and mercy that he so often missed among men. And he was convinced that he did not look in vain. In Jehovah, the God of his fathers, was an abiding power that sooner or later would punish lawlessness and vindicate innocence. The daring thought that inspired Micah's words, ' What doth Jehovah require of thee but to do justly, to love mercy, and to walk humbly with thy God ? ' had been finding its way into the Hebrew mind and religion long before the seventh century. The very name Jehovah is personal ; unlike Elohim, ' god ' or ' the divine,' and ' Baal ' or ' lord,' it is the name by which personal character is expressed. Hence, so far as this was recognized, to get into touch with Jehovah in sacrifice was to approach to the source of morality. The sacrifice was thus an act of moral renewal. When the worshipper laid his hand upon the victim, sending it, as it were, as his own forerunner into the divine presence, and identifying himself with it, he was offering himself to a God who asked, not for tribute or payment, but for conduct and obedience. We must not lay too much stress on a conception which is not the common possession of religion even yet ; and we must remember that until the later years of the monarchy very few Hebrews had reached the distinction expressed in the well-known question of Samuel, ' Hath Jehovah as great delight in sacrifice as in obeying the voice of Jehovah ? ' To sacrifice was to obey. But for a Hebrew who knew anything about Jehovah at all the peace-offering was companionship with the best and most righteous that he knew, and in the burnt-offering he invoked the presence of the highest and the most merciful.

This conception of Jehovah's character and will, and its development, is the most significant thing in the Old Testament, as it is the most central thing in the New. It is not, indeed, reflected in the ritual legislation. This was hardly to be expected. That legislation had simply to lay down the accepted praxis. But when we come to the Deuteronomic code, we find it clearly marked in the civil and humanitarian sections. There the right attitude of the Hebrew to Jehovah, and the constant attitude of Jehovah to the Hebrew, except when disturbed by disobedience, is felt to be love. And love, or something corresponding to it, was, therefore, the true attitude of one Hebrew to another. The earlier prophets—Nathan, Elijah, Amos—had paid little attention to the thought or the possibility of the divine love; Hosea had, indeed, been profoundly conscious of it, and so, to a certain point, had Isaiah. It was reserved for a group of legal authorities, after their country had been for years a vassal of Assyrian imperialism, to turn the dream of an inspired seer into the principle of a religious community. To do this was to make it impossible to confuse Jehovah with Baal, or with the deity in whose name the false prophets of Jehovah had been accustomed to speak. And it was also to rescue sacrifice from being the means of a commercial transaction or bargain between man and his Maker. When they are referring to sacrifices, the authors speak of rejoicing as the natural mood in which to appear before Jehovah. It was the result of their view of God, as one who did not look for personal satisfaction or gain through the sacrifices of His worshippers, but for a personal intercourse which was as much to His delight as to theirs. Lastly, it laid the foundations for the transformation of the older conception of sin. It did not accomplish that transformation. The habit of thinking of sin as involved in a ritual failing or error was too deeply rooted. But where others thought of sin as some act of disobedience quite possibly inadvertent and unintentional, as when Uzzah raised his hand to prevent the ark from falling out of the jolting wagon, and was struck dead for breaking the 'taboo,' the man who has learnt the lesson of Deuteronomy comes with a heart broken for moral disobedience. Love always means penitence; and where there is no love there is no forgiveness; only fear, or bargaining.

This element in Deuteronomy brings us back to the distinguishing mark of its legislation which we have already noticed. Hitherto in Israel, as in ethnic religions, sacrifice could be offered in any 'clean' place. The altars of the Hebrews, like those of the Vedic Hindus and the Romans, were raised beneath the open sky, wherever God had already made His presence known. Abraham and Jacob, Gideon and Samuel and Solomon, offer sacrifice on the site of some theophany, recent or traditional, just as the fellachin of modern Palestine bring their offerings to some

THE HEBREW SACRIFICES 109

sacred spot which they think of as the grave of a Moslem saint, or as the Catholic peasant brings his own offerings to Loretto or Lourdes, or some other place where the Virgin has deigned to manifest herself. In Palestine this meant the use of Canaanite sanctuaries, with the constant danger of religious corruption. This danger was threefold; it involved immoral rites and practices; it threatened a lower conception of the character of Jehovah; and it meant ritual uncleanness.[1] There was only one remedy, and that was to bring all the sacrifices to Jerusalem, which had already inherited the prestige of the old central sanctuary at Shiloh. In the old days the peasant would come up to Jerusalem as a churchman from the provinces would visit St. Paul's or Westminster. The Christian can go back to his parish church, and the Hebrew could go back to his village altar. But now that altar was to be no altar. The advance was first attempted under Hezekiah; it was naturally favoured by the Jerusalem priesthood; but a reaction followed under Manasseh. The idea, however, lived on; it was felt to be a genuine Mosaic principle. It was embodied in the code which was lost and subsequently found in the reign of Josiah, and it became, later on, so much a part of Jewish religion that Jewish writers spoke of the history of the northern kingdom as one vast sin because of the altars set up at Bethel and Dan.

The change thus introduced was more far-reaching than Josiah or his clergy suspected. Sacrifice was now no longer something popular, as before, or even the natural expression of religious feeling. Although distances in Judah were not great, since the whole kingdom was not much larger than the county of Yorkshire, a visit to Jerusalem, and therefore the opportunity, or even the sight, of a sacrifice, would be comparatively rare for most people. No other

---

[1] It would be beside our present purpose to discuss the details of the Hebrew conceptions of holiness and cleanliness. Originally the holy is that which is specially reserved for divine use; the unclean is that which a man cannot touch for fear of some pollution. It is clear that one and the same object, if segregated from common use, might be regarded now as holy, now as unclean. The practical results would be the same. But the two conceptions move farther and farther apart. Behind the Israelite horror of objects and states regarded as unclean we can see a quasi-aesthetic loathing, as for contact with a corpse or with filth; a religious reaction, as against anything connected with pagan rites; and a tribal or national memory, from the early experiences and superstitions of the desert.

religion has ever taken such a step. The country was loth to acquiesce, as can be seen from the writings of Jeremiah. We are reminded of the unwillingness of the Catholics in England, at the time of the Reformation, to give up their familiar rites. The change also meant a new stress on holiness and ritual avoidances or taboos. The moral element, in spite of the desires of the authors of the code, became correspondingly less prominent; for how could an evil conscience wait for leisure to travel to the capital to confess its sin? The approach of sin is independent of any periodical visit, and its results must be dealt with at once if they are to be dealt with at all. Still, if the worshipper would now of necessity think less of forgiveness, he would think the more of the other and older purpose of the sacrifice, to get into touch with God; as the journey to the shrine became more of a pilgrimage, the experience at the shrine would move him the more deeply.

The local centres, however, were not finally killed by Josiah's reform, but by the exile. But the Deuteronomic legislation had an important effect on the priesthood and on priestly restrictions. These rise into prominence for the first time in the so-called Holiness Code, and in the work of its authors' contemporary, Ezekiel. Many of these restrictions, both on priests and people, seem to be ' taboos ' and nothing more, depending on a conception of holiness that was merely material—a kind of contagion that must be avoided unless special precautions are taken, just as the Moslem worshipper who runs round the sacred stone embedded in the Kaaba at Mecca will put off his usual garments to prevent their becoming holy. But it cannot be denied that, with a real sense of religion beneath it, such scruples would increase what the wiser priests were now growing very anxious to cultivate—a pious and awestruck reverence in all human dealings with God. To us they are artificial enough; but they spring from the rising conception of the exaltation of Jehovah and the gulf between Him and all other deities.

If the Deuteronomic code set out to destroy local worship, the exile made all sacrifice impossible. There could be no sacrifice in a foreign land.[1] But exile could not destroy the thought of sacrifice. Development of that thought went

[1] Cf. Ps. cxxxvii. 4 and 1 Sam. xxvi. 19.

THE HEBREW SACRIFICES

on all the more vigorously when the possibility of performing the rites was removed. The imagination could play more freely around the ritual in Babylon than in the Temple courts. But such imagination was the work, or the privilege, of the priests, not of the people. Popular zeal may transform actual rites; only the specialist interest of the priest will devote itself to transforming their memory. Hence the things which now occupy the attention are the distinctly sacerdotal elements—ritual, holiness, sin—rather than what made the sacrifice of unique worth to the layman—the progress into the presence of God. The extent of the change is clear if we contrast a peace-offering as described in the book of Samuel with its reduction to a formula in the earlier chapters of Leviticus. The emotional effect would be enormously increased by the place and the occasion, the throng of worshippers in the clean white court, the dignified movements of the priest with his spotless robes, and all the punctiliousness of the intricate series of actions. It would be natural to compare the effect of High Mass in a spacious cathedral on a peasant lad who had never previously left his native village in the hills.

On the surface, the Priests' Code seems to care for nothing save ritual correctness, like the Hindu Yajur-veda. But this must not suggest that the sacrifices of the code were merely a form. The formal interest of the legislators could not kill the vitality of their functions. We have only to turn to the Psalms to see how vital these were to the pious Jew. The code is, indeed, what it professes to be—a manual for the altar, partly for priests, partly for laymen. And in two instances at least the language of the code suggests explanation or instruction. The sacrifices are to cause a 'pleasant odour' to Jehovah; and they, or the priests who officiate, are to 'make atonement' for sin.[1] The first of these phrases is a survival of a cruder conception of the deity; others will meet us in the code later on. The second is ambiguous. As regards derivation, the word used may mean either 'cover' or 'smear'; the sacrifice, that is, may

---

[1] We may compare the account in the earliest of the Genesis documents of Noah's sacrifice (Gen. viii. 21) and also its Babylonian parallel, 'The gods gathered like flies over the sacrifice,' in the so-called Gilgamesh Epic. See. pp. 111 and 45.

be thought either to cover the sin for which it is offered, or to be like a hand held up in front of the face of God, or smoothing out the angry frown.[1] But we may well doubt whether the word had, for priests or for people, any distinct connotation. Theological and ritual terms, especially when they become traditional, easily pass into algebraical symbols.

It has often been urged, indeed, that at least in a number of the sacrifices in the code, to atone must mean to propitiate or appease. God is justifiably angry, and the sacrifice removes His anger. In support of this, attention has been called to the two sacrifices which are met with in this code for the first time—the sin-offering, as it is called, and the trespass-offering.[2] But in this case also we must not be misled by nomenclature. The manual does not explain the two terms, but it shows clearly what it means by ' sin.' What it has in view is not sin in our sense of the word at all; in fact, the sin-offerings are to be offered ' if any one shall sin through error, in any of the things which Jehovah hath commanded not to be done, and shall do any one of them.' Later on, the cases for which sin and guilt offerings are necessary are specified—contact with an unclean animal or some other kind of defilement; the discovery of the omission to carry out the terms of an oath uttered carelessly or rashly; and concealment of the truth by a witness subpoenaed, as we might say, in a trial. This last, it is true, is not a case of ' error,' and its connexion with the other two reminds us of the fashion in which Ezekiel joins ritual and moral faults together in his list of sins. The sin-offering often accompanies other sacrifices, evidently so as to avoid any risk of impurity.[3] It is clear, however, that the majority at least of these ' sins ' do not need any atonement in our sense of the word. Jehovah would be no better than a pagan deity if His wrath should

---

[1] For a valuable discussion of the representative passages in which the Hebrew word occurs, see Driver, *Deuteronomy*, p. 425.

[2] The general character of the ritual of all four classes of sacrifice is very similar. All seem to have been developed from one type. The most striking difference lies in the fact that the peace-offering was shared by the worshippers; the other three were devoted entirely to Jehovah.

[3] Lev. iv. 1 ff., v. 1 ff.; and see vi. 6 f.; also Ezek. xviii. 6 ff. The Babylonian polytheist went farther, and not only provided against sins which he might have committed, but included in his prayers gods and goddesses whom he might have offended. Cf. also Acts. xvii. 23.

THE HEBREW SACRIFICES

blaze up when a Hebrew had unintentionally touched the dead body of an owl or a mouse, claiming the innocent life of some dumb creature in return. The ' guilt ' which demands a guilt-offering is defined with equal care ; it is either an unintentional fault, or the wrongful withholding of some property. In this case restitution has to be made, with an additional payment,[1] and an animal is offered to Jehovah. But this offering is hardly one of ' atonement,' in our sense, for the culprit has already made the appointed restitution, and why should this particular piece of wrongdoing rouse a species of anger in Jehovah that others, to us more serious, do not ?

The emphasis thus laid on ' sin ' and ' guilt,' however, brings into the light a very important characteristic of the view of sacrifice held in the Priests' Code. Ritual cleanliness and ' holiness ' have to be understood as semi-material. If the ' sins ' in question do not need atonement as we use that much-disputed term, they do separate from Jehovah. The horror of uncleanness, as we have seen, is physical as well as religious[2] ; holiness is a quality possessed by Jehovah Himself, His priests, His worshippers (if they have taken the proper means to ensure it), and certain objects ; it is contagious, like uncleanness ; and an object which has been solemnly devoted to the service of Jehovah, or has been in contact with another article so devoted, and is then used for common or ' profane ' purposes, becomes as dangerous as an unclean thing. The great problem is how to get rid of uncleanness when it has been acquired. No unclean person can venture into Jehovah's presence ; that would be to invite disaster. And the problem cannot be solved by simply passing over the taint to the victim ; there is not a word to suggest that the worshipper thought that he was doing this when he laid his hands on the animal he offered ; and the stress laid on the purity of the animal makes it impossible to think that the animal could be regarded as ceremonially unclean at the very moment when it approached Jehovah. Nor was the victim given to be punished instead of the offerer ; for many of these ' sins ' the punishment could not possibly be death, and sacrificial

[1] Lev. vi. 1 ff.
[2] We may compare the repulsiveness, to a high-caste Hindu, of the suggestion of eating beef or working on leather.

death is nowhere connected with the thought of punishment. The sin-offering of the Priests' Code is simply the opening of the way to Jehovah; the unclean person cannot approach to his deity as he is, any more than a guest could come into a royal wedding feast with unclean garments and soiled hands; but where he cannot go he can send the clean animal which he offers, and with which he identifies himself; and when the animal's blood is splashed or sprinkled, both on himself and on the altar which represents Jehovah, the transaction is complete and the uncleanness is removed.[1]

We must not expect to arrive at an entirely homogeneous theory. The elements in the rites are far from homogeneous, and the rites have a long history behind them. Curiously enough, the Priests' Code, which is the latest in point of time, contains the oldest elements. The ceremonies after the forty or eighty days of uncleanness that follow childbirth, the letting loose of one bird in the purification of a ' leper ' and the killing of another over running water, the shaving of the hair, the elaborate precautions after contact with death, notably the administration of water mixed with the ashes of a red cow, and the ordeal of ' jealousy,'[2] all find abundant parallels in pagan practices; and they probably have their origin in the very early ' riddance ' ceremonies—the attempts to banish demons or harmful spirits, to whom sickness and death were alike attributed. This belief has moulded a large number of the Babylonian religious texts; it seems to lie behind the expressions of Ps. xci.; and it has existed, more or less unformulated, through the Christian centuries. This is shown by the treatment of witches, and the precautions still widely taken against the evil eye. The inclusion of pagan elements is, however, nowhere more striking than in the ritual for the Day of Atonement. For the most part, indeed, this ritual is in accordance with the ruling ideas of the code; the main sacrifices all have their place on that day; and the conception of holiness is conspicuously dramatized by the high-priest's entrance into the ' Holy of Holies '—forbidden even

---

[1] In earlier times the single stone or the heap of stones which served for the altar was regarded as the dwelling-place of the god (cf. Gen. xxviii. 18, 19, xxxi. 13), or as the god himself.

[2] Lev. xiv. 4 ff.; Num. xix. 1-22, v. 15 ff.

THE HEBREW SACRIFICES 115

to him save on that day—with the sacrificial blood. But the treatment of the second of the two goats, ' for Azazel,'[1] recalls a crowd of pagan associations. It was not sacrificed; it took the community's guilt away into the wilderness. It was not punished, any more than the other goat which was duly offered on the altar; but, like the scapegoat whose ritual has been found in all parts of the world, savage and semi-civilized, it was the vehicle for carrying off ' sin ' (in this case the accumulated uncleanness of a whole year contracted by priests and people alike) into some secluded region where its consequences were no longer to be feared.[2]

Were not the sacrifices, we may ask, enough to secure this riddance? The answer appears to be that in such a solemn matter as this it was advisable to take no risks, and the old rite was too popular to be allowed to die out. That it should have been invented by the authors of the code is as unlikely as that it should have been directly revealed to Moses in the desert. In this, as in other matters of purification from uncleanness, where the beliefs of the priests in the half material nature of the pollution coincided to a certain extent with those of the populace, the authors had to choose between being too revolutionary and drastic, attempting perhaps quite unsuccessfully to banish the familiar and trusted rites that had lingered on in popular practice for centuries, and baptizing them, as it were, into their own system. The latter was doubtless the wiser course; it was, at any rate, the course which the leaders of the Catholic Church have consistently followed in dealing with the more primitive peoples in Europe and Asia. It would certainly attract the worshipper to a system where much was already strange to him; and, in the special instance of the Day of Atonement ritual, the emotional effect on the crowd, as they watched the goat being led farther and farther away, till it disappeared from sight, must have been enormous. The special importance of the rite is shown by its subsequent elaboration. Such elaboration was inevitable. The process of ritual definition, having gone as far as it did in the code, could not stop there. Much

---

[1] This seems to have been originally the name of a desert demon.

[2] Lev. xvi. See p. 75. Some illuminating paragraphs will be found in C. F. Burney, *Old Testament Conception of Atonement fulfilled by Christ*, 1920, pp. 18 ff.

remained unsettled in the biblical text, and the careful provision that no single act, however minute, should be left to chance, is seen clearly in the Mishna tractate ' Yoma ' or ' Day of Atonement,' where directions are given, not only for the detailed instruction of the officiating high-priest, to avoid any possibility of his forgetting a single word, but for the mixing of the blood of the several victims, the exact movements on this side and that of the altar, and the steps to be taken in case one of the two goats, after its selection, should unfortunately die.[1]

In the post-exilic age there is thus a gradual change in the spirit of sacrificial worship, as of the whole religious outlook. It can be seen in the contrast in the Hebrew traditions of the creation, the flood, the patriarchs, and the plagues in Egypt, as given in the narratives compiled in the early monarchy, and the more formal history connected with the Priests' Code itself. It is equally clear in the transformation of the festivals from family or agricultural gatherings to solemn and awe-inspiring commemorations,[2] where the succession of services would entirely prevent the unseemly merry-making of the past. To us, with our memories of the ' puritan Sabbath,' these ' holy convocations ' will suggest gloom and the awful sense of a deity whose wrath can only be escaped with difficulty and bloodshed. The effect on the Jew was certainly very different. True, he was not allowed to forget the dreadful possibilities of carelessness and ignorance, possibilities which are, of course, equally involved in our conception of the automatic action of the ' laws of nature ' to-day. But the sacrifices were the provision of the way out of these dangers mercifully vouchsafed by their fathers' God, the source of the most important instruction that man could receive. To most of the worshippers, at any rate, the sacrifices would suggest chiefly the return again into happy relations with God which lies at the heart of all religious satisfaction, Pagan or Christian. We must bear in mind the physical effect of the spacious and

[1] Cf. Lev. xvi. with *Yoma*, v. and vi.

[2] The Passover is the only house festival which the Priests' Code (P.) has allowed to survive, and it preserves other characteristics sternly ruled out by P. elsewhere; see Driver's *Exodus*, *C.B.S.*, pp. 405 ff. In Deut. (xvi. 1-8) the Passover is regarded as a sacrifice to be offered at the central sanctuary; in P. it is still killed there, but eaten at home.

THE HEBREW SACRIFICES

white Temple court, the bright, warm sunshine, the singing of the birds round the altar, and the Temple chants and hymns; joined to the psychological effect of watching, as one of a great crowd, a series of acts which brought God objectively into the midst of His people.[1] The Protestant has often been bewildered as he has seen the rapture of the Catholic witnessing the 'sacrifice' of the Mass. The pious Jew found an equal delight in his sacrifice, eloquent of the goodness of Jehovah in enabling His people to dwell in the intimacy with Him which was their true life.

There was thus a real connexion between the earlier and the later sacrifices. This, indeed, was only to be expected. There was no such discontent with the established order as caused the hostility to their clergy manifested in the French or Russian Revolutions, nor even in the reaction against Catholicism at the Reformation. But the connexion was the community of ritual rather than of theory. There was no doctrine of sacerdotalism or apostolical succession. Cyprian knew little of the spirit of the Old Testament when he developed a view of the Christian priesthood founded, as he supposed, on the Levitical hierarchy. The only principle was, 'This must be done, and in this way.' The approach to God is the central thing, as, in Christianity, the reception of the grace of Christ; but the former had a much closer connexion with external rites than the latter, and never occasioned the same bitter divisions.

In this approach, a special rôle was attached to the blood. If the animal had been merely killed, we might perhaps have imagined that it was a gift to the deity. But why this manipulation of the blood? 'The blood is the life.' It was 'taboo'; not to be 'eaten.' It may be that the later Jew did not know the reason for the special treatment of the blood at the altar; but the rite must have had some origin. To the early Hebrew the blood was alive; when it was shed, it could cry from the ground.[2] It was, indeed, the living bond of union for the whole tribe. When a murder was committed, the serious thing was not that a man had been killed, but that the tribal blood had been spilt. It seems, indeed, that physical contact with blood, or the sight of blood flowing, arouses an instinctive awe, or even horror, in the human breast; how much more when

[1] See Pss. lxxxiv., cxxii. [2] Gen. iv. 10.

the spectator regards that blood as his own? It would thus be quite natural that when the god is to be approached, it should be by means of this mysterious fluid, at once a part of man, and removed from him into the sphere of the supernatural.

All this would seem, indeed, to point, not only to blood, but to human blood. We have already noticed the traces of human sacrifice in the Old Testament, the most perplexing of which refer to the sacrifice of the 'first-born.' But this could never have been carried out regularly, especially where population was thin and men were valued. The remains at Gezer only show that infants were sometimes sacrificed, but not of necessity with any regularity. The story of Abraham and Isaac, and the language of the Book of the Covenant, prove that the existence of the rite had not been forgotten in historical times. It could even be revived in a crisis, as by Mesha, or in dark and troublous years like those of Manasseh.[1] We have, indeed, no data that would warrant us in deducing the practices of Semitic or of Hebrew sacrifice from human sacrifice in general. There can be little doubt, however, that the ritual emphasis on blood among the Hebrews and other Semites points back to the idea of the consanguinity between man and animals. The Hebrews sacrificed domestic cattle; and it has been suggested that domestication resulted from totemistic beliefs. The blood of the bull or the goat would thus be regarded, literally, as the blood of the community offering it. It would be too much to suppose that a practice so widespread as domestication has resulted from totemism alone. But it is certainly difficult to see how animal sacrifice, with its special rites of the blood, could have arisen at all, unless the animal was a substitute for a human victim, or regarded as 'of one blood' with the tribe and the god. From the fact that Jehovah was constantly figured as a bull, and that the blood of cattle was by preference brought to Him, it may well be that from far antiquity the pastoral ancestors of the Hebrews, as of other peoples, believed in some bond between themselves, their cattle, and their god. This sense of kinship, at once admiring and grateful, would naturally be

---

[1] See 2 Kings iii. 27, Mic. vi. 7 (cf. Gen. xxii.); 2 Kings xvi. 3, xvii. 17, xxi. 6; Jer. xxxii. 35.

THE HEBREW SACRIFICES 119

strengthened by the energy of the bull, more prominent than that of most wild animals of the desert, and perhaps with the usefulness of the milch cow. Such a feeling could be compared with the Hindu reverence for the cow, the curious semi-deification of the cow among the Todas, and the special and often curious rules for the treatment and safety of cattle among all pastoral people.[1]

It is difficult to say how the above theory, or any other, could be made more than probable ; but, be this as it may, the central point of most Israelite sacrifices was the offering of the blood of domestic animals. Vegetable or meal sacrifices were at best accompaniments ; the use of incense was late ; libations of wine were rejected altogether by Ezekiel ; and the story of Cain and Abel points to a view that animal sacrifices alone were valid. This can only imply that what Jehovah is pleased to accept from His people is the blood, the life, of some chosen animal. But there is more in the rite than this ; the blood is not only brought to Jehovah ; it is sprinkled on the worshipper himself. Evidently the blood, the life, is regarded as in some way joining together, or reconciling, bringing into right relations with one another, the worshipper and his God.[2]

One special characteristic of the Priests' Code has often escaped notice ; as a result, the code has been greatly misunderstood and misjudged. As we have seen, it introduced the ' sin-offering ' and the ' guilt-offering.' These sacrifices are for ritual or involuntary misdemeanours, and with one unimportant exception, for no others. ' Highhanded ' or deliberate sins are expressly excluded.[3] In the older religion it was not so ; Mic. vi. and Ps. li., to name no other passages, show that the idea of sacrifice

---

[1] See Frazer, *Folklore in the Old Testament*, vol. iii., pp. 111 ff., as illustrating the ' taboo ' of Exod. xxxiv. 26. Perhaps, later, the bull was thought of mainly as a domestic animal, and thus, by analogy, other domestic animals, like sheep and goats, were regarded as acceptable.

[2] It is remarkable that the fat of the kidneys is also looked upon as holy, and reserved for the deity. Regarded as it is by Oriental people as a dainty, its reservation meant that the Israelites denied themselves that part of the animal that they would have liked the best. Some have suggested that the kidney fat was ' holy,' i.e. reserved for the deity, because the kidneys were connected with the soul. But the fat part of the animal's tail was thought to be set apart in the same fashion.

[3] Num. xv. 30 ; cf. vv. 24, 26 f. Cf. Deut. xvii. 12 f.

for moral shortcomings was not unfamiliar. And if
sacrifice was regarded generally as for the purpose of
reconciliation, the need for it would be specially felt if the
guilt of some previous sin lay heavy on the conscience.
True, there are few or no examples of this in the early
books. The instance of David and Bathsheba, and even
of the census, are not decisive, for in each case sacrifice
followed punishment and repentance. The sacrifice, as
the last act of the drama, simply brought David actually
into touch again with Jehovah. Yet we can hardly imagine
that, if the sacrificer had any conscience at all, he could
have failed to suppose that his sacrifice must make up
for sin. In the Priests' Code this supposition is ruled out.
' So much the worse for the code,' one is inclined to add.
But this would be an injustice to the authors of the code.
They saw that their system could not touch actual and
deliberate sins. On this point they agreed with Micah.
For such acts the code has only two consequences;
the sinner is to be ' cut off,' excommunicated, or he is to
' bear ' his iniquity. Deliberate acts which do not necessi-
tate one or other of these are not mentioned. The code
knew how to secure purification after leprosy; it was
silent as to purification from lewdness. It knew nothing
either of penitence or of forgiveness in our sense of the
word, for it knew nothing of the sins that need the one
and the other.

The fact appears to be that the priestly authors of the
code regarded these sins as outside their purview. But
they did at least see, as no one save some six of the prophets
had hitherto seen, the difference between the ritual and
the moral. The code saved the moral by ruling it out.
To the wicked it said, ' I can give you no help. No mere
sacrifice will avail you. Look elsewhere.' Its presupposi-
tion is that of Ezekiel, whose vision of the new order follows
his prediction of national repentance. When the only
sins are involuntary or inevitable, sacrifice and sacrifice
alone will be needed. This is the reason why the Priests'
Code has none of the moral exhortations of Deuteronomy
or the Holiness Code; and for the same reason Ezekiel,
save in his social laws, has no references to morals after
his section on repentance.

' If sacrifice means no more than this, what a monument

THE HEBREW SACRIFICES 121

of misplaced ingenuity is the code.' Such a comment is natural to all who have read the Gospels. How much better it would have been, we say, to have spent the time and energy given to these precepts in working for morality. But sacrifices took up only a small part of the time and the attention of the later Jews; and it was surely right that they should be carefully ordered, without haste or carelessness or unseemliness. At the great festivals of the sacred year, when Jews from all parts of the world assembled, a large intellectual and emotional effect had to be secured. How could this be done save by the solemnity of the traditional and developed rites? We may even see a psychological fitness in these elaborate preservatives from ritual uncleanness; for if these ritual ' sins ' could destroy communion with God, how much more the deeper sins of the disobedient purpose and will? The code was, as we may say, the ' minute scholarship ' of religion. We may readily admit that it was not so regarded universally. For many, both priests and people, it was an end in itself. The due performance of its rites came to be looked on as the one thing God desired from man, as a Catholic may regard attendance at the Mass. This is the perpetual danger of all ritual. Still, at the end of the development of Jewish religion, as it is recorded in the Old Testament, we have a consistent theory of sacrifice, which finds no place for atonement or propitiation, for gift or penance, and all that we hold to constitute a ' sacrifice,' but which clings all the more to the thought of sacrifice as a means to communion—the removal of the last obstacle to the presence of Jehovah in the midst of His people. It is no wonder that to the later Jew the law was a source of joy and thanksgiving.

If all this is true of the Priests' Code, is it true of the Judaism that followed? We have little information on which to rely for an answer to this question until the Christian era. There is, indeed, an ample literature between the middle of the fifth century B.C., the date of the promulgation of the code, and the end of the first. But it consists chiefly of ' Wisdom ' books and Apocalyptic; and both these classes of writing neglect the code and the ritual law in general. For the right ordering of life, and the fulfilment of national hopes, sacrifice, save as the traditional practice of religion, was to them only secondary. The view of the Priests' Code, that sacrifices were for inadvertent offences, would seem to have been in the main accepted. But, as every reader of the New Testament knows, the Temple and its services survived undiminished in the affections and reverence of the Jews, both inside and outside Palestine. And, what is more remarkable, we hear of other temples, notably two in Egypt; a temple at Assouan, as early as the end of the fifth century, was the seat of the worship of a Jewish colony there, the members of which did not feel themselves to be in the least heretical, in spite of Deuteronomy; and at Leontopolis, some twenty miles north of Memphis, there was another temple from 160 B.C. onwards. The outstanding event of the period was the Maccabean revolt in 166 B.C.; its immediate cause was the attempted enforcement of idolatry by Antiochus, and the whole of the patriots' enthusiasm centred round the determination to keep their worship undefiled and conformable in every detail to the demands of the law. The original aims of Judas Maccabeus were continued and transformed by a line of royal high-priests. Till its destruction in 70 A.D. the Temple at Jerusalem was the centre of all Jewish hopes and national functions, and the priests were its only officials.

But while the sacrificial system was thus the symbol of the nation's fealty to God, it was steadily losing ground, in the practical religion of the greater number of the Jews, to the synagogues. The synagogue services could be attended regularly and frequently, and, full of comfort and encouragement as they were, they relied for their effect on praise, prayer, and instruction. The synagogue worshipper was thus being trained to do without sacrifice. Naturally, this significant discovery aroused much discussion as to the religious value of sacrifice in relation to forgiveness. To every serious man comes, at some time or other, the consciousness of guilt. If he lives in the atmosphere of sacrifices, he may naturally be expected to suppose that sacrifice is intended to make up or atone for his sin. And when he advances to the sacrifice with a penitent heart, it is not strange if he attributes to the rite, at least in part, what penitence has itself secured for him. Many thinkers, however, doubted the possibility

THE HEBREW SACRIFICES 123

of forgiveness through sacrifice. How could the blood of bulls and goats take away sin ? The more deeply sin was felt as affecting the mind and heart of the individual, the more futile would seem the manipulation of some material substance to remove it. This finds striking expression in some of the Psalms, the 'hymns of the second Temple': 'Sacrifice and offering thou hast no delight in . . . burnt-offering and sin-offering hast thou not required'; 'I will take no bullock out of thy house, nor he-goats out of thy folds. . . . Will I eat the flesh of bulls, or drink the blood of goats ? '[1] Even Psalms which refer to sacrifice as part of the practice of religion sometimes speak of it as the consequence rather than the cause of acceptance with God : 'I will wash mine hands in innocency ; so will I compass Thine altar '; 'And now shall mine head be lifted up above mine enemies, and I will offer in His tabernacle sacrifices of joy'; elsewhere they are expressions of gratitude for deliverance.[2] But the Jews were neither theologians nor schoolmen, and the generally accepted view would seem to have been that expressed in Ecclus. xxxv. : sacrifices are seemly and necessary ; but they are of no avail without personal goodness ; and goodness is the real sacrifice. 'He that requiteth a good deed offereth fine flour . . . and to forsake unrighteousness is a propitiation. Thou shalt not appear empty before the Lord. . . . The sacrifice of a just man is acceptable.'[3] There is an important passage at the close of the treatise on the Day of Atonement which lays down the rule that without repentance the 'day' can do nothing ; and that while the 'day' atones between man and God ('the place '), it does not avail between man and man until reconciliation or reparation has taken place.[4] Again death, or death with repentance, or the death of the righteous, makes atonement.[5] And atonement may result from the merits

[1] Pss. xl. 6 ; l. 9.
[2] Pss. xxvi. 6, xxvii. 6, lxvi. 13-15.
[3] Cf. Luke xi. 42 : 'These ought ye to have done, and not to leave the other undone.' Doubtless many a Christian thinks of the Eucharist, or the Mass, in a similar way ; it is necessary, but without the grace of God it is futile ; and grace is independent of it in the last resort.
[4] *Yoma*, viii. 8. cf. Matt. v. 24.
[5] 4 Macc. vi. 28, 29, xvii. 22. The idea that death alone can make atonement is curious ; are the wicked, one asks, to be free from further punishment? On the other hand, it would be easily felt that after death one would be 'quits'; there would be nothing more that one could offer or do.

of the fathers, as the Christian theologian may point to the merits of the saints, or the supererogatory work of Christ.[1]

What strikes us most forcibly in all this is the Jewish refusal to theologize, as Christian theologians have theologized unweariedly in connexion with the sacrifice of Christ. The Jews were satisfied with the statement in Leviticus : ' The life of the flesh is in the blood ; and I have given it to you upon the altar to make atonement for your souls ; for it is the blood that maketh atonement by reason of the life.'[2] How it does this is not stated, nor apparently asked. There is, however, no suggestion of substitution, or of anything that could be called propitiation, in the classic words. It is an explanation that does not explain. It would not be too much to say that no further explanation was required. For this reason little is to be gained from a discussion of the origin of the Hebrew term *kipper*, the word which is translated 'atone.' In historical times, when the ritual codes as we have them were being worked out, as little thought was given to the Arabic meaning of the root, ' to cover,' as to the Babylonian 'to smear,' and it is best to leave these obscure matters out of account in expounding the Hebrew technicality. Any light that Arabic and Babylonian usages have to throw is beneficial for the ethnological stage of Hebrew religion ; it is an anachronism when we are dealing with the religion of Israel. There sacrifice has its place, either as the accompaniment and symbol of the repentant heart, or of the desire for some gift of the divine goodness and power, or of the longing to be assured of the escape from ritual imperfection, because it is the divinely appointed means for entrance into that relation of communion and intimacy with God without which no gift could be received and no prayer offered.

---

[1] The principle is expressed clearly in *Tractate Sanhedrin* (tr. Danby, p. 88), where the man condemned to death by stoning, when ten cubits from the place of execution, is told to confess, for every one who confesses has a share in the world to come. If he does not know how to make confession, he is told to say, ' May my death be an expiation for all my sins.' It should be noticed that in the prayer of confession in the Day of Atonement service (*Yoma*, iii. 4) sins are confessed which were otherwise held to be unpardonable, and forgiveness is asked for all. Cf. L. Abrahams, *Pharisaism and the Gospels*, xix., ' God's Forgiveness.'

[2] Lev. xvii. 11. Cf. Bertholet's note *ad loc.*, in the *Kurzer Hand-Commentar*.

VI

THE REACTION AGAINST SACRIFICE

THE foregoing chapters have shown that the rite of sacrifice is all but universal, and that if sacrifice is fundamentally a means of getting into touch with the god, we can explain the various species of sacrifice as we cannot if we start from the conception of gift or bribe. It is clear, too, that sacrifice has a large survival value; what other rite has shown the same capacity for development and the same power of resistance? The more advanced the race, the more elaborate the sacrificial ritual. To the student, in spite of the Christianizing of the idea in theology, all this may seem one more proof of the folly of the human race, based on an erroneous and anthropomorphic idea of God which strangely persists when men ought to know and do better. He may regard them much as the puzzled and exasperated missionary may regard the rights and duties of the maternal uncle or the woman's carrying of the load on the march while the man carries only his weapons. Still, if anthropology teaches anything, it is that rites and customs are the expression of emotions and desires. Even when the expressions change, the emotions themselves remain. But when a rite is itself so persistent, the emotion of which it is the expression must be taken all the more seriously. Augustine's famous words about the heart that cannot find rest till it finds rest in God would seem to be illustrated by all the fantastic history of sacrificial practices that we have been passing in review.

The validity of sacrifice, however, did not remain unchallenged till Christianity came to transform it. Three separate attacks have been directed against the institution, and this just in the regions where we might have supposed the institution to be the most secure—in India, where its ritual had, even in Vedic times, become so imposing; in Greece, where its survival was itself a triumph; and in

Israel, where it had become the centre of the deepest and most pervasive religious feeling. It will be instructive to trace the fortune of these attacks, to see where and why the sacrificial idea failed to commend itself, and how far, when attacked, it was able to maintain its ground.

In India the attack originated with Buddhism in the sixth century before Christ. Buddhism was indeed far more than a reaction against sacrifices. It challenged the whole edifice of Brahman religion. Yet it sprang from Brahman thought, and it could not deny its parentage, any more than Christianity could deny the Judaism which had given it birth. On the philosophical side it was a logical elaboration of Brahmanism; on the ritual and institutional side, it was a denial; and of all the Brahman ritual, the most obvious section was sacrifice.

Buddhism accepted from Brahmanism the doctrines of *karma*, the deed which must work itself out in the subsequent life of the doer; transmigration, coupled with the non-continuity of conscious life; the illusory nature of present existence; and the merging of the soul, at its end, in the One which is the All. It also gave great emphasis to the thought, widespread in India, that the root of misery is desire. These doctrines were not fundamental in Brahmanism. Brahmanism possessed a highly organized pantheon, which, indeed, has steadily extended; the gods of India are now numbered by the million; and where there were gods, there were and are necessarily sacrifices. Again, the circumstances of the Aryan invaders of India had led to the creation of caste and numberless ritual 'taboos.' Brahmanism is, therefore, in reality a combination of three religious tendencies or attitudes—the mystical desire for union with the divine; the approach to the god through the priest and the altar; and the complex of ceremonial restrictions, partly aesthetic and hygienic, partly racial, which religious conservatism always tends to keep alive and fertile. The same is true of modern Hinduism, which, it must be confessed, has little understanding, and even less reverence for logical consistency.

Buddhism, on the other hand, was thoroughly logical. Moreover, it threw over all the caste system of the Aryans. All men are alike, it taught, in relation to existence. This was not to assert the democratic doctrine that all men are 'free and equal,' or the Christian doctrine that in the sight of God there are no distinctions of race or social standing. It was philosophic rather than religious or political; and with it went another doctrine even more radical—that there are no gods at all; man's whole fate depends on man himself. Thus if, in addition, it is held that life means misery through the tyranny of desire, man must be freed from desire. How can this be accomplished but by killing desire—by asceticism? Further, the strongly altruistic and humanitarian feelings which, as all Buddhists hold, have been inspired by the example of the Buddha himself, have made them shrink from the idea of taking even animal life. Thus there is no place for sacrifice, and since there are no gods to be the source of any blessing, there is nothing to be gained by it. Life consists in lessening the denominator, as Carlyle said, rather than in increasing the numerator. It follows that priests disappear likewise; only religious mendicants are left, as the examples and reminders of self-mastery, and the material for acts of beneficence and merit.

Buddhism might well have been expected to be an utter failure. It surrendered the very elements which could be thought to make an appeal to the masses. It was Christianity with all its uncompromising zeal, more than all its austerity, and none of its attraction; with no 'dynamic' or promise of more than human power to face the ills and foes of life; and with no redeemer. The same thing might be said of it in relation to Islam. It called to no earthly conquests; it offered no heavenly paradise; it manifested no pride of religion or of orthodoxy. Yet it was an amazing success. Within three centuries of its rise it had passed over to Ceylon, to Burmah and Thibet; and though it was expelled later on from its native land of India, it found an enduring foothold in China and Japan.

Only a small part of this success can be attributed to the national and racial character of the peoples among whom it was gained. It has been customary, until the last few years, to talk of the unchanging and contemplative East; but the character of the populations of China and Japan cannot be considered naturally self-effacing and ascetic; and with regard to Burmah (for we can speak with even less confidence about Thibet) the calm, pensive, and childlike traits about which so much is heard[1] may well be the fruits rather than the seed-ground of the invading religion. Its only strength lies in its emphasis on self-mastery as a means of escape from the uproar of desire, in universal goodwill and harmlessness, and on devotion to the Buddha himself. It is remarkable that with this alone the religion—if we can call that a religion which denies the need for worship of any kind of god—should have spread so far. Christians may well recollect the emphasis which their own faith lays on self-mastery, goodwill, and devotion to the person of Jesus. And if Jesus was always preached as a saviour, the Buddha was a saviour also. The Buddha's salvation, moreover, was into the realm of the spiritual. The famous 'noble eightfold path' is purely spiritual.[2] Buddhism has no rites apart from conduct. Its only sacrifices are the offerings of flowers at a shrine, along with a prayer, either for general wellbeing or some immediate need. In a Buddhist religious song we read, 'For one flower offered I have enjoyed eight million years in a heaven, and by the remnant of his merit I now attain Nirvana.'[3]

If Buddhism knows no sacrifices, it also knows no reconciliation. Its doctrine of *karma* forbids both. It is at once 'individualistic and anti-social.'[4] Each man must 'dree his own weird.' True, every religion may be, and in some sense is, self-centred. Every religious man desires to gain

---

[1] See the writings of Fielding Hall, who is more of an artist, however, than a student of religion.

[2] Its steps are as follows : right views, right aims, right speech, right conduct, right manner of life, right effort, right mindfulness, right contemplation.

[3] Quoted in Saunders, *Buddhist Ideals*, p. 152. The offering of the flower is properly the expression of religious love to the Buddha. We may compare the gift of a cup of cold water in the name of a disciple (Matt. x. 42). Compare also *Dhammapada*, 54, 56 : ' A slight thing verily is this scent of incense and of sandal-wood, but the odour of the righteous pervades the heavens.' The true Buddhist is at one with many of the Psalmists in holding that the only acceptable sacrifice is a pure life. But when the Buddhist, on the failure of his monks to secure his wishes, has recourse to demons, he forgets all this, and brings animal sacrifices such as the demons may be thought to desire.

[4] 'By oneself the evil is done ; by oneself one suffers. By oneself evil is left undone ; by oneself one is purified. Purity and impurity belong to oneself ; no one can purify another ' (*Dhammapada*, 163). Ps. xlix. 7 as the context shows, is not a true parallel to this conviction.

REACTION AGAINST SACRIFICE

something for himself from God, either in the way of a gift or blessing, or in friendship and protection and intimacy. But theoretical Buddhism has no place for God at all. Properly speaking, it is a philosophical way of life rather than a religion. Yet we cannot help suspecting that if Gotama had not found the doctrine of *karma* already too strongly entrenched for him to attack it, it would have been ejected from his system. For he demands, and Buddhism has actually produced, the fruits of the reconciling spirit, kindliness, gentleness, simplicity, and the avoidance of the angry word or act. Buddhism has known no religious wars and no organized persecutions.

Yet, like Christianity, it lost its first love and purity. It is held as faith by hundreds of millions, yet the Buddhism of Gotama and the earliest Buddhist books can hardly be found. Modern Buddhism has coupled it with demon worship and animism. ' It is the devil-priest and not the religious mendicant or Bhikkhu who is the real pastor of the people.' As the Buddhist has no rites provided for him in his religion, he has recourse, in his hour of need, to magic. And although Gotama taught his followers to have no care of the gods, they have turned the Buddha himself into a god, with his temples, his priests, his services of prayer, and his solemn meditative images. Mankind cannot live by self-abnegation. He must get into touch somehow with higher powers. If he is allowed no sacrifices, he will find some substitute, generally something worse. For a thousand years Buddhism lived on in the land of its birth; then, from the assaults of the Brahmans on the one side and the Moslems on the other, it began to die out, and, some two thousand years after the death of Gotama, Buddhism was represented in India only by the small sect of the Jains.[1] The longing to be absorbed in God and to receive the gifts that God had to give were too strong for it; and, we must add, the sacrificial impulse also. It had indeed, however, left some mark. Caste, with which Buddhism proper can have nothing to do, was too powerful to be ejected; although shaken in some respects by the

[1] Jain worship offers many close parallels to the worship of Buddhism; but whether Jainism should be classed as a form of Buddhism is uncertain. See Farquhar, *Outline of Religious Literature of India*, p. 119.

influence of Europe, it is as strong to-day in India as ever it was. But the religious feeling against the taking of life, which Buddhism did not so much originate as accentuate, has become universal. In this way Indian sacrificial practice has completely changed. The Vedic rites, with their animal sacrifices, are gone. Yet Indian religion is still essentially a religion of the ritual worship of the gods. The life of the peasant cultivator is one long sacrifice, while the millions of the aboriginal inhabitants—the 'depressed classes' and the outcastes—are untouched either by Buddhism or Hinduism, save for the merest veneer.

Even in Hinduism, however, something of the same reaction against the worship of the altar can be traced, though it had a very different starting-point. The fundamental conception of Hinduism is neither atheism, as with Buddhism, nor polytheism, as one would conclude from the bewildering tangle of worships and devotions to be observed to-day in India, but pantheism. The supreme desire of the instructed Hindu is for liberation. This has led to a succession of philosophic movements since the third century of our era, some of which have announced themselves as the true successors of the Vedic religion, while others have sat loosely to all orthodoxy. Most conspicuous of these has been the Sankhya system, which rose into prominence at the beginning of the philosophic period, but has now almost entirely died out. It maintained a kind of atheistic dualism, in which there could be no more place for sacrifice than in Buddhism itself. Other philosophies, however they might emphasize the all-pervading and impersonal nature of the deity, found no difficulty in reconciling their views with the popular and traditional practice of sacrificing. Later on the principle of *bhakti*, or loving personal devotion to God, culminating in a kind of mystical union with Him, gained great influence, while Hinduism has universally held in the highest reverence the ascetic, who leaves behind all social and earthly ties and goes out into the jungle or the forest to live a life of isolated meditation, and for whom temple and altar have no longer any meaning. Indeed, orthodox Brahmanism regards this as the fourth or final stage of the earthly life of every religious man. The modern movements of the Arya and

REACTION AGAINST SACRIFICE 131

the Brahmo Somaj, which have given up caste, at least in theory, have also given up sacrifice.

The truth is that sacrifice, though surviving because of, or in spite of, the beliefs of those who offer it, is something different in post-Vedic Hinduism from what it is in any of the religions we have hitherto examined. It is, in the first place, like all Hindu worship, a thing primarily for the individual. There is in Hinduism no common worship, and no common sacrifice. It is a possible and very valuable means, but not the only means, of approach to God. The common man may regard it as the most obvious path to God for him to take; but the privileged and advanced, and especially the saint, may regard it as quite inferior to the road which he is able to travel. In the second place, sacrifice is not the way of reconciliation. To the Hindu, reconciliation with God is unmeaning or impossible. With him, as with the Buddhist, the nature of the deity makes it inconceivable. Liberation can only be obtained by unwearied patience lasting through innumerable existences, and indomitable self-mastery. These secular processes may, of course, be aided by sacrifice; and if the Hindu mind valued consistency even less than it does, the impulse to offer some sort of sacrifice to the gods, and to expect something from them in return, would suffice to ensure its continuance even under a system that had no place for such hopes. But if we would find anything in modern India that corresponds to sacrifice as we have found it in the rest of the world, we must go to the half-civilized and half-Hinduized communities who dwell on the fringe of orthodoxy, despised by the Brahmans, and only tolerated by them because of their perfunctory respect to the sacred caste, but who in the obscurity of their remote villages retain the belief, however monstrous its manifestations, that their god can bless them, here and now, and that the barriers which have kept off those blessings can be removed by acts which man can perform and god will recognize.

In dealing with the religious movements of India, it is thus truer to speak of the reaction against sacrifice than of an attack on sacrifices. The same is true of Greece. In Greece, as in India, when once philosophy came to be studied, an interpretation of life grew up in which there was no place for sacrifice or what sacrifice represented,

132 ALTAR, CROSS, AND COMMUNITY

implied or was understood to secure.[1] Indeed, to the Greek philosophers, as to Gotama, gods to whom sacrifice could be offered did not exist. The process of this new interpretation of the world began with the Ionian philosophers, who were contemporaries of the greater Hebrew prophets. What was at the heart of all the variety of this puzzling and many-formed world? Water, air, fire, or some quasi-personal principle of strife, or a half-material substance called mind? Such speculations had little effect on popular practice or even on the religious attitude of the speculators, who could conceivably continue to sacrifice, undisturbed by their own suggestions. It would not have been the first time in history that a change of theory had failed to be followed by change in outward action. But such thoughts none the less, to the quick Greek mind, suggested daring and impiety. Behind these 'elements' were there really gods at all, and if so, were they not quite different from the village and clan gods and heroes, and even from the Olympians themselves? The real force of these questions was made clear by Heraclitus, in his doctrine of opposites and flux. Nature, he taught, is like a river, always flowing past you, so that you cannot dive into the same river twice—or even once! 'War is father and lord of nature,' alike in the physical as in the social world.'[2]

The effect of all this was like that of Darwin on his contemporaries. How could sacrifices avail when the world was organized on so austere and inhuman a system? Heraclitus himself saw the contradiction plainly enough. He also saw the patent weakness of popular sacrifices. How could a bad man offer acceptable sacrifices to any god who was worth believing in at all? A good man would not need to bribe heaven; a bad man could not hope that

---

[1] 'One of the largest interests of the later history of Hindu worship is the slow but steady weakening of the old sacrificial cult under the pressure of the more attractive temple-system.' 'There is one point which is absolutely clear, namely this, that the essential elements of the temple cult are so distinct from the sacrificial cult as to betray an alien origin.' This tendency is clearly seen during the period from the third to sixth centuries of our era. At its close, 'everywhere temple-worship and the presentation of offerings to images tended to take the place of the ancient ordinances' (Farquhar, *op. cit.*, pp. 51, 140, 170). Farquhar holds, as is most probable, that the ritual of sacrifice, on a holy spot, but without temple or image, was properly Vedic, but that temple and image worship belonged to the aborigines.

[2] See Arist., *Met.* iii. 5, 1010*a* Plutarch, *De Iside*, 48.

his bribe would be accepted. To cleanse oneself from pollution with blood is like cleaning with mud a mud-stained foot. This theological argument was reinforced by his younger contemporary, Xenophanes, in the familiar contention that the gods of current religion are mere products of human imagination. 'God is in truth invisible and one, neither finite nor infinite, neither motionless nor moving.'[1] To a thinking man the whole system of anthropomorphic gods, who could be influenced and pleased with offerings, was inconsistent with the facts of life, and therefore, to an intellectual Greek, inconceivable.

Later Greek physicists were even more radical; we can only suppose that they escaped the charge of treasonable impiety because they lived in communities which, unlike Athens, were not in the habit of taking a man's speculations seriously, or because they took care not to let their opinions affect their conduct. Xenophanes himself was no atheist, though he might easily have been attacked, like Socrates, for atheism; but when Democritus, still as early as the fifth century before Christ, and only about a century later than Gotama, affirmed that the universe is made up of atoms, each one carried downwards independently, but swerving aside so as to clash and unite with others, thus making up things as we know them, the study of nature and the denial of the gods had clearly met. Some five centuries later the cultivated Roman Lucretius hailed this system as a means of escape from the tyranny of religious practices, and the fears which gave them birth. But such attacks could have little hope of popular success, either in Greece or Rome. Widespread religious cults and institutions are not to be brought down by theory; and conservatism and the love of a common and awe-inspiring ceremony are too strong for logic. It was not by logic or theories about the constitution of the physical universe that Gotama produced the impulse to his way of self-abnegation, but by the relief he offered to the weariness of life, as Christian Science offers its relief to-day. A religion that promises liberation from the ills of which men are actually conscious will never lack adherents, unless its promises are patently vain and false. Greek thought could never have understood

[1] Quoted in Ritter and Preller, *Hist. Phil. Graecae*, pp. 39, 84.

the Buddhist eightfold path; it had no desire for the kind of liberation that attracted the Oriental mind. Its real strength lay in its ethics. The movement started by Socrates and developed in different directions by the Cynics, by Plato and Aristotle, and later by the Stoics, was unlike that of the Buddha in laying stress on the kind of action that would lead to satisfaction here and now; but like it in producing a view of conduct in which sacrifice could find no place. Speculation, however daring, might very well leave a man's religious practices where it found them. A new way of life could not but affect them in one way or another.

None of these thinkers, indeed, had anything in common with the fanatical reformer. But they saw the inherent weaknesses of the sacrificial system as it worked out in practice. Could prayers and gifts bend the gods? Then bad men would bend the gods to their own bad will. Yet Socrates, in his last moments, could arrange, surely not altogether in sport, for a cock to be sacrificed to Asclepius, and Plato describes the lads' sacrifice of Lysis and his friends, and the dignified rites of the aged Cephalus, with evident interest, and without a trace of disapproval or criticism.[1] It was not for his attitude to accepted religious worship that Socrates was charged with being an atheist. None the less the charge was plausible, and to an average Greek even more than plausible. Socrates not only brought down philosophy from heaven to men; he did the same for ethics. Virtue, to refer to one of his most frequently quoted maxims, was knowledge. Let a man once fully understand the nature of right conduct and he will practise it. He needs neither priests nor rites nor means of reconciliation with heaven. Gods, in the sense of beings with whom he must get into touch before he can act rightly, do not exist. All that a man needs is self-knowledge and the dialectic of his own experience.[2]

The Cynics handed on the tradition, with a strong emphasis on a rather repellent kind of dour asceticism. But the core of their teaching, like that of their master,

---

[1] See Plato, *Phaedo*, 118, *Lysis*, 207, *Rep.*, i. 331.
[2] The same view—that a man can form, or receive, a new conception of life, and cut himself off at once from the entail of his past life—is implied by Ezekiel (ch. xviii.).

was 'You can, if you are willing; you must, if you are wise.' That conduct is affected by the attitude of heaven to past failures or present wishes, or that duty depends on a personal relation to an unseen being, is not even considered.

To suggest that the systems of Plato and Aristotle were atheistic would be to misconceive them utterly; and yet in their schemes of conduct they allowed no more place for the gods of the orthodox Athenian than did Socrates. They reached conceptions of life and action infinitely more subtle than that of the average Greek or the average Englishman; yet, even when the fullest justice is done them, their view is not unlike that of many an earnest Christian who cannot acquiesce in a universe in which God is not the central and controlling factor, however obscure, but who also holds that in matters of conduct he must fight his own battles and work out his own salvation. Plato would have us aim at the harmony of all the parts of the soul—thought, emotion, and desire; and this a wise system of education, he held, may be expected to secure for us. But how can we set any reliance on mendicant prophets who 'go to rich men's doors and persuade them that they have a power committed to them by the gods of making an atonement for a man's own or his ancestor's sins by sacrifices or charms, with rejoicings and feasts . . . with magic arts and incantations binding heaven, as they say, to execute their will?'[1] Aristotle bids us construct an elaborate habit of choosing naturally the middle path between the extremes offered by pleasure or threatened by pain. Plato may speak of being friends with the gods; and Aristotle may encourage us to play the immortal, in imitation of the superbly contemplative life of the great first cause.[2] We can as little conceive of Plato and Aristotle offering sacrifice to get into touch with God as a means to the blessed life, as we can think of Kant kneeling at the elevation of the host.

What Plato really thought of the function of sacrifices can be readily seen from the references he makes to them when sketching his ideal state: 'To Apollo there remains, then, the ordering of the greatest and noblest things of all —the institution of temples and sacrifices and the rites

[1] Pl., *Rep.*, ii. 364.
[2] Pl., *Rep.*, x. 621; Arist. *Eth. Nic.*, x. 1177b.

which have to be observed by him who would propitiate the inhabitants of the world below.'[1] That he is quite serious here is shown by his further statement that when the 'rulers' of his city depart to the islands of the blest, 'the city will give them memorials and sacrifices, and honour them, if the Pythian oracle consent, as demi-gods.' In his later work, the *Laws*, he speaks of sacrifices and feasts as the natural expression of the friendship between good men and the gods (' like to like '). They are, indeed, to form the spiritual bond of the community. They are social and not individual. From the bad sacrifice will be abhorrent.[2]

Plato and Aristotle have exercised an influence on subsequent thought out of all proportion to the number and importance of their professed followers in Greece. As intellectual and moral leaders, Platonists and Peripatetics were soon superseded by Stoics and Epicureans. This is not the place to discuss these two schools, as profound as they have been misunderstood. Profound as they were, we miss in them the subtlety of their predecessors; but for this very reason, perhaps, the circle they affected was wider. All can understand the simple connexion between satisfaction and duty; there are moods when we admit the Stoic paradox that the wise man who has trampled the fear of death under foot can be happy on the rack; and though in rags, can be the equal of the lord of heaven. And however rigorously we reject the teaching of Epicurus, as popularly represented—namely, as an appeal to hedonism and the cult of physical pleasure —we can admire the ideal of a mind at leisure, with simple delights that arouse no passion, excite no envy, and are threatened by no disappointment. All that has here to be pointed out is that Zeno and Epicurus alike made no more demands on heaven than did Plato or Aristotle. Epicurus, indeed, like Gotama, left the gods out of account. He did not deny their existence; he denied their interest in human affairs or hopes. The Stoic position was very different. To the earlier Stoics, Zeus was nothing else than the whole universe, the cosmic order[3]; and when Stoicism migrated to Rome, its best-

---

[1] Pl., *Rep.*, iv. 427; cf. vii. 540 and *Laws*, viii. 828. [2] *Laws*, iv. 716.
[3] Cf. the well-known ' Hymn of Cleanthes.'

known exponents wrote as pure theists.[1] But the god of whom they wrote so eloquently, and whom they sought with such pathetic zeal, was not one to whom any man could sacrifice, or who would have known what to make of a sacrifice if it had been offered. Their thought of God was either too deep or not deep enough to find room for the need of a reconciliation between an offended and neglected power and a disobedient and rebellious servant.

Greek ethics was naturalistic. It had at once the strength and weakness of naturalism. It repudiated the idea that the favour of heaven could ever be secured by an *opus operatum*, performed either for the worshipper or by him, or that the help of heaven, if the expression were allowable at all, could be secured save by justice, self-control, and goodwill. What could God require of man, if He required indeed anything at all, save courage and wisdom and gentleness and proper self-respect and pride? On the other hand, Stoicism made nothing of human frailty and despair, the footsteps that have wellnigh slipped, and the evil past that no mere effort to reform can obliterate or neutralize. For these it had little sympathy and no cure.

And it failed. The sacrifices continued. Not a single city put an end to its rites because of the Stoic creed. Not a single god went without his dues. The reason for the decay of state sacrifices, and their supersession by new religious impulses, with a new conception of the place and effect of sacrificial rites, we have seen already. But the philosophers as a class stood aside from the Oriental mystery religions, as they stood aside from Christianity. Marcus Aurelius would have been horrified to think of coquetting, as his son coquetted, with Mithraism.[2] Perhaps the philosophers' attack on sacrifice was not sufficiently resolute. They had not the courage of their convictions. They did not really desire to see the rites come to an end. Like Plato, they felt their value as civic and political institutions. And when it became the custom to offer sacrifices to the divinity of the reigning emperor, few of

---

[1] 'Remember that you must behave like a guest at a banquet. If anything is handed to you, take a portion of it. When it is removed, do not clutch at it' (Epict., *Man.*, 15). 'External affairs cannot take hold of the soul, nor have they any access to it, nor can they turn or move it. It alone turns and moves itself' (Marcus Aurelius, *Comm.*, v. 19).

[2] Cumont, *Textes et Monuments*, vol. i., p. 281.

them dared to run the risk of what might be put down as treason. Only Jews and Christians would do that. After all, they might argue, so long as men do not look to sacrifice to atone for their past, what harm can they do? And since, in sacrifice, it is the ritual that matters, and not any individual belief as to its efficacy, the philosopher could play the part demanded of him like a good citizen, and even found it difficult to understand why the fanatical Christians could possibly object to sacrifice when the state so commanded.

In this acquiescence, however, the philosophers misunderstood or were unjust to their own contentions, and to the popular religion which they in their hearts despised. To the common man sacrifice had more than a merely manward aspect. It brought him to God. He might have little idea how this was accomplished. He might think that the main thing to do was to repeat the old words and actions. The great innovators in politics are often the most conservative in religion. But he was not going to take unnecessary risks. He was not prepared to stake his hopes on the efficacy of morality as the philosopher or any one else defined it. He had not sufficient trust in himself; or else he felt that life needed something more than harmonious relations between man and man. The unseen had its claims which could not be denied without leaving an immeasurable void. The theories of the schools were doubtless interesting and valuable; but his soul cried out for God, and he could not get at God save by something more concrete and dramatic than self-control and justice and what was rather vaguely talked of as 'virtue.' He could even worship the 'unknown god,' as the Babylonian sufferer had done. When he became conscious of the appeal of a unified world under a central government, he turned that appeal into a religion and deified the emperor. When he trembled, in all the loneliness and ignorance of frail humanity, before the face of death, he found relief in the great sacrificial dramas of the communal mysteries. When he came to feel the bondage and guilt of passion, self-seeking and lust, he turned to a greater deliverer, whose salvation, as he now saw, had been wrought in the most stupendous sacrifice ever offered upon earth.

The sacrifices remained, as they remained in India. And Greek philosophy gave rise to nothing corresponding to Buddhism. It did not challenge the established order of things by a new organization and system. It had no conception of the spiritual force and intensity which won for Buddhism its surprising triumphs. It did not move masses of men; but it performed a work perhaps not less important. It broke the very power which it seemed hardly able to shake. It undermined the defences from which it recoiled. Gradually and imperceptibly the belief in sacrifice, either as a state function or the mystery of a fraternity, lost its vitality. The ponderous edifice seemed impregnable. The assaults of six hundred years had made no visible effect on its walls. But when a new attack was made, resting, not on ' wisdom,' but on faith, a faith in a sacrifice, indeed, but in a sacrifice very differently conceived, offered once, and never to be offered again, for the deliverance of all mankind from every foe that they could need to fear, the walls fell down; not with the suddenness suggested by Milton's ' Ode on the Nativity,'[1] but with the steady crumbling of fortifications which had neither defenders nor repairers.

We must now turn to the reaction against sacrifice in the religious life of Israel—the most important, because of its lasting effect on Judaism; because of the convictions which lay behind it, at once moral and religious; and because of its influence on the teaching of Jesus, the last and greatest of the succession of the prophets by whom the reaction was led. In Jesus His followers have recognized at once the fulfilment of prophecy and the archetype of the sacrifices against which prophecy launched its unwearied protest.

The rivalry between prophet and priest is a commonplace in most presentations of Hebrew history. But this rivalry only appeared in the course of the development of the two institutions of prophecy and priesthood; and though it seems to us inevitable, it was not lasting. The priest stood for the regular and controlled element in

[1] ' In urns and altars round
   A drear and dying sound
Affrights the Flamins at their service quaint;
   And the chill marble seems to sweat,
While each peculiar power forgoes his wonted seat.'

religion, the prophet for the irregular and spontaneous. The priest was to be found at the place of sacrifice, to direct and supervise and to intervene when necessary, and to give oracular responses and judicial decisions when required. Since he stood in a special and official relation to the unseen world, to him belonged the ephod, the Urim and Thummim. The spirit of the prophet was one which was not subject to him. It came and went. It might give an answer when it was requested, or it might inspire a message when no inquiry had been made. Naturally, therefore, the priest, dwelling beside his shrine, would emphasize the rite as the important element in worship; the prophet, with no settled factor in his life save attentive waiting to hear the word of Jehovah, would emphasize obedience to a command which might be as strange as the priest's rites were familiar. The contrast can be clearly seen in Samuel's rebuke to Saul's excuse for sparing Agag.[1] This rebuke, however, was only occasioned by a definite clash between two duties, as they seemed to the Hebrew of the time. Ordinarily, the earlier prophets were accustomed to offer sacrifices, like every pious Israelite. Samuel at Ramah or Bethlehem had no more thought that he was compromising with a lower form of religion than Elijah on Carmel.

It is only when we come to deal with the prophets of whose addresses we have actual reports or epitomes that we find the genuine prophetic protest against sacrifice. And in the century that divided Amos from Elijah a great change had been coming over religious ritual. Sacrificial feasts had always been seasons for merry-making and business, convenient and pleasant social gatherings. Now, with the rapidly growing wealth of the country, they became opportunities for luxury, display, and a self-indulgence that easily developed into vice. Since the holy places of Israel, their equipment, and their appointed and solemn acts, were often almost identical with those of the Canaanites, the licence of the devotees of the Canaanite Baal would quickly be reproduced by the worshippers of Jehovah. Further, in the eighth and seventh centuries, the sacrifices of Jehovah were invaded by the worst elements of heathenism. The prophet, therefore, could not regard the sacrifice as a second-best approach to

[1] 1 Sam. xv. 22.

God ; it was no way of approach at all ; it was positive impiety. Gilgal and Bethel were places of transgression. The idolatry which the prophets denounced was not merely the worship of false gods, nor of Jehovah under the form of an image ; it was the worship of Jehovah in a false spirit— the spirit in which a confident purchaser might approach a rich but benevolent merchant, and which therefore made everything, on both sides, of payment, and nothing, on either side, of moral attitude and character.

If this is true, it implies something more. If sacrifices had simply been regarded as contaminated by idolatrous processes, we should have expected a distinction to be made by the prophets between the true and the false. ' Substitute,' they might have cried, ' an altar on Carmel for the calves of Bethel,' just as Paul protested against the abuses in the Eucharist at Corinth, but not against the Eucharist itself. We find no such distinction in the writing prophets, and no hint that there might be any better sacrifice than the existing sanctuaries had to offer. The inference is clear. But we are not left to inference. If the earlier prophets did not make a distinction, they constructed an antithesis between sacrifice and righteousness. This is not to assert ' ritual will not avail without morals,' or ' ritual will not avail ; only morals.' It expresses a deeper conception. Sacrifice, as we have seen, was an attempt to ' get into touch.' Hence the prophetic assertion : ' You try to get into touch with Jehovah by prayers, backed by lavish gifts. You cannot do it. No rite, no prayer, is of any use ; only justice and honesty and goodwill.' They do not say ' No rite is of use while the heart is wrong.' They never imply that it will be of any use when the heart is right. What they would have said if they had been discussing pure and untainted sacrifices we do not know. But the fact that in discussing debased sacrifices they spoke of sacrifices as a whole suggests the answer.

So much for Amos and Hosea. But they spoke of Israel, where religion was confessedly at a low ebb. What of Judah ? There is no difference. This is shown by the remarkable summary of the state of religion in Judah which is prefixed to the prophecies of Isaiah. There, as in Israel, the prophet finds ritual lavishness, moral laxity, political madness. This is the sin, not the schism which is so vigorously emphasized in the historical writings. As in Amos and Hosea, the cry is 'turn,' 'wash you,' and, though in no ritual sense, 'make you clean.' True, the vision which gave to Isaiah his call was in the Temple. And he uses a ritual term, though doubtless in a sense of his own, 'The Holy One of Israel.' It was hard for one high in court society not to look on the rites of the established religion with favour. All the more significant is Isaiah's condemnation. But in that condemnation there is a new note. The chief stress in his attack on Judah's sin is not laid on idolatry and false worship. Here he differs from Hosea, who, himself a northerner, feels, as it were, a personal pollution in the idols of the northern sanctuaries. In this respect he is nearer to Amos. Amos attacks the luxury of the shrines at Gilgal and Bethel with the bluntness of a puritan peasant who loathes display in religion or anywhere else; but he could not have spoken as he did, without hypocrisy, unless religion in Judah had been at least relatively pure. Perhaps in spite of the appalling description in the first chapter of Isaiah, the southern ritual was less debased at the time. In any case, Isaiah attacks the sacrifices, not because the ritual was debased, but because the heart was wrong. With him, the antithesis of rite and conduct as means of approaching and pleasing Jehovah is even sharper. Conduct alone can reconcile. That sacrifices played no part in his thought is clear from the later narratives which are appended to his prophecies, where, either as a protection against invasion or as a remedy for sickness, they are unmentioned. How far we have moved from the closing chapters of David's reign![1]

This is the more remarkable because a real attempt at reforming the sacrificial system from within took place in Isaiah's lifetime. Whatever abuses might have crept into the rites of the Temple at Jerusalem, the proceedings at the country shrines were worse. There the worship of Jehovah was exposed to the daily contamination of the foul practices of the older inhabitants of the land. 'We must get rid of these at all costs; religion must be centralized.' The cry was one with which any earnest man might have been in sympathy. Yet not a word of

[1] Isa. xxxvii. f.; cf. 2 Sam. xxiv.

REACTION AGAINST SACRIFICE 143

approval or encouragement from Isaiah has come down to us—nothing to suggest that even a purified sacrifice can bring man near to God. Isaiah's younger contemporary, Micah, is even more emphatic. What possible difference, he asks, can sacrifice make to God? What God does need is perfectly clear—honesty, goodwill, and reverence. It may be objected that Micah thought of sacrifices as gifts or bribes, not as a means of reconciliation. It is probable that this is how, in his day, most people thought of them. If so, he has no idea that they could be anything better. They are wholly vain. Jehovah is a God with character. What Jehovah desires is really likeness to Himself; the intercourse of human beings who embody the qualities which are conspicuous in Him. To show these is the only way of being acceptable to Him. The conception may seem thin and inadequate to us. It leaves as little room for forgiveness as for sacrifice. Man can turn from his wickedness; then he will live. But, at all events, it is different from the philosophy of Gotama, or the ethics of the Greek thinkers; and the confident longing for forgiveness, even at the expense of logic, dwelt by its side.[1]

But, like Gotama and the Greek philosophers, the eighth-century prophets failed to root out the practices they abhorred. The centralizing reformers failed also. Under Manasseh things were worse than they had ever been in Judah before. The old local sacrifices were revived. New and hideous practices were introduced; and there was not a prophet to protest. None the less, a party existed in Judah which was opposed to all this; and at last it found itself with a new king, Josiah, under its influence. Apparently, little change was at first effected; for with the new reign a new and sinister prophetic voice was heard. Jeremiah reiterated the old rebukes, and made the old simple appeal. But when a document was discovered, containing the principles, in a developed form, of Hezekiah's reformation, and insisting on the centralization of

---

[1] Micah's prophecies themselves contain much moral denunciation; no moral appeal. The hope of restoration and forgiveness, however, is clear from Mic. iv. 10, v. 12 f., vii. 18. For our purpose it makes little difference whether the last two chapters of Micah date from a later period or not. For the presence of appeal and promise in the same preaching cf. Isa. i. 16, 25; Ezek. xviii. 21, xxxvi. 26.

worship and drastic measures for abolishing all the Canaanite and debasing elements at the shrines, Josiah accepted it at once as authoritative, and carried it out to the letter. Worship at the high places, where Baal and Jehovah had disputed for supremacy, suddenly ceased, and in Jerusalem, under the eye of a reforming and reformed priesthood, the scandals of the past received their death-blow.

Such a change would naturally attract a prophet who saw in the sacrifices of his time a corrupt ritual, and could find in the reforming zeal of his contemporaries evidence of the long-looked-for change of heart. But we have no word of commendation from Jeremiah on the subject. It may be, indeed, that he devoted the remaining years of Josiah's reign to addresses in favour of the reformation, which have all been lost.[1] Perhaps earlier hopes of the covenant were dashed by its subsequent failure to touch the heart of the nation. In any case, after Josiah's untimely and disastrous death, when the old impieties were renewed, we find Jeremiah denying that Jehovah ever gave any command about sacrifices at all, even to Moses[2]; that is, he explicitly refuses them any divine sanction. Henceforth his attitude is that of his predecessor. No rites can avail; unless a radical conversion takes place, destruction is certain. The nation is doomed, as Hosea had said a hundred and thirty years before about Israel. But Jeremiah goes farther. He cannot believe in final doom, though the Chaldeans draw nearer and nearer. And he cannot believe in a change of heart. How, then, does he escape from the dilemma? A *new* covenant is to be made, by which the heart will be changed.[3] But it will not come from or through sacrifice; it will be the pure act of Jehovah. Jehovah must have His people back, reconciled to Him at last. He makes them turn. Thus, at the last, reconciliation is seen to be only through the reformation

---

[1] See Jer. xi. 1-8. This mission, which Jeremiah evidently regarded as a failure, certainly points to the Deuteronomic reformation. Erbt thinks that the failure of the reformation was a distinct element in the formation of the prophet's later convictions on the subject of ritual and the law; Duhm and Cornill question the authenticity of the passage, pointing to a certain tameness in its style, which we can observe if we compare the verses in question with ch. x. 12-25 or ch. xi. 15-23; and Cornill asks how such a mission could be consistent with the authorship of ch. viii. 8.

[2] Jer. vii. 22.   [3] Jer. xxxi. 31.

REACTION AGAINST SACRIFICE 145

and forgiveness of the heart. Sacrifice is simply ruled out.

The note thus struck never ceased to find echoes in Hebrew devotional literature.[1] But it was unheeded by Jeremiah's contemporaries. A centralized and purified system of sacrifice perhaps persisted through Josiah's reign. After his death the old abuses revived, and when, at last, the blow fell, and Jerusalem was sacked, and with a small party of fugitives Jeremiah was dragged into exile in Egypt, the last glimpse we have of him is the raising of a vain protest against the sacrificial worship, not of Jehovah at all, but of the ' queen of heaven.'[2]

While Jeremiah was still preaching to the unheeding crowds in Jerusalem, in the feverish days of Zedekiah, his message was being urged in a new accent among the exiles of the first deportation in Babylon. A disciple for Jeremiah might have been looked for in any one rather than Ezekiel. The unsparing opponent of the sacrificial system found his successor in a young priest. Jeremiah himself had sprung from a priestly family in Anathoth, a village outside Jerusalem ; doubtless some of his relations had been dispossessed by the reformation of Josiah.[3] But Ezekiel belonged to one of the highest priestly circles in the capital itself, who would naturally be the custodians of whatever ritual purity there was, and who would look with contempt on the inferior and disestablished ministry of the country. And Ezekiel was imbued with the ideas of his caste. Unlike the earlier prophets, he shows in a hundred expressions his sensitiveness for ritual considerations, and he places ritual by the side of moral faults and virtues, as if he saw no difference between them.[4] His only divergence from the other priests would seem to have been that he took the ideas of Deuteronomy and the sacerdotal conception of holiness much more seriously than they did. The misuses of the Temple against which he inveighed could not have taken place without at least their connivance.[5] Such was the man who echoed Jeremiah's

---

[1] Ps. xxxiv. 18, xl. 6, l. 9, li. 16, 17 ; Isa. lvii. 15, lxvi. 2.
[2] Jer. xliv. 15 ff.
[3] If so, this would deepen the resentment of his native place to any advocacy of the measures of Josiah which he might undertake.
[4] Cf. Ezek. iv. 14 ff., xviii. 5 ff.
[5] Ezek. viii. 6 ff., xliii. 7 ff.

K

arraignment of his country's sin in the exiles' settlement on the Chebar.

Ezekiel is generally spoken of as heralding a new movement in prophecy ; subjecting the old free moral ideas of his predecessors to the bondage of the law; introducing legalism into the religion from which it had been banished by the burning condemnations of Isaiah and Jeremiah. It was certainly a new movement which Ezekiel initiated, but not one of this nature. With legalism, in the sense in which his critics accuse him of it, he had as little sympathy as any of the prophets who went before him. What he did was to find a place for ritual beside the older prophetic ideas, but also to give those ideas a new elaboration before they were brought into touch with ritual at all.

The older prophets had held that sacrifice was of no value for an approach to God or an atonement for sin. It had no relation to forgiveness, for forgiveness was an entirely spiritual matter, and could not be affected by any transaction in the material world. Ezekiel was in entire agreement with them. He differed only in working out in a scheme what to them had been merely an intuition. Their message had been ' Cease to do evil ; learn to do well ; sin brings destruction ; repentance and return bring restoration.' Jeremiah went farther. ' How can we return ? When Jehovah makes with us a new covenant.' Ezekiel went farther still. Not till the independence of the city was finally quenched in 586 did he hold out any hopes. Then, when the whole nation was in exile and, as it seemed, on the brink of actual annihilation, he had to consider the problem of reconciliation for himself, and for them. How was it to come about ? To Ezekiel, the simple answer ' A new covenant ' was not enough. How did he know that the covenant would be kept ? Or how could it be written on the heart ? His answer was remarkable. First will come the return to Palestine ; then prosperity ; this will produce self-loathing ; and self-loathing (as by some inner psychological necessity) will produce the new spirit.[1] It is not necessary to consider this pronouncement in detail, but only to point out that it involves sacrifice or ' legalism ' as little as his own earlier

[1] Ezek. xxxvi. 22 ff.

REACTION AGAINST SACRIFICE 147

statements, or those of the other prophets. It could only be called legalism if legalism means ' doing that which is lawful and right ' ; in which case all the prophets are legalists.

He is like the other prophets in another respect. His attacks on sacrifice seem to be directed only against false and debased cults. The vivid description of chapter viii. shows how much of sheer paganism had invaded even the Temple courts, and illustrates clearly enough the ruthless language of Isaiah. These sacrifices could not reconcile. They were an obvious abomination. But, it may be argued, that is not to say that other sacrifices might not have reconciled. The reply to this suggestion, for Ezekiel as for the rest, is that when he describes reconciliation he does not mention sacrifice at all. He is priest enough to hold that what we call ritual offences are as serious as offences against morality. But all that is necessary for salvation from them is to avoid them. If he did not think of sacrifices in such a context as this, would he be likely to do so at any other time ?

But surely, it will be objected, this is just what Ezekiel did in the concluding chapters of his book, in the vision of the new temple and city. Here is a whole code of law, and, except for a few passages, not a word about morals. Ezekiel now seems to part company from the other prophets altogether. What would be the feelings of Jeremiah if he had read all this ? But the inconsistency is not as great as it seems. Jeremiah would probably have taken no interest in the ' house ' or the altar, or the ' taboos ' for the priests ; but he would find no unfaithfulness to the spirit of his message of repentance. For the vision, with all its insistence on ceremony, applies to the state of the nation after the reconciliation is complete. The new heart and spirit have already been given. Israel's one desire is now to serve Jehovah and to fall into sin no more. Her oppressors also have been swept away. All that is necessary is to preserve her from temptation. To the mind of the priest, as to many others, some worship is inevitable. History has shown that worship always tends to grow corrupt or over-elaborate, till the act obscures and defeats the intention. Hence special rites must be provided by which worship will be kept pure, and the laws of holiness will not be transgressed.[1] His attitude is the same to the old social evils of princely oppression and taxation. The old bad times have gone; it is only necessary to take care that they have no chance of returning.[2] And in all this legislation there is no mention of sin or atonement. No reason is given for the sacrifices which are described with such loving care. Nor could there be; for these last chapters are describing an ideal city, the origin of the heavenly city of the Apocalypse. The city of John's vision had no need of a temple; Ezekiel could not get beyond that need; he could not conceive of worship which should have neither temple nor sacrifice nor priest. But there were no sins to be atoned for. He had not to think of cure, but prevention. The very name of the city was 'Jehovah is there'; and its most striking feature was the river of life, which flowed 'from under the threshold of the house.'

It has been necessary to go into this detail with Ezekiel because while he, rightly understood, completes the prophetic protest against ritual, he also profoundly affected the development of ritual itself. In his view ritual does not atone for sin; but right ritual prevents unholiness. In the pre-prophetic age ritual had done more than this. If there had been sin, there was happily sacrifice, precisely as for the Greeks of Plato's time. The sacrifice might be either a sign of repentance or a substitute for it. But if, in the later codes, sacrifices are for ritual sins alone, while in sacrificial language, 'high-handed' sins cease to be thought of at all,[3] Ezekiel is mainly responsible for the change of view. The inefficacy of sacrifices as such had taken a deep hold of the Jewish mind. For that reason, even while the 'doctors of the law' pondered over its precepts, and tithed their mint and cummin, they could canonize the prophets; for they knew what the prophets and the Psalms told them with one voice, and what the law itself could not deny—that 'the sacrifices of God are a broken spirit.'

[1] It is quite true that Ezekiel's conception of holiness is not that of Isaiah. It comes at times very near to the material or semi-material ideas of primitive religion which the priestly cultus preserved, although at other times he rises far above this level. But this does not mean that Ezekiel had also a different conception of reconciliation or even of sacrifice; only that the contents of his code of right and wrong were larger and less homogeneous than theirs.
[2] See Ezek. xliv. 9 ff., xlvi. 16 ff.   [3] See p. 120.

Thus the reaction against sacrifice in Palestine was not the failure it had been in India and Greece. In India the Buddhists had taught that there was no deity and therefore no reconciliation, and that therefore sacrifices were needless. The philosophers had taught that to unite with the one divine essence, reconciliation was not a possible method, and therefore that sacrifice, if it persisted at all, must be something different from what it had been in Vedic times. The Greek teachers, whether they professed any definite theism at all or not, looked to education, communal or individual, to mould the will in the right direction, and sacrifice meant nothing to them. In each case popular instincts were too strong. Philosophic teaching helped to bring about a great change in sacrificial practice in India. Buddhist propaganda drove out sacrifice by the front door, to allow it to enter again by the back. Greek sacrifices simply went on, in spite of the philosophers; and if, in the later mystery religions, they assumed a new form and rôle, the philosophers had nothing to do with the change. In Palestine the sacrifices continued, and were, indeed, more elaborate after the prophetic activities than before. At the centre of Judaism was the Temple; and the proper work of the Temple was sacrifice. But the prophets had done two things. They had destroyed all sacrifice save in one place; and they had driven out of sacrifice the idea of a general atonement. In doing so, they had gone far to rob the whole system of its religious value. For what is the value of a system which only contemplates what are not really sins at all?

The answer to this question is partly religious. The sacrifices laid stress on ceremonial holiness; and though to us holiness is not a matter of fluxes and contact with corpses, its symbolism was very valuable. It was a constant reminder of the majesty and transcendence of God. And a system that tended to place sin and dirt together, in the mind of the worshippers, as equally displeasing to God, was not more misguided than the mediaeval sanctification of dirt, and it certainly anticipates with startling clearness the modern discovery of the connexion that often links physical dirt and disease to moral delinquency. But the answer is also psychological. A sacrificial pilgrimage and feast is of vast use in keeping up social and personal religious feeling. All the greatest teachers have known this, from Moses to Plato, and from Plato to Mohammed and the Catholic missionaries and administrators of the Middle Ages. The Jews had neither king nor judge, nor land nor army nor government of their own through the long ages that followed the exile; they had not even one language. But they had a law; and the law prescribed sacrifices. And if the sacrifices have been for centuries at an end, their renewal is still eagerly looked for.

We cannot, however, close this chapter without reference to another prophetic voice. We have implied that Ezekiel's was the last word of prophecy that was likely to affect the authority of the sacrifices. This was not so. Towards the end of the exile another great word was uttered which forms at once the profound and moving conclusion to the whole body of teaching, and the most powerful of Old Testament influences upon the thought of the first generation of Christians. But we have kept all mention of it to the end, because it stands curiously out of relation to the rest. It cannot be called a protest. It does not refer directly to sacrifice at all. And it had no effect on the sacrificial practice of the Jews. It did not even mould their subsequent theological thought in any respect, as far as that thought is represented in the Canon. It stands like some solitary monument by an unknown sculptor, left unnoticed by his brothers in art, until the ideals of a later age suddenly seize upon it and know it for their own.

In the prophecies of the second half of Isaiah are four songs describing the career of one who is called the ' servant of Jehovah.' The last of these contains a doctrine of reconciliation at which no other Old Testament writer ever hinted. The ' servant,' who is spoken of in all four brief compositions in terms so vague that it is impossible either to identify him with an individual (whether historical or ideal) or with the whole nation, is here represented as a figure of utter humiliation, who, at the terrible crisis of his history, is recognized as bearing the sins of the very spectators who are horrified at his fate. In doing this he is fulfilling the divine will, exactly as the whole Christian Church has held that six centuries later Jesus did it upon the cross; and by an amazing intuition the poet sees that

REACTION AGAINST SACRIFICE 151

in doing so the sufferer actually saves the men with whose sins he has thus identified himself. That this passage should have been recognized as a prophecy—perhaps the single Old Testament prophecy—of the Atonement, was inevitable. But its interpretation has been affected by the current Christian interpretations of the Atonement.[1] As a type or prophetic picture of Christ, the world's sacrifice, the mysterious victim has been regarded as himself a sacrifice, bearing the sins of mankind as the Levitical sacrifice bore the sins of the offerer or the community.

To understand the conception in this way, however, is to miss its whole force. The sufferer is compared to a lamb, it is true. But this is not the sacrificial lamb. The point of the comparison is the helplessness of the servant, as a lamb marked down for slaughter, or as a sheep helpless beneath the shears. Had the poet been thinking of a sacrifice at the altar, this second figure would hardly have occurred to him. And the picture of the humiliation of the victim is quite foreign to the idea of sacrifice ; for though the Jews did not garland their victim, like the Greeks, they never thought of it as polluted. Nor are the sacrificial victims said to ' bear ' the sin of those who offer them. To ' bear ' sin is to be responsible for it. Only in rare cases in the Priests' Code can one be responsible for another's sin,[2] like a husband for the rash vow of his wife which he has not at once annulled, or the children who ' bear ' their parents' ' whoredoms ' in the wilderness, or the priests who eat the sin-offering to ' bear the iniquity of the congregation.' The scapegoat also ' bears ' the sins of the whole community on the Day of Atonement ; but the scapegoat is not sacrificed ; and there is nothing to suggest the Atonement ceremony in the poem before us. But indeed the phrase has too wide a meaning to be confined to the animal at the altar. If the sinner must carry his sin like a load, until he can find some means of putting it off his shoulders, and if, when no sacrifice will avail for it, he must continue to carry it indefinitely, the unique discovery of the poet of Isa. liii. consists in the belief that the sin of a guilty person can be removed from him—the load can be taken from his

[1] For Jewish interpretations see Driver and Neubauer, *The Fifty-third Chapter of Isaiah according to Jewish Interpreters*.
[2] Num. xiv. 33, xxx. 15 ; Lev. x. 17.

shoulders, so to speak—not by a sacrificial animal, but by an innocent person.

The sufferer of Isa. liii. has often been spoken of as if he were being punished for the sins of others. The thought of the author goes much deeper than this. There is really not a word in the poem to suggest that the poet is guilty of the superficial confusion between consequences and punishment. The consequences of sin, indeed, the sufferer must bear, or he would not be bearing sin at all. And since to the Hebrew mind all uniformities of antecedent and consequent are brought about by God, it must have been the divine will to 'bruise' him and put him to death. But a vicarious endurance of punishment would never have evolved that marvellous identification of the guiltless with the guilty. He saved those whom he perplexed and outraged, not by bearing punishment for them, but by bearing (a far greater thing) their sin. There is no humiliation in bearing another's punishment, if one is known to be guiltless oneself. But what appals the writer is this very humiliation; and out of it springs the magnificent triumph of the servant and the deliverance of the world. And if we press the vicarious bearing of penalty, we must at all events give up any analogy with sacrifice, since the animal certainly was not thought of as bearing the penalty due to the worshipper. Unless we do this, we shall confuse penalty with the ground of penalty in the most dangerous fashion, and raise insoluble problems both for psychology and ethics. To speak of the vicarious bearing of sin, on the other hand, is to attempt to penetrate one of the deepest and most illuminating mysteries of human life and (as we may well add) divine love.

It is not surprising that the Jews of later ages did not reach the heart of the mystery. Some of them fell into the confusion between sin and punishment, always difficult for a Jew to avoid. Others came near to guessing the great secret. None of them could use the light which for every Christian was thrown upon the passage by the redeeming activity of Christ. But, whether understood by its readers or not, the song fulfils and transcends all that the older prophecies had proclaimed. Like them, it sees that escape from sin is a matter of the heart and the disposition, not of the ritual act. Like all his predecessors, except Ezekiel, the poet refuses to consider arbitrary ' taboos ' by the side of moral delinquencies. Unlike them all, he sees that the change of heart can only come through the healing and reconciling act, with all the suffering it involves, of another.

VII

JESUS

THE parallel has often been drawn between Jesus and Socrates. And it is certainly true that of the actual words of both teachers we are told so little that we feel what we do know to be extraordinarily out of proportion to the influence it has exerted on the world. Socrates, indeed, through Plato and Aristotle, has affected the world of thought more profoundly than any one except Jesus. But the effect of Socrates has been wholly different from that of Jesus. Socrates was a philosopher; though always respectful to the gods of popular belief, he had little interest in religion, and he hardly left a mark on the religious practices of his countrymen. Sacrifice, as a means of approach to the divine, remained what it was, in spite of his equivocal attitude to it.

The effect of Jesus on men was religious; if it was anything else, that was only because of its import for religion. Jesus made no direct contribution to abstract thought. He was no more of a metaphysician than any other Jew. He appears to have been as little influenced by Greek thought as was Socrates by the Hebrew conception of God and the world. Though Gentiles were all round Him in Galilee, we seldom read of His mixing with them. But He did claim, as the most penetrating of His disciples saw, to show to men the Father. And even the agnostic who denies that we can ever know what God is like must confess that the conception of God which Jesus gave to the world is far more appealing and inspiring than any other; and that all other conceptions of God are valuable only in so far as they embody elements which we find welded together in the view of Jesus.

To show men what God is like, however, means also to show them how to approach God. If, as we have seen, sacrifice is the method of such approach which is the most

JESUS

widespread and widely followed, we should expect to find in the words of Jesus a doctrine of sacrifice as clear as the doctrine of the will and purpose of the Father in heaven. Not the least of the surprises in the teaching of Jesus is that no such doctrine is to be found. This is not to deny that, unlike Socrates and his followers, Jesus has made an abiding and very startling difference in the sacrificial practice of all the communities who have in any way come under His influence. Throughout Christendom, sacrifices from the earliest age have entirely ceased. No attempt was made to Christianize the rites of either the pagan or the Jew. The beliefs and theories, festivals and current practices of Christianity have been influenced by both Jews and Gentiles in a thousand ways; in this one way, not at all.

On the other hand, Jesus Himself has been recognized as the world's great sacrifice. The only altar known to Christendom is the cross. Sacrificial terminology has been applied for centuries to the Eucharist, but those who have used it most zealously would be the first to admit, and even to claim, that the Eucharist is no equivalent of an ethnic sacrifice; it is simply a representation—perhaps with some it would be truer to say a re-presentation—often regarded as dramatic or symbolic, of Christ's sacrifice of Himself on Calvary, and that all its efficacy is derived from that one supreme act, of which no repetition is possible or thinkable.

The production of this vast effect in the sphere of religion is the more remarkable because Jesus said very little about sacrifice, and certainly made no definite attack upon it as a religious institution. We may speak of Him as the last and greatest of the prophets, or as the fulfilment of that goodly fellowship. But on the theme which inspired their keenest and most searching eloquence He was almost silent. He did, indeed, on two occasions quote one of the most striking prophetic utterances on the subject: 'I desire mercy and not sacrifice,'[1] but it was to rebuke Pharisaic scruples about eating with unwashed hands and intercourse with 'publicans and sinners'; the question of sacrificing was not involved. Otherwise, Jesus seems to have taken sacrifices for granted, and to have assumed

[1] Matt. ix. 13, xii. 7, quoted from Hos. vi. 6.

that like fasting and prayer, they would continue as the natural expression of religious devotion.[1] If He did not actually offer sacrifices Himself, sacrifice was offered for Him at His circumcision, and His disciples, and at least one of His patients, were bidden to carry out the requirements of the law of which sacrifice was an integral part.[2]

We never read of His offering sacrifice when He was at Jerusalem for the festivals; nor, on the other hand, with all the complaints that were made about His attitude to the law, was a neglect of sacrifice included among the charges. His attitude was that of one who was not really interested in the institution which was the glory of His nation; who did not waste time or thought over it; who had much more important things to occupy His attention, and who was quite content that, if His general teaching was assimilated, the practice of sacrifice, like one of the Stoic ἀδιάφορα, or acts which did not count either for or against virtue, should go on as before. Our accounts of His life, whose fidelity is at once deeper and more subtle than is often recognized, have caught and reproduced this attitude by their silence.

Since, then, there was no open attack on the institution, the effect of the teaching of Jesus must have been produced indirectly. In studying how this effect was produced, it will be well for us to confine ourselves first to the Synoptists, and then to consider the fresh elements introduced in the fourth Gospel. The differences both in terminology and outlook between the first three Gospels and the fourth are unmistakable, and it is now usual to regard the former as containing actual reminiscences of the words of Jesus, gathered from early sources, and the latter as representing a deposit of His teaching, influenced by decades of Greek thought, and put forward, in his old age, by one who had ceased to distinguish between his convictions and the original words, so far as he remembered them, of his master.

This is not the place for a detailed examination of these views; even the more recent books on the subject form a

---

[1] Matt. vi. 2–18, cf. v. 24.
[2] Matt. xvii. 24 and viii. 4; Mark i. 44; Luke v. 14; where the words 'for a testimony unto them,' which occur in all three accounts, simply mean 'to show them that you are healed.' See Lev. xiv., and above, p. 114.

JESUS

small literature of their own. And the question is complicated by the various sources from which the Synoptic information is drawn, so that it becomes necessary to examine each passage, and not simply each document, on its merits. The view just stated, however, underlies nearly all modern study of the Gospels and the life they enshrine. That the Synoptists contain authentic words of Jesus cannot well be denied; and the figure that rises before us as we combine the materials they have each of them left to us could never have been invented—certainly not by writers of their somewhat limited intellects and imaginations. But each of them, and perhaps more particularly the first, contains sayings which have been felt as hard to understand on the lips of Jesus.[1] We may indeed shrink from such an assertion as dangerously subjective; for who are we that we should decide what Jesus could or could not have said? But after all, it involves nothing more than the attempt to compare scripture with scripture; and the mere comparison of parallel reports of the sayings of Jesus in the different Gospels shows how often, by one or other, or even all the three, they were misconceived. It is not pride but reverence which moves us to criticize the materials which they have put into our hands.

When we turn to the fourth Gospel, the difficulty of separating the reflections of the narrator from what he intends us to receive as the actual words of Jesus is well known.[2] We can hardly help asking whether he seriously intended us to place any part of his book in the latter category. The question is more insistent when we note, lying on the surface, the differences between the style and the subject-matter of the discourses of Jesus in the fourth Gospel and the other three. These differences have been felt to give its chief support to the contention that the author of the fourth Gospel was not even an actual companion of Jesus, but some one who had learnt His inner teaching from the lips of the 'beloved disciple.'

Whether the words, as we have them reported, are the words of Jesus Himself, or of the son of Zebedee or of one of his friends, is a matter for scholarship to decide. It is clear that in several of the episodes, such as the conversation

---

[1] e.g. Matt. xvi. 18, 19, xxi. 19, or parts of the invective in Matt. xxiii. Cf. Luke xi. 42 ff.   [2] e.g. John iii. 13 ff.

with the woman of Samaria or with Nicodemus, we have nothing more than a bare summary of what was said on those occasions. How much of that summary is given in the exact words spoken, if we may suppose that the exact words were retained for years in the adoring memory of a disciple, cannot be settled. Perhaps it is as well. Jesus, like Paul, would never subject His followers to the domination of the letter; they were to be left, however audacious the plan might seem, to the freedom of the spirit. But the tenor of the conversations must certainly be attributed to Jesus. For, if this is not so, we shall have to find in some one else than Jesus one who has been felt in all succeeding ages to have the words of eternal life. Who could create such a picture as that of Jesus in the Gospel save an equal of Jesus, or a superior? It could as little have been invented, save by an extraordinary religious genius, as the portrait of the Synoptists. And it must in fairness be added, though the fact is sometimes hidden from us by the minute study of texts, that its remarkable kinship with the central figure of the Synoptists—a kinship amounting to positive identity, though the obvious divergences rule out anything like interdependence or collusion—points to the conclusion that we have a representation of Jesus Himself as well attested as it is convincing.[1]

The Synoptic Gospels, like the fourth, show us Jesus as a youthful, vigorous, and perfectly fearless personality. Like the prophets and unlike Buddha, He is always prepared to take the offensive. He speaks of Himself in our records as 'meek and lowly of heart'; but His meekness was like that of Moses, who could with equal courage defy Pharaoh, rebuke the Hebrews, or expostulate with God. It was the meekness of one who did not care what might happen to Himself personally, and who, therefore, could endure without either flinching or resentment any contradiction

---

[1] Are we to suppose that by some miracle of literary power we were presented, in one of the simple naïve sources that lie behind our present Gospels, with an imaginary portrait? This would surely be the greatest triumph of imaginative insight ever gained. But even if this is possible, can we conceive it possible that in all the various sources which have been used to produce our Gospels, 'Q,' the Matthean document, the Lukan travel document, the minor documents, and the Johannine material (whose substantial independence of one another we are never allowed to forget), a single and harmonious character, and that the most subtle and arresting ever described, should have been achieved?

JESUS 159

or insult; but who would refuse to allow to pass unchallenged a single word against the cause to which He was committed.

But while His teaching was like a two-edged sword, flashing upon the unreal with an entirely ruthless devotion to sincerity, He was still content, as we have seen, to leave the sacrificial system alone. He reserved His attacks for the ethical, or rather the casuistical, elements in the Jewish law. In what is described as His first public appearance He fell foul of the Sabbatarian restrictions of the time, and He seemed never to tire of dragging into the light their innate irreligiousness. But He was as emphatic in challenging the accepted ideas of the religious leaders of the people on worship, fasting, oaths, the punishment of crime, and divorce; and the populace, amazed at His extraordinary cures, was equally amazed at His unabashed criticism of the influential classes and His audacious assumption of authority.

It is thus the more surprising that a scheme so open to attack as the Levitical system should have been left in peace. Did Jesus really believe that the blood of bulls and goats could take away sin? Or was He in accord with the authors of the Priests' Code that while deliberate sins could only be purged by repentance, involuntary infractions of the law of holiness must be atoned for by the aid of the complicated sacrificial tariff of the Temple? The truth is that Jesus did not attack the system in face. He undermined it. The whole business of the cleaning of pots and pans (in Mark's expressive and contemptuous phrase[1]) He dismissed with a word. He would not stay to discover the possible hygienic value of the Levitical rites. With regard to wilful sin, He simply passed over the idea of sacrifice in silence. Like the Baptist, He never hinted that anything else could be necessary than repentance and forgiveness.[2] He did not argue the point. He assumed it. In parable, in discourse, and in His actual dealings with individuals, He laid stress on forgiveness alone—a forgiveness that could even anticipate any expression or experience of repentance. He spoke as if the old prophetic polemic against the sacrifices was universally accepted. He was more anxious to convince men of the practical truth

[1] Mark vii. 4.   [2] Cf. Matt. ix. 2, xii. 31; Luke iii. 3.

that the power to forgive sins is shared by God with the 'Son of Man' than of the theoretical proposition that forgiveness alone, without sacrifice, can do away with sin.[1]

The above statements, however, do not cover the whole facts of the case. Some months at least before the end of His brief but marvellous career He became convinced of the nature of its tragic termination. It could only end in death. But the death to which He looked forward was in His eyes more than a martyrdom. In the first place, He clearly felt till the last hour that He could avoid it if He chose to do so. And His cry of anguish at the very moment when He was taking the irrevocable step shows that the possibility had been seriously considered by Him. And secondly, it had some connexion with the mass of human sin. For the most part He was content to announce the coming tragedy (a tragedy as terrible for His followers as for Himself) without any comment on it[2]; but once or twice He used in connexion with it a term represented by a Greek word which we translate 'ransom.'[3] The conclusion has been drawn from these passages that Jesus here meant a good deal more than the larger part of the Synoptic teaching would suggest; that sin asks for something more than repentance and forgiveness, namely a transaction carried out for the sinner by a third person, and that this transaction is sacrificial; i.e. that it involves the offering of a pure life, namely, His own, in exchange for the impure life of the sinner.

It is safe to say that this view could never have been gathered from the language of the Synoptists alone. It needs the support of other and more explicit expressions in John and Paul, where Christ is said to die for the ungodly, or the Good Shepherd lays down His life for the sheep.

---

[1] Matt. ix. 6; Mark ii. 10; Luke v. 24. On the meaning of the phrase 'Son of Man' see below, p. 176; but that the power in question was not in later times thought to have been regarded by Him as absolutely and always confined to Himself seems plain from Matt. xvi. 19, xviii. 18.

[2] See Matt. xx. 19, xxvi. 2, xvii. 22; Mark ix. 31, x. 33; Luke ix. 44, xviii. 32.

[3] Matt. xx. 28; Mark x. 45; cf. Luke i. 68, ii. 38, xxiv. 21; in the last three instances at least, the word appears to mean little more than 'deliverance'; and Delitzsch, in his translation of the New Testament into Hebrew, reversing but confirming the process of the Septuagint, renders it by the Hebrew words *p'duth* and *g'ullah*, which have no substitutionary or sacrificial significance.

JESUS

Where these are taken into consideration, the conclusion seems less forced. For Jesus was sinless. He did actually die. He did connect His death with forgiveness; therefore His death accomplished what was by the Jewish system attributed to the sacrifices; and therefore it was sacrificial; and a sacrifice, or at any rate, the most exalted sacrifice conceivable, is necessary to forgiveness.

But did Jesus, as we know Him from the Synoptists, actually hold this view? It is true that an interpretation in harmony with it may be placed with no apparent violence upon the passages in question. But the argument is very precarious. Because certain words of Jesus can be interpreted in accordance with convictions which became explicit later on,[1] can we conclude that Jesus held those convictions Himself? It is only by such a mode of reasoning as this, for instance, that the Catholic doctrine of the Church or the ministry can be traced to Jesus. But the argument neglects two very important questions. If Jesus had really meant this, would He not have been bound to state it more fully and frequently? And would He have expressed Himself elsewhere as He actually did?[2] Such questions are fatal to the Catholic theory of the Church, as something that can be deduced from the lips of Christ; they are equally fatal to the sacrificial theory of Christ's death. Is it possible that if He Himself had held and taught this doctrine, any one who knew anything of His teaching could restrict it, in a ministry abounding in references to forgiveness, within a couple of passages? To speak of forgiveness as He did, if forgiveness is imperfect or even impossible without some sacrificial transaction, would positively mislead. If such a transaction were necessary at all, it would be central, and economy of truth on such a point would be as sinister as it is perplexing.[3]

[1] The question whether Paul and John actually held this sacrificial view is discussed on pp. 167, 190.
[2] On His teaching that forgiveness needed no sacrificial rite, cf. Rashdall, *Idea of Atonement in Christian Theology*, pp. 23, 26.
[3] Sanday, *Divine Overruling*, calls attention to the fact that there are only two passages in the Synoptists which refer to a ransom. Mark x. 45=Matt. xx. 28 and Mark xiv. 24=Matt. xxvi. 28=Luke xxii. 20. He notes the influence on the passages of Isa. liii. Rashdall, *op. cit.*, pp. 40 ff., is led by critical considerations to reject the words which have suggested a substitutionary interpretation of the words of the institution of the Eucharist, and then asks if a doctrine vitally necessary to salvation can be founded on one passage, and that by no means above suspicion.

162 ALTAR, CROSS, AND COMMUNITY

It may, however, be asked whether the word 'ransom' used by Jesus refers to the sacrificial system at all. This has been generally assumed, but it is highly doubtful. We do not know the actual Aramaic word used by Jesus, but the Greek term, when used in the Septuagint, represents Hebrew words which have no necessary connexion with sacrifice, and suggest, as the English word 'ransom' suggests, the price paid for the emancipation of a slave, or the deliverance of a prisoner. No one familiar with Jewish sacrificial rites would ever think of a lamb or a kid as giving its life as a ransom for sinful human beings. True, such an expression, applied to the deliverer from the spiritual tyranny of death or sin, would inevitably suggest the language of Isaiah liii., where the suffering servant, led as a lamb to the slaughter, or like a dumb sheep beneath the shears, 'bears the sin' of many. But the atmosphere of this passage is not Levitical.[1] It is by hs knowledge that the righteous servant makes many righteous. The idea that 'ransom' in the passage before us is intended to suggest the sacrifice on the altar cannot be found there unless it is imported from outside.

At this point, however, we shall be reminded of words still more familiar and solemn: 'This is My body which is given for you; this is My blood which is shed for you.'[2] In view of the prevalent interpretation of these words in every age of the Church, to deny that they have any reference to Levitical sacrifices may seem very bold.[3] But

---

[1] See p. 151.

[2] It should be noted as not unimportant that in each case the present tense is used—'which is being given . . . which is being shed.'

[3] The critical questions raised by the differences between the words actually used by our authorities in the parallels—Mark xiv. 24=Matt. xxvi. 28=Luke xxii. 20, with 1 Cor. xi. 24 ff.—are not here considered. The argument in the text assumes that the special features of each passage can be carried back to our Lord's own words. But this is not to be taken as axiomatic. In a matter as vital to the Church as the Eucharist, and our Lord's words in connexion therewith, it is almost incredible either that the evangelical records should have omitted anything of which their authors were aware, or that they should not have been aware of anything which our Lord had impressed on the disciples on that occasion. Either of these suppositions really causes more difficulty than the omission of all mention of the institution of the Eucharist in the Fourth Gospel. It is noteworthy that, as P. Gardner pointed out in *The Origin of the Lord's Supper*, 1893, Paul, in writing to the Corinthians on the institution, claims to have received his own knowledge of what was said and done in the upper room, not from the tradition of the Church, but directly from Christ

JESUS

when we take them as they stand, apart from later expositions, we shall see that the denial cannot well be avoided. For those who are accustomed to think of sacrifice in the abstract, but have never seen or even imagined the ritual of slaughter at the altar according to the ' Jerusalem usage,' the analogy may seem tempting ; but to any one familiar with the Temple rites, as were all who were gathered in that room, the action at the table during the Last Supper would repel the analogy rather than suggest it. The sacrifice for sin was never eaten by the worshippers ; blood was never drunk, but only poured out or sprinkled or dashed on the worshippers and the altar; bread was never an equivalent for the body of the animal victim, but only an accompaniment ; there was no suggestion in the ritual of any connexion between the blood of the victim and the wine used in libations ; and the idea that a human being could be offered as a sacrifice in any sense lay outside all but the most primitive Hebrew ideas. To Christian thought the sacrifices have only been of interest as symbols of the death of Christ ; they have, therefore, been interpreted in the light of the ideas which have gathered round His death, and they have rarely been studied by Christian theologians save with a view to that interpretation. If Jesus had intended to explain His death to the disciples by means of the sacrifices, as any pious Jew of the time would necessarily understand them, we should have to follow the reverse order. We should then see how inapplicable were all the leading conceptions and practices of the altar to the death upon the cross.[1]

Himself, by revelation. This would imply that for what took place on that occasion our chief authority is not the Synoptic sources, but Paul, who is also the earliest in point of time and the fullest, and who alone lays stress on the periodical performance of the rite. We should still have to ask why, unless the original tradition were imperfect or little known, such a special revelation was necessary. For the purposes of our argument such intricate discussion is happily unnecessary.

[1] It is worth while to notice that in the two ' Manuals of the Altar ' in Leviticus, for the layman (chh. i.-vi. 7), and for the priest (chh. vi. 8-vii. 38), the meal-offering is only mentioned in connexion with the burnt-offering, but neither with the peace-offering, which the worshippers joined in eating, nor the sin-offering, which was regarded as specially ' holy.' The cakes, for whose ingredients and cooking precise directions are given, were to be burnt, and what was left was to be eaten by the priests, but not by laymen. Wine is mentioned in the Holiness Code as an accompaniment of the heave-offering, and in the Priests' Code, of the daily sacrifice, the monthly sacrifice

164 ALTAR, CROSS, AND COMMUNITY

It is true that the Synoptists, unlike the fourth Gospel, represent the last supper as coinciding in time with the Passover celebration; but this is hardly equivalent to saying that they regarded Jesus as constituting Himself the Paschal lamb. If such a purpose had been in His mind, we should have to admit that Jesus did not regard Himself as a sin-offering, since the two sacrifices were quite distinct, and the lamb was in no sense a substitute for the worshippers nor was it offered to atone for their sin. It was, according to the familiar narrative, a means to keep off the destroying angel from the houses where it was eaten.[1] Doubtless on the anniversary of that great deliverance from Egypt, and in the last hours before His arrest and condemnation, the deliverance which His own death was going to effect would be in the centre of the thoughts of Jesus. But to conclude from this that He regarded His death as Paschal—that is, as keeping off the destroying wrath of God from those who were enabled to 'appropriate its benefits'—would be to place an unwarrantable burden on the simple words which Jesus actually employed. And indeed the analogy between the old story of the destroying angel, who had to be prevented, so to speak, from entering the wrong houses by the sign of the sprinkled blood—a purely external contrivance which some Egyptian might have been fortunate enough to be able to imitate—and the deliverance of the whole human race from the empire of sin, wrought by the Son of the Father's universal love, is one which we can hardly suppose to have been much in the mind of Jesus at that time. If the Passover is to help us to understand the spirit of Him who died on the cross, we shall remember the deliverance which it preceded, but we shall forget the blood sprinkled upon the door-post. Such an analogy might strike a rabbi. It could not weigh with Jesus. Those who prefer to lay stress on the sacrificial idea in general rather than on the specifically Paschal

and various others. A stated quantity of wine (ranging from a quart to two quarts) is poured out at the slaughter of the animals, but no special directions are given as to the manner in which this is to be done. Clearly it was a minor part of the ceremony. The ritual could never have suggested a symbolical equivalence of wine to blood, and Jesus' identification of the wine and His blood would never suggest the ritual.

[1] The question of the original significance of the 'Passover,' before it had come to be connected with the Exodus, does not concern us here.

JESUS

analogy point out that the two words 'do' and 'remembrance'[1] both appear in sacrificial terminology. This suggestion, which first occurs as early as Justin Martyr, might perhaps carry some weight if the connexion of these acts with sacrifice were less feebly marked in the passages concerned. But their usage in the sacrificial manuals is limited; 'remembrance' is applied only to the frankincense and the meal-offering, not to the victim; and 'do' is a term of wide application, which often indicates the preparation of any kind of food. And the mere fact that two such common and all but inevitable words can be used in the language of the altar can hardly suffice to give a sacrificial colouring to a phrase in which otherwise it would never suggest itself.

Truth to tell, the attempt to connect the thought and purpose of Jesus at this supreme moment with the cumbrous and already outworn Jewish system robs it of its transcendent value. For if Jesus had it in His mind, or intended His disciples to have it in theirs, He must of necessity have been thinking of the contemporary form and object of the rite. This, as we know, had moved far away from the simple impulse to come into *rapport* with God by the aid of some external medium of communication. That the sacrifices of the second Temple were meant to be types of His vicarious death He had, as far as we know, never suggested; nor could His language on this occasion give His friends any hint of this desire. But even had this been His wish, it would be strange that He, who had repudiated so definitely the idea that ritual 'sins' had any religious significance, could have looked to a system in which these 'sins' occupied so large a place. He was facing an event which had enormous value for the whole race, as we can see from the Synoptists as well as from the fourth Gospel,[2] and which far transcended the bounds of Jewish ceremonialism, however pious and well meaning. That event was to make a difference to mankind to which the difference made for the Jewish worshippers by their sacrifices was not even remotely comparable. What that difference was must be considered later. We may, indeed, admit that the Temple

---

[1] 'This do in remembrance of Me' (1 Cor. xi. 24; Luke xxii. 19). The words do not occur in Matthew or Mark.

[2] John xii. 32 and Matt. xx. 28, Mark x. 45, referred to above.

sacrifices would powerfully stir the imagination of the worshipper, as well as remove his anxiety and soothe his conscience. But such a result could not be mentioned by the side of the emotions which would be roused in the disciples by the death of their master, or even by its prediction in their startled hearing. Through the last week their minds had been full of other things than those preparations for the festival rites in the Temple which presumably occupied most of the visitors to the city. But even if it were possible that what was going on at the time outside their perturbed circle influenced His speech or their own understanding of it, their later experiences, when they saw that glorious being, *sans peur et sans reproche*, amid every circumstance of horror and degradation, hideously done to death, would have obliterated all more superficial associations.

Theologians have been accustomed to divide the functions or 'offices' of the Saviour under three heads, prophetic, royal, and priestly. The third they have naturally connected with the Jewish rites. The first suggestion for this was made as early as the Epistle to the Hebrews.[1] But to attempt such a division is a serious error. If we would think of His work, we must start from the many-sided but unified picture which Jesus gives us of Himself—the Son of Man, the Lord of the Sabbath, forgiving the sins of men, coming into their midst as the great deliverer, betrayed and killed, rising from the grave, and seated finally at the side of His Father to judge all mankind. If, in this imposing list, there is no mention of officiating priest or selected victim, it is surely because Jesus would have us look upon our deliverance as wrought, not according to the terms of a time-honoured ritual, but by some marvellous condescension in which strength and weakness were wedded, and the gates of new life were opened to us by a hand like our own.

In the foregoing pages we have expressly avoided critical discussions. The careful and, we may add, reverent study of the Synoptists leads us inevitably to the necessity of distinguishing between the spirit and the letter of sayings which appear in divergent forms in our different accounts. But where all that we have is the result of more or less

[1] See the discussion of the passages in question below, p. 206.

JESUS

reliable reporting, based on the recollection of the witnesses, it is impossible to draw with finality the dividing line between what we may accept and what we must reject. On the other hand, if we accept everything that has come down to us as claiming approximately equal authority, we shall still have to be guided by the general tenor of the teaching which we possess, interpreting the obscure or less frequent language by the more familiar or certain.

We shall follow a similar course with regard to the fourth Gospel. It may be that the fourth Gospel gives us no one sentence which we can assert to have been spoken, in the form in which we there read it, by Jesus. Indeed, unless the author, whether an eye-witness or not, were working on some earlier notes of his own or of some one else (and of this there is no trace), we can hardly suppose that he would be likely, after the lapse of half a century, to recollect more than a few striking sentences. But we must repeat that the author has either given us a trustworthy and surprisingly detailed impression of his master, or that he has achieved a creation so marvellous that it could demand, in its own right, the closest study that we can give it.

At first glance the fourth Gospel seems to have less to offer to our search than the other three. No sacrificial terminology is employed. The institution of the Eucharist is unmentioned; and especial care is given, it would appear, to point out that the Last Supper was held on another day than the Passover, and therefore, presumably, to be regarded, in spite of the Synoptic accounts, as distinct from that festival. Even when Jesus goes up to Jerusalem, and is in the atmosphere of the feasts, there is no more reference to what was going on than in the Synoptic parables of the last week. The reference to the living water in the discourse on the last day of the Feast of Tabernacles has been connected with the ceremony of ' the libations of water brought in a golden vessel from Siloam which were made at the time of the morning sacrifice on each of the seven days of the feast.' But there is more explicit teaching on the living water in the conversation with the woman of Samaria, and there is certainly nothing sacrificial in either account.[1] There are, however, three familiar passages which have

---

[1] John vii. 37, and Westcott *ad. loc.*; John iv. 10, 13 f.

often been taken as pointing to the sacrificial work of Jesus, and which cannot be lightly passed over—the discourse on the eating of His flesh and the drinking of His blood; the words about laying down His life as the Good Shepherd for the sheep; and what is known as the high-priestly prayer.[1] If these are read in the light of each other, we seem to learn that Jesus was the true sacrifice, to be eaten by the worshippers like a peace-offering under the old covenant; that His life was laid down like that of the victims at the shrine; and that He was also the priest officiating at the stupendous rite. Thus He appears to gather up into Himself the whole significance of the sacrifices. In this case we should have a striking instance of a doctrine passed over or misunderstood by the Synoptists and emphasized by John.

No one will deny the suggestiveness of this interpretation of the three passages; each has a force, when taken in conjunction with the others, which it has not when taken alone. None the less, they must be examined separately. The author gives no hint that they are intended to elucidate each other. They have nothing in common in their language; and an interpretation cannot be founded on a combination of the three—it can at best be suggested by such a proceeding—unless it is discovered in each of the three taken apart.

Let us then turn to the first of the three—the discourse which followed the feeding of the five thousand. A comparison with the Eucharist is inevitable; yet no reference is made to that rite in the text. If the author had connected these words with the Eucharist in his own mind, he could hardly have avoided at least alluding to the connexion. Elsewhere he allowed himself to comment on the words he reported, as where he explained the reference to 'the temple of His body,' or to the quotation about the 'rivers of living water.'[2] Possibly we have here one of what Dr. E. A. Abbott calls the silent corrections of the Synoptists, and while treating them, and Paul as well, with all gentleness, he may mean his readers to gather that the rite which commemorated the dark close of Jesus' life had its foundation in something even more profound. Be that as it may, the connexion is too dubious to allow us to argue

[1] John vi., x. 15, and xvii.   [2] John ii. 21; vii. 39.

JESUS 169

from the Eucharistic words as they are given in the Synoptists and Paul to this discourse.

In any case, if we follow the dialogue between Jesus and the Jews as it is found in the sixth chapter, we must conclude that the Jews suspected no sacrificial reference. To them the language of Jesus was simply puzzling; but had they detected the sacrificial reference, their perplexity would have been of a different kind. It could hardly have avoided repelling them. 'How can this man give us His flesh to eat?' they asked. A human being as a burnt-offering might be barely conceivable, though nothing more, to those who had read the stories of the offering of Isaac and of the son of the king of Moab; as a peace-offering, when the sacrifice was eaten by the offerers, a human victim would suggest the most odious cannibalism. The sin-offering, as we have noticed, was never eaten. To us modern European Christians, who, though we have never seen a sacrifice, have behind us centuries of metaphysical and mystical renderings of the phrases, the difficulty does not even arise. To men who were neither metaphysicians nor mystics, who had never heard of transubstantiation, but who had seen animals killed at the altar and certain parts of them devoured every year of their lives, the difficulty would be unavoidable.

And how easy it would have been to insert a word of explanation! 'As the sacrifice is eaten by the offerers, so must the Son of Man be eaten by His disciples'; we have only to remember the other explanation of a difficult phrase, 'As Moses lifted up the serpent in the wilderness, even so must the Son of Man be lifted up.'[1] John does not, like the Synoptists, represent Jesus as being content on occasion merely to puzzle His hearers. He reads the question in their minds and answers them by what is, to the genuine disciple, a clearer and profounder statement of truth. But here, instead of pointing out the difference between literal and spiritual sacrifices, He went on at once to speak of an intimate relation between Himself and His followers to which sacrifice offers no analogy. The whole passage is only explicable on the supposition that neither

[1] John iii. 14. The other analogy, between bread and teaching, was noticed, as familiar to Jewish writers, by Lightfoot in his *Horae Hebraicae*.

Jesus nor His hearers were thinking of victim and altar and ceremonial meal.

The second passage, about the life of the Shepherd laid down for the sheep, seems more explicit. Does it not refer to what happened at every sacrifice, when the victim's life was offered? The answer is surely, however, that it can refer to nothing of the kind. The laying down of the life is a proof of love; and it is performed on behalf of one's friends—two conditions which can never be represented in any sacrifice. The central part of the sacrifice, the solemn self-identification with the victim, is here left unnoticed, and is indeed out of the question. In these great words the thought of Jesus cannot be fitted into any sacrificial scheme. The victim in the sacrifice is at best a means of mutual approach. The important persons in the transaction are the offerer and the receiver. All that is necessary with regard to the victim, who is purely passive, is to make sure of its eligibility—its age, its sex, its species, and its freedom from blemish of any kind, and of the correctness of the mode of slaughter, and the disposal of the blood, the fat, and the entrails. After that not another thought was given to it, save that the remains had to be put away in the most rapid and inoffensive manner. No sentiment was ever wasted over the kid or the heifer.

How different is all this from the Good Shepherd's self-sacrifice! The initiative, instead of springing from the offerer, belongs to the victim. Instead of being a means for bringing offerer and deity together, the victim places Himself in the centre, and speaks of an abiding relation with Himself as the one thing necessary. The whole centre of gravity is changed.[1] The words naturally connect themselves with the conversation in the upper room, where the relation envisaged is not that of victim and offerer, but the more intimate one of vine and branches. The more we think of a lamb or a heifer on the altar, the less we shall understand the essential union with the disciples to which Jesus here looks forward. The less attention we pay to the sacrificial figure, the more we appreciate the amazing

---

[1] It is equally impossible to find, in an idea of the shepherd being sacrificed for the sheep instead of the sheep for the shepherd, a bold and touching epigram like that of the little lamb, looking as if it had been killed, actually seated on the throne (Rev. v. 6). See p. 173 n.

JESUS

demands and offers of Jesus. Here, as in the 'Good Shepherd' discourse, we are not simply dealing with the absence of any reference to sacrifice; we are only able to understand the meaning of Jesus if we keep that reference out of our mind.

But are we not bound to admit it in the 'high-priestly' prayer? 'For their sakes I consecrate Myself.' In these words, as it would seem, though He, as usual, avoids the term, Jesus implies that He is at once the priest who consecrates and the victim who is consecrated. But here also we must remember that the disciples knew something of sacrificial ritual. Even if we may assume that they would have understood, without further explanations, the subtle identification of priest and victim, they would know that there was nothing in the ritual which corresponded to the consecration of the victim. If it had the necessary qualifications, it was simply brought to the altar to be killed. A victim either possessed or did not possess the conditions for being regarded as holy when that approach was performed. It may be urged that in the case of the priest consecration was all-important. This is true, but it is not to the point. The consecration of the priest aimed at removing, at the outset of his official career, all unfitness for the continuous performance of his duties.[1] Its nearest analogue is the ordination of the Christian minister. But no one could argue that Jesus needed to have any unfitness removed, or that the consecration of which He spoke was some act which was to enable Him to discharge a function of which He would otherwise have been incapable.

The prayer in the seventeenth chapter is indeed worthy of being called 'high-priestly'; but not in the sense of this one verse. The reason carries us farther. All through that prayer, Jesus is making Himself, so to speak, the representative or spokesman of the disciples, putting into a series of simple yet far-reaching requests all that He Himself could desire for them. But the gifts which He asks for them are gifts which He already possesses. He is the

---

[1] Before the ceremonies of the Day of Atonement the high-priest observed certain restrictions and underwent special 'coaching,' so as to make no mistakes in his duties (*Yoma*, i.); but even if Jesus could be thought of as regarding Himself in the light of the Jewish high-priest, the word He here uses would be quite inappropriate to such preparation.

172 ALTAR, CROSS, AND COMMUNITY

'priest' in the sense of being the intermediary between the source and the recipient. All that He has from God He has passed on, or desires to pass on, to them. All whom He has received from God He has kept, to hand them back to God. This can hardly be called a sacerdotal idea. Certainly it does not correspond to the function of any Jerusalem priest.[1] Jesus did not dwell in thought within the Temple. He went there regularly while in Jerusalem. He could not have avoided doing so, if He wished to take part in the public or social life of the city. It was the one open place in that town of huddled streets and lanes. And it was to Him His Father's house. But to watch its services must have given Him little pleasure. He could hardly have had more sympathy with the official hierarchy and their ideas than with those who carried on the *bureaux de change* within the precincts. It is not surprising, therefore, that even in the Temple discourses, when offerings were perhaps being made before His eyes, His language is unaffected by what He saw, and that His thoughts must be recognized as belonging to another sphere. The word 'holy,' the key-word of the whole system of the altar, is conspicuously rare in the Gospels and Acts, save as the epithet of the Spirit; and John's use of 'consecrate' ('make holy') is almost confined to this passage.[2] It is accomplished 'in the truth,' the sum of Christ's own revelation; and it denotes the process of admission into the new society, which He undergoes on behalf of His disciples and as their representative.

Before leaving the subject of the language of the fourth Gospel, we must notice the tribute of the Baptist to Jesus: 'Behold the Lamb of God.' The words are evidently intended by the author, who sets every testimony which he records to Jesus in a definite scheme, as striking the key-note of the whole work. We need not stay to ask here if the words were actually spoken by the Baptist on this occasion. But if they were, and if, at the same time,

---

[1] 'If a sacrifice is pointed to, it is a sacrifice which all Christians are called on to offer' (Rashdall, *op. cit.*, p. 182). If the expression in John xvii. is reminiscent of the Temple services, the reminiscence is certainly vague.

[2] See Westcott *ad. loc.* The only other passage in John is x. 36: 'Say ye of Him whom the Father hath consecrated,' i.e. hath set apart for His exalted mission? The word does not occur in Mark, and in Matthew and Luke only in the Lord's Prayer, and in one other passage—Matt. xxiii. 17, 19—where it is obviously used in the technical sense of the ritual law.

JESUS 173

we are to follow the common interpretation of them, they are very difficult to understand. 'Behold the man who is to die like a sacrificial victim, and this for the sins of all men, Jews and Gentiles alike.' But the lamb as a sacrifice was specially associated with the Passover; and, as we have already seen, the Paschal lamb did not 'bear sins' at all. What the Baptist really had in mind must have been Isaiah liii. He who was there compared to a lamb did 'bear the sin of many.' To bear sin is to bear the weight and responsibility of sin, like the man who without benefit of sacrifice bears his own, or the scapegoat who carries off the sin of the whole community.[1] The Baptist points out Jesus as some one, meek as a lamb, who takes on Himself all the weight of the world's sin, and in whom at last the vision of the prophet is translated into reality. As with other passages, the idea of the Levitical sacrifice has to be read into the words before it can be extracted from them. We can see the influence of Isa. liii. on the fourth Gospel as on the rest of the New Testament; it is, indeed, the foundation of the earliest Christology; but wherever we find it, the sacrificial suggestion, which might have been so easily made, is not made at all.[2]

So far, then, our results would seem to be merely negative. Jesus does not, like the prophets, attack the sacrificial system. He ignores it. The language in which He speaks of His death neither suggests nor illustrates Levitical ideas. We have not a single word from Him which leads us to suppose that He thought of Himself, or wished others to think of Him, as a Levitical sacrifice; and the ideas that centre round the Levitical rite are absent from the context, and interfere with the proper course of His teaching.

To admit this, however, raises a very serious difficulty.

---

[1] See p. 115.

[2] We cannot here discuss the theological language of the Apocalypse, where the contrasts to that of the fourth Gospel are as striking as the similarities. The very term for 'lamb,' which reminds us constantly of the fourth Gospel, is the diminutive 'lambkin.' The central figure in the whole vision is this 'lambkin,' 'as it had been slain,' set on the throne. Here, too, the thought is dominated by the impulse which starts from Isa. liii. Redemption has been gained for the world by one who was as meek and unresisting as a helpless little lamb, who yet bore our sin, and in doing so met a death which in the eternal purpose of God was the inevitable outcome of His unique work. The signs of that death will never be removed; but the Redeemer now sits as king over the universe, and all the hosts of heaven do Him reverence.

It does not only set on one side the Hebrew sacrificial system as out of relation to Christ; it would seem also to set aside the whole institution of sacrifice as an accompaniment of human religion in general. If, as we have seen, sacrifice is so widespread as to appear the result of an almost universal instinct of mankind in its search for God, must we not now regard that instinct as entirely mistaken, or else conclude that Christ showed at best only one of several ways to the Father? To the student of religion neither of these conclusions will necessarily be unwelcome. All ethnic beliefs about the approach to God have their interest for him, but they have no permanent validity; and Jesus, like all great religious leaders, is worthy of their study; He is not the one unerring guide to the world's desire. The Christian student, however, looks at the matter differently. To him, Christ came to fulfil, and not to annul or set aside, the works and the hopes of the generations that had preceded Him, outside as well as inside the favoured nation of Israel. The way which He opened is not one of several possible ways to God. Christ does not jostle Buddha and Confucius in the market-place, with directions which may or may not be more useful than theirs. All that others have ever hoped or desired finds its sole and authentic speech in His victorious words.

If, then, Jesus is to be thought of as fulfilling, instead of as destroying, all the sacrificial practice of mankind, how was that fulfilment carried out? Has He given us any guidance Himself, or are we to look for an answer only in the thought of later ages? The course of theological history is strewn with the wrecks of conceptions which cannot be traced back to Christ Himself; and of any guidance which He has not chosen to give us Himself we may well be chary. But with regard to the question of sacrifice, the guidance is really there.

Hitherto we have been thinking of the words of Jesus in relation to the Levitical system. To His hearers, and, we must probably add, to Jesus Himself, sacrifice meant the Levitical system and nothing else. They were not interested in the sacrificial rites of other nations, nor in the ethnological study of their origins and essentials. Therefore, if His words about dying for mankind did not, save in some remote degree, suggest the Levitical sacrifices, they

JESUS 175

would not suggest sacrifices at all. But it has become clear to us that the Levitical system is only one member of a very large and diverse class; and elements common and even constitutive of sacrifice as a whole may well, in such a highly elaborated rubric as that of the second Temple, take a very subordinate place. A little reflection will show that this was the fact. Sacrifices in general are a means for attaining communion with God, for becoming *en rapport* with Him. The special need which prompts the sacrifice may be some definite gift, or more generally, health, success, prosperity, or the diffused sense of power and effectiveness; or it may be desire for deliverance from the chilling sense of failure or wrong-doing or stupidity, individual misery or national disaster. The Levitical system had forgotten most of these springs of sacrificial action. Sacrifices could still be scenes of joy and national and patriotic elation[1]; but they meant to the ordinary Jew ceremonies which were mostly performed at stated times—daily or on special and periodic occasions—and their purpose was to 'atone' for conduct which the offerer or onlooker did not, for the most part, feel to be morally wrong, and which certainly roused no deep emotion.

Jesus stood for just that side of sacrificial religion which the Levitical system had neglected—the free approach to God, as children might come to a father for whatever they needed, comfort, forgiveness, food, gifts, and sheer affection or safety. Indeed, Jesus goes far beyond ethnic ideas in the simplicity—we had almost said the *naïveté*—of the childlike trust in God which He teaches. ' Ye shall ask what ye will '; ' Seek and ye shall find '; ' Shall not God avenge His own elect ? '; ' Your Father knoweth what ye have need of.' But the sacrifices demanded an intermediary —something by which the *rapport* could be established, and the lines of communication opened; something which had its rightful place, so to speak, in the spheres both of God and man. This was found in the animal victim; less frequently in the bloodless offering; and also on occasion in a human being. When the offering was merely a valuable object, or even a present of fruit or cakes or wine, the offerer may have simply expected that it would put the deity in a good humour with him. But, as our second

[1] As is clear from Ps. cxviii.

chapter made clear, even apart from the other difficulties of the gift view, the fact that sacrifice was generally more than a valuable object or a dish of fruit shows how much more deeply rooted was the other conception of sacrifice as a medium between the two parties involved.

It is here that the teaching of Jesus gives validity to the ethnic sacrifices, for if He has made anything clear, it is that He expected to be regarded as 'at home' in the two spheres—of God and of man—and that He was the ideal means of communication between them. This brings to our mind His constant use of the phrase the 'Son of Man.' There is no need to discuss its exact meaning here. If the meaning had lain on the surface when the phrase was first used, or if Jesus had intended every one to understand at once all He meant by it, the discussion about His use of the term would hardly have been so prolonged and obscure. But it is quite plain that, whether the term suggested to His hearers 'the man in the street,' the ideal man, the representative man, the apocalyptic man, the prophet who sees visions of God, or the human being who is highest in the order of created things, Jesus meant by using it of Himself to identify Himself with humanity; whether humanity at its lowest and weakest or its highest and most favoured really makes little difference.

The corresponding term, Son of God, is rarely used (save by demons, who are always rebuked for it) in the Synoptists,[1] and only sparingly in the fourth Gospel. Jesus never uses it there of Himself, though He does not rebuke its use in others. But though He does not use the actual term, He is not afraid of what is implied by it. In the first three Gospels, as in the fourth, He claims to know, and to reveal, as no one else can, what God is like. He knows what God will do, and whom He will accept or reject. He even feels Himself free to exercise the functions of God Himself, such as forgiveness and judgement. If we could imagine the Creator speaking among men, He could not use terms of more authority and decision. To put into simple yet adequate words the thought that lies behind the statement, 'Jesus is divine,' we can but say that Jesus was 'at home' with God.

---

[1] On Matt. xiv. 33, cf. Mark vi. 51; on Mark xv. 39, cf. Luke xxiii. 47; on Matt. xvi. 16, cf. Mark viii. 29, Luke ix. 20.

JESUS

Thus Jesus is in the world of religion what the victim was in the sacrificial ceremony. He made it possible for man to 'get at' God, because He was Himself the road. He joined together the two sundered points. The fact that they could reach God through Him, and only through Him, He made as clear as He made the intimacy of His own relation to God. 'Through Me'; 'in My name.' The phrase occurs constantly; but the idea which informs it is still commoner. Every religious act, and every act of goodwill and neighbourliness not ordinarily thought of as religious at all, gains its value from being mediated through Christ. The Christian who prays, or receives a disciple, or gives a cup of cold water in a disciple's name, does so in virtue of his recognition of what Christ really is. This is more than to say that he is acting in the spirit of Christ or at Christ's bidding. He is brought into touch with God because he puts himself in touch with one who is in touch with God already.

It is in this sense that Jesus, if we may follow the records in the Gospels, is the great sacrifice. As such, He is the fulfilment and explanation of the conception that is embodied in the sacrifices by which, in all ages, humanity has endeavoured to draw near to God. He fulfils it, because every actual sacrifice is at best imperfect. The sacrificial victim can only symbolize the required medium. Its death is no more than a clumsy and barbarous way of emphasizing its ideal function as a medium. Jesus is all that the sacrificial victim was supposed to be; and, if we may allow His own claim, He was more than they could even suggest in a metaphor. The real function of the victim is naturally liable to be forgotten or misunderstood. The attention is generally concentrated on the dramatic moment of the rite —the animal's immolation; and the belief easily grows up that the immolation is somehow in itself pleasing to God, or will make amends for the folly or inadvertence or disobedience of the offerer. When, however, we turn from these dramatic rites to the simple teaching of Jesus, we find the emphasis laid elsewhere—namely, on the fact that Jesus, so to speak, holds God with one hand and ourselves with the other. When we recognize this, we can look back upon the ethnic sacrifices and find in them something of greater religious value than a gift, a *douceur*, or an expedient for making amends; they become symbols that enable the worshipper to feel, as he must feel if his worship is to give him any satisfaction, that he has been brought over the gulf that separated him from God into harmony and peace.

But before we leave this subject there are three questions briefly to be considered. We must, for the moment, set on one side the question that will probably occur to the reader first of all. If the death of the victim is really only an incident, why is the fact of the death of Jesus made so much of in the religion of which He is the centre? Does the account which has just been given assign enough importance to the reiterated statement that Jesus died for our sins? In the Gospels, as we have seen, this aspect of Christ's death receives comparatively little emphasis, and it is with the Gospels that we are dealing. It receives quite a new emphasis in the Epistles, and the discussion of its meaning there will naturally follow our study of them. The analogy, however, which we have drawn between the functions of Christ and of the sacrificial victim suggests other difficulties. First, Jesus is presented for us, and not, like the animal on the altar, by us. If the mediation of Jesus is thought of specially in connexion with His death, this objection may be allowed considerable weight. The fact that it is often not felt results from the prevailing looseness of the sacrificial interpretation of the death on the cross. It is certainly true that while the sacrificer led the animal to the altar and then killed him, the Christian does nothing of the kind. All he does is to plead the fact, even though from one point of view he deplores it, that Jesus was put to death. But there is a sense in which the ethnic, and certainly the Jewish sacrifices, were, like Christ Himself, 'provided' by the deity to whom they were offered. That is to say, the worshippers were instructed that a certain rite or rites, and no others, would be accepted if performed. And though the Christian does not identify himself, save in some moods of mystical devotion, with those who 'pointed the nail and fixed the thorn,' he does in a sense himself 'present' Jesus; he feels Jesus explicitly to be what the offerer saw in his victim—the medium between himself and God.

This last assertion, however, may be called in question.

JESUS

It may be doubted, that is, whether all or even many Christians have thought of Jesus in this way; and surely, it may be urged, if this is not the case, the actions of the Christian, since not consciously related to the sacrifice of Christ, will be like the actions of a respectable agnostic; even though ethically good, they will be without religious value. That Jesus is not habitually thought of as the means of communication between man and God need not trouble us. To multitudes He is rather the example or the friend, the helper, the consoler, or the deliverer. He stands in the place of God. He has, as Ritschl put it, the value of God. But the results of what He did are not conditioned by the theological knowledge of His followers. And though they may not think of Him in any sense as a sacrifice, the mere fact that they draw from Him that comfort and help and deliverance of which God is the source shows that to them also He is at least implicitly the mediator.

As a matter of plain fact, men do come to God apart from Christ—Jews and heathens who lived before His birth, pious Buddhists, Moslems, and Confucianists who have never heard of Him, and pay no more heed to Him than the simple Christian would pay to Buddha or Mohammed; and Europeans like J. S. Mill or Mazzini, who, on intellectual grounds, rejected all belief in Him as a mediator. But the reply to this is not far to seek. To accept Christ does not mean to accept certain statements about Him which would be unsuspected by the ancient Hebrew, the Moslem, and perhaps, we may add, the educated European to whom the facts had only been presented in a distorted fashion. It means to accept the principles which He taught and the way of life which He laid down as authoritative and as the true path of obedience to God.[1] If, therefore, Jesus is so accepted, He really becomes thereby the means of communication between man and God.

For a man may learn of Christ, even if he has never heard the gospel story; and those who come from the East and the West may take, as their one hope of salvation,

---

[1] Peter, in the Acts (x. 35) is represented as putting this truth more generally still: 'In every nation he that feareth Him and worketh righteousness is acceptable to Him.'

meekness and poverty of spirit and purity of heart, with a devotion to which many ' children of the kingdom ' may be entire strangers. Such men are surely coming to God through Christ. This is not to assert that salvation is by ' works,' and that men do not need Christ. For meekness and poverty of spirit are not ' works,' nor are the acts they inspire performed like ' works,' in the hope of some external reward. They are learnt, as no Christian can deny, from Christ, and Christ alone ; and for such meek and pure-minded men, though they have never heard the name of Christ, Christ is none the less the way by which they come to God. If we have learnt to find in Christ the medium for every good and perfect gift, we shall not be greatly perplexed to discover that these gifts are sometimes bestowed outside the circle of His professed followers ; we shall be distressed and humiliated by the reflection that inside that circle they are not more often to be found.

We are now in a position to attempt to sum up the impression which the teaching of Jesus as to His death actually did leave on the disciples. If He did not give them any hint that they were to regard it as sacrificial, He at least made them understand clearly that it was to be more than what we should call a martyrdom, however glorious. It was, indeed, a martyrdom in one sense ; it was a great act of witness to all for which His life had stood. It was the supreme act of obedience to the Father's will, which was the mainspring of His being. But all that the martyr can do by his death is to put the seal on his conviction of the truth of those principles by which he has lived. Jesus taught His disciples to think of His death as their ransom or deliverance. We must not, indeed, exaggerate the importance He attributed to it. Our familiarity with the passages in which He referred to it must not blind us to their paucity. There is little ground for supposing that the Synoptic records, which represent the early teaching about Jesus, give a disproportionately small place to what He said on the mysterious subject. In view of the immense impressiveness of the circumstances of His death and resurrection, and the detail with which they are described, we should have expected the teaching to give too large rather than too small a place to them in its accounts of His discourses.

JESUS

It is quite possible, on the other hand, that the silence of Jesus on the subject till the latter part of His ministry resulted from the fact that He did not Himself envisage what His end was to be at the first.

However this may be, He was far more explicit as to the general character and purpose of His life on earth. His death was a deliverance; but so was His whole life. His death would have meant nothing to us, it would have done nothing for us, apart from His life. To separate the two, and to say that His life was our example, and His death our redemption, is to misunderstand the unity of all that He 'began both to do and to teach' and to suffer on earth. His whole life, from the manger to the cross, and from the cross to the Mount of Ascension, was the great sacrifice. It was because He was at once the Son of Man and the Son of God that He has brought men to God. What the victim was supposed to become in the sacrificial moment at the altar Jesus was through the long, sacrificial years of His life—the mediator between God and man.

Later Christian thought has put all this into explicit expression; and the early teaching would be unintelligible without it. But the early teaching could never have arrived at it apart from its exemplification at Calvary. Even before those awful hours, His companions might be forced to the pathetic question which the fourth Gospel puts into their mouth: 'Lord, to whom shall we go? Thou hast the words of eternal life.' But Jesus Himself had to wait for the terrible loneliness of the crucifixion to reveal to the world how absolutely He was at one both with man and God. Only when all the accidental accompaniments of every-day life were removed could He be fully seen as the mediator. Undoubtedly He knew this Himself. All His pondering over the song of the 'Redeeming Servant' had shaped the knowledge in His mind. Only when He was actually facing and enduring death could He fully take on Himself the sin of the world. It was His death that was to be, as without it His earthly life could not have been, the ransom for mankind.

It is, therefore, a sound instinct that has led both Christian art and devotion to draw their deepest and most triumphant inspiration from His hour of mortal weakness, and to see in the cross not only His humiliation, but His throne. And when we gaze at the masterpieces of a Perugino or a Tintoret we forget the heifers and kids that were brought lowing into the Temple courts. What we do not and must not forget is the life that was laid down from the moment when, in the midst of the crowds waiting to be baptized at the Jordan, Jesus heard the voice from heaven, or, more truly still, as the Christian will add, the life that was laid down before the foundation of the world.

VIII

THE BEGINNINGS OF THEOLOGY

It would be a useful study to draw a comparison between the relations of Buddhism to Brahmanism and of Christianity to Judaism. Though the parallels might easily be over-emphasized, both Buddhism and Christianity took over with them very much that has remained characteristic of them from the soil from which they sprang. Sacrifices, deeply embedded in the two older systems, disappeared in the others. But while, in Buddhism, they had from the beginning no place at all, they lingered on, as it would seem, among the Jewish Christians for at least a generation; and, when no one thought any longer of offering a sacrifice, sacrificial language came to take a central place in doctrine.

The continuance of sacrifice is not difficult to understand. Many of the earliest Jews to believe thought of Jesus mainly as the fulfilment of the Messianic hope, and saw no inconsistency between that view and the punctilious observance of the Mosaic law to which they had been trained.[1] The total disappearance of sacrificial practice from Christianity was due to the general, though perhaps still only half-conscious, recognition that the teaching of Jesus had removed all ground for it, coupled with the fall of the Jerusalem Temple, the mighty influx of the Gentiles into the Church, and Paul's vigorous assertion of the inapplicability of the Jewish law to the faith of the new converts. The persistence of what may be called the theory of sacrifice when its practice had come to an end demands closer consideration.

Historians of doctrine have been apt to forget the influence

[1] The Anglican will perhaps reflect that many of the English Reformers could call themselves Protestants, and intercommunicate with non-episcopal churches on the Continent, without any sense of inconsistency; and the Methodist will remember that many of the early followers of John Wesley were ready to protest, with the founder of their 'religious societies,' that they were members of the Church of England.

of imagination on religious reformers. In most of us the evil practices which we see arouse a much keener opposition than the doctrines which on reflection we feel to be erroneous. Luther would never have been that fiery protagonist of the new ideas which all Germany saw in him, had it not been for his personal contact with indulgence-mongering, and his disillusionizing experiences in Rome. Amos and Hosea would never have urged their attacks on sacrifice with such impetuous ardour if they had not watched the display and the licentiousness of the shrines at Bethel and Gilgal. The accounts which underlie the Synoptic Gospels, however, have come down to us from men who were more familiar with the religious aims and discussions of the synagogues of Galilee than with the rites of the Temple at Jerusalem. The author of the fourth Gospel, though he chooses to report for the most part what took place in Jerusalem, and has preserved a wonderfully clear memory for the life that was lived there so many years before his work was written, clearly takes no trouble to envisage for himself and his readers the long-past Temple ceremonial.

It is, therefore, easy to understand why the gospel tradition contains none of the impressive declamation of the eighth-century prophets. The protests which we do find there are rather against the laws of clean and unclean, of Sabbath and common days, which were enforced at least as rigorously by the Jewish puritans of the north as by the Jewish priests of the south; and against the pride and hardness of heart and contempt for the claims of the poor, which were confined to no religious centre. The early evangelists did not think it worth while to point out that the sacrifices which were carried out at Jerusalem were left in a position as insecure as that of the formal observances which could be carried out even in the Diaspora. And we can hardly doubt that in this, as in other respects, they have given us a trustworthy representation of the attitude of Jesus.

Paul was no Galilean. He had studied theology in Jerusalem itself. He had drunk in his knowledge of the whole system of Judaism at the fountain-head. But he himself has shown very clearly that it was not the sacrificial part of that system that had any special attraction for him. His Judaism was the Rabbinism of the schools rather than the sacerdotalism of the Temple. He was a Pharisee, and

THE BEGINNINGS OF THEOLOGY 185

not a Sadducee or a priest. The questions that interested and often almost engrossed him, right onward into the period of the maturity of his powers as a Christian theologian, were the familiar Pharisaic topics of the limits of human freedom, faith as opposed to works, and the origin of sin. And when he found himself involved in controversy with the Jews of the Dispersion, he thought as little as they did of the other question—of the abiding or transitory validity of the Temple worship, which, after once leaving Jerusalem, he, like them, could only see on rare occasions and by taking special journeys. Their attention, like his, was fixed on other aspects of the law, dealing with Sabbaths, circumcision, food previously offered on heathen altars, which could be observed as carefully in Antioch or Thessalonika as on the sacred soil of Palestine itself. He was certainly enough of a Jew, even to the end, to value the opportunity, when it offered itself, of going up to Jerusalem ' to the feast.' The magnetism exercised on him by Jerusalem, and the certainty of the opposition there, which grew on him during his preparations for his last journey thither, remind us of the tense experience of Jesus when He set His face to go to the holy city, outside whose walls no prophet could perish. But such visits, to all Jews who lived outside Palestine, were more than the mere chance of witnessing the sacrifices ; they meant a sort of ' gathering of the clans,' a quickening of national enthusiasms and patriotic hopes, the meeting of long-sundered friends, and the possibility of discussion and of doing business at the one spot where all Jews were really ' at homo.' In such crowded days the sacrifices of the festivals, however important and impressive, were only an incident.

Paul was a theologian. His letters, though most of them the very opposite of set treatises, present us with a theology, or at least the prolegomena to a theology, as the Gospels do not. The Gospels propose to themselves to give us a picture of Jesus as He was, as others saw Him, leaving us to draw our conclusions ourselves. This is true even of the fourth Gospel. Its purpose is that its readers may believe that Jesus is the Son of God. But the system on which it is arranged, with its orderly exposition of Jesus as the son, the light, the life, the good shepherd, the vine, is not the system of a theological treatise, or even of a theological mind. Paul, on the other hand, took the representation of Jesus for granted. He knew, as he sat down to write to his friends, that he and his colleagues had seen to this already. His great task was to make clear to his readers the inner significance of those two main facts about Jesus that they had already learnt, namely, that He died and rose again. And now that they had begun to have a Christian ' experience,' and were beginning to discover in his absence the truth of what he had taught them while he was with them, he had to press upon their minds the connexion between experience and fact, and to teach them that they could now approach God with ' boldness,' as sons, instead of with fear and trembling, as unsatisfactory and disobedient slaves who could never be sure of their reception by their master.

For this purpose it was almost inevitable that a teacher in Paul's position should have fallen back on sacrificial language. He did not, like his master, live in the one country in the civilized world where heathen sacrifices were unfamiliar. He spent his life in Gentile cities, the majority of which did not come far behind Athens in the number of their altars. His Gentile disciples, before their conversion, had suspected nothing of the special road to communion with God which was well known to every pious Jew from the Psalter and the teaching of the more spiritual of the Pharisees. Their only idea of access to God had been by the medium of sacrifices, whose purposes were often obscure and their rites unintelligible, but which, in some strange fashion, could yet make themselves felt as bringing men into touch with God. And the Gentile, unlike the Jew, did not altogether shrink even from the thought of a human being given in sacrifice. In some dark and secluded spots the rites which demanded a human victim still survived. Many a man in Thrace and Calabria knew of groves which had echoed to the shriek of the slave or the child beneath the knife of the priest, and every one of any education knew the stories of Iphigeneia, or of Curtius, who had offered himself to the gods of the underworld for the safety and prosperity of the Roman people.[1]

---

[1] The remark of Caiaphas that it was expedient that one man should die for the people (John xi. 50) would sound natural enough to those who knew of the old Roman custom of ' devotion ' as carried out by Decius and other Roman heroes. See also p. 188.

Living in a world, therefore, where sacrifice and religion were almost identified, as they had ceased to be identified in Palestine ever since the Reformation of Josiah, and having even had on one occasion the experience of being himself the recipient of a sacrifice, he could not have hoped to keep his preaching of the death of Christ on the cross, in the minds of his hearers, distinct from the idea of a sacrificial offering. For the preacher to say 'The Son of God died for us' was for the hearer, untaught but interested, to interpret, 'This great hero evidently offered himself as a sacrifice.' Every public speaker, and every missionary, knows that the relation between speaker and hearer is mutual, and that the hearer's interpretation has a way of invading the speaker's thoughts. Paul could have hardly addressed a succession of Gentile audiences, as he was constantly doing, without being conscious of a fresh connexion between Christ's death and a divine sacrifice in his own mind. And no Jew could preach the death of Christ as the final means of escape from sin, in any sense of that word, without being conscious of the older sacrifices which had held out a hope that they could never fulfil. This did not mean that either Paul or any other Christian brought up in Judaism would be inclined to draw a parallel between Calvary and the altar in Jerusalem. He would be readier to emphasize the distinction. But the very fact that the first subject would call up the associations of the second, if only by way of contrast, would suggest the transference to the first of language appropriate to the second.

Let us, then, inquire to what extent Paul's teaching about the death of Christ was influenced by the ceremonial of the altar. We need not for this purpose examine the whole of Paul's doctrine of the Atonement; but we cannot overlook the fact that he held Christ's death to be 'for our sins' with the force of a 'pivotal' conviction.[1] This regular representation of Christ's death as connected with deliverance from our sin has been held to prove, of itself, the sacrificial aspect of that death. Such a conclusion, however, must not be too hastily drawn, since in the first place nearly every reference to the death of Christ is immediately followed by a reference to His life or His resurrection,[2] as if expressly

[1] See Rom. v. 6; 1 Cor. xv. 3; 2 Cor. v. 14; 1 Thess. v. 10.
[2] Rom. viii. 34, xiv. 9; 1 Cor. xv. 4; 2 Cor. v. 15; 1 Thess. iv. 14.

to exclude a sacrificial interpretation; for in the sacrifices there is no suggestion of such a rising again, nor is it necessary for the fulfilment of any idea connected with the ritual. And such a conviction, as it stands in the familiar phrase, 'Christ died for our sins,' is little more than a formula. Death for our sins could be explained in half a dozen ways—as the death of a victim on the altar, or of a soldier in battle, like Decius for his country or a leader for his followers, or of a friend for his friend, or a wife for her husband, like the Alcestis of Euripides. And if it be replied that only the first of these kinds of death could be regarded as delivering from sin, we must remember that in the mind of the Jews of the period other kinds of death could be regarded as removing sin.[1] The very phrase, indeed, 'for' or 'on behalf of' 'our sins,' interchangeable as it is with 'for' or 'on behalf of us,' refuses to confine itself to a sacrificial reference.

The result of such an examination shows that Paul was much less influenced by sacrificial language than might have been expected. In his contact with Gentiles he yet retained the religious outlook of the Jew and the Pharisee. He refused to be affected by Gentile conceptions, or to express his message in Gentile terminology. He could have done so with the utmost ease, and, we might have thought, with great advantage. He made himself 'everything to everybody,' as if he were like the most versatile of Greeks in Rome,[2] and completely broke with the unbending sternness of the Rabbi. He might have pointed out in a dozen speeches and letters that Christ had been immolated at the head of the world's great altar-stairs, and that what the Gentile priests had never done was now accomplished on Calvary. In this way he might certainly have commended his gospel to the more religious among his hearers at Athens and elsewhere. But that is not how he preferred to express his message. His interest was moral and religious instead of ceremonial; and in this respect he would make no concessions to the expectations or prejudices of his audiences. In the passages where they might have welcomed the sacrificial metaphor he prefers to talk of the sinner's being 'put in the right' before God, of the

---

[1] See above, ch. iv. fin. [2] 1 Cor. ix. 22; cf. *Juv.* iii. 75 ff.

THE BEGINNINGS OF THEOLOGY 189

condescending love which moved God to give up His own son for us, or of our being made (amazing phrase!) the 'righteousness of God' in Him.

To the Gentiles he is still a Jew. And to Jewish sacerdotalists he is still a Pharisee. He cannot avoid all sacrificial language, chary though he is of its use. But when he does use it, he does not use it as a ritualist. He neglects the very points which a Jew, really interested in the service of the altar, would have considered important. Only in one passage does he seem to speak of Christ as a sin-offering.[1] But if he intended to connect the cross and the altar by those words, he had evidently not thought out the answer to the question which a Jewish ritualist would certainly have asked, What kind of a sacrifice was it that was really offered upon the cross? For elsewhere he speaks of Christ as if He were to be compared to the lamb of the Passover.[2] But the Passover was quite a distinct sacrifice from any sin-offering. The ritual was also different. In the sin-offering the victim was wholly consumed; in the Passover it was eaten by the worshippers; and the same animal could not serve both purposes. Moreover, the Passover was not eaten at the altar in the Temple, but in private houses. A careful ritualist could never have confused the two. The fact that Paul does not seem to have made up his mind whether Christ is one or the other shows that he is not expressing a theory to which he attached any

---

[1] Rom. viii. 3. This interpretation is not free from doubt. The words Paul actually uses are 'for sin'; but those words are regularly used in the LXX to represent the Hebrew for 'sin-offering.' But, as Sanday and Headlam point out *ad. loc.*, the object of this sacrifice was 'to make atonement especially for sins of ignorance' (see above, p. 119); and they add: 'We need not suppose the phrase here specially limited to the sense of sin-offering.' It is, however, worth noticing that though Paul never uses 'sin' in the Levitical sense, his conception of sin as 'reigning over' the race suggests the state of being in wrong relations with God rather than some deliberate defiance in the individual.

[2] 1 Cor. v. 7. The verb 'to sacrifice' is used by Paul only here, and in another passage (1 Cor. x. 20) where he is referring plainly to heathen sacrifices. Paul only uses the noun θυσία five times—three times of the sacrifice of a devoted life, offered by the Christian (Rom. xii. 1; Phil. ii. 17, iv. 18), once of heathen altars (1 Cor. x. 18; see above), and once of Jesus (Eph. v. 2, where the reference is apparently not specifically to His death, but to His love, as an example of unselfishness to His followers, and therefore, it would seem, to be compared to, e.g., Rom. xii. 1). προσφορά is used twice, in Eph. v. 2 (see above), and Rom. xv. 16, of 'the offering of the Gentiles' made possible by his ministry. For the Hebrew Passover, see p. 116.

weight, but hinting at an analogy, the details of which he does not think it worth while to press.

So far from using language, either as part of his systematic teaching or by way of illustration, which people who were familiar with the practice of the altar would understand, he occasionally almost goes out of his way to puzzle them. Christ, we read, was 'made sin' for us. This could certainly not be said of the sacrifices. The sin-offerings were and remained holy; the worshipper did not hand on to them his sin; he received their holiness. The only sacrificial animal to which the word could be applied was the scapegoat.[1] Christ is also said to have been made a curse for us.[2] This, too, is not true of the sacrifices. And in the same passage Paul explains his meaning. Our disobedience had brought us under a curse. The fact that Jesus had hung upon a tree, according to the old legal maxim, had brought Him under a curse. We could thus be 'bought off' by Him from the curse which rested on us. However we treat the argument, it obviously had nothing to do with the sacrifices. To a Jewish mind there could be no connexion at all between a criminal condemned to a degrading death and the pure animal, inspected by the priest to make sure that it had no blemish, led to the sacred place of immolation. Paul's problem was too serious, and his experience was too profound, to allow his thoughts to rest in the world of sacrifice and ritual. The subject with which he was continually wrestling was one with which, even to the ritualist, the sacrifices had little to do. How can man escape from the sin which results from his paralysing inability to obey the moral law? Violations of the ritual law caused him no trouble. And those violations were never regarded as deserving of death. It was otherwise with disobedience to the moral law. Deliberate disregard of God's commands meant death. And it was with that deliberate disregard that Paul was concerned. The death of Jesus naturally came to be central for this deliverance in his thought, as the death which disobedience had deserved was central in his thought

---

[1] 2 Cor. v. 21. It is noteworthy that the comparison of Christ with the scapegoat is made in *Ep. Barn.* vii., but not in the New Testament.

[2] Gal. iii. 13, quoted from Deut. xxi. 23, with the significant omission of the words 'by God.' See Lightfoot *ad. loc.*

THE BEGINNINGS OF THEOLOGY

of man's bondage to sin. 'To suggest that Jesus had borne that threatened death for all, and that that was the reason why a just God could also show Himself to be a merciful God, seemed to him to meet the difficulty.'[1] This interpretation of Christ's death, as we shall see later, cannot be considered exhaustive; and if Paul, in working out his view, uses language that can only be called substitutionary, he is far from confining himself to it. But we must at least recognize that his view, in so far as it can fairly be called substitutionary, arises from the moral conviction that the consequences of sin are too serious to be made to stop short of death, and not from the supposed ritualistic belief that God cannot forgive the sinner unless a victim has been offered up on some altar in his place.

We have thus found that into the majority of expressions which are usually classed as sacrificial the idea of sacrifice has to be imported from the outside. What then, it will be asked, of the references to the blood of Christ in the Epistles? These, it should be observed, are far from numerous in Paul's writings. Christ was set forth as a propitiation 'in His blood'; we are justified, 'put in the right,' 'in His blood'; we have our redemption 'through His blood'; we became near 'in the blood of Christ'; and Christ made peace 'through the blood of His cross.'[2] These passages certainly point to the conclusion that Paul regarded Christ's blood, shed on the cross, as analogous to the blood of the victim shed on the altar. No one can fail to be reminded of that careful manipulation of the blood which was vital in both Jewish and pagan rituals.[3] Are we, then, to conclude that while for the most part the apostle avoided the terminology of the altar, he made use, on occasion, of the one word which would suggest the altar and nothing else?

This is a possible supposition; but it is not necessary, nor indeed, on examination, very probable. A Jew did

---

[1] Rashdall, *The Idea of the Atonement in Christian Theology*, p. 108.

[2] Rom. iii. 25, v. 9; Eph. i. 7, ii. 13; Col. i. 20. The only other reference in Paul is to the blood and the Eucharist (1 Cor. x. 16; xi. 25). Peter speaks of the 'obedience and sprinkling of the blood of Christ' (1 Pet. i. 2, 19), to which must be added 1 John i. 7: 'The blood of Jesus, His son, cleanses us from all sin.' Outside these the only references not in the Gospels are in the Epistle to the Hebrews and the Apocalypse.

[3] See above, chh. ii., iii., v.

192 ALTAR, CROSS, AND COMMUNITY

not need to be specially interested in ritual to be acquainted with the ancient traditional belief that an animal's blood is the vehicle of his life. 'The blood is the life.' If he had never seen a sacrifice performed, he yet knew that neither he nor any other Jew was allowed to eat meat from which the blood had not been carefully drained.[1] Blood thus became for him something completely removed from ordinary contact or use. It had the mysterious quality of 'taboo,' common to the holy and the unclean. To let the imagination dwell upon the crucifixion was, of course, to see the blood flowing down the limbs, and how was it possible for Jewish believers, conscious that something had passed over from Christ to them—something which had transformed, not only the world, but their own weak and sinful characters—to avoid uniting their joyous but solemn experience with the thought of that sacred life-blood, flowing for them and for all mankind? We may call the language sacrificial if we will. If so, it was the result, not of theology, but of an overmastering emotion. It was much more than theological. It expressed an experience which might to some extent be felt when the blood of a sacrificed bull was sprinkled on the worshipper's clothes. But it passed beyond that into the region of those deep and fundamental emotions which a ceremony can arouse, but which no ceremony can exhaust or confine. For in that moment, perhaps really ecstatic to some worshippers, and certainly so to the initiates of the later mysteries in which blood played so important a part, the faithful were conscious that the very life of the sacred thing, or of the divinity himself, was being communicated to them. To them, as to the pagans who first brought to their primitive altars their communal sacrifices, the blood was not the sign of a death inflicted upon a victim, but of a life shared among the members of a society.[2] And however little attention Paul might pay to the details

---

[1] The early Christians were at one with the Jews in their horror of consuming blood. See the resolutions of the Jerusalem Council, Acts xv. 20 and 29, if the text be reliable. The refusal of Jews and the 'weaker' Christian brethren to eat meat previously offered in a heathen temple was not merely because to do so was to imply some countenance of the idol to whom it might have been dedicated, but because it would have been killed in heathen fashion, with the blood (see 1 Cor. viii. 1 ff.)

[2] See p. 47.

A## THE BEGINNINGS OF THEOLOGY

of the sacrifices in which he had once participated, he, too, knew that blood stood for life and not death; for sharing, so to speak, and not for substitution; and the blood of Christ could mean nothing but the life of Christ now made available for him.

But did not Paul say much also about the cross in connexion with Christ's redemption? Surely, it will be argued, his language here can be nothing but sacrificial; to preach the cross is to preach Christ's sacrificial death; the message of the cross is the message of Christ as our substitute, or it is nothing. Now if, by the cross of Christ, we mean His death upon Calvary, the preaching of the cross will have as much, or as little, substitutionary character as we give to the Pauline doctrine of His death. But if we examine Paul's language more carefully, we shall see that, to him, Christ's cross is not synonymous with Christ's death, nor is the cross merely the object on which, like some glorified altar, Christ's blood was shed. Paul is the only New Testament writer outside the Gospels, and one other passage, to refer to the cross at all.[1] His reticence, and the refusal of the other New Testament writers to use the word, are not strange. For the cross was the most revolting thing in the world of antiquity. The idea that a man of any social or political standing could be condemned to death on the cross—a fate usually reserved for the most despised and notorious criminals—was felt to be monstrous. That the claim to be the Messiah should be put forward on behalf of one who had suffered in this horrible way might well rouse the synagogues of pious Jews to fury. Neither when he spoke in Athens or when he wrote to Rome did Paul ever allude to the disgusting topic. When he actually forced himself to it, it was not to emphasize the sacrificial aspect of Christ's death. It was to compel his hearers to recognize that the object of their adoring reverence was regarded with horror and contempt by the world as a whole, and to bring his

---

[1] It is instructive to refer to the actual passages—1 Cor. i. 17 f.; Gal. v. 11; vi. 12 f.; Eph. ii. 16; Phil. ii. 8, iii. 18; Col. i. 20, ii. 14. The verb is found in 1 Cor. i. 13, 23, ii. 2, 8; 2 Cor. xiii. 4; Gal. iii. 1, v. 24, vi. 14. It will be observed that Paul does not use the word in Romans or Thessalonians. It is avoided by all the other New Testament writers save in Hebrews xii. 2, where it is placed in strong contrast to Christ's joyous exaltation, and once in the Apocalypse, xi. 8, 'where also their Lord was crucified.'

194 ALTAR, CROSS, AND COMMUNITY

own natural self-esteem and pride to rest in a spot which all others would look upon as plague-stricken.

It was his chosen way of reminding his friends and himself that the new religion meant an absolute break with all the standards of the world, and the 'transvaluation' of all its values. To preach the cross is not to preach that we have found a substitute or God another victim; it is to preach a loyalty to Christ which entails a point-blank defiance of everything that the world esteems, an enthusiastic acceptance of everything that it loathes. Those who argue as if it were simply an element in a deliberately calculated scheme of salvation are oblivious of the passion which in every instance sweeps Paul into the realm of this paradox, and which alone could keep him there. And it is significant that the cross, to his thought, should be also the chosen instrument of reconciliation between Jew and Gentile, as if the ancient and deep-rooted quarrel could never be made up until the two parties had met where each was stripped alike of every prejudice and every claim.[1]

This brief study of Paul's references to the cross has led us to what was always his central idea—reconciliation. His main interest was not ceremonial, or forensic, or even, in our modern sense of the word, theological. It was personal—to bring sundered parties together. The sense of separation from God had entered so deeply into his soul, and the marvel of reconciliation with God, in Christ, had so firmly taken possession of all his thoughts, that he could conceive of religion in no other way. To reconcile man to God, to reconcile Jew to Greek, and to reconcile opposing individuals, parties, and groups to one another, became the master passion of his life. Naturally, the first of these aims dominated the rest. But it did not only dominate them; it inspired them. It became one with them. For, as he needed no teacher to inform him, reconciliation with God could only be effected through Christ.[2] But Christ was also the medium for all reconciliation among men. Christ produced the atmosphere in which all quarrels and misunderstandings inevitably vanished.

[1] Eph. ii. 6; Col. i. 20; cf. Col. ii. 14. In the Epistles of the Captivity, the cross as a means of reconciliation takes the place of the cross as a token of humiliation, common to the earlier letters.
[2] Cf. Gal. i. 16.

THE BEGINNINGS OF THEOLOGY 195

Sufficient weight is seldom given to the ethical exhortations which comprise the second part of most of Paul's letters. These are not added by way of appendix. Paul comes in them to close quarters with his readers. They might have been puzzled by what had gone before. These they could all understand. The value of the preceding dissertations consists in the fact that, if they are understood at all, they must issue in conduct. When these exhortations are studied, it will be found that they are almost wholly occupied with two subjects—chastity of the body and harmony in all personal and social relations. Emphasis on the first was inevitable for any teacher of high ideals who knew the pagan world in which he moved. Perhaps, if our modern preachers read their own society more correctly, they would find themselves drawing nearer to Paul in their own warnings and rebukes. The second was simply the result of Paul's conception of the Christian life. That Paul was right, and that self-seeking, enmity, suspicion, and greed make havoc alike of the moral life and of the Christian Church as nothing else can do, is written in characters only too legible, for those who care to read them, across the distracted history of the Christian centuries.

In other words, Christ, as the great mediator of that essential harmony, is the fulfilment of the fundamental idea and aim of sacrifice. The details of the developed Jewish practice of the altar, the differences between the four classes of sacrifice, or the respective parts in the ritual to be performed by worshipper and priest, were of little interest to Paul. Of the original purpose and the almost universal degradation of pagan sacrifices Paul knew and cared even less.[1] But his own spiritual history and his unerring insight into the secrets of the religious life led him straight to the heart of the secular Godward movement of humanity. 'Whom ye ignorantly worship, Him declare I unto you.' For all his Jewish upbringing, he forgot the narrow Jewish hopes of escape from spiritual uncleanness and moral inadvertence when he gazed at his master dying on the cross. He saw instead a stupendous act of love and self-devotion inspired by One who would stop at nothing, even the torture and ignominy of His own Son, to break

[1] Though compare Rom. i. 24, 26.

down the barrier between sinful men and Himself.[1] Before such a passionate and heroic longing for reconciliation one could hold off from his fellow men in pride or selfishness as little as he could hold off from God. All became inevitably one in Christ Jesus. Thus Paul's conception of the sacrifice of Jesus, we may say without exaggeration, is one with the conception held by Jesus Himself. Both avoid the word; both make no clear allusion to the practice. And both use quite different language. But beneath the teaching of both lies the thought of mediation. Christ is our sacrifice, not because He dies instead of us ; but because He makes it possible for us to come with boldness into the presence of God.

We have said that Paul neglected sacrificial terminology ; but there is one significant exception to this rule. In one group of passages the terminology is freely used ; and these passages refer, not to sacrifices at all, but to conduct. He speaks of his own work as a sacrifice ; λειτουργία, προσφορά ; and even of himself as being offered up. This may well surprise us, in view of his own language about Christ. But if he claims that he himself is a sacrificial victim, it is not because of any functions of his own as an apostle ; his followers are called on to perform the same solemn rite. What this rite is, is seen quite clearly from his own exposition of it in the first verses of Rom. xii.[2]

Nothing could be more striking than the fashion in which, having put aside the whole altar-praxis and the group of ideas connected with it, when he is dealing with the death of Christ, he restores it when he comes to the subject of conduct and Christian morality. It has often been pointed out that his references to the Atonement are allusive, as if the doctrine were already familiar to his readers. The same thing is true here. If he had thought that there were any other important element in sacrifice, as, for example, its Eucharistic application, he could hardly have avoided mentioning it. Here, as elsewhere, his silence is as eloquent as his speech. When he deals with

[1] Rom. viii. 32.
[2] See Rom. xv. 16, xiii. 6 ; 2 Cor. ix. 12 ; Phil. ii. 25, 30. He is even the libation at the sacrifice which is offered by their faith (Phil. ii. 17). In 2 Cor. ii. 15, and still more clearly in Phil. iv. 18, we meet the suggestion that the Christian's life is itself the fragrant sacrifice on the altar ; cf. the technical phrase used of the sacrifices in Lev. i. 9, &c.

THE BEGINNINGS OF THEOLOGY 197

the law itself, as far as it relates to conduct, he is explicit enough: 'Touch not, taste not, handle not.' But he calmly reduces the ceremonial to the level of a metaphor. True, the insistence on the importance of conduct does not of itself prove that Paul thought nothing of ritual. Ezekiel and the authors of Deuteronomy would caution us against this conclusion. But neither in Ezekiel nor Deuteronomy is good conduct spoken of as a sacrifice; the two spheres are kept quite distinct. Paul not only uses the sacrificial phrases for conduct; he leaves the ritual of sacrifice, apart from them, without a mention.

The metaphor is striking, but not altogether original. It occurs in a noteworthy passage in James; the genuine and unadulterated practice of religion does not consist in offerings and pilgrimages, but in visiting the friendless and unprotected, and in moral rather than ritual cleanliness.[1] It is not always recognized that both writers are linking themselves with the earlier prophets. They can hardly have forgotten that they are repeating the teachings of a class of men who saw nothing in sacrifices as such. James is simply echoing Micah[2]; and though the echo is a comparatively faint one, for there is far more in Micah's resounding statement, the implication as to the invalidity of all sacrificial rites is equally clear.

It may be urged in reply that the thought of conduct as a sacrifice appears elsewhere in the Old Testament[3]; that is, presumably, in circles where actual sacrifices were still practised. Such passages, in their relation to contemporary Judaism, are certainly difficult. They suggest that the thoroughgoing teaching of the eighth-century prophets lived on, even when the reformed sacrificial law was gaining quite a new hold on the religious life of the community. For all we know they may have been protests, as brave and as ineffectual as were the protests of the earlier prophets, against ritualism, loved all the more because it was purged of its grosser abuses. But, in any case, the fact that a certain number of Jews after the exile could sit lightly to the ritual law can hardly be used to prove that

---

[1] James i. 27. The last words, 'from the world,' show that the connotation of keeping oneself unspotted is moral. It is related that when some one in Theodore Parker's presence spoke of 'mere morality,' he replied, 'Mere morality! One might as well speak of mere God.'

[2] Mic. vi. 8.   [3] e.g. Ps. li., Isa. lviii. 6.

Paul and James attached to it an importance which their words nowhere imply. We must needs believe that if the apostles had meant to perpetuate sacrificial ideas in the new communities, they had enough command of language to have said so.

Another point, however, must be noted in this connexion. The passages in question may be few. They are not casual. And the ideas which inform them are of cardinal value. When we were considering ethnic and Jewish sacrifices, we could not overlook their psychological value. No idea can maintain its existence without some expression. This is as true in religion as elsewhere. The sacrifices at the altar were admirably fitted to afford that expression. Formal, leisurely, dramatic, with all the aids of solemn acts and half-understood words, ' taboos,' preparations, ceremonial robes, the sudden passage from life to death, and the heightened emotion resulting from the presence of a subdued and expectant and awe-inspired crowd, conscious of its nearness to the unknown and the menacing, the sacrifices had an effect which the modern religious service can hardly hint at. It was equally potent for the Jews, accustomed to the periodic feasts, as for the Gentiles of Ephesus or Corinth or Pergamum. But all this was now, for the Christian, at an end. Jewish converts from the Diaspora were not forbidden by their new faith to go up to the feasts.[1] But they were few in number. They could hardly help feeling like exiles ; and if they understood anything at all of Paul's teaching, they would be conscious of no need which these sacrifices could meet. Gentile Christians were debarred from the rites both of the Jews and of their own communities. To enter within the screen in the Temple was death, and to return to the dangerously impressive sacrifices of heathenism was to worship devils.

We know how the Jews, when they were cut off from the opportunities of sacrifice by the exile, or after 70 A.D., retained the benefits it had conferred on them. They had the other practices of the law on which to fall back—the Sabbath, circumcision, the Passover, the Day of Atonement, the services of the synagogues which sprang up to replace the Temple, and the various restrictions of the law, which, rapidly multiplying, became instead of a burden a sheer

[1] Compare what is said of the Epistle to the Hebrews below, p. 201.

THE BEGINNINGS OF THEOLOGY 199

joy to the pious. They were of course expedients; but for the Christian in apostolic days such expedients as these were impossible. The time-honoured observances of the Jewish law had no meaning or attraction for them; and the attempts of Jewish Christians to introduce them had to be vigorously repressed. Later on, the rite of the Eucharist was to be used to supply this need. But Paul makes no reference to such a use; his comments on what took place among the Corinthian Christians do not suggest that anything of the kind was in his thoughts, or in theirs. To him there was but one way for the Christian to express his religious emotion. The place that sacrifices had previously held, both with Jew and Gentile, must now be held by conduct—the new ritual in which no one would be a spectator merely, or even an offerer, privileged to take a certain part in the presentation of his victim; but each would be the priest who brings the offering right into the presence of God, and the offering itself which is blessed and sanctified.

It would be too much to say that this view of conduct is fundamental or even habitual in the early Christian writings. If it had been, we should probably have had more references to it. But Paul was a man of so fertile and luxuriant a mind that he could throw off, almost as an aside, what would have sufficed others for the central idea of a lifetime. It has remained where he left it in Christian thought—a suggestion. But it is none the less an essential part of his teaching on sacrifice, whether he himself recognized its importance or not. His system (if we can use so formal a term for what grew up piece by piece) was the result of the impact of errors and perilous tendencies, natural and even inevitable in ignorant but extremely vigorous communities, on a few deeply rooted convictions. Had he been confronted by the precise problems that taxed the author of the Epistle to the Hebrews, we might have had a development of the point just considered which would have added several chapters to our standard theological treatises. As it is, when we look back on his writings, in order to sum up his references to the sacrificial system, we find that he worked out no theory (as he did with the other great section of the law) of its place in religious development or as a *preparatio evangelica.* In spite of his unwearying emphasis on Christ's death as ' for us ' and ' for our sins,' he avoided all words reminiscent of the rites of the altar; he filled the space they might have occupied with a definite system of moral activity. Had he been a student of comparative religion he would have been able, had he cared, to point to a profounder connexion between his teaching and the sacrifices which he was transforming. The thought of reconciliation as the main function of the victim had passed to the periphery of the circle of Jewish ideas, or even outside the circle altogether; and therefore it did not occur to Paul. But to Paul this reconciliation was at the heart of Christianity. We have seen that it was as near the heart of the impulse to sacrifice as we can get. Could we have presented him with the striking parallel, it may be that he would not have refused to accept the gift.

We have already referred to the problem of the Epistle to the Hebrews. We must now return to it in greater detail. In that Epistle we meet with references to the sacrificial system more numerous than in all the rest of the apostolic writings put together. The purpose of the Epistle, on the face of it, is to give an interpretation of the work of Christ in terms of the rites of the Jewish altar. Writer and readers alike are familiar with these rites, and in one way or another attach great importance to them. By the side of them the other provisions of the law to which Paul paid so much attention, the prohibitions in the sphere of conduct, slip out of notice altogether. Sin, to this writer, is not so much disobedience to a command too exacting to be perfectly obeyed by any one; it is, as we might expect in a student of ritual, the uncleanness which must be purged away before God can be safely or properly approached. He seems to have chiefly in mind the ceremonies of the Day of Atonement; but he also refers to the daily sacrifices, the consecration of the priests, and the sacrificial ratification of the divine covenant, and he is quite familiar with the scholarly Levitical view that the sacrifices were for inadvertence, and not for ' high-handed ' sins. The startling expression that after wilful turning away from the light there avails no sacrifice for sin, but only a terror-stricken expectation of judgement, is a plain

THE BEGINNINGS OF THEOLOGY 201

reference to the fate of the sinner under the old law who had been guilty of an act for which no sacrifice could be offered, and whose necessary consequence was excommunication or death.

Yet, as we read him, we cannot avoid the feeling that he was not really at home with the Temple sacrifices, or else that he took no interest in their details. Although he refers to the different kinds of sacrifice, he makes no attempt to distinguish them; his treatment of them, so far from being exhaustive, is no more than allusive.[1] His references throughout are not to the Temple in Jerusalem, but to the Tabernacle in the wilderness. Like Philo, he is an Alexandrian Jew; and though in his quotations from the Old Testament he does not allegorize with the same freedom as Philo,[2] he regards all that he reads of in the old dispensation as a passing shadow to suggest the eternal realities of the gospel. Christ is not properly the fulfilment of the sacrifices. The sacrifices are signposts to point to Christ; and therein lies for the author their sole interest.

On the other hand, the theoretical contentions of the Epistle result, as with Paul, from a very practical purpose. The author evidently thinks of his readers as perplexed by their exclusion from the sacrifices of the Jewish Church. They seem to be in the position of dissenters, told that they have cut themselves off from the time-honoured and valid ministrations of a Catholic community. They are left orphaned, with neither priest nor altar[3]; and

[1] For instance, in speaking of the Day of Atonement, he says nothing of the scapegoat, although it might have materially assisted his argument; and his language is at times inexact, as when he connects the 'tamid,' or daily sacrifice, with the high-priest (Heb. vii. 27).

[2] He is not, however, averse to the use of the allegorizing method, as when he compares the burning of the bodies of sacrificial victims outside the camp to the suffering of Jesus outside the city (xiii. 11 f.) or the high-priest's passing through the curtain of the Temple to Christ's passing into heaven (ix. 24).

[3] This is true, whether we regard the readers as Jewish or (with Pfleiderer, von Soden, and others) as Gentile Christians. It will be noticed in any case that they are not warned against joining in the sacrifices of the altar; apparently this was not possible for them; and nothing is said about the other Jewish regulations, to which so many references are made in the Gospels, which could be carried out by Jews, proselytes, and also Jewish Christians anywhere. The actual dangers against which earnest cautions are given are lack of zeal and unreadiness to meet persecution when it comes. This seems to make against the view, e.g., of Nairne, in *The Faith of the New Testament*, pp. 129 f., that the readers were Jewish Christians, tempted to throw in their lot with the Jews shortly before the rebellion of 70 A.D.

202 ALTAR, CROSS, AND COMMUNITY

they are threatened with severe persecution. He proposes to show them that they have both a priest and an altar in a far richer sense than their ecclesiastical critics. Hence his main stress is not on the victim demanded by the rites, but on the position of the priest. Jesus is thought of primarily as the priest who offers the sacrifice (Himself), and only secondarily as the victim sacrificed. In Jesus Christians have a priest more exalted than any Levitical functionary. His argument is not intended simply to prove that Christ was the true high-priest, but that all which the high-priest did under the old régime (in which, for its own sake, he appears to take no interest) Christ has done, and still does, much more completely.

The high-priest did not choose or appoint himself; his office was conferred on him. This, the writer points out, is still more conspicuously the case with Christ.[1] The high-priest was chosen to make an offering; this, too, is true of Christ; but while the former was transient and unsatisfying, Christ's is complete. The difference noted above is important; for if the writer were anxious to prove that Christ was really a priest, he would be emphasizing an aspect of Christ's work which is not only unmentioned in the accounts given of Christ's teaching in the Gospels, but with which that teaching seems entirely out of accord. The same thing must be said of the Pauline doctrine. Jesus brings men to God, not as worshippers to a deity who refuses to be approached by them directly, but as sons to their father, to whom they have immediate and confident access. The relation is not ritual; it is moral and personal. This is shown clearly enough in our Epistle, where Christ is contrasted with Moses as a son is opposed to a servant. The distinction is even clearer where the author, in the second part of his argument, treats of the functions of the priest. The offering of Christ is Himself; and to emphasize this the author chooses to refer to one of the distinctly anti-sacerdotal passages in the Old Testament, in which the offering is not a victim but a moral life.[2] Thus the notion of the priest who presided over the slaughter of a victim by which the deity is induced to look favourably

---

[1] Ch. v. 4.
[2] Ch. x. 5, quoted from Ps. xl. 6–8. Compare the references to Jeremiah's prophecy of the new covenant (xxxi. 31) in viii. 8 ff., x. 16 ff.

THE BEGINNINGS OF THEOLOGY 203

on his worshippers is replaced by that of a son who, by his own life of obedience and love, brings his brothers into a communion to which, by themselves, they could not attain. And in order to work out the appeal of this 'sacrifice' he lays stress, in the passages which have most endeared themselves to generations of readers, on the temptations and sufferings of Jesus, which are as inapplicable to the conception of a priest as they are to a victim, but which are regarded as actually training Jesus for His work of obedience.[1]

To modern readers the arguments of the earlier part of the Epistle will always lack cogency. They are of great importance as showing the nature of the considerations which had weight with certain sections in the early Church, and which were used to give support to beliefs of undying significance. But our views of scholarly Old Testament exegesis are not those of the writers of his day. We can almost smile when we follow his eagerness to prove that Aaron was a lesser figure than Melchizedek, or that Melchizedek, king of righteousness and king of peace, really stood for Christ. He touches us more nearly when he breaks loose to speak of Christ as a leader and a son, winning His position and fulfilling his task by that moral devotion with which the priest at the altar had nothing directly to do, or when he emphasizes that confidence and reliance on the invisible for which the sacrificial system could find no place; and when he describes the great community in heaven, where Christ has made His own never-to-be-repeated and yet eternal offering.

The line of approach to the law, and the law itself, is thus one thing in this Epistle and another thing in Paul. In one respect, the two writers seem to draw near to one another in their use of the distinctly sacrificial term—blood. Even here, however, the resemblance does not carry us very far. Paul's use has already been discussed. Our writer, in accordance with his general standpoint, thinks of the blood as the accompaniment of all sacrifice, and is impressed with its profound inadequacy. After the briefest period its effect wears off entirely. But he is also, as a

---

[1] Cf. Nairne, *op. cit.*, 'The sacrifice is hardly a sacrifice at all; it is the off-scouring of a sacrifice. But it means the Lord Jesus, glorious in humiliation' (p. 142).

Christian, insensibly reminded of the blood of the covenant ; he does not usually call it the *new* covenant.[1] Christ's blood is the blood of the covenant. But in so describing it he is guilty, from the point of view of a strict logician, of a curious though almost inevitable inconsistency. For, according to the Hebrew and the pagan idea, covenant involved sacrifice; but this sacrifice was quite distinct from those sacrifices for sin with which the author has hitherto been dealing. The covenant sacrifice was not to atone or make amends for any kind of sin or misdemeanour ; it was to ratify a bond or contract between those who, hitherto foes, were now to live as friends. The precise connexion between sacrifice and contract has been disputed. The two parties often passed between the sundered portions of a slaughtered animal, either to emphasize their new union, or, less probably, to doom themselves to a similar fate if they should either of them be unfaithful.[2] But there can be no doubt that the blood sprinkled on the covenanters, or even shared by them, was the symbol and the means of uniting the two parties ; they became of one blood, of one and the same life.[3] The rite could be carried through even though one of the parties was divine ; and as such it appears in the Old Testament. In the mind of the prophets such anthropomorphism could have no place. Holding as they did that the covenant made at Sinai had been broken, they were convinced of the necessity of a new one, which needed no shedding of blood, but only the outpouring of Jehovah's spirit. With these passages the Eucharistic formula was naturally connected ; and our author, as his thought passes away altogether from the expiatory sin-offerings of the old covenant, urges that the only true way of understanding the blood of the covenant is to think of it as that magnificent life of suffering, temptation, and heroism, which did not shrink from the horrible loathsomeness of the cross itself, through which the two sundered parties, God and man, are reconciled at last and for ever. Hence, when he is

[1] See ch. ix. *passim* ; x. 4, xiii. 20 ; xii. 24.

[2] Many instances are given in Frazer, *Folklore in the Old Testament*, vol. i, pt. ii, ch. 1 ; see also H. C. Trumbull, *The Blood Covenant*.

[3] Wellhausen, *Skizzen* (3te Heft, p. 122), quotes an Arab formula : ' The blood of the covenant animals is their own blood ; and when they bring the two bloods to one divine place, God binds them together.'

THE BEGINNINGS OF THEOLOGY 205

describing all that is to be found within Mount Zion, the city of the living God, the mention of the mediator of the new covenant, even Jesus (the order of the words is significant), is followed by the covenant blood, sprinkled on the covenant-makers, which, as he points out in a noble parenthesis, does not perpetuate a feud like the blood of Abel, crying out for vengeance against his brother from the ground, but turns foes to friends in an indissoluble unity.[1]

It is clear that the author had very little sympathy with Ezekiel, the one great prophetic writer of the Old Testament who had any interest in sacrifices, or with the Levitical system as a whole. The old sacrifices, he says, could never take away sin. Sin, as he understood it, they never proposed to be able to take away, save under conditions. The sins that they did propose to remove were not to him sins at all. There is no sign that he attached any importance to the ritual mistakes or misdemeanours which the code classed as sins. The attempt made by many theologians to show that Christ by His sacrifice did what the Jewish sacrifices had tried to do in vain cannot be attributed to him. He was assured that Christ had done what the sacrifices had never offered to do. This is, indeed, his most characteristic contention. The most that could be said for the ritual system centring round the Tabernacle was that it was a shadow cast beforehand by the great event which had been so long in coming. But what the priests had not thought of doing was now being authentically accomplished by the Son. And although His death, infinitely more potent than any sacrifice, had been attended with every circumstance of horror and infamy, so that His followers must perforce go to Him even now 'outside the camp,' he had really entered, once and for all, the holy place above, as the representative of the people of God.

The author uses ritual analogies frequently enough

[1] A further inconsistency, as it may appear to us, takes place when the author passes, in ch. ix. 15 ff., from the sense of 'covenant' to that of 'testament' or 'will.' The Greek word he uses may carry both meanings, though the former is the regular Jewish use. But a will, unlike a covenant, does not come into force until the testator has died; it was thus easy for the change of meaning to be made (see verses 15, 16 in the R.V.). It will be noticed that in order to work out this further implication of the death of Christ the author passes away from the sacrificial aspect altogether.

but one after another they break down. What he is concerned to prove is that Jesus is a priest of a totally different τάξις, or order. And yet, if the title is still used of Jesus, there is a singular appropriateness in it. In the case of one priestly function after another, the likeness between the Jewish functionary and Jesus is shown to be one of language only; notably in the quotation from Ps. xl.—the offering of the 'body,' where all thought of a dead victim is out of place. But there is one function of which this cannot truly be said, the function of mediation. The priest was a mediator in the sense of standing between man and God. Christ was the mediator in the sense of bringing man and God together. It was through Him, he says, that God has in these last days spoken to us. Through Him we have entered the heavenly world, the new Jerusalem. He is the mediator of the new covenant, in which, as our 'forerunner,' He opens the way for us to enter where He has already passed. Thus, while He annuls the sacrifices as they appear in the Jewish ritual, He carries out the idea which, as we have seen, underlies the whole institution of sacrifice, Jewish and Gentile. Sacrifice is the staircase which human yearning for God has set up between earth and heaven. Divine messengers go up and down on it, carrying up all the wistful devotion and desperate hopes of mankind, and bringing down all the reassuring goodwill and mysterious power and efficacy of God. That is precisely what Jesus does. On this point our Epistle is as explicit as Paul's writings or the fourth Gospel. The notion of a surrender or bribe, a daring bargain founded on the principle of *do ut des*, has no real place in the large meaning of sacrifice. It certainly has none in the great offering of Himself accomplished by Jesus. But when we think of Jesus prolonging His unflinching obedience right on to death, and doing so avowedly as our representative, like the tragic yet victorious sufferer of Isa. liii.,[1] and so setting God by the side of man and man by the side of

---

[1] It is noteworthy that there is in our Epistle only one definite allusion to this poem; but that occurs in one of the most significant passages in it (ix. 28=Isa. liii. 12). And the conception of the work of Christ throughout the Epistle, like that which meets us in the rest of the New Testament writings, is infinitely nearer to that of Isa. liii. than to that of the Levitical priest.

THE BEGINNINGS OF THEOLOGY 207

God, we can see how the pathetic and blundering yet genuinely religious impulses of every age have found their explanation and, we may add, their justification, in the reconciliation of Christ.

In one passage, indeed, the writer seems to forget his main contention—that Christ's sacrifice is unique and final, and that there is no need for repetition, by Himself or any one else. At the close of the magnificent chapter about the entrance to Mount Zion, he comes back, as his manner is, to practical exhortation, and bids his readers offer sacrifice themselves 'with reverence and godly fear.' ' For indeed,' he adds, ' our God is a consuming fire.' The addition of the last clause is striking. The words have been understood as explaining the reason for the fear. Offer these sacrifices, he is thought to be saying, or God will consume you in His anger. This, however, is a way of speaking about God which, though not altogether foreign to the writer, certainly seems foreign to his thought at this moment. The words do not refer to the offerer, but the sacrifice.[1] It is for you, he says, to offer it; it is for God to come down, as before Elijah on Mount Carmel, and accept and consume it. With such sacrifices as I bid you offer God is well pleased. What sacrifices are these? His readers might well have been puzzled to know, if their knowledge of Christian, and even Jewish, thought had been confined to this Epistle.[2] But if, as is probable, they knew their Old Testament, they would immediately think of the meek and quiet spirit, or the broken and contrite heart. And if echoes of Paul's teaching had reached them, they would remember the exhortation to present their bodies (as they had learnt from our author that Christ had presented His) as a living sacrifice.[3] For the thought of our author, moving along tracks so different from those of Paul, reached at length the point to which Paul was wont sometimes to return. The Christian has his sacrifice. It is the sacrifice

[1] The words occur in Deut. iv. 24, but the author omits the conclusion of that verse, 'a jealous God.' Cf. also 2 Macc. ii. 10, ' the fire came down from heaven and consumed the sacrifices.'

[2] That even Gentile Christians were expected to understand allusions to the Old Testament is abundantly clear from Paul's use of Old Testament quotations.

[3] It is at least a tenable theory that the destination of the Epistle to the Hebrews was Rome, as von Soden holds and Zahn and Harnack think possible.

of the obedient life, reproducing the very life of Christ. There are no animals or birds for him to bring, no heifers or turtle-doves. But the life of goodwill and peaceableness and honesty and hospitality, carried out with the awe in which the most pious of the saints of the old covenant would approach their ancient altars, will be at once accepted. The offerer will not be left in doubt as to its finding favour. God Himself will give the authoritative sign that in such an offering worshipper and deity are at one.

We are now in a position to see more clearly the relation of Christ's sacrifice to human sin. As the Gospels seem to reveal, Jesus did not explicitly connect His death with men's sin. Even in the words of the institution of the Last Supper, His blood, we read, is shed, not for our sin but for us. And our examination of the epistles has led us to lay more emphasis on the results of the sacrifice in producing a new relation to God than on bringing the old one to an end. To some, this will seem like making too little of sin. Christian thought, as we shall presently observe, has occupied itself chiefly with the retrospective effects of the work of Christ. To minimize the importance of those retrospective effects, indeed, would ill become any exponent of Christianity. But no feeling of horror at the loathsomeness of sin, or delight at being freed from it, must make us forget that we are saved from sin by being saved to righteousness. The Gospel looks forward and not backward. It does not drive out the evil spirit and then leave the room swept and garnished. It comes to fill the room, and not to empty it.

The state of being freed from sin was not in itself the object of Christ's work. It cannot properly be called a state at all, if sin is interpreted as the Christian would interpret it. If sin means simply the infringement of a command or a taboo, a man can doubtless be free from sin when he is doing nothing at all. But to the Christian, sin means far more than this. It means a way of life which neglects the commands of God, and refuses to serve the needs of one's fellow men. It means the proud and self-centred mind, the uncontrolled and lustful desire. To be freed from sin can only mean to take the way of life which fulfils these commands and serves these needs. The only way of securing that freedom is to win over the man

THE BEGINNINGS OF THEOLOGY

who is to be freed to the new activities of obedience and service. Jesus saves us from sin because that 'winning over' is precisely what He has done for us.

What then, some will ask, of forgiveness? If all that Jesus came to do was to make us capable of living the life which God requires of us, what need for any dealing with sin? It might be answered with truth that to make us capable of living such a life is the greatest service that could be rendered to fallen humanity. But it is also true that, to make us capable of such a life, it is the very dealing with sin which is in question. We can love the new life when we are persuaded of its desirability, when we are assured that it is possible, and when we no longer feel ourselves, in the eyes of those whom we have wronged, as tied down to the bad and guilty past.[1] This last point brings us to forgiveness. Forgiveness is not the same thing as salvation. But without forgiveness, salvation is impossible.

Moreover, to take the forward look, as Jesus is represented in the Gospels as taking it, is not to overlook the 'exceeding sinfulness' of sin. It is rather the only way by which that sinfulness can be recognized. Sin may be dreaded for its outer consequences of physical suffering, or its inner results of mental dissatisfaction or pollution. It is never known to be what it really is, until it is confronted by an ideal, or law, of goodness. As Paul puts it, Christ condemned sin in the flesh because, in conditions with which we were all familiar, and which had proved too much for the morality and resolution of every one of us, He once for all lived the perfect life.

---

[1] This argument is developed on pp. 278 ff.

IX

THE SACRIFICIAL DEATH OF CHRIST

THE view to which we have been led in the preceding chapters may now be briefly summed up as follows. The purpose of sacrifice has always been, in essentials, to form a medium between man and God. As such a medium Christ is represented throughout the New Testament. Other functions which have been associated with sacrifice can claim no universal validity, and their various appearances can generally be explained by quite intelligible psychological considerations. These functions, too, are never emphasized in the New Testament, though often alluded to in connexion with the reconciling work of Christ. And further, in the case of ethnic and Jewish sacrifices, whether the offering is living or non-living, reconciliation is effected by the single act, duly prepared for, of handing over the object to the deity; an act which, if the object is living, is naturally accomplished by ritual slaughter. The offering of Christ, however, if our view is not mistaken, is not fulfilled merely in His death at Calvary, but involves His whole life of obedience—His humiliation, as we might call it from one point of view, or, from another, His manifestation of His Father's glory.

This conception of Christ as the world's sacrifice we have been led to recognize alike in the representations of His life in the Gospels and in the reflections on it in the rest of the New Testament. And we have seen how the emphasis of the earliest Christian writers on His death for our sins and on His atoning blood developed quite naturally from this conception. But when we pass from these first writings we find ourselves at once in a period in which the characteristic note of the Epistles seems to have been forgotten. Neither Barnabas, Hermas, nor Justin moved far beyond the Christology of the earlier chapters of the Acts of the Apostles; the profound thoughts

SACRIFICIAL DEATH OF CHRIST

alike of Paul and John they failed to grasp. But they were quickly followed by another set of writers who sounded the key-note, so to speak, of the Christian devotion and theology of the succeeding centuries. And here also we have to observe an alteration of emphasis (though of a different kind from that which preceded it), great enough at times to suggest a wholly new way of thinking of Christ's work. It is hardly too much to say that since the fourth century Christ's death has been the dominating certainty of Christian thought.

Artists, hymn-writers, mystics, have been at one in emphasizing Christ's sufferings, and more particularly His death on the cross. 'I determined not to know anything among you save Jesus Christ, and Him as crucified.' Such words as these have often been taken to justify the unique insistence upon the tragedy of Calvary. To dwell upon the Galilean or Jerusalem activities of Christ, save as preparations for His death, or to hold up for imitation the main features of His conduct while He went about doing good, has seemed a kind of unfaithfulness to the marrow of the gospel. Unlike one another in so many ways, yet united more closely with one another than either suspects, Catholic and Protestant have both tended to call attention away from what He did in the three years of His activity to what He suffered at its close. And if this is true of popular thought and exposition, it is equally true of more serious theological work, from Augustine to Dr. Denney.

Popular devotion and scientific theology, indeed, have always influenced one another. The theological treatise is completed in the study or the monastic cell, but it is written to be transferred to the pulpit; and if the message of the pulpit is to find its way to men's hearts, it must be capable of being worked out in a form that can be used in the hymns, the pictures, the devotional tracts, and even the ecclesiastical jewels and the wall-texts of the Christian community. On the other hand, theologians have generally sprung from the people, and have mixed with the people; their deepest convictions have been learnt from simple and pious persons rather than from the writings of philosophers; they are as familiar as others with the popular aids to piety and worship—images, pictures, or favourite hymns;

not even a theologian can emancipate himself altogether from his fellow-worshippers. To think of Christ's death on the cross as constituting His sacrifice, or to think of His sacrifice as a sacrificial death, may be the result of one kind of appeal in the mind of the simple worshipper, and of quite another in the mind of the systematic thinker; but we can never afford to neglect the subtle interaction between the two.

The emphasis which has always been laid on the death of Christ in popular and missionary propaganda, and the response which has greeted it, is not difficult to understand. In the first place, a crisis is always more impressive than a continuous action. Human nature welcomes the dramatic. An impulsive and isolated act of bravery will attract thousands where a life of silent self-repression goes unnoticed by all. Thus it happens that the hero himself will often be commended for what is by no means the most heroic part of his life. Moreover, the tragic elements in the story of the crucifixion make an irresistible appeal to the emotions of the most careless. The exhaustion on the road to Calvary, the blood flowing down the emaciated and tortured limbs, the rent of the spear in the side next the heart, will touch those whom even the melodramatic sometimes leaves cold. It is natural to rely on the effect of pity and horror, and there is little of pity and horror till we come to Gethsemane. And, quite apart from this, few can resist, at least for the time, the constraining power of the thought, 'He died for me; all this pain and agony were for my sake.' Gratitude is one of the noblest instincts (the psychologist will perhaps pardon us for calling it an instinct) of our nature. The story which makes such an unerring call upon our gratitude will enter in at the lowliest doors. If we reflect, in addition to all this, that for a man to face death for the sake of another, especially for the sake of the ungrateful, the hostile, and even the murderous, is to reach the height of what we all feel to be heroism, and to make us conscious of an eager wish to follow so exalted an example, we shall understand why Calvary does within us so much more than Galilee.

Now it must not be supposed for a moment that this appeal is to be deprecated. Heroism is not so common that we can afford to suggest that the laying down of the

SACRIFICIAL DEATH OF CHRIST 213

life is not the greatest thing of which humanity is capable, even when that humanity is taken up into Godhead. And if, when we think of the Man of men, we remember that the fashion of His leaving His earthly life was all of a piece with His sojourn in it, and that the glory of the last hours was different only in the compelling splendour of its manifestation from the glory of all the spotless three or three and thirty years, it will be impossible for us to overestimate it. None the less, that concentration of the mind upon those last hours which has been so characteristic of Christian devotion has brought with it certain disadvantages, both for thought and practice. It has drawn away attention from the large ethical and religious contents of Christianity. We have been in danger of forgetting the 'Jesus of history'—the startlingly simple life of courage and purity and unselfishness lived against the complex and fascinating background of Palestine in the first century—and we have forgotten to ask how that same simplicity could be carried out in the equally complicated world of to-day.

After all, to lay down our own lives is not, for most of us, a practicable proposition; and the spectacle of the cross, when it ceases to be an example, may become a dangerously short-lived excitement. Further, the marvellous series of words and acts which made people say that the world was gone after Him comes to be looked at as something that has no saving power apart from the catastrophe that brought it to an end. Secondly, it must be confessed that emphasis on the saving power of the death of Christ, considered by itself, has often resulted in an individualism and a selfishness which the Master would have been the first to check and denounce. The man who is taught to believe more particularly that faith in Christ's death, regarded by itself, is the means whereby his soul can be saved, comes perilously near to the fate which Christ pronounced on those who were anxious to save their own souls; it concentrates his mind on his own escape from more or less clearly envisaged evils; it makes him see in Christ, as a pagan devotee might see in the animal dying on the altar, the chance of securing some blessing which he desires for himself, and in salvation something to lead to what he can receive and enjoy, rather than to a new way of life.

The Church is not a heaven-appointed boat, to use an ancient figure, into which a shipwrecked sailor, battling with the threatening waves, must scramble as best he can, leaving others, less fortunate or less instructed, to perish. To assert that such a view of the Church, indeed, is the necessary result of regarding Christ's death as the one availing sacrifice for sin would be to contradict a thousand facts. Piety constantly shows itself superior to both logic and psychology. The new life of service and self-forgetfulness which Christ bestows is not limited by the mistaken doctrines set before him who receives it. But it cannot be denied that the emphasis which Catholics as well as Protestants have placed on the merits of Christ's death, whether appropriated personally or mediated through the Church, has tended in every age to produce this self-centred view of religion, and with it to foster a carelessness for the 'outsider' which in other quarters has been felt to be the severest reproach to which Christians could be liable.

Further, Christians who have been, through their zeal for the salvation of others, conspicuously free from this reproach, have yet been prone to overlook the claims of society and the world. If the supreme necessity is that the individual should learn to trust in Christ's merits and death, he may be tempted to pay very little attention to the life and needs of his country. He is waiting for the entrance into another country which has been assured to him. He may even come to think that the less he concerns himself with what he considers only as 'social amelioration,' the more true he will be to the demands of his Saviour and the real needs of perishing mankind; and, in these days of growing social enthusiasm, he will sadly point out that the social enthusiast, high-minded and unselfish as he may be, is apt to think very little of organized religion and its worship. It is certainly true that the present tendency is to choose the service of man, for the sake of man, and to move away altogether from a religion which centres round faith in the cross of Christ.

And it is undeniable that the view of Christ's sacrificial death which is commonly identified with popular evangelicalism has raised almost insuperable difficulties in the minds of multitudes of earnest people—difficulties which are not less real because they are not always advertised.

SACRIFICIAL DEATH OF CHRIST 215

yet they hardly need enumeration. How can it be just that some one else should die for my sins? If it is, how does the faith that Christ did so die save me? Or, if Christ's righteousness is imparted to me through my faith, how can God regard me as something which, in fact, I am not? That these difficulties exist, the long series of works on the Atonement makes clear enough. That they have not been met in a way that will satisfy the non-theological mind is equally clear from the fact that the series continues.

To all these questions, however, the advocate of what we may call the traditional view has two replies. He will ask, first, Can you who connect Christ's sacrifice with His whole life and activity, and regard His death as only one incident in that life, though doubtless the most important, answer these questions any better than you suppose others to be able to answer them? Can you bring forward any interpretation of that sacrifice which will be more successful in making men eager to lose their lives and to serve the interests of the community, if that is really the aim which the Christian ought to set before him? Can you explain salvation in any way which will not leave, to human reason, an unfathomable mystery? Secondly, he will urge that the appeal of the death of Christ has had a unique and continuous influence in the history of Christianity. It has steeled the tenderest and melted the hardest hearts; it has inspired a devotion and a sense of gratitude which no other consideration has aroused; and it has proved its efficacy with obdurate sinners whom no other argument seemed able to touch. The very fact, he will contend, that representations of the cross in art and references to it in devotional literature are so constant shows that it must possess some deep psychological affinity with the springs of our religious emotions.

The former of these two questions we must keep for fuller treatment later on, only observing at this point that the truth of a doctrine cannot be finally tested by the success of the results which have followed some presentation of it. We should at least have to consider at the same time possible instances, not so readily collected, of its failure. The second question involves more than has always been apparent at first sight to those who have asked for it. If it is brought forward as a psychological justification for a certain interpretation of the death of Christ, we have to ask whether the psychology is sound, and what precisely is the interpretation which it is held to justify.

Now we have already admitted that the appeal, 'He died for you,' is one of the most powerful that can be made; and when some one else, who has done nothing amiss, lays down his life for sinners, of whom I am convinced that I am one, and that with every circumstance of pain and ignominy, only the grossest unimaginativeness or the basest ingratitude could remain untouched. To contemplate the cross, when the extreme of human brutality only calls forth from the unresisting and heroic sufferer the prayer 'Father, forgive them,' and to realize that I myself share the guilt of that brutality and am the object of that prayer, excites the deepest emotion and can arouse, one would think, the dullest conscience. All religions live by rousing the emotions and touching the conscience; but in its power to do this, Christianity has left all other religions far behind.

Why, then, has it not succeeded more signally? How can we account for the melancholy fact that after all only a small minority of those to whom the appeal has been made have responded to it? Human selfishness and greed, it must be confessed, oppose even to the most powerful call a dead mass of hostility. What we may call the psychology of response, indeed, has not been worked out. But it is only the heroic in a man, even though latent and previously unsuspected, that can reply to the heroic. The sower must cast his seed on every kind of soil; he cannot tell, till it springs up, whether the ground on which it has fallen contains the elements which its growth demands. Nor is it always easy to secure the consent of the contrite heart. To look at the cross may mean that I feel pity for the sufferer and indignation against His murderers; but these emotions may be quite distinct from any feeling that I share in the guilt and deserve the indignation myself. The appeal of the cross implies something more than the emotional presentation of a good man's death for the sins of others. That something more will at times arise spontaneously; at others the best efforts of the preacher fail to rouse it.

We must notice, however, that the appeal, as it is described to us, has no necessary connexion with any one

SACRIFICIAL DEATH OF CHRIST 217

interpretation of Christ's death. 'Christ died for you; therefore give your lives to Him.' These commanding words do not imply any elaborate 'plan of salvation.' As a matter of history, the sacrificial death of Christ has been expounded, not in one, but in many ways, and almost all of them could be enforced by this plea. If, then, we are to understand how Christ's sacrifice has come to be so closely connected in thought with His death, or why it is that the sacrificial rite, as a visible act, though never finding an entrance into Christian practice, has established itself as a theory at the centre of Christian thought, we must observe the transition from the New Testament, where sacrifice occupies such a minor place, to later writers, where it is so constantly met with; and we must then, if our task is to be properly performed, study the successive theories of justification and atonement. Those theories often prove melancholy reading. Conceptions are brought before us which seem repellent or bizarre. We find, for example, the pagan conception of a god who must be propitiated or appeased, and who will not be satisfied without the shedding of some one's blood[1]; the striking of a bargain, sometimes open and 'above-board,' sometimes involving an ingenious ruse, with the rightful lord of sinful humanity, who can be none other than the devil; a struggle between the divine justice and mercy, as if they were two opposite impulses or moments in the one divine nature; a payment to God which was greater than He could demand from the payer, and which had, therefore, to be met by a corresponding boon on the part of God Himself; and a long series of attempts to unite disconnected scriptural passages, most of them charged with meanings long since lost sight of, and regarded as possessing a divine authority which was free to be communicated to any explanation of the words given by those who used them.

But all this must not blind us to the real services rendered by the succession of Christian thinkers. Inevitably subject to the limitations of their age and their outlook, they yet

---

[1] To describe this demand in terms of an august but impersonal 'moral law' which must be 'vindicated' by some penal suffering, does not bring it any closer into the atmosphere of the New Testament, for which an impersonal moral law does not exist. All that is done is regarded, there, as done by the living and personal God, the Father of mankind.

worked with a deep resolve to discover the solution to the greatest of all problems—namely, how, in a world where sin appears to have the upper hand, we can find assurance, in the suffering and death of an historical character, Jesus of Nazareth, that the present dominance of sin in the human race and the individuals who compose it will come to an end. We shall not attempt to trace the history of the doctrine as a whole. That has often been done, and its results are readily accessible.[1] We shall only try to show how, in its leading exponents and its different forms, the sacrificial character of Christ's death has become so important an element in the development of the exposition of His reconciliation.

The early Christian fathers, like the New Testament writers, had no articulated view. That Christ died for our sins they were all assured ; they did not trouble to ask how our sins were affected by His death. Nor had they grasped the meaning of the developed Jewish law of sacrifice. The distinction between the various sacrifices was unknown to them. A sacrifice simply meant an animal whose death on the altar somehow effaced or wiped out the sins committed by the person who offered it. Now this was precisely what they felt had been done for them by Christ. It was natural, therefore, for men whose experience of the new life was deeper than their knowledge of biblical antiquities, to use the language of the altar about Christ. It was all the easier because the Old Testament was regarded by the earlier Christian writers as on an equal plane of inspiration with the New. At first, indeed, the Old Testament enjoyed the respect which the New had not had time to acquire. The very fact that in the Old Testament law the death of the victim was all-important was calculated to give a fresh emphasis in their minds to the death of

[1] A good summary of the different classes of interpretation will be found in J. K. Mozley's *Doctrine of the Atonement* (1915). An earlier lecture in this series, Lidgett's *Spiritual Principle of the Atonement*, contains an appendix on ' The Doctrine of the Atonement in Church History ' (60 pp.). More elaborate is R. S. Franks' *History of the Doctrine of the Work of Christ*, which appeared in 1919 ; and Rashdall devotes the central part of his Bampton Lectures (*The Idea of Atonement in Christian Theology*, 1919) to a very full analysis of Patristic Theories, the Later Greek Fathers, Latin Theology, Scholastic Theories, and Luther and the Reformation, the last of these chapters, perhaps, showing a certain bias from which the rest are free. The most recent work is that ot R. Mackintosh, *Historical Theories of the Atonement*, 1920.

SACRIFICIAL DEATH OF CHRIST 219

Christ as opposed to His life, and the language of Paul would naturally encourage this tendency.

Yet it is surprising that, in spite of quotations from prophecy, and statements already becoming traditional about Christ's cross and death, there is really no attempt at theory. The diversity of the thoughts in the phrases which the writers use when they are obviously urging their own personal convictions about Christ's salvation shows that no such attempt was contemplated, 'He Himself cleansed their sins by the performance and endurance of many labours'; 'That we might be sanctified by the forgiveness of our sins, which is in the blood of His sprinkling'; 'He suffered that His wound might make us alive'; 'Him who died on our account, in order that believing on His death ye might escape death'; 'Gain possession of yourselves in faith, which is the flesh of the Lord, and in love, which is the blood of Jesus Christ.' Rashdall justly remarks that ' as soon as the early fathers attempt to explain precisely how the death of Christ contributes to the forgiveness of sins, it is always some subjective, ethical, and quite intelligible effect upon the believer to which the saving efficacy is attributed.' This is true even of the most explicit of the references to the language of ransom or exchange. ' In pity He Himself took on Himself our sins, He Himself gave up His own son as a ransom on our behalf, the holy for the lawless, Him who was without evil for the evil, the just for the unjust. . . . For what else was able to hide our sins but His righteousness? . . . What a delightful exchange!' ' The ram by its slaughter ransomed Isaac; so the Lord also by His slaughter saved us; by being bound He loosed us, and by being sacrificed He ransomed us.'[1] It is also noticeable that in these references to Christ's death, as a ransom or sacrifice, there are no allusions to expiation. Christ's death shows the Father's love as much as His own. If they had any knowledge of the tendencies of Jewish thought which found completer expression about the fifth century A.D., the writers would find further confirmation for this conception in the Jewish teaching that God had arranged the sacrifices in His pure love to the chosen people, so that nothing might keep them

[1] Hermas, Sim. 5; Barn. 5, 7; Ign. Trall, 3, 8; Diogn. 9; Iren. *ap.* Routh, *Rell. Sacrr.* i., pp. 123-4, quoted by Rashdall, *op. cit.*

from the joy of worshipping Him in unclouded communion; what thought could more fully suggest the free grace which assigned Christ as the great sacrifice through whom mankind could regain communion with God?

The leaders of the Church, however, were from early times what the Jewish doctors never were—men of philosophic and juristic temperament. The Jewish doctors, indeed, were possessed of keen intellects, and from time to time thinkers of conspicuous power arose among them, like Maimonides, who could meet the Christians on their own ground. But for the most part the Jewish intellect worked along one or other of two lines, correlating passages in the sacred writings of the Old Testament, or the hardly less sacred comments added thereto, in order to elaborate some rule of conduct or casuistry or to illustrate some obscure text; or else examining apparent contradictions, in the spirit of the well-known story about Hananiah's reconciliation of Ezekiel with the Pentateuch. Such a method was not wholly alien to the Christian theologians, though happily it could not affect the insight of the greatest men among them; and its results, for good and evil, though never carried to the extremes familiar to the students of the Rabbinic writings, may be found in the productions of many a church council. But the problem of the Atonement necessitated a more philosophic consideration. In the Christological controversies, men were battling about terms which could be but little more, by their very nature, than algebraical symbols. The question of the purpose of Christ's death forced their minds into creative thinking.

They were all familiar with the thought of that death as a ransom; it was indeed a ransom rather than a sacrifice. But if so, it implied to them the paying of a ransom price. To whom could that price be paid? Only to some power from whom Christ wished to deliver men. And what could that power be, save the devil? The question did not trouble the first Christian thinkers. They were more interested in interpreting their own experience than in working it into a scheme. But when the premisses are granted and taken seriously, it seems impossible to avoid the conclusion, both as to the means by which the devil was supposed to have gained his power over mankind, and

SACRIFICIAL DEATH OF CHRIST

the diplomatic arrangements, so to speak, by which the price of redemption was paid into his hands and the concession so purchased was carried out. 'But to whom did He give His soul as a ransom for many? Certainly not to God. Could it, then, be to the evil one? For he had possession of us until there should be given him the ransom for us, the soul of Jesus; though he was deceived by thinking that he could have dominion over it, and did not see that he could not bear the torture caused by holding it.'[1] To modern ways of thinking the whole conception is so grotesque that we wonder how intelligent Christian men could ever have entertained it. And it would be wholly unfair to suggest that it was the central part of the thought of Origen or any of his contemporaries. Like his teacher Clement, Origen is constantly emphasizing the importance of the example of Christ. 'He is called the lamb of God because His will and goodness, by which He rendered God propitious to men and bestowed the forgiveness of sins, rose up before the human race like the stainless and innocent offering of a lamb.'[2] 'Christ justifies only those who have entered on a new life by the example of His own resurrection, and have flung away the aged garments of their injustice and iniquity as being the cause of death.'[3] But we must remember that belief in the devil was very real to the Christian thinkers of the time. The whole pagan world believed in demons; to multitudes of Christians the greatest service which the new religion had rendered was deliverance from demons; and it was, therefore, quite natural to think of the ransom paid by Christ at His death as the arrangement by which the tyrannous grasp of the lord of all the demons was relaxed. And New Testament language was not wanting to lend support to the interpretation. What would have saved Origen and many others from the error would have been a more insistent recognition of the sacrifice of Christ as involved in His whole life, and not simply in the last stages of it.

The energy of the new experience of Christian freedom, indeed, naturally inclined minds even of a high order to welcome a view which seemed to do justice to what they felt every day with renewed thankfulness. Those who

[1] Origen, *in Matt.* xvi. 8. Cf. Rashdall *ad. loc., op. cit.*, pp. 259 f.
[2] Homilies on Josh. viii. 3. [3] *In Rom.* iv. 7.

can appreciate the psychological background will be more inclined to wonder that the theory went no farther than that it went so far. The Western Church, however, took a somewhat different course. The great thinkers of the West, many of them actually trained as lawyers and all of them influenced by the atmosphere of a church which had already come to pay much more attention to administration and status than did the Easterns, fastened upon Paul's great question, How can a sinner be pronounced just in the sight of God? And though they did not penetrate to the centre of his thought, and were more deeply influenced by his compelling phrases and the meanings which they found in them or brought to them, yet they saw that the question could not be answered by the suggestion of a successful bargain with the devil. It was not enough to ask, What can the devil do to man? They had to discover what God thinks of man. Their acquaintance with the law-courts and their knowledge of their own inner life combined to tell them that God can regard men only as condemned criminals before His judgement seat, who cannot be allowed to go free until the due penalty has been paid by them or by another in their behalf. Thus the Atonement was to them essentially the satisfaction of God.[1] But to them, as to the Greek theologian, the Atonement still involved the propitiatory death on the cross; their reading of Paul left no other conception open to them. It followed that Christ's death must in some way satisfy God; that is to say, it must remove His dissatisfaction and wrath towards sinners. To imagine that the holy God could ever cease to be angry with sin, or with the sinner, was impossible. It was, therefore, the work of Christ's death to dissociate man, collectively or individually, from his sin. Agreeably to the feeling of the time, this process was conceived in a forensic rather than a psychological fashion. It called into prominence all the New Testament expressions which appeared to emphasize the piacular character of Christ's sufferings. His death could only be thought of as propitiating God.

---

[1] ' You have offended, but you can still be reconciled; you are dealing with one who can be satisfied by you, and that with no great reluctance ' (Tert., *de paen.* 7). Tertullian does not forget the satisfaction which a man can pay for himself. ' In so far as you have not spared yourself, so far believe me, God will spare you ' (*ib.* 9).

And here there entered another doctrine, equally prominent to those who found in Paul the type and the explanation of their own inner history. This was the Fall. Christ had to redeem the whole human race, lost in the sin which had entered into the world with Adam's disobedience. To provide a reasoned account for redemption, the Greeks had laid more stress on the Incarnation than on the death of the Son of God. God became man, they had taught, to deify humanity. But to the Western teachers, more at home with forensic practice than with metaphysics, sin is something for which a penalty has to be paid. And the heavenly council chamber, just as Milton has described it, became a kind of law-court, in which the amount due is assessed, and the manner of paying it decided. To the Western theologians, Christ is the man who presents Himself as the sacrifice of the guilt-offering to God. They were not troubled by the fact that the guilt-offering, as it appears in the Old Testament, was not in their sense propitiatory at all, and that their argument, if interpreted with fidelity to the Old Testament sacrifices themselves, would have destroyed their theory. Until that sacrifice was paid, they held that the wrath of God remained on the children of disobedience, the whole sinful human race. Few passages reveal this manner of thinking better than a sentence of Augustine's : ' Since men through original sin were under this wrath, and that sin was the heavier and the more hurtful according as they had added greater or rather more sins, a mediator was necessary, that is, a reconciler, to placate this wrath by the offering of a unique sacrifice, of which all the sacrifices of the law and the prophets were shadows.'[1] Augustine goes on to point out that Christ was Himself free from original sin, and therefore able to offer this sacrifice, because born of a virgin.[2]

The most elaborate working out of this idea of propitiation in the West is that of Anselm. By his time, feudal conceptions were as powerful in theology as in political organization. Sin, therefore, meant a kind of treacherous

[1] *Enchiridion*, 33.
[2] ' Augustine distinctly explains the phrase " He was made sin for us " (2 Cor. v. 21) as meaning " He was made a sacrifice for us " (*Ench.*, 41), thus defining Paul's doctrine more clearly than does Paul himself, who does not often actually use the terminology of sacrifice ' (Franks, *op. cit.*, vol. i. p. 124).

unfaithfulness to man's duty of homage to God. Hence, to Anselm, the need for satisfaction. Complete obedience was man's recognized duty; and, therefore, even if in the future this complete obedience could be offered, it could never make up for the past. The position of man would be hopeless, were it not for Christ. But not even the complete obedience of Christ could make up for man's treachery. Only one thing, indeed, could do so, and that was something more than obedience. And this Christ presented. Christ was divine, and God could not have asked of Christ more than eternal conformity to His will. When Christ went beyond that, and actually gave Himself to death, this something more was attained; it could be presented, and accepted, as the required satisfaction; and man was thus freed from the ruinous past.

Aquinas, on the other hand, with a less political and more philosophical view of God, denied that He was bound to seek some satisfaction of His own honour, as a judge might feel bound to secure the satisfaction of the honour of his sovereign. God could have forgiven us without any satisfaction at all. But the passion of Christ incites our love, sets us an example, and wins for us grace and glory. It was therefore fitting (a favourite word with Aquinas) that He should satisfy for our sins, and this He did when He took upon Himself the penalty due for the sins of others.[1]

Most readers will feel almost as much unreality and artificiality in these dealings between God and Christ as in the older theory of a ransom to Satan. And no one can fail to be conscious of the gulf which separates these elaborate schemes of salvation, carefully adjusting the honour or holiness of God to a rebellious and ruined humanity, from the undeniable fact of forgiveness, lit up with the simple beauty of the picture of the Servant who loads Himself with the sins of His brothers, as we have it in both the Old Testament and the New. Not even the scholastic emphasis on love and grace can alter this impression. For

---

[1] 'Deus non habet aliquem superiorem . . . convenientius fuit, quod per passionem Christi liberaremur, quam per solam Dei voluntatem' (*Summa*, iii. 46). As Loofs says (*Dogmeng.*, p. 295), ' that even at the period of her full maturity the mediaeval Church had not reached a distinctive dogma of the work of Christ is shown by the explanations of Aquinas in the *Summa*. Aquinas employs in describing the work of Christ all the representations which tradition had offered, with the exception of the legal transaction with the devil.'

SACRIFICIAL DEATH OF CHRIST 225

love and grace themselves come to be simply elements in the scheme, playing their appointed part along with others, and so rendering the whole thing workable. The appearance of such a gulf is inevitable as soon as mediation is exchanged for satisfaction. But, none the less, the schoolmen were making an honest attempt to solve the problem within the limits set by the presuppositions of their time. The narrowness of those limits makes their achievement all the more remarkable. And, partly because of its clear articulation, partly because of the hesitation and indecision of other thinkers, the position of their statement, essentially homogeneous in spite of individual modifications, as the outstanding theory of the first fifteen centuries in the West, is assured.

But though it goes farther than those of the Greeks in taking account of the effect of the death of Christ on God rather than on the enemy of mankind, it does not ask an equally necessary question, What was the effect of that death on man? God might acquit man, but would man be able to live thereafter as an innocent man should live? If Christ's death only availed to reverse the sentence of condemnation, admittedly deserved, it was obviously far from securing man's salvation from sin. The scholastic teachers might have shown how this could be done, had they realized its necessity, by their doctrine of grace. They borrowed the term from the New Testament, but the New Testament content of the term, unfortunately, they seem never to have seriously studied. With them it becomes an external gift, with definite functions to perform, administered, one might almost say, like a kind of tonic, to ensure the due activities of the health already acquired. To do them justice, however, this was not the difficulty to them that it seems to us. To secure and preserve this salvation was the business and prerogative of the Church. Once inside the Church, and able to benefit by her sacraments and penitential discipline, the believer was assured of all the grace he needed. For although Western thought was far from faithful to every detail of Augustine's system, and gave to good works (especially in the controversy with Augustine's great disciple, Luther) an emphasis which was more than semi-Pelagian, the lack of good works could always be made up for in the faithful by more diligent use of the varied ordinances of the Church. The general sentence of condemnation on all the sinful race having been revoked, the Church could be trusted to secure the rest.

This was enough for most mediaeval thinkers. It was not enough for one of the most original and 'modern' of them, Abelard, a younger contemporary of Anselm. Abelard threw over the idea of the satisfaction of God, and regarded the work of Christ as a revelation of love. The love of God, as Abelard was the first of mediaeval thinkers to urge, was indeed the source of the whole process of reconciliation. Christ's work was the manifestation of this love, the means by which it could make its saving appeal to men. God did not need to be satisfied. He wanted to be able to forgive. Christ's death made men feel that horror of their sin which alone could make them seek forgiveness. And when that forgiveness was sought by men, it could not be withheld by God. 'When God's Son took our nature on Himself, teaching us both by precept and example, He persevered till death, and more largely bound us to Himself by love. . . . And so our redemption is that supreme love manifested in our case by the passion of Christ, who not merely delivers us from the bondage of sin, but also acquires for us the liberty of the sons of God, so that we may fulfil all things from love rather than from fear of Him.'[1] The only ransom needed, or possible, was deliverance from the paralysing power of sin which prevented men from believing that any escape from it by way of repentance and forgiveness was practicable or even desirable. This was in reality to work back from the apostles as they were and still are generally understood to the simplicity of the Gospels ; or, rather from Christ's death, regarded as something detached, to the whole teaching and activity which culminated in His death. He demanded faith ; but this faith involved no assent to any view of His atoning person and work. It was simply confidence in Himself and His power to declare the guilt of past sins annulled, and their influence over future conduct broken. This faith, as Abelard was psychologist enough to see, would doubtless be enormously stimulated by the spectacle

[1] Abelard, *Expos. in Rom.*, Lib. ii. (Ed. Migne, col. 836 A).

SACRIFICIAL DEATH OF CHRIST 227

of the cross. But the cross simply magnified the impression which had been made on the contemporaries of Jesus by His life of unselfish service and devotion. It was a new and mighty inducement to them to break with their sin and throw themselves for mercy and forgiveness on the love which that life had made plain.

The influence of Abelard was much smaller than the originality and, we may add, the profound loyalty to Scripture of his teaching. To suggest that Christ's death was not in itself a satisfaction seemed heretical; to identify salvation with a change of attitude and conduct that did not require ecclesiastical ministration to make it effective was to endanger the functions and privileges of the Church; and to minimize the ' sacrificial ' validity of Christ's death was to neglect, as it appeared to Abelard's contemporaries, the plain implications of biblical texts. The general mind of the Christianity of the time found more satisfying expression in Aquinas.

The statement of Aquinas, already quoted,[1] had two great advantages over that of Abelard, though these were both more readily appreciable by theologians than by plain men. It seemed to give more weight to the doctrinal statements of the New Testament; and it recognized that sin had brought a deep disability on the human race, from which, therefore, the human race as a whole needed to be delivered by some act of universal significance. At the same time, by leaving a place for the healing efficacy of the Church it emphasized the value of grace, as something that came to man from without. It was necessary that God should be satisfied; but, once that satisfaction had taken place, God could show Himself, through the appointed channels, the Father of light and love. Yet we cannot but see that Abelard was the nearer to the spirit of the New Testament, for the texts which he appeared to neglect were expounded by his critics in accordance with a mistaken theory of sacrifice; and Abelard, in refusing to interpret sacrifice as satisfaction in the forensic or governmental sense, and in going back to the direct appeal to ' Him who loved me and gave Himself for me,' avoided what had become a traditional anachronism in the Catholic theology.

[1] p. 224.

228 ALTAR, CROSS, AND COMMUNITY

The age that followed Aquinas did little to advance the special conception of the Atonement. In the gradual but sure decay of the scholastic theology, men's minds were torn between the controversies of realism and nominalism, and both the parties were concerned with other questions than the sacrifice of Christ. The Scotists, indeed, asserting that whatever God's will determined, as by some arbitrary fiat, was therefore right, freed the exponents of the sacrificial satisfaction of Christ from the necessity of justifying it either to the conscience or the reason. Such a dangerously short cut, however, was far from commending itself to Luther. Luther, whose views on the Atonement have had an immense influence on the whole of evangelical thought, was less of an original thinker than has sometimes been supposed. Like Wesley, he was content to take from others the systems by which he worked, so far as he found it possible to work by them at all. When they collided with his experience they had to be reconstructed. This explains the measure both of his acceptance and his rejection of the scholastic theory of the Atonement.[1]

That Christ's death was primarily a sacrifice, and that His sacrifice was primarily in His death, Luther never doubted. Nor did he doubt that the merits of that sacrificial death availed for the whole race. But while he gave due weight to the question that was fundamental for Anselm and Aquinas, his own inner conflicts pressed on him the question that was fundamental for Abelard, How does the death of Christ affect me? He could not answer the question as Abelard did, just because he felt

---

[1] Luther revolted against the doctrine which the schoolmen had derived from Aristotle (the 'philosopher,' as they loved to call him), that good works might help a man to reach God. He fell back on the teaching of Augustine that grace alone could lift our fallen and ruined nature. To Luther the doctrine of original sin was vital. 'The devil had brought us all into disobedience, so that we lay under the wrath of God, condemned to perpetual damnation; and it was Christ who won the favour of God by placating His wrath.' God's law must receive satisfaction. 'Therefore, since that satisfaction was impossible for us, He has ordained one for us in our place, who should take upon Himself all punishments that we had deserved and fulfil the law for us, and thus turn them from us and reconcile God's wrath' (quoted in Franks, op. cit.; see also the Larger Catechism, ii. 2, 27 f.). To change the emphasis from God's private satisfaction to the vindication of public right was a distinct gain; but that satisfaction is still a matter of the vicarious bearing of punishment or suffering, to Luther as to Augustine.

SACRIFICIAL DEATH OF CHRIST

that Christ's death was sacrificial; Christ was the victim slain for man's sin. On the other hand, he could not take refuge in the Catholic view that, once God was satisfied, all needful grace could be given through the Church. Some personal dealing was necessary.

The place for this Luther found in faith. Faith, however, was not to him what it was to Abelard. It was not a simple reliance on the love of God in Christ for forgiveness. It was a more complicated thing, which he thought he had found in Paul. By Christ's death God was reconciled to the race. So far Aquinas had gone. But this did not mean that He was thereby reconciled to any and every individual, such as Aquinas himself or Luther. Before this could take place the individual must by faith appropriate the merits of that reconciling death. That is to say, he must, by a mental act, transfer his sins to Christ, or recognize that his own sins, in common with the sins of the whole world, were borne by Christ on the cross, and received their due punishment at Christ's death there. He is then pronounced righteous by God, and the righteousness which is thus 'imputed' to him, which is indeed not his own, but Christ's, becomes actual through a further exercise of faith. The good works, which even if they had existed, could have done nothing for him in his previous life of sin, are now naturally produced in him, as faith seats Christ at the centre of his new life. But even now he places no reliance on them. They could be of no avail without that saving faith in Christ from which they spring, and which alone can keep him in the favour and love of God. Faith in Christ is thus no more simply reliance on Christ, but self-identification with Christ, first, as Christ is the bearer and bearer away of sins, suffering their penalty in His death, and secondly, as He is the perfectly righteous and obedient Son of God.

In this brief account of Luther's teaching we have purposely laid emphasis on the elements which connect him with Aquinas and the accepted Catholic theology on the one hand, and with the main current of Protestant and evangelical doctrine on the other. Luther contributed to the doctrine of Aquinas his stress on saving faith. But this was not his only contribution. To evangelical thought the sacrificial death of Christ was not merely a satisfaction;

it was a punishment. This thought was not unfamiliar to the Catholics. Satisfaction and the endurance of penalty lie very close to one another. But while it was easy to speak of Christ as suffering and dying for men, it was not so easy to speak of Him as being punished for them. Luther, however, had felt the guilt and pressure of sin as few great theologians seem to have felt it since Augustine. Sin, to him, was something that called aloud for punishment. Therefore, if he was not punished for it by actual and eternal ruin, some one must be punished for it instead. Who could that be except Christ? Thus the satisfaction wrought on the cross was penal and vicarious. Looking back on the cross, the sinner knew that all the sins he had ever committed, all the sins that any one had ever committed, were heaped on that guiltless victim. 'The Lord hath laid on Him the iniquities of us all.'

It is easy to see how this conception of vicarious punishment might harden into an exaggerated and even grotesque schematism, which should emphasize the exact equivalence between the sins of the world and the sufferings of Christ, and would allow no merit in any of the ordinarily accepted virtues of mankind, either before or after a knowledge of the fact of the great sacrifice. Indeed, that sacrifice, so interpreted, would end by eliminating virtue altogether as a factor in human life, since before the exercise of faith in Christ's death there could be no virtue in the true sense of the word, but only what Augustine called *splendida vitia*; and after it there were only the merits of Christ in those who had been saved by it. Most men are better and saner than the extreme statements of their creeds would suggest. This was certainly true of the men of the Evangelical Revival, both on its Arminian and its Calvinistic side. Indeed, we cannot doubt that many of them would have repudiated the logical consequences of their own tenets. As if to illustrate the constant element of paradox in religion, the Arminians, who were never tired of depicting the wrath of God as resting on Christ in His death on the cross, yet exhausted language, in sermons and hymns alike, in their adoration of His pardoning love to all the sinful race, even though they held that, for the sake of the race, Christ believed Himself for one awful moment forsaken by His Father. The Calvinists, convinced that

SACRIFICIAL DEATH OF CHRIST 231

the eternal lot of man was fixed for him from his birth, were untiring in their efforts alike for social improvement and individual salvation.

The Evangelical Revival added nothing directly to the doctrine of the Atonement, unless we call this insistence on Christ's salvation of men by His sufferings for them an addition. But the sinner who was saved by Christ's death and sufferings might be, and ought to be, assured of his salvation by the Holy Spirit. The Spirit bore witness with his spirit that he was now a child of God. And it produced in him those fruits of righteousness which could assure him and others that his sins really were forgiven, and that he was not the simple victim of 'enthusiasm.' This insistence on the actual consciousness of salvation, which could become explicit in the believer, and could be substantiated by convincing demonstration to others, was the most arresting and individual thing in the preaching of early Methodism. It gave as much offence on the side of doctrine as the 'field preaching' and its remarkable results on the side of practice. But its critics were slow to do justice to Wesley's defence against the charge of 'enthusiasm' or wilful self-deception. Any one might imagine himself purged by the entrance of the Spirit from his sins; but no one who had not really been so entered could exhibit a life of holiness; and that was what Wesley claimed for the genuine Christian.[1]

---

[1] Like so many other characteristic Methodist doctrines, this is admirably expressed in a hymn by Charles Wesley:

> How can a sinner know
>   His sins on earth forgiven? . . .
> What we have felt and seen
>   With confidence we tell,
> And publish to the sons of men
>   The signs infallible. . . .
> Whate'er our pardoning Lord
>   Commands, we gladly do;
> And guided by His sacred word
>   We all His steps pursue.

To urge such a proof as this of the reality of his conviction might well make any man tremble. But in his well-known sermons on the 'Witness of the Spirit,' Wesley lays it down in the clearest fashion that the 'testimony of our own spirit is the consciousness of the fruit of the Spirit.' Wesley's insistence upon morality has seldom been adequately appreciated. Without morality, and morality in the sense of entire loyalty to Christ's two great commandments, there could be no witness of the Spirit, nor anything for the Spirit to witness to. The same reliance on conduct as a proof of sincerity is seen in his *Rules of Society*, in which it is stated that the only

This insistence on the work of the Spirit made the work of the Church, as the Catholic understood it, needless. The redeemed sinner needed no ecclesiastical ministration of grace; he was as little dependent on the sacraments of the Church as he was concerned about the validity of ministerial orders. And though the communities of the Reformed Churches, with the striking exception of the Quakers, provided carefully for a definite and separated ministry, it was in every case pastoral and regulative rather than mediatory and sacerdotal.

In the last century the evangelical conception has been attacked from many sides, but the main tendency of thought has been on the lines of Abelard. The most important and elaborate work has been that of Ritschl. Ritschl, whose writings have had a larger effect on the doctrine of the Atonement than those of any other writer in the nineteenth century, held that the idea of the vicarious punishment of Christ in any and every form breaks down upon the rock of Christ's personal innocence. His priestly work must, therefore, be subordinated to His prophetic work.[1] We are justified through God's taking a favourable view of our case—that is, by adopting us. The knowledge that God is our Father makes us His sons. This knowledge Christ gives us. He is conscious 'of standing in the closest possible relation to God and of being called to receive others into the same relation, so that their sins shall present no obstacle to their trust in God and to God's communion with them.'[2] Ritschl was at one with Abelard in opposing an interpretation of Christ's sacrifice which, however appealing and powerful, is not that which Christ, the great mediator, has left us Himself; or, in other words, where others spoke of expiation and satisfaction, Ritschl

---

condition for entrance into membership is the desire to be saved from one's sins; but that desire, he adds, must be evidenced by doing all possible good to one's neighbours, avoiding all kinds of harm, and making use of the 'means of grace.' Here, indeed, the theologian in Wesley might have asked how this could be done, unless the salvation had actually taken place. But the theologian was never allowed to interfere with the moralist.

[1] This does not follow, unless we make the double identification of Christ as a priest with Christ as a victim, and of Christ's death with a penal infliction of suffering. But it cannot be denied that Ritschl had found reason for making these identifications in the views which were in possession of the field in his day.

[2] Ritschl, *Justification and Reconciliation*, Engl. Tr., vol. iii., p. 542.

SACRIFICIAL DEATH OF CHRIST 233

spoke of reconciliation and fellowship. The clearest statement in quite recent times of this contrast has been given by Rashdall.[1] But it will not be denied that, in the main, evangelical theology, at any rate in its more generally accepted statements, has remained true to the sacrificial conception of both Catholicism and Protestantism, and that the question which it still suggests is that which the majority of the great Christian thinkers have set themselves to answer, How can we express the effect of the death of Christ, regarded as a sacrifice to God, on God and on man?

From the point of view of our argument, however, the problem demands a somewhat different statement. That the sacrifice of Christ is to be identified with His death, and that the altar on which that sacrifice was offered was the cross, is an assumption which was not made, as it would appear, by the New Testament writers. What we have really to ask is how the mission of Christ reconciled sinful man and the sinless and holy God. This may be stated in three ways—as a theological question : How can we fit the New Testament language and conceptions into one satisfactory formula? As a moral one : How can the action of divine love, anger, and forgiveness be joined into one harmonious process? Or as psychological : How can we express in terms of atonement or reconciliation the deliverance from sin which the Christian actually experiences?

---

[1] *Op. cit.* Many readers will feel that Paul is not in such strong antagonism to the simpler teaching of the Gospels or the author's own beliefs as this book suggests, or that Paul is so close to the ' hard-shell ' side of Luther. But its contention that Dale's exposition of the Atonement in his widely read work is self-contradictory and untrue to the teaching of Christ will prove very difficult to answer. Rashdall explains Peter's words in Acts iv. 12 to mean ' There is none other ideal given among men by which we may be saved except the moral ideal which Christ taught by His words, and illustrated by His life and death of love ; and there is none other help so great in the attainment of that ideal as the belief in God as He has been supremely revealed in Him who so taught and lived and died. So understood, the self-sacrificing life which was consummated on the cross has indeed power to take away the sin of the whole world.' If Wesley himself had not been previously led to suspect erroneous doctrine, he might have accepted this statement of the moral influence of Christ's saving work. But here Rashdall is as much an individualist as Dale. He does not recognize that Christ, as a mediator, is more than an example and an inspiration. It is perfectly true that for forgiveness nothing is necessary but repentance. But the repentance which precedes forgiveness, and the works which follow it, are the result, if our own argument is correct, of the new relation in which Christ sets us to God.

As to the first of these, it is not necessary to be a believer in verbal inspiration to recognize in Gospels and Epistles the most illuminating as well as perhaps the most baffling documents on this subject that have been produced. More than this, they have an authoritative character that has never been equalled. But their authors would be the last to claim that this authority is absolute, and the first to insist that their conclusions must commend themselves to the moral judgement of their readers. Our own attempt to answer the question has been made in the two previous chapters.

The second demands more careful consideration. The sacrificial view of Christ's death has for some time been undeniably losing its hold, as we have already been reminded, upon large numbers of those who have been brought up in Christian circles. This is due in part to the arbitrariness and artificiality which many have come, rightly or wrongly, to find in it, and to the wide distance which separates sacrificial categories from modern habits of thought; but still more to the moral difficulties which are felt to be inherent in it. Apart from the question (psychological rather than moral) whether love and anger are consistent, and whether God, if He genuinely loves mankind, can be angry with it or wish to punish it, there are more serious difficulties. Can the punishment even of eternal death be rightly withheld because another has suffered in the place of the sinners? Or how can we suppose that perfect justice would ever wish to deny what perfect love would bestow, or vice versa? Or could either justice or love consent that the innocent should ever be punished at all? The time has gone by when an act can be considered moral because God is alleged on some authority to have performed it. Any conception of God is bound to suffer which cannot maintain itself before the bar of man's moral consciousness.

The third setting of the problem will, however, seem of chief importance to most persons. Religion is increasingly construed in terms of psychology. And rightly so; for religion is a matter of experience, and must, therefore, admit psychological criteria. If we desire to bring about the relief of conscience and the sense of deliverance from

SACRIFICIAL DEATH OF CHRIST

sin, we must ask under what conditions these results can be expected. How far does any doctrine of the Atonement that may be offered to us conform to these conditions? Does this sense of relief follow one or more than one presentation of Christ's work? And if the preaching of this doctrine or that sometimes fails and sometimes succeeds, what is the common element whose presence or absence must be held to determine the result?

If we now apply the first of these three tests to the doctrine of the sacrificial death of Christ, we observe that as soon as we press the analogy between Christ's work and a sacrificial death it breaks down. The sacrifice is passive; what is vital in the self-surrender of Christ is the love which led Him to that great act. The sacrifice is offered by the worshipper in his own behalf through the mediation of a priest; Christ gave Himself, with no priest or intermediary, and on behalf of men who, so far from wishing to approach God, were alienated from Him. The barrier was not merely in what they had done. It was in their hearts. The analogy is still weaker if we apply it to the expiatory view of the Atonement. For the victim, though it might be said to render God propitious, was not regarded (as Jewish writers knew) as satisfying God's desire for blood, but man's wish for cleansing by the shedding or sprinkling of blood.[1] Still less could it be said to be punished in the place of the worshipper. It was killed, but it was not made to suffer; and to any suffering which might accompany its slaughter no one paid any attention or made any reference. The only conception of sacrifice which fits either the practice of the Jewish altar or the New Testament allusions is that of reconciliation. The death of the sacrificial animal, and the loving and filial obedience of Christ, carried up to the extreme point of self-renunciation, are the means by which man and God can be brought together.

Secondly, the questions suggested by the theory before us from the side of morals raise the subject of retributive justice, which is only another name for punishment. God, as the personification of moral law, has been outraged by

[1] This will only be doubted by those who wish to interpret in the crudest possible manner the Old Testament references to the blood as the portion of the sacrifice specially set apart for God. See p. 104.

human disobedience; and that outrage demands satisfaction. This belief, as we have noticed, is not essential to the validity of the rite of sacrifice, either inside or outside Judaism; but it is prominent in the theological writers who have interpreted Christ's death as a sacrifice, and therefore it cannot be put on one side. Retributive justice takes us as far back as Aristotle,[1] and the still older law of an eye for an eye and a tooth for a tooth and the general principle, which never seems to die, of reprisals. In a court of summary justice, where an act is regarded as an isolated event for which the agent is entirely responsible, the principle may be roughly defensible. But in any careful discussion it must be admitted that acts cannot be regarded as isolated. Behind the act lie the motive and the intention, and behind these again all the complexities of the upbringing of the agent and the standards of the society or group of which he is a member. The guilt of the same act, in one set of circumstances, may be very slight; in another, heinous. It is impossible to establish a quantitative standard by which the act and its punishment can be equated.[2] It has been replied that at the bar of the supreme moral law all human beings deserve death. The reply is easier to accept in the study than in the marketplace or the street. But, apart from this, we have to ask whether God, as the representative of complete holiness, can be 'satisfied' by the death of a sinner, however guilty. The only thing that can 'satisfy' God is goodness. It might be necessary for God to doom some sinners to death in order to induce others to amend their ways; but in that case the death of the sinner would really be deterrent, not retributive. It might also be necessary for Him to inflict suffering on the sinner in order to induce him to amend his own ways. In that case, the suffering would be remedial, and it would not be death. Retributive justice, when neither deterrent nor remedial, is nothing but vindictive. Such 'justice' may be tolerated, though deprecated, among men; it cannot be attributed to God. But in that case the whole theory of the need of satisfying God falls to the ground, and we are brought back to think

---

[1] *Nic. Eth.*, bk. v., ch. 4.
[2] This consideration vitiates Aristotle's 'arithmetical' argument, *loc. cit.*

of sacrifice as not punishment at all, either for the victim or the offerer.

But surely, it will be argued, God must punish sin. Everything depends on what is meant by punishment. If every act must be judged by the end it is hoped to secure, we must ask what is the end of this divine punishment of sin. If the end is deterrent or remedial, the punishment is intelligible and possibly moral. The only thing to be decided is the likelihood that the end will be reached by such means. But such 'punishment' is not penal, in the ordinary sense of the word. It is not inflicted to take vengeance on the sinner, but to diminish the extent of the sin. On the other hand, if it is properly penal—that is, if it involves an element which is neither deterrent nor remedial—it falls under the *lex talionis* again. It is impossible on ethical grounds to suppose that God could inflict suffering and death in order to repay those who had injured Him, or for any reason except to serve the cause of goodness and to overcome evil. The case against the penal aspect is even stronger when it is joined, as in the case of the Atonement it usually has been joined, to the substitutionary. Some rude and elementary instinct of fairness is certainly satisfied when the wrong-doer is made to suffer, however hard it is to carry out with any exactness the sentence 'Be done by as you did.' But no such instinct can be satisfied when some one else is made to suffer. Such a misdirection of justice, except among savages, would only rouse indignation. There is but one justification for substitutionary suffering—the possibility that the spectacle of another, enduring the pain caused by my own wrong-doing, may shame me into penitence and may win me to the love which made such endurance possible.

To argue in this way may seem equivalent to emasculating the whole idea of justice. What is justice, it will be asked, save doing by others as they themselves have done? The real answer is that true justice always takes the forward and never the backward look. It is concerned with the future, not with the past; with the goodness to be produced in the sinner, not with the punishment which may make his heart still harder and his hatred of goodness more deep-seated. To treat a man justly, to 'do the right thing by him,' is to act towards him so that he will be the most likely to do right himself.[1] That is why, in the profound argument of Paul in Romans ch. iii., God's justice is manifested by the death of Christ. That death is the means by which God makes it possible for man to do right, when the flesh and the law combined to make him to do wrong. Justice is not the antithesis to mercy. When justice and mercy are seen in their true proportions, they are one and the same thing. The work of justice is not to punish the guilty, or even to let the innocent go free; the work of mercy is not, by punishing the guiltless, to let the guilty go free; the work of both is to deliver the sinner from his sin and reconcile him to the goodness he has rejected. Complete justice is doubtless only possible for God; but human life will not be moralized till men try to be just as their Father in heaven is just.

The discussion of the moral aspect of the death of Christ has led us insensibly within the domains of the psychological. Justice consists in carrying out a course of conduct which will have a certain effect on the mind of those who witness or experience it. That effect may be described as threefold—loathing or horror for sin; gratitude to the person who has delivered the sinner from his load and its consequences; and the resolution to avoid evil courses in the future.[2] But how is this effect to be brought about? No single answer can be expected to such a question. Human nature is too complex. The same emotions can be roused by the most different incentives. The same incentives will at different times rouse the most different emotions. Punishment itself may harden or soften. It may produce repentance or remorse or defiance. Kindness may overcome resistance or nourish contempt. In such a welter of opposing possibilities any guidance from

---

[1] Aristotle's discussion of justice, noticed above, was preceded by the more penetrating treatment of Plato in the *Republic*—too penetrating and subtle to have influenced any but the minority of the like-minded. Plato throws over the ' repayment ' theory in every form, and decides that justice, whether in the community or the individual character, consists in that inward harmony that enables all constituent parts of the common life —the faculties of direction, control, or acquisition—to attain each its own proper excellence by due co-operation with the rest.

[2] These three elements can be well studied in Ezekiel (ch. xxxvi.); they are implied in Isa. liii.; the second and third are prominent in Paul; but when Paul is thinking, as he generally is, of his own mental history, he is inclined to place the first, in point of time, before the recognition of the work of Christ; cf. Rom. vii. 23, 24.

SACRIFICIAL DEATH OF CHRIST

psychology might seem hopeless. But this is not the case. When the same treatment has differing results, it is because of differences in those who inflict or those who receive and endure. The appeal of the spectacle of another bearing the suffering which I have deserved or caused has always been powerful. One of the strongest arguments for chastity is ' Your sin may bring its consequences, not on you, but on your innocent wife and child.' But we can go farther. Human nature will always be attracted by offers of friendship or help or deliverance, if it has reason to believe the offers sincere and likely to be effective. The infliction of pain, however richly deserved, will only repel unless the sinner recognizes, in the person who inflicts it, some friendliness or goodwill quite independent of the wish to cause suffering. The sight of another's suffering always tends to rouse sympathy, if any social bond is felt between the sufferer and the spectator, and with that sympathy is produced resentment against the cause of the suffering. If, however, I recognize that the cause is my own wrong-doing, resentment and sympathy combined, recoiling, so to speak, upon myself, produce a determination to reform; and this draws me with a new and subtle force to him in whom I see the suffering my own misconduct has brought about.

The effect of punishment is more simple and less certain. Its appeal is frankly to the self-regarding side of consciousness—the fear of pain and love of ease. The thought of punishment simply suggests a calculation. Is the satisfaction I desire worth the threatened or expected painful result? It depends on the answer to this question whether a man forgoes the satisfaction or, to use Bentham's phrase, pockets the consequences. The fear of punishment may thus result, as a deterrent, in preventing the performance of many wrong acts; but it has in itself no moral value, except in so far as continued turning away from certain acts from fear of their consequences may induce a habit of self-control and dislike of the acts for their own sake.[1]

---

[1] When the punishment expected or threatened is eternal suffering it is more difficult to gauge the psychological effects. On many evil-doers, even though they profess no doubts as to its certainty, it appears to exercise no influence. The history of religious revivals and a study of conversion suggests that, whatever power it may have as a deterrent for future conduct (and this it is, of course, impossible to estimate), the dread of it

A penal system is thus entirely different from the appeal based on the suffering of the innocent for the guilty.

The effect of all this, in the brief analysis we have given of it, may seem cold and hard; in reality, its emotional possibilities are enormous. We cannot, indeed, assert that they are universal.[1] Many persons are too unimaginative, and many others are too much set on their own immediate comfort or their other concerns, to be touched by this spectacle when it is presented to them. There is no type of the preaching of the cross which is universally effective. But the unimaginative, it is safe to say, could be moved by no appeal save that of personal and immediate pain; and that appeal would be neither moral nor abiding. The emotions which fire and transform the soul, till it glows with indignation at the approach of selfishness and greed, and flings itself enthusiastically into some generous and holy cause, are the very emotions which are naturally roused when we watch one who was wounded for our iniquities and bruised for our transgressions.

We are thus brought back to that deeper view of sacrifice which does not consist in the attempt to appease God, or avoid punishment, but is the means of being reconciled to Him. True reconciliation is precisely that hatred for sin, that longing to be united to goodness, which we have seen to be the result of the work of Christ. We have learnt in the present chapter why this, the dominant element in the life of Christ as most of the earliest Christians understood it, was replaced by less profound and moral ideas of expiation and penalty and substitution, and how the expressions, so frequent and touching, in the New Testament writers, ' by His death,' ' by His blood,' were changed into the forbidding terms of a legal document. And we have seen to what perplexing consequences this process of thought inevitably leads. The clue to the understanding of the Atonement as the world's great sacrifice is not the

---

will lead to horror for the sins of the past. In mediaeval Catholicism the doctrine was modified by that of purgatory, which led to a widespread practice of religious bargaining rather than actual avoidance or loathing of sin. When Protestantism destroyed the belief in purgatory, it did not find hell a sufficiently powerful motive even to preserve its own adherents from wilful sin. The story of Faust, as treated both by Marlowe and by Goethe, shows how ready a man may be, until some special crisis overwhelms the imagination, to ' jump the life to come.'

[1] Cf. Matt. xiii. 19 ff.

SACRIFICIAL DEATH OF CHRIST

Levitical sacrifice as interpreted by the Christian thought of any age, but the impulse, as widespread as mankind itself, to find the mediation by which man can obtain ready access to God.

To suggest that the traditional interpretation of Calvary, which in one modification or another has characterized every age of Christianity and most schools of Christian thought, is founded on a misconception may seem a piece of unpardonable boldness. But if the argument of the two preceding chapters is correct, we can be led to no other conclusion. And we can see the way in which the mistake, as it now appears, came into being, the services it has rendered, and the reason for its perpetuation. Special emphasis on Christ's death was almost inevitable; and when so emphasized and isolated, it was naturally regarded as propitiatory. And as the Christian ministry came more and more to be described in terms of the Levitical priesthood, the Levitical or pseudo-Levitical interpretation of Christ's death lay all the nearer to hand. Once firmly embodied in Christian theology, the doctrine could hardly be questioned, for theology has always shown a marked tendency to conservatism. The points which have divided Christians have been for the most part subtle and of secondary importance. Athanasius, indeed, forced the world to see that a single 'iota' involved an essential difference of outlook and belief. But to-day those who are the most anxious to heal the 'unhappy divisions' of the Church know that, as far as the main doctrines enshrined in the creeds are concerned, there is little difficulty. Protestants took over far more of the Catholic faith than they ever thought of rejecting. And even when the traditional beliefs seemed open to every kind of objection, as in regard to the inerrancy of Scripture, the virgin birth, the omnipotence of God, the depravity of the whole human race, the fore-ordination of man to eternal bliss or eternal damnation, they held their ground as if by virtue of their having once been accepted by large sections of the Church. Protestants have acted consistently on the maxim of Bacon, which every Catholic would support: 'Reason, not to criticize, but to substantiate and defend.'

It is not surprising, therefore, that this view of the Atonement persisted. But there was another reason.

It allowed full weight to a factor in human experience which Christian theology, to do it justice, has never permitted itself to forget—human guilt. All theories like that of Abelard, which have shrunk from the substitutionary view, have had to meet one serious challenge: 'You are making light of sin.' The doctrine that Christ bore the punishment due to the actual sin of the individual was felt to answer to that deep consciousness of sin which no theology can venture to neglect. The more a man felt his sin and its ill-desert, the more he thought of his deliverer, if he could find one, as bearing it; and the more natural it was for him to say, 'It was there, on the cross.' We may use hard words about the substitutionary theory; there is one thing we cannot say of it—that it dulls a man's mind to the heinousness of his own past. It is true that the doctrine has sometimes been made to express a less penetrating experience: my sin deserved punishment; Jesus bore the punishment, and so I am free. But the real nerve of the doctrine is not in such words as those. 'My soul ... knows her guilt was there.' If it be the function of religious instruction to make men feel their sin, there can be none more effective and eloquent than that which bids them 'see all their sins on Jesus laid.' The thought that 'my sins were laid on Jesus' is not necessarily connected with a substitutionary doctrine at all.[1] But it has been so connected for centuries, and this connexion, constantly looked on as axiomatic, has been the chief and the most creditable reason for its vitality.

But to return. This long discussion has made it possible to distinguish between the doctrines of the Church on the subject of Christ's sacrifice, left even till now without authoritative definition, and the references to that sacrifice in the New Testament. We can see, too, how far these doctrines travelled from the actual sacrifices of the ethnic and the Hebrew religions. Between those sacrifices and the redeeming work of Christ there are wide differences—differences which are all the wider if we interpret that

---

[1] This has become clear from our consideration of Isa. liii. (p. 150). Sin is not like punishment, however often the two have been confused. One person may bear the sin of another, feeling its shame *with* the sinner, and more deeply, perhaps, than the sinner himself. The penalty is the only thing that he can bear *instead of* the guilty individual.

SACRIFICIAL DEATH OF CHRIST

work in the terms of the theology of the schools. But when we are content to study the sacrifices by themselves, apart from what later ages have imagined about them, and to disentangle their central purpose, we can detect the glow of light which is shed from their ancient altars on the Galilean peasant. He knew that His task lay apart from all rites and altars ; but what the men who built those altars had sought for—the transference of the holiness of the consecrated bullock or goat to their own lives—He accomplished through a sinless sequence of love and self-sacrifice, that human beings, purified from uncleanness and sin, might enter with boldness into the holy place.

X

THE EUCHARIST AND THE MASS

In the last two chapters we have considered the theology of sacrifice. We have observed how, in the thought of the Christian Church, the world-wide conception of sacrifice as the accomplishment of mediation between man and God for the attainment of some end desired by one or both was effected in Christ, and more particularly in Christ's death. But sacrifice is an act, and not the mere thought about an act; and to understand its real place in Christianity we must turn from the controversies of the theologians to the worship of the congregation. The controversies often broke into the thought and affected the practice of the congregation. In times of sectarian hatred and persecution a formula might become a matter of life and death, and would exercise a strong influence, positively or negatively, on liturgical phrases and even acts. Doctrine and worship have always influenced one another. What worship demands, doctrine will sooner or later supply. But the abstract and fine-drawn doctrines of the Atonement were little understood by the simple Christian. What is felt in religion is inseparably connected with what is seen and heard.

Christianity is a religion of but one sacrifice. Yet that sacrifice, never to be repeated, is repeated endlessly. The service has many names—the Communion, the Eucharist, the Mass; yet from an early age the term sacrifice has existed with the rest. The Eucharist was not a rite enforced from above; like others, it grew from beneath, and then was rationalized and systematized by authority.[1] Strikingly as the first Christians outside as well as inside Palestine were

---

[1] Even if we were to accept the theory that the Eucharist, in the general form given in 1 Cor. xi., Matt. xxvi., and Luke xxii., was founded by Paul, the earlier gatherings from which sprang both Eucharist and Love-feast, no less religious because intensely social, went back to the very birth of the Church. There is no reason for doubting the narrative of Acts ii. 42, 45, 46.

influenced by Jewish practices and by the Jewish liturgy,[1] the earliest and most characteristic Christian service was not a repetition or modification of the worship of the Synagogue; it was more than prayer, praise, and instruction. A memorial of the redeeming love of the Master, it became inevitably a family gathering, in which the union of the Master with His disciples was as real as that of the disciples with one another.

We might well have expected that so central a rite would have been mentioned more frequently in the earliest Christian writings as we have them collected in the New Testament. Beyond the definite accounts of its institution in the passages already referred to, we have hardly an allusion to it. This can only be explained by the fact that none of the New Testament writers set out to give a formal account of Christian practice, or even a careful analysis of Christian experience. Even so, it is curious that they should not have appealed oftener to what must have been so familiar and precious to their readers. It is really impossible to suppose that to Paul or John the Eucharist was the great event of the week; still less that its due administration by 'apostolically ordained officials' was the mark of the true Church. Perhaps, like Paul, the other writers also were a little out of touch with the main currents of popular thought and devotion.[2] But there is no doubt of the importance, even in that period, of the Eucharist. Apart from the brief but unmistakable reference in Pliny's well-known letter to Trajan,[3] both the Didache and Justin give a detailed description of the service. The former, which places the communion in the cup before that in the bread, and implies that the Agape, or Love-feast, and the Eucharist were still parts of the same service, if not identical,[4] gives the words of the liturgy recommended,

---

[1] See Oesterley and Box, *Rabbinical and Mediaeval Judaism* (1920), p. 142.

[2] It has already been remarked that the sub-apostolic age gives us few echoes of characteristically Pauline preaching. The same thing is true of the Petrine and Johannine writings and the Epistle to the Hebrews (see p. 200). Barnabas, Clement, and the Didache would suggest that the Epistle of James was more typical of the regular Christian thought and preaching of the time.

[3] *Ep.* x. 96; *c.* 194 A.D. After assembling to sing a hymn to Christ and to bind themselves to a moral life—*sacramento obstringere*—' they are accustomed to depart and to meet again to take food.'

[4] 'After they have eaten what they want' (sec. 10).

246 ALTAR, CROSS, AND COMMUNITY

which is entirely one of thanksgiving; but in a later passage, confession and reconciliation with adversaries are enjoined before the actual participation, 'in order that your sacrifice may be pure . . . in order that your sacrifice may not be defiled; for this is the sacrifice mentioned by the Lord, "in every place and time to bring Me a pure sacrifice."'[1] No reference is made in this account of the Supper and the death of Christ. Justin's account is more detailed.[2] The service as he describes it has six parts—the introduction of the newly baptized, the kiss of peace, reading from the memoirs of the apostles and instruction, the production of the elements, the thanksgiving, and the participation. Justin does not use the term sacrifice. Here he is loyal to the language of the New Testament, which never uses the term of the Eucharist, but (when it is used at all) only of Christ's death on the cross. Other sub-apostolic writers, however, Barnabas and Ignatius,[3] use the term of the praise and prayer offered at the Eucharist. The first Epistle of Clement[4] shows how naturally the meal could be thought of under the guise of a sacrifice; and the same thing is true of Ignatius' Epistles.[5] Later, in the Apostolical Constitutions,[6] the sacrifice is explicitly separated from the praise and prayer which formed the earlier part of the service. 'After this, the sacrifice is to take place, all the congregation standing and praying quietly. When it is offered, each section of the congregation is to take part separately in the Lord's body and the precious blood in order, with modesty and reverence, as if approaching to the body of a king.'

How, then, did this sacrifice come to be envisaged?

---

[1] The quotation is from Mal. i. 11; the mention of reconciliation before sacrifice is doubtless an allusion to Matt. v. 23 f. (See p. 25.) The date of the Didache is still uncertain. The most recent German editor, R. Knopf, places it between 100 and 150 A.D., though Anglican writers often regard it as considerably later, and reflecting the practices of a small and unimportant section of the Church. See J. Armitage Robinson, *Barnabas, Hermas, and the Didache*, 1920. A convenient translation is published by the S.P.C.K., edited by T. W. Crafer.

[2] *Apol.* i. 65–67; *c.* 160 A.D.

[3] Cf. F. Wieland, *Der vorirenaeische Opfersbegriff* (1909).

[4] Chh. xl., xli., xliv. The epistle was written from Rome to Corinth *c.* 100 A.D.

[5] *Eph.* 5, 20; *Philad.* 4; written *c.* 120 A.D.; and see Justin *Dial.*, 41, 117.

[6] Dating probably from the earlier half of the fourth century.

THE EUCHARIST AND THE MASS 247

There is a striking passage in Justin[1] which suggests the answer. After quoting the words in the service, ' This is My blood,' he adds, ' And this is what, in the mysteries of Mithra, the evil spirits have instituted in imitation of us. The bread and the cup of water are used in the initiation ceremonies, as you know or can easily ascertain.' 'We are reminded at once by these words that Christianity did not grow up in a world where the only competing religion was Judaism. It had to maintain itself in a jostling crowd of sects and systems. As Cumont has remarked[2], we can best understand the religious world of the first and second centuries if we imagine our own country invaded by troops of Brahman priests, Mohammedan devotees, grave Chinese scholars, and Buddhist monks, leading noisy processions through the streets, erecting halls at every street corner, and finding disciples in every class of society and almost every family. We have to remember also that although the rites and organizations differed, their general type was so similar that a convert could pass from one to another without difficulty,[3] and that the religious ideas underlying them all had gained a large hold upon the more seriously minded section of educated people. We might compare the wide influence enjoyed at the present day by the ideas which are common to the various schools of spiritual healing. Now, to this whole *entente* of mystery religions, Christianity stood in direct and determined opposition. To the Church, the means by which these cults offered deliverance were not the result of a purification of the older and cruder idolatries of paganism, but the invention of devils. Individual Christians were as little likely to be attracted by the neo-paganism of the time as the Jews who were brought up in the atmosphere of the ' Aboda Zara.' If this is true of their religious conceptions in general, it is still truer in regard to the Eucharist. If the New Testament phrases about the ' reasonable service ' could be supposed to have been current coin, they were used expressly in the New Testament of conduct and reverence, without any distinct reference to the Eucharist. And even the performances of the mysteries were not commonly thought of as centring round a sacrifice.[4]

[1] *Apol.* i. 66 ; cf. *Dial.* 70.   [2] *Les Religions Orientales*, ch. viii.   [3] See p. 92.
[4] In the Mithra liturgy already referred to, the word $θυσία$ does not occur.

Nor can we suppose that the official cults of the pagan altars had more influence over Christian thought or language. In an age of syncretism the Christian Church stood for relentless independence and opposition. Its adherents had heard the command 'to come out from among them and be separate.' Anything that reminded them of their previous way of life was suspect. The fact that many of them before their conversion must have been familiar with both the official and the mystery cults would make them less liable to be influenced subconsciously by the praxis of the heathen altars. To them the very word sacrifice would suggest the tremendous alternative, ' Diana or Christ '—' Throw the incense on the altar and be false to your Saviour, or refuse and gain the glory of the martyr's death.'[1] They were in a somewhat similar position to the group to which the Epistle to the Hebrews was addressed. They had turned away with loathing from the altars of the market-place and the theatre. They had indeed an altar of their own, but in its sacrifice they could only contemplate something entirely different from anything which the world around them could suggest. Naturally, therefore, they fell back upon the Old Testament, which belonged, they felt, as much to them as to the Jews, and with which the heathen had nothing to do. There they read of the calves of the lips, the sacrifices of praise and thanksgiving, of the broken spirit and the contrite heart. This brought before their minds the services of the church as well as private devotions ; and in particular the service of the Eucharist. But the Eucharist, even in the first age, was felt as more than a prayer and praise meeting. It involved the solemn consumption of articles of food, and not only their consumption, but their presentation before God, like non-living sacrifices upon an altar.

The path to the identification of the bread and the wine with these offerings seemed therefore open. But it was not taken. The act of sacrifice was in these first days identified with the spoken words or with a

---

[1] Compare the well-known reply of Polycarp when he was being exhorted to save his life by sacrifice : ' Fourscore and six years have I been his servant, and he hath done me no wrong. How can I then blaspheme my king who saved me ? ' (Mart. Polyc. 9).

THE EUCHARIST AND THE MASS 249

good life, not with the gift. Of the idea that the gift, or the sacred food, is one with the body of the victim upon the cross there is as yet no hint.[1] We are thus led to the paradox that the original use of the term sacrifice was a protest against the sacrificial view of the service; and this is emphasized by the Apologists, who urge that God, unlike the heathen gods, needs nothing from man, and therefore Christians bring to Him only praise.[2] Similarly, Irenaeus regards the Eucharist as the thank-offering of the redeemed creation. It does not give God what He lacks, but acknowledges His sovereignty. 'It is His will that we, too, should offer a gift at the altar, frequently and without intermission. The altar is in heaven; for toward that place are our prayers and oblations directed; the temple likewise is there, as John says in the Apocalypse.'[3]

But a change began to make itself felt about the end of the second century. The gradual separation between the Eucharist and the Agape had tended to place new emphasis on the mystic character of the elements[4]; and with large numbers of heathen converted, and in periods when persecution was forgotten, the difference between heathen and Christian sacrifices was less marked. The words 'Do this in remembrance of Me' are connected with the offering of the bread, itself

---

[1] See R. Knopf, *Lehre der zwölf Apostel* (1920), p. 24. He concludes: 'In particular, bread and wine were brought before God with prayer. Hence inevitably arose the conception that the sacrifice and sacrificial meal of us Christians is the common eating with the eucharistic thanksgiving.' This is true if we underline the sacrificial aspect of the meal and the prayers, as opposed to that of the objects involved. To Clement the supper is a φάρμακον ἀθανασίας, a 'drug' to confer immortality, rather than a means for forgiveness of sins; and this remains true of Irenaeus. What the early writers value in the Eucharist is the present experience of union with God which it expresses. 'The mysteries of natural religions seem generally to have acquired moral significance by elaborate and conscious interpretation; those of Christianity were from the first either moral or meaningless.'—Alice Gardner, *Hist. of Sacrament* (1921), p. 51.

[2] *Min. Felix*, 32 (qui fraudibus abstinet, propitiat Deum: qui hominem periculo surripit, optimam victimam caedit; cf. p. 123); Tert. *Adv. Marc.* ii. 18. Cf. Ps. l, 10; Mic. vi. 6 f.

[3] *Adv. Haer.* iv. 34.

[4] Cf. A. V. G. Allen, *Christian Institutions*, p. 533: 'When there was no longer occasion for those contributions (to the Agape), the bread and wine intended for the Eucharist, as distinct from the supper, became invested with a new meaning and a higher solemnity.'

thought of as the body of Christ. The thought of Irenaeus is partly concrete, partly symbolical.[1] Tertullian, holding that the sacrifice which is brought is made up of the prayers of the congregation, yet emphasizes the offering of bread and wine and the enjoyment of the body and blood of Christ. Cyprian, however, here as elsewhere, goes much farther. The spiritual and the physical had not been distinguished in the thought of the Church fathers; Cyprian was the first to regard the supper explicitly as the offering of the body and blood. The Eucharist, he says, represents the passion of Christ; it is celebrated in wine and not in water, because wine is always a figure for the passion. The priest does what Christ did—he offers a true and full sacrifice to God the Father in the Church.

In the East thought did not move so quickly. Clement of Alexandria says that 'in the Eucharistic offering the Christian enjoys the purification of the sacrifice and the word, the food of immortality, of this divine knowledge.'[2] Origen regards the Christian as bringing the bread to God with thanksgiving, and receiving it back as hallowed food, as the Logos makes His offering on the heavenly altar. The altar, it will be noted, is still in heaven; Christ's entrance to heaven is His ascent to the altar. That Christ is in the Eucharist on the altar Origen does not assert. Origen, however, uses the term 'mystery.' In the third century, 'mystery' in the Greek Church, and its equivalent 'sacrament' in the Latin, had become firmly embedded in Christian usage. Cyril of Jerusalem speaks of his five catechetical instructions to the newly baptized as 'mystagogic.' The singing of the hymns at the Eucharist, he teaches, conducts us to the 'fellowship of the holy mysteries,' and in the final prayer the worshipper thanks God who has 'made him worthy of such great mysteries.' Cyril, too, employs the term sacrifice with a new freedom. The table around which the presbyters sit is the altar ($\theta\nu\sigma\iota\alpha\sigma\tau\eta\rho\iota\nu$) of God. He goes on, 'After the spiritual sacrifice, the bloodless offering, has been made ready [by the descent of the Spirit upon it, to make the bread the body of Christ and the wine the blood of Christ],

---

[1] See, for instance, *Adv. Haer.* v. 2.   [2] *Strom.* v. 10, 11.

THE EUCHARIST AND THE MASS 251

we invoke God at that Sacrifice of propitiation on behalf of the common peace of the Church.'[1]

But it will be noticed that here also, however the actual terms used may be reminiscent of paganism, the associations are all different. The convert might be led, or misled, by the fact that the Eucharist was only open to the baptized,[2] and involved eating food which was somehow regarded as one with the body of Christ, into imagining that he was present at something not very different from a celebration in a Mithraic grotto. But if he had ever been in such a grotto, and had seen the bizarre figures and the central group, and if he knew anything of the subjects that took up the attention of his new co-religionists and their teachers, he would be struck by the differences far more than the resemblances. That there were special seats in both places for clergy and laity, that the lighting of the building was dim and impressive, that precautions were taken to keep out all who had not been specially prepared, would seem to him natural enough in any religious service. But the commemorative nature of the Eucharist, the solemn recital of words once veritably spoken by the Saviour, the absence of any suggestion of the worship of nature or the sun, and the decorum and quietness of the whole proceeding, would effectually prevent him from making any confusion between the two.

Still, through all its slow liturgical development, with its caution and its daring, the Eucharist was doing for its participators what the mysteries at their best had been trying to do—establishing, by means of a solemn act, replete with the holiest associations, the sense of unity between man and God. On this point, as elsewhere, Augustine joins the old and the new conceptions, even when they might seem irreconcilable, in a form which has affected all subsequent thought. The heavenly altar is God, and

---

[1] *Catech.* v. 2, 7, 8, 22. Cyril's date is the middle of the fourth century. An example of the manner in which this language travelled through the Church may be found in the liturgy of the Syrian Jacobites: 'Commemorating thy death and thy resurrection . . . we offer thee this fearful and unbloody sacrifice, that thou deal not with us after our sins. Look upon the sins and look upon the offering for them, for the offering and the sacrifice is greater far than the sins. . . . By thy living sacrifice dispel my passions and heal my offences' (Hammond, *Western and Eastern Liturgies*, ed. Brightman, 1895, vol. i.).

[2] Cf. *Lit. of St. James* (Syrian), Hammond, *op. cit.*, μή τις τῶν ἀμυήτων κτλ.

252 ALTAR, CROSS, AND COMMUNITY

man who gives himself to God is the true burnt-offering. The altar is also the means for uniting man to God; to come to the altar is to unite oneself with God. Before the Fall, and after the Last Judgement, right offerings can be brought to God by men; between these events, only by Christ and baptized infants. But, for us, death is a necessary accompaniment of sacrifice. Christ is daily offered—that is, symbolically slain in the sacrifice of His body and blood. The sacrifice of the body and blood is the formal means of our incorporation with God, corresponding to the sacrifice performed on the cross. And for us, suffering in the sense of the suffering Christ, in so far as it is freely willed, imitates the sacrifice of Christ.[1] The Eucharist as the sacrifice of the body of Christ is the Church's offering of herself.[2] The combination of mysticism and realism in the view of Augustine was doubtless too delicate for popular thought about the sacrament; it was too delicate for the practical administrators of the Church. By the time of Gregory the Great, who impressed on the Roman Eucharist, now become the Mass, the character it still wears, and whose robust influence was dominant in Western theology for five centuries, the finer distinctions were pushed on one side, and the realistic conception was alone and completely emphasized. The Mass became an actual repetition of the sacrifice of Christ. Augustine's caution against thinking that the bodily presence of Christ was on the altar was forgotten. The way was open for a thorough-going doctrine of transubstantiation.[3] In fact, from Gregory we pass without hindrance to the full sacramental position of the Council of Trent, namely, that 'the sacrifice of the Mass is the propitiation for the living and the dead not yet passed through purgatory.'[4] The Tridentine doctrine is that there is an objective act of offering in the Mass. The offering on the cross was not constituted by a concrete gift, but by Christ's death. As a Catholic author[5] puts

---

[1] Aug., *de Civ. Dei*, x. 19, 20.

[2] As Miss Gardner (*op. cit.*) says, the change, to Cyril, is in the elements, to Augustine, in the worshippers.

[3] References will be found in Loofs, *Dogmengeschichte*, p. 247. The old phrases, however, still linger. Gregory can still emphasize, in dealing with the Mass, the regenerating power of grace.

[4] The document adds, 'Whoso shall say that the Presence is symbolical, let him be anathema.'

[5] Wieland, *op. cit.*, pp. 175 ff. (This work has been placed on the Index.)

THE EUCHARIST AND THE MASS 253

it, all sacrifice has for its object union with God. The sacrifice is a symbol. By the Hebrews and pagans the symbol was mistaken for a gift. Against this, he says, the Old and New Testaments are one long protest. On the side of man, therefore, the sacrifice can be regarded as a sacrament of atonement, praise, prayer, and thanksgiving. It consists in the voluntary death of God's Son, which was an act of atonement. Hence the Christian must speak, not of *a* sacrifice, but of *the* sacrifice.

Such words will help to explain the immense impressiveness, so unintelligible to the convinced Protestant, which the Mass has exerted in the past and still, for vast numbers, exerts in undiminished strength. Newman has given an eloquent and arresting description of its effect in his semi-autobiographical novel, *Loss and Gain*: ' I declare, to me nothing is so consoling, so piercing, so thrilling, so overcoming, as the Mass, said as it is said among us. It is not a mere form of words—it is a great action, the greatest action that can be on earth. It is not the invocation merely, but, if I dare use the word, the evocation of the Eternal. He becomes present on the altar in flesh and blood, before whom angels bow and devils tremble. Words are necessary, but as means, not as ends. They are instruments of consecration, of sacrifice. They hurry, as if impatient to fulfil their mission. Quickly they go ; for they are the awful words of sacrifice ; they are a work too great to delay upon ; as when it was said in the beginning, " What thou doest, do quickly." '[1] Newman goes far in this passage to reveal the secret of the popular influence, not only of the Mass, but of all sacrifice. It is a mysterious and awful action, set in operation by human wills and words, and then proceeding, as by its own inner momentum, to join together man and God, and pour upon the human heart divine grace. ' By an actual change, a cleansing and renewal of our manhood, a transformation which we can mark in human lives and human faces, or trace in that strange trait of saintliness which Christianity has wrought into the rough fabric of human history, may the reality of sacramental grace be known on earth.'[2]

A study of the order of the Mass as it appears in the Roman Missal, the authoritative rubric for every part of

[1] pp. 327 f., 10th edition, 1891.   [2] F. Paget, in *Lux Mundi*, p. 433.

the Catholic world, will show how all the stages in the development of the office, culminating in the Council of Trent, after which there was to be no further change, have been preserved—even certain heathen elements which had made their furtive way within; and how all the theological conceptions which we have rapidly passed in review have been employed for producing a profound effect on the mind, however untheological the worshipper or spectator.

The first part of the Mass, or 'Antiphon,' was, until the sixteenth century, sung in the sacristy; it contains a confession, as old as the sixth century, in which Michael is invoked between the Virgin and St. John the Baptist. It concludes with the kissing and the censing of the altar, both of which practices suggest pagan veneration. This is followed by the Introit, containing the invocation of the Trinity which occurs towards the end of the Anglican service. Then comes the reading of the Scripture—this, as we have seen, goes back to the time of Justin—with or without a sermon, and the Nicene creed, introduced into the Mass in the eleventh century. This part of the service concludes with the words 'Let us pray.' No prayer follows them, but in the fifth century they introduced the main prayer for the congregation, as in the Anglican order. Next comes the Offertory, that is, the ceremonial offering of the host, which begins the Mass proper, and at which only baptized persons are supposed to be present. Next, the Preface, commencing with the words 'Lift up your hearts.' It contains the 'trisagion,' or thrice-repeated 'holy,' which was uttered as early as the first century.[1] What follows is known as the Canon of the Mass, the central portion which contains the consecration and elevation of the host, 'which we offer to Thee for those also whom Thou hast deigned to regenerate by water and the Holy Spirit, giving unto them remission of all their sins,' and, later, the words 'command these things to be carried by the hands of the holy angel upon this lofty altar, in the sight of Thy divine majesty.' The different parts of this

[1] 1 Clem. 34. 'Praefatium' in the Roman cults was the term applied to the warning to the ceremonially impure to depart; also to the preliminary offering of wine, cakes, and incense at the sacrifice. The words of the 'Preface' are found as early as Cyril of Jerusalem (*op. cit.*), but in a different part of the service.

THE EUCHARIST AND THE MASS 255

section of the Mass show much displacement and omission when compared with the earlier liturgies. After this is the act of communion, which includes the dropping of a portion of the bread into the cup, a relic of the Eastern ' communion of the sop '; the ' Agnus Dei,' or ' Lamb of God ', at least as old as the eighth century; and the kiss of peace, inserted since the time of Innocent III, *c.* 1200. The conclusion, too, belongs to the eighth century; its last words are the first fourteen verses of the fourth Gospel, which were anciently used as an exorcism and specially as a protection against storms. They were written on the walls of churches, and are still framed under glass and kept upon every Roman altar.[1]

This somewhat lengthy account of the development of the Mass has been necessary in order to show the steady advance of the conception of sacrifice therein. At first the word was used in a clearly metaphorical manner; the sacrifice consisted in the worshipper's attitude of thankfulness, though this was soon joined to the words of praise which were uttered, and the offerings of food which were to form the meal or to be given to the poor. At the same time Christ, once crucified on Calvary, was felt to be present. This led to the second stage, towards the end of the second century—the symbolical bringing of Christ as a gift to God. In the third stage, while Christ's sacrifice of Himself is still one, it is identical with the Mass, which is the sacrifice on the cross itself, made present through the prayer of consecration, and needing regular and constant repetition. Thus the conception of sacrifice in the Church is steadily assimilated to that of the pagan and Hebrew ceremonies, where a victim is presented in death to the god, and where the actual presentation of that death, rather than the attitude of the worshippers, is the important thing. The chief difference between them from this point of view is that while at the Hebrew and pagan altars the worshippers had a real and important part to play—for example in the slaughter of the animal—in the Mass they have simply to repeat certain responses, and stand or kneel as tradition demands.

[1] For a more detailed account of the Mass see Duchesne, *Christian Worship* (5th edition, 1919), ch. 6. The actual words of the Roman Missal are conveniently given in H. Lietzmann's *Kleine Texte*, No. 19 (Bonn, 1911).

But not all the reaction on the Mass, with its gains and losses, of what may be called paganism, but should really be called the instinctive desire of the heart for the performance of a great and impressive action which brings the seen into the unseen, can conceal the fact that the Mass is, after all, Christian; and because it is Christian it lays a stress, of which paganism knew nothing, on reconciliation by redemption. There is, throughout its ritual, a sense of the forgiveness of sins, purchased at a great price. Here is the secret of its spiritual power. The weakness of the Mass as of the older sacrifices is that if religion means the offering of oneself to God in a devotion which turns every act into a communion based on joyous obedience, it is not here represented. Yet the contrast which Lactantius draws between the heathens and the Christians in 300 A.D. can be applied to the devotion of the Middle Ages. The heathen, he says, sacrifice and leave all their religion in the Temple. 'Our religion is safe from shock and change because the mind is its sacrifice, and it dwells enshrined in the breast of the worshipper'[1]

To join in a Protestant Communion service is to feel ourselves, at first, in another world. The combined mystical and dramatic impressiveness of a great act is repudiated. What it affirmed made the service more valuable, doubtless, to the completely religious temperament, but it inevitably made a narrower, and to most minds a weaker, appeal. The Protestant theologians, following Luther, laid their main emphasis, as they were bound to do, upon faith. 'The validity of the rite springs from faith, not from its mere performance.'[2] That the Mass could be considered in itself as a good work and a sacrifice was to them a profound error. They found it, however, less easy to define what the sacrament was than to protest against what it was not. One of the weaknesses of Protestantism has been the absence of any official doctrine of the Eucharist

---

[1] ' Nostra religio eo firma est et solida et immutabilis, quia mentem ipsam pro sacrificio habet, quia tota in anima colentis est' (*de Justitia*, v. 19).

[2] 'Non implentur dum fiunt, sed dum creduntur' (Luther). Luther was assured that the true service of God is the whole Christian life, in its trust in God, repentance and faith, humility and faithfulness in our calling (see Harnack, *Dogmeng.*, 2nd edition, 1893, p. 368). To this end all outward worship is but the means.

to oppose to the clear and imposing Roman doctrine of the Mass. The obscurity of the doctrine of consubstantiation to which Luther found himself driven is well known, and it is questionable whether it has ever possessed any validity for the average Lutheran. Equally obscure is the difference between the Calvinist and Zwinglian views for any but a trained theologian; and trained theologians are not the only persons for whom the Eucharist is intended. Zwingli's teaching, indeed, is the clearest and the most meagre of the reformed views; the Communion was to him the commemoration of the sacrifice of Christ. Yet he could say, 'If we firmly believe, our soul receives food and drink with the flesh and blood of Christ'[1]; and in spite of his opposition to transubstantiation he held that no Christian could doubt that the body and blood of Christ were actually consumed. With the discussions of the Protestant teachers, which reproduced much of the subtlety and the unreality of the mediaeval schoolmen, we have nothing to do. We have only to observe that their result was, for the ordinary members of Protestant congregations, to empty the Eucharist, for better or worse, of its sacrificial significance. However valuable a solemn commemoration may be, it is not a sacrifice, and cannot claim the advantages which participation in a sacrifice, pagan or Catholic, will produce.

The same thing cannot, however, be said of English Protestantism. The Anglicans, true as always to their principle of the *via media*, set themselves to preserve all that they could of the sacrificial element in the Mass. They did not allow themselves to hint, in the Eucharistic liturgies which appeared in the various Prayer-books, that the mere performance of the rite ensured the ' real presence,' or that through the priest's words Christ's body was made out of the bread and eaten. In the sacrament the pledges of the love of Christ were received; the service was for the comfort, that is, the strengthening, of those who repented, who were in love and charity with their neighbours and intended to lead a new life. The participants were bidden to pray that they might so eat and drink the sacred flesh and blood that their sinful bodies and souls might be cleansed and washed by Christ's body and blood. The

[1] Works, Zurich edition (1828-1842), i. 252.

right attitude was necessary if the act was to be valid. The Anglicans were at one with the continental reformers in asserting that Christ's sacrifice on the cross was the one sufficient satisfaction for the sins of the world; Jesus Himself is 'our spiritual food and sustenance in that holy sacrament'; and that the bread and wine on the altar were nothing but created things, taken in obedience to Christ's command and in remembrance of His passion ; but, by taking them aright, the worshipper became a partaker of His body and blood. Yet they retained many of the invocations of the Mass ; they held the service to a rigid form ; and they made it, as the Romans had done in opposition to the Greeks, distinctly penitential ; the thrice-repeated prayer for mercy comes at the conclusion of the whole liturgy ; and the concentration of the thought on the benefits to be received by Christ's death for sinners must have made it possible for many who had been brought up in the older form of service, but were untouched by its complicated corporal acts and genuflections, to feel that no serious change had taken place.

In one respect, however, the Anglicans have made a notable advance. Until the act of participation they shrink from the word 'sacrifice.' It is only used once—in the prayer of consecration. But in the following prayer it occurs three times ; first, reproducing the conception of the Eucharist in Barnabas and Justin, 'to accept this our sacrifice of praise and thanksgiving,' and then, recalling the language of the New Testament, 'we present ourselves a reasonable, holy, and living sacrifice unto Thee '; and finally disclaiming worthiness to offer any sacrifice, but praying that this 'bounden duty and service,' reminiscent of the λογικὴ λάτρεια of the Epistle to the Romans, may be accepted. This is the distinct Anglican contribution to the liturgy of the Eucharist, and it is one of which English Christians may well be proud. In the elaborate harmonies of Eucharistic praise it sounds two notes which had been unheard for centuries. The true sacrifice which God requires is not some material object ; it is not even exhausted by gratitude ; it is the worshipper himself. There can only be one sacrifice—the sacrifice of Christ, once offered, not on the cross only, but in the perfect obedience of His entire life on earth, and throughout the eternal existence that was manifested in time when His sinless feet trod those holy fields. But if His sacrifice is understood in this manner, in His continuous life of obedience and love, which links and reconciles us to God, we can see how it can and must be repeated, how His sacrificial attitude and its expression become ours, and how we, made through Him the sons of God, offer like Him the sacrifice of the devoted and reconciling life. Thus understood, the sacrifice of Christ is no longer an act which we have simply to contemplate, and from which we receive passively the benefits it has to bestow. It is an act which we ourselves also perform ; in which we, like Christ, are at once the offerings and the priests. And although that act is not performed simply at the Eucharist, but in every moment of the redeemed and reconciled life, the deep self-consecration which it involves, made at the culmination of that intense period of concentration on Christ's redeeming love, brings to the mind all the gain of the repeated sacrificial act, while it leaves unimpaired all the majesty of an act that never can be repeated.

When this has been grasped there can be no fear of the results of emphasizing the real presence or the actual consuming of Christ in the sacred elements. The reality is so intense that the symbol can never blur or obscure it. And it is perhaps not remarkable that the leaders of the Evangelical Revival in the Church of England, passionately devoted to the Protestantism of Luther as they understood it, should have used, to express their delight in the Eucharist, language which seems at first sight to embody the devotion of Rome. It is incorrect to say that the Eucharistic hymns of the Wesleys are the survival of a high and almost Romanist Anglicanism which they shed, little by little, and, as far at least as Charles Wesley was concerned, reluctantly. They were the expression of the inner faith and experience of the Revival itself, and of its characteristic doctrine of assurance and the indwelling of the Spirit of Christ. To that faith the Eucharist was as far removed from magic as it was from sentiment. It breathed the complete union with God wherein the sacrifice of Christ found its fulfilment and its end.

The leaders of the Evangelical Revival were not mystics. They had, indeed, the mystic's sense of intercourse—they would not have called it intimacy—with God, and his consciousness of a heart filled with the overpowering love of Jesus. But they were saved from the extravagance and the ' unpregnancy '[1] that always lie in wait for the mystic, because they knew that what they had was mediated to them. They needed a sacrifice, a victim; they had not made their way to God by themselves—they had been reconciled to Him by another. Their religious consciousness rested on a great act which had been performed for them; and therefore it necessarily issued in a series of acts to be performed by them. The love of the Redeemer was no impersonal thing. It was manifested in ceaseless activity and a magnificent death. It must manifest itself in like fashion in the lives of the redeemed, or it ceases to be.

There is another aspect of the history of the Eucharistic rite on which we must now touch. The Eucharist, the august seal of the oneness of the Church, has been all through its existence a sign of division. There is no more sinister word in the vocabulary of the Church than the word excommunication. Strong as was the feeling, in the mysteries as well as in the official cults, that the uninstructed and unprepared must be kept away, we do not hear of any permanent exclusion of persons who had been accustomed to participate in them. But the Church early laid down the rule that certain acts unfitted a man from sharing in her mysteries, until he had submitted to her discipline. Such a practice was not without its moral value. But with certain acts were quietly joined certain beliefs, and since beliefs, unlike acts, were generally shared by large numbers of people, anathematization and excommunication no longer excluded irreligious individuals merely, but also religious communities, from the one Church. A large section of church history is the record of intellectual differences in which each party excommunicated the other, and often it has been little more than an accidental superiority in numbers that has decided which of the two sets of disputants should go down to history as orthodox, while its opponent was ranked with the heretics. The most disastrous instance was the schism of 1054 A.D., when the two halves of Christendom permanently broke off relations with each other.

[1] ' Like John-a-dreams, unpregnant of my cause.'

At the Reformation, Rome refused all relation with those communities who were no longer able to recognize the supremacy of the Pope. In the Anglican Church the point which is considered most vital is not doctrinal ; it is connected with the validity of ministerial orders. The question is discussed with the eagerness, the deep feeling, and the subtlety which marked the dispute about the sacerdotal intention at the end of the Middle Ages.[1] But in every case the sign of this breach of relations with the erring brother, and his treatment as a heathen man and a publican, is the express refusal to allow him to kneel by the side of the orthodox, or the adherents of what is known as a valid ministry, at the table of the Lord. The same attitude was manifested in the stricter of the Reformed Churches, but it has happily been disappearing of later years ; and at present the only non-episcopal Churches of any note that refuse to welcome other Christians to their Eucharist are the close Baptists and the Plymouth Brethren. To-day the ' scandal ' of exclusion is deeply lamented in many quarters, especially in the Anglican Church. And naturally, for it is no longer mutual. Anglicans would willingly communicate with Romans and Greeks, but both Romans and Greeks refuse to allow them to do so, while Free Churchmen, who know of no bar to communion with Anglicans, are as rigidly excluded from Anglican altars. The Anglicans are thus in a peculiarly isolated position.[2]

The cause which has made such a stumbling-block possible is less widely appreciated. It is the failure to recognize the true character of the Christian sacrifice. If the Eucharist is regarded as an act which the Church, and the Church alone, can perform, and which, by its mere performance, secures for the faithful blessings otherwise unattainable, we can readily see how the fatal exclusiveness would arise. What is more easy than to say to the party whose opinion you condemn or whose opposition you dislike and hate, ' We are the appointed stewards of certain blessings ; and until you submit to us you shall be deprived of them ' ? But the Eucharist is more than this. It is a

[1] See Report of the Lambeth Conference, 1920, pp. 131 ff.

[2] This is equally true as regards both the Roman and the Greek Churches, although interesting but tentative overtures have been made between Anglicans and Greeks.

sacrifice in the truer and older sense of the term—an act whereby, through some august mediation, a group of men are united to God, and therefore to one another, for the exercise of some power which God wishes to bestow. And the Eucharist is a Christian sacrifice; that is to say, participation consists in sharing the spirit of the mediator Himself, the spirit of one who would stop at nothing in order to bear the follies and sins of the obdurate and ungrateful and to win their friendship and love. A sacrifice so understood could not fail to be the mechanism of union and the bond of peace. For union, like life, is dependent on action. Receiving is a matter for individuals; it leaves us, as it finds us, separate and divided. Giving, obeying, serving, imply an end to be gained by common action; they are a matter for a community. They find us separate individuals; they leave us allies. Neither union nor what is now called reunion is possible on any other terms.

It may be that a more sympathetic study of John xiii. would make this clear. As is well known, the fourth Gospel does not record the institution of the Eucharist at the Last Supper. As far as the language of chapter vi. goes, apart from considerations of the practice of the Church from the end of the first century onwards, it would be just as likely that the author intended to deprecate the celebration of the Eucharist as to 'spiritualize' it. But he records another incident at the Last Supper which he seems to regard as at once sacramental and institutional. The incident of the feet-washing is introduced with all the solemnity and sense of a deep symbolism which the Synoptists apply to the bread and the cup; and its definite repetition is enjoined on the disciples in the most explicit manner. The reader is inclined to ask, What would have been the result if the Church, instead of fixing upon the reception of the elements as her central ceremony, had followed the fourth Gospel, and had perpetuated some act or class of acts which should have embodied the spirit of Him who was among His own disciples as one that serveth?[1]

But to return, and to sum up. We have seen that the underlying ideas of the Eucharist, at once the oldest and

[1] This suggestion has also been made by J. H. Moulton in *A Neglected Sacrament* (1918).

THE EUCHARIST AND THE MASS

the youngest in the history of sacrifice, were those of the mysteries rather than of the altar—the dying god, the blessings made possible by that death, the actual meal by which the worshippers come to share his powers, and the new and 'risen' life spread through the whole favoured community. There are, however, three noteworthy differences between the mysteries and the Eucharist. First, the difference between the character of the divine victim celebrated in the Eucharist, and the character (if the use of that term is not a positive absurdity) of the dying mystery gods; second, the difference that Jesus, commemorated in the Eucharist and felt in the heart, was a definite historical person, while the mystery gods could never be drawn out of the region of myth and shadow; and thirdly, the difference that the Eucharist was saturated with the conception of forgiveness and redemption. These conceptions do not belong to the circle of the suggestions of any sacrifice, ethnic or Hebrew. They arose in entire independence. Sacrifice may be understood to accomplish expiation or appeasement. But expiation is not forgiveness, and appeasement is not redemption. To understand the work of the great sin-bearer we must look to one who, in the days of the Jewish exile, stood apart from all sacrifice, but by whose words, as penetrating as any that have ever been uttered save on the Master's own lips, all sacrifices have been transformed.

Transformed, yet not abolished. The coming of Christ did not change man's religious nature, nor the way to the satisfaction of his religious needs. Nor is it true in every sense to say that all the predecessors of the Good Shepherd who laid down His life were thieves and robbers. Even to-day the one hope for mankind is union with God. That union can only be effected through the mediation which is the heart of all sacrifice. And that mediation, appropriated by the worshippers as the spirit of their own lives, still needs embodiment in some formal and even ceremonial act. They who truly repent and are in love and charity with their neighbours must still draw near with faith, and take the holy sacrament to their comfort, and present their bodies a living sacrifice unto God. What is implied by this sacrificial action of the Christian believer, in the world in which we find ourselves to-day, we have now to consider.

XI

FAITH AND FORGIVENESS

THE long discussion now coming to an end suggests that religion is one vast example of needless complexity. Why cannot we aim at simple goodness and be satisfied, bending our energies to being honest and kindly and chaste, loving God and our neighbours? What has the race really gained by sacrifices, so elaborate and cumbrous, and all the apparatus for union with the divine? It is to many a sheer relief to turn to the childlike wisdom of the discourses in the Synoptists, or the blunt common sense of the prophets: 'Bring no more fruitless offerings; but let justice flow as a mountain torrent.' If God simply demands justice and love, why should we think about anything else? And can we suppose that He would think about anything else either?

This is a question which is being asked by the majority of serious people to-day. It is frequently heard inside the Church; and by the larger number of persons who believe strongly in morality and are by no means prepared to give up their belief in some kind of God, however little they may care to affirm about Him, but who are not attracted at all by churches as institutions, it is almost assumed to admit of but one answer.

But before we decide whether simple goodness is enough or not, we must make up our minds as to what simple goodness is. It is an old and even elementary inquiry in ethics: Does goodness consist in doing or being? Careful thought has always answered, In being. Such at least was the verdict of the most considered and systematic of Greek moralists; mere formal goodness—the goodness of the act apart from the intention—is not worth calling goodness at all.[1] It may have very convenient and desirable results, as when a trader, anxious to drive his

[1] Aristotle, *Nic. Eth.* i. 1105a.

FAITH AND FORGIVENESS 265

competitors off the field, sells his goods below cost price, or when a barbarous power, desiring to get rid of a detested and subject race, reduces to helplessness a number of unscrupulous money-lenders in the process. But no one would call this goodness, though the acts of selling cheaply to the poor and of putting down usurers might conceivably be praised. Without staying to distinguish between motive and intention, we can see that both must be taken into account in deciding the goodness of an act. And that is as much as to say that goodness depends on what we are, and not on what we do. It is not a matter of conduct but character.

This will prepare us for a further discovery. Goodness is not an affair of a single person, however estimable. It is concerned with the relations between persons. A person is only possible in a society of persons. Goodness has to do with the attitude of such persons to one another. It could almost be asserted that complete goodness is only possible in a society of good people. Here it is enough to say that goodness always implies an attitude of goodwill, kindness, patience, and comradeship. The Decalogue is content with setting forth a list of things to be done or avoided. Later exponents of the Mosaic Law rightly emphasized the sentiments of friendliness and forbearance which underlie any adequate performance of its duties; and the profoundest of Jewish moralists knew that the foundation of all these duties is the one attitude which is also their fulfilment, namely, love. The frigid correctness of the Pharisees may remove a man farther from the true moral society than the misguided and aberrant impulsiveness of a publican or a sinner. Devotion to duty may end in the most repellent self-seeking. Even the moral man who would save his life is in danger of losing it. No virtue is safe that is not passionate. There is nothing good except the good will; and to accomplish this good will, there must be a conversion, a definite turning of the mind away from the interests of a man's own self, however exalted or purified, to the interests of the community or communities of which he is a member.

It is a mistake to think of all this as if it were the principle of Christian ethics as opposed to ethics in general; or to argue that while ethics set before the world an ideal of straightforward good conduct, Christianity asserts that something else is needed, without which good conduct in some mysterious way ceases to be good. It would certainly be but a poor compliment to Christianity to regard Christian ethics as only one species of a wider genus. The ethical system of the New Testament is not the ethics of Utilitarianism or Stoicism, or even of Kant. But there is no ethical system which does not lead, when carefully thought out, to the position that the good man is the man who shares with his neighbours whatever of value he may possess. This is the conception of goodness in the New Testament, and it demands a definite attitude and direction of the will. The main problem of ethics is not the problem of the end. To change from the search for satisfaction in physical pleasure to satisfaction through blessedness, or εὐδαιμονία, demands no change of will; only a change of mental outlook or a recognition of facts unsuspected before. It is the willingness to place the happiness of others in the same position as my own, however I understand that happiness—to love my neighbours as myself—which is the real test of my goodness. Such goodness may still be called simple; but it involves more than a readiness to perform certain actions. It demands a certain relation to other persons which has to be maintained deliberately, and may readily be destroyed.

To say this, however, carries with it more than is often understood. It means receiving as well as giving, feeling as well as acting. To be, in the full sense of the word, is to experience as well as to function. Comradeship is a relation in which each man should take as much as he gives. The sense of being trusted and of being able to trust, the consciousness of having a common aim and of being, as we say, a part of a larger whole, imparts a mysterious satisfaction which can never be obtained by aiming at it directly. Even so rudimentary a form of comradeship as making one of a crowd enables a man to feel, for the moment, that he is living life on a wider and higher plane. And when he is not one of a crowd but of a community, when he is a member of a larger body, he finds a satisfaction which men often miss, but which, once enjoyed, can never be forgotten, and which, indeed, gives the only real value to everything that is called pleasure. We have

FAITH AND FORGIVENESS

been slow to recognize the transforming effect of comradeship. But we have most of us experienced it. The very pleasures of the senses bear witness to this truth. A man may study a work of art or a great musical composition in solitude ; to enjoy it he must have companionship. The Roman satirist was speaking more wisely than perhaps he knew when he said that you cannot even enjoy a wild boar (*animal propter convivia natum*)[1] if you eat it by yourself. For the essence of pleasure is nothing that can be expressed in terms of the physical or chemical effect on our sense organs, but the enlargement and transformation of certain sensations which in themselves would soon leave us cold, with ' a heart high-sorrowful and cloyed.' Joy is not joy until we call our neighbours to rejoice with us. This is perhaps one secret of the appeal of the theatre. Who would enjoy either a Shakespearian tragedy or a revue if he were the only member of the audience ?

This transformation of experiences by sharing them applies in other instances also. 'A friend,' it is said, 'doubles our joys and halves our sorrows.' This is not strictly or universally true. A sorrow does not lose its poignancy because it is felt by a number of people at the same time. But the familiar effect of sympathy shows that sorrow which is felt by other people is somehow easier to bear. A certain quality is imparted to it which renders it even perhaps different in kind as well as in degree. The discovery that it brings the sufferer nearer to others goes far to neutralize its bitterness. This is equally true of toil, suspense, and the pursuit of an uncertain end. The patience and resolution that few men save the strongest can compass in solitude can manifest themselves in the weakest when they are in the company of allies. And with every increase in strength and effectiveness comes an increase in that subtle satisfaction and sense of wellbeing which is the salt of life. But to experience this in any completeness or security, something more is needed than mere membership of a crowd or group. One must be a partner in a society, subordinating one's own interest, ceasing to play for one's own hand, as in any intelligent team-work, losing oneself in the larger and richer whole.

[1] *Juvenal* i. 141.

To maintain the right attitude to the community, to enter into fellowship with it, means what the moralist calls goodness, and what the plain man feels as a glow and thrill that, at its highest, is more precious than life.[1]

These considerations are familiar to all who have been attracted by recent studies of the 'group-mind.' But we cannot do justice to the group-mind without recognizing that in all the larger and more influential human groups one of the members has been a deity. What is true of the totemic groups of Australia or North America is true of the great religious societies of Christendom. The interests which the individual shares with his society are not the interests of men only, but of a divine being, and the life which circulates through all the members of the body is a life which is more than human. If this seems a paradox or an absurdity to us, it is only because we are out of touch with any group-life save that of our own time— and often with even that! The satisfactions gained in such an alliance are therefore of a higher order. Men can grow conscious of a joy and hope and elation and 'power over the hour' which can only have its source in some region beyond the world of human sense. To such an exalted society belong all the deepest experiences of which mankind is capable. The raptures of the saint, the poignant bliss of the martyr, the assured hope of everlasting life, equally with the religious abandonment and exaltation of the savage, the fiery energy of the old Hebrew warrior filled with the spirit of Jahveh, or the calm serenity of the man who enters upon his daily task 'with joy to do the Master's blessed will,' are all of them the results of the higher social experience. In every age men have purchased thereby deep delights for which they would willingly have bartered all other possessions. Life does not exist for the sake of pleasure. Pleasure—whatever we mean by the term —exists for the sake of life. And life, which at its best is only found when we are willing to throw it away, is reached when we have attained and can preserve the right relation to the members of our society. That society takes very different forms; and the life it produces will differ accordingly. It may be a totem group, a clan, a

---

[1] See for a discussion of the possibilities of the group-life in politics and society, M. P. Follett, *The New State*.

mystic cult, a brotherhood, or a religious denomination. But all are alike in producing, in their own degrees, that large and massive wellbeing which lives alike in the actions it inspires and the blessedness it affords.

'Simple goodness,' therefore, is not enough; first, because, in the sense in which mankind has sought it, it is not nearly so simple as people have been inclined to suppose; and secondly, because it cannot be produced by a direct act of will. It involves an attitude, a relation, between persons. How is that attitude to be brought about, and how—equally important—can it be restored? To restore it, indeed, is a more pressing problem than to bring it about. For a study of human life shows that the relation is not so much non-existent and unknown as jarred and broken. Enmity and clashing interests, jealousy and selfishness are obvious and commonplace enough; humanity has never been able to make up its mind that they are original. Religious men, indeed, have always been clear on the matter. Hebrew story-tellers, in the dim Eastern past, and Christian thinkers in the intellectual enlightenment of the Roman Empire, have been sure of some sinless garden of Eden, or could beseech men to be reconciled to God, to put aside an enmity which, at least ideally, never ought to have been there.

And even apart from religion, the belief in a state of comradeship and goodwill, somehow anterior to the strife and self-seeking which disfigures and tortures life to-day, refuses to be rejected. Hobbes might tell us of a state of nature in which every man's hand was against his brother; but the study of societies which appear to resemble the primitive most nearly has revealed much of social solidarity and mutual aid within the group unit. Group may wage unceasing war against group, but the group is the primitive man's real world, and within that world it is felt that peace comes before strife; and when peace follows strife, it is not an advance; it is a restoration.

We must, therefore, assume the priority, either in fact or idea or both, of a relation of concord between man and man, and between man and God. Everywhere it is thought of as existing; everywhere it is broken. To restore the broken relation between man and God has been in every religion and age the main function of sacrifice. Sacrifice, we have seen, is not a gift nor a surrender.[1] It is the solemn act or rite by which the gulf between man and God is bridged. Since we have to do with an institution which takes us far back into the childhood of the race, we are not surprised to find reasons for that gulf which seem to us puerile. At a period when the distinctions between a sin and a mistake, between deliberate disobedience and innocent inattention to an arbitrary rule, and between a moral principle and a traditional convention, are hardly suspected, the reason may as easily be a ritual misadventure—like the eating of food on which a 'taboo' has been placed or contact with unhallowed blood—as an act of criminal violence. Quite probably, among men acquainted with the waywardness of their barbarian chieftains, the latter might be held less repugnant to their gods than the former. The important point for religion is that when the gulf exists, sacrifice is there to bridge it.

But is such a sacrifice more than magic? Once the stress is laid on the correctness of the appointed word or act (and, as we have noticed, in sacrifice it nearly always is), the act and word begin to take on a magical significance. And once the act or word, to ensure correctness, is confined to some specially appointed class of persons, they begin to take on the character of magicians. But religion moves in a different world from magic. It tries no experiments; it relies on no blind forces. Unhappily, what is to one man an act of religion may be to another a piece of pure magic; or the worshipper may come to regard with a magician's confidence what was once the expression of a religious need. Among the throng of patients at the pool of Bethesda, a holy well on the anniversary of its patron

---

[1] In our modern sense of the word, as something to be given up unwillingly under the pressure of necessity or duty or fear, sacrifice has no true place in religion. It is true, indeed, that men have often dreaded lest heaven should be jealous of human happiness. The Greeks called the action of this jealousy Nemesis, and the recognized way of avoiding it was to fling away some cherished possession or forgo some advantage or delight. (See the story of Polycrates, *Herod.* iii. 40, and Aesch. *Agam.* 931 ff.) But such a precaution was not thought of as a sacrifice; and when the Jew, with his more assured religious instinct, thought of a wealthy and prosperous man suddenly plunged in adversity, he attributed the tragedy to the mysterious adversary of mankind rather than to the jealousy of God. Jahveh was a 'jealous' God because He would not share the devotion of His people with any rival, not because He demanded sacrifices lest they should be too happy.

FAITH AND FORGIVENESS 271

saint, or the grotto at Lourdes, who shall decide where magic ends and religion begins? And when at the Eucharist itself the communication of divine grace is regarded as dependent on the fact that the liquid drunk is true or fermented wine, or on the ordination by consecrated episcopal hands of the officiating priest, who can deny that the conceptions of magic are very near us? [1]

Sacrifice, however, is more than the attempt to control the brute forces of nature. Such a desire is strong and natural enough, of course. Mankind will always seek for some way, wise or foolish, of escaping from disease, accident, or disaster. But no one can contemplate the part played by sacrifices in Homeric Greece or Vedic India, on Mount Moriah, or even at Carmel and Bethel, without being convinced that sacrifice is the secular expression of the yearning of the human spirit for God. This is the clue which the investigator of the rite must never allow to slip from his hand. Sacrifice is the means to fellowship. Judged by its obvious and tangible results, it might seem hopelessly inferior to magic. It makes no such tempting offers to hate or fear or lust as magic is always ready to make. But over against the offerer and his priest stands the god; through the blood-shedding it involves his will is done; in the august words or frenzied cries that accompany the rite he draws near to his servants. It may be to bring them no definite boon, to protect them from no perceived danger; it may even be to bring near to them the peril of his holiness. But it gives them the blessing, craved by ignorant and clouded hearts as by eager and serene faith, of fellowship between God and man.

Fellowship is a word oftener used than clearly understood. Like all terms which attempt to pierce their way towards the centre of religious experience, its meaning has eluded discovery with Protean persistence. And yet, for all its high and mystical associations, it means nothing more than sharing. The pagan devotee is as anxious to experience this sharing as the Christian saint. The things the two men desire and expect to share with their god may be as far asunder as the poles. What the god can share with his worshipper depends on what the worshipper conceives

[1] See p. 309, and Headlam, *The Doctrine of the Church and Reunion* (1920), p. 261.

about his god. But if the god deserves his name and his worship at all, he will certainly have some attributes, and his approach to his servant will mean that something from one or other of these attributes is bestowed. This may be some access of physical strength, clear vision or supernatural illumination; some power over inanimate nature; the assurance of fertility in crops and herds, superiority to enemies, skill to attract and capture the wild creatures of forest or desert or sea; self-control and patience; the stern virtue that can resist all the temptations of the flesh; the clean heart and the pure thought, or the overwhelming sense of more than mortal breath that fills a man as with new wine. These are among the ends for which men sacrifice; to gain these ends they carry out the antique and often cumbrous and expensive rites whereby they purify themselves and confess their sins, negligences, and ignorances, prepare their victim for the altar, consume it by fire or tear it limb from limb and devour the quivering flesh, never doubting that in such appointed mode the channel is opened through which divine grace can flow into their bodies and hearts and restore the relation in which alone such attainment can be looked for.

Simple goodness, then, is something which man has never desired or expected. His hopes and wishes have been wider; they have aimed at that intimacy with the divine by which whatever divine qualities he needs—goodness or power or wisdom or love—can be his. This intimacy he establishes by sacrifice. We have seen the process at work in religious systems both less and more fully developed. The Old Testament offers the clearest and most convincing example, because the Old Testament exhibits the development of sacrificial ideas and practices with a detail which meets us nowhere else. The recognized and regular method of approach to God, until the exile, is sacrifice. The Hebrew knew, indeed, that God might visit him at any time, of His own divine accord.[1] He would then make his offering, in order to be put on good terms with his majestic visitor, as a subject might greet a king who came to his dwelling; or he might simply receive the grace with humble thanksgiving and praise. In the century and a

[1] Cf. Judges vi. 18.

FAITH AND FORGIVENESS

half before the exile he learnt through the prophets that his whole scheme of approach to God through the sacrifices was really useless; that God did not desire them and that they could never secure forgiveness; and that he must make his approach to fellowship in some other way. He was strangely slow to learn the lesson; but after the exile he did learn enough to doubt whether sacrifice was the sole means for fellowship, and to suspect that while it would remove barriers raised by negligence and ignorance, it might be quite unable to remove those which had been raised by wilful sin. In the New Testament we have watched the whole doctrine of sacrifice disappear. There, sacrifice can remove no barriers at all. That removal is the result of faith in the redeeming work of Christ, in His death or His 'blood,' and it is perpetuated and celebrated in the periodical breaking of the bread. But, subsequently, the doctrine of sacrifice reappeared in a new form. The Church fixed on two foci of Christian thought—the death of Christ and the Eucharist. The one she interpreted as a sacrifice, offered once and for all, for the human race. The other she came to speak of as a sacrifice offered continually in order to secure for believers the merits of the sacrifice on Calvary.

In studying the results of this re-introduction of the idea of sacrifice into Christian thought and practice, we have seen how far the Church has wandered from the combined clearness and profundity of the New Testament. We could trace the influence upon the leaders of the Church of practices with which they were familiar among Jews and pagans, and of many expressions in the Old and New Testaments which they seriously though quite naturally and innocently misunderstood. But to observe this was not to be led to desire to expel the conception of sacrifice altogether from Christian thought. We saw, indeed, that sacrifice as the presentation of a piacular victim to appease the wrath of God and counteract the penal effects of sin had as little place in the New Testament as in the Old. We also saw that the older and wider ethnic idea of sacrifices, as the means of approaching with confidence to fellowship with God, though seldom referred to in the New Testament, is everywhere implied and fulfilled. What these animal sacrifices were intended to become, Christ was and is. That astonishing impulse—instinct, we might almost call it—to offer sacrifice does not stand before us dumb and witless; the redemption of Christ has given it a language and tongue which we can understand and rejoice in.

But there is one word found on every page of the New Testament which that language does not contain. It is the word 'faith.' We need not deny that there must have been something corresponding to the saving faith of the Christian in many a worshipper before altars both pagan and Hebrew. Indeed, without it sacrifice would be unintelligible. Whatever view is taken of sacrifice, more is meant than meets the eye. Sacrifice is the entrance for multitudes into the unseen world. The relations established by sacrifice are relations with the invisible. This is not to assert that every pagan who brings his offering —his few leaves of tobacco, his pig, his horse, or even, like the Thonga, his saliva—is consciously venturing out upon an uncharted ocean. He has custom to rely on. He can doubtless point to previous instances where sacrifice has secured for him what he wants it to secure now. It has appeased the anger of his god; it has brought at least an alleviation of his suffering, or some gift otherwise unattainable. But this is not to weaken the element of faith in his action. It could only do so if we regarded faith as the opposite of reason. Faith is not opposed to reason, if we may follow the New Testament account of faith. It is opposed to sight. Unless nourished by reason, faith could not be expected to survive, either in the pagan or the Christian. Faith is not less faith because it can point to scores of instances where its venture has been justified. It would cease to be faith only when it ceased to deal with what in the last resort can never be touched nor seen.

If the view of sacrifice to which we have been led is correct, the place we must assign to faith is really more rather than less important. To perceive in sacrifice a means to the establishment of friendly and gracious relations between God and man implies three beliefs—that such relations are possible; that they are intended by the unseen power; and that they can be secured in a certain way, that is, by an offering of a particular and prescribed

FAITH AND FORGIVENESS

nature. For none of these beliefs can there be a shadow of direct proof, nor can they be regarded as in any sense the result of experiment. The method of trial and error could not be applied to establish any one of them. How, then, did they come to be accepted? We must search below the level of experiment and verification, and approach the region of convictions which lie too deep for argument and almost for words. When man says 'God,' he does not think of a power as capricious and alien as the wind or the storm or the plague; but of one who will, under conditions, be favourable to himself—who cannot, he would often add, be anything else; and those conditions are fulfilled when he approaches God in the right frame of mind—that is to say, when he is anxious to give to God what he understands God to demand. This gift is what we call the sacrifice. Why God demands this and not something else it is not for the worshipper to decide. It may be an animal; it may be a cake or a plate of fruit or vegetables; it may be his own eldest son or a lock of his hair. In any case, it involves faith, and faith, as we must admit, of a somewhat elaborate nature. Ask him how he knows that his god will accept such a sacrifice, and he will probably be able to give no answer that will be satisfactory to you, or even to himself. Reflecting on this, we may point to the innate tendency of human beings to find the ground for phenomena they cannot understand in the will of personalities they cannot see. But the Christian will find in this reaching out after an unseen and powerful friend the glimmering of that conviction of the love of God which is his own ground of assurance for the present and hope for the future. Such a conviction is not the result of argument. It is an affirmation. This is not to say that it is contrary to the reason which argument demands. It is an interpretation of our experience and our life. It is an act of will. It is the statement that we choose to regard the world as dominated by a power which is fundamentally friendly, and whose friendliness we are under certain conditions able to enjoy, and that in any different world we refuse to live.

Now, what is at best implicit in the ethnic and the Hebrew sacrifices is made explicit in the New Testament. 'The righteousness of God is revealed in the gospel from

276 ALTAR, CROSS, AND COMMUNITY

faith to faith.' The validity of the sacrifice of Christ depends on the faith of those for whom it is offered. This, indeed, is so clear that the great Protestant doctrine is that of salvation by faith, rather than by the sacrifice of Christ, as if Christ's death were useless without faith.[1] What, then, is this faith? 'Believe, believe the record true.' But this is misleading, in so far as it implies 'You cannot prove that Jesus died for your sins; but you must take it as true.' It is that opposition of faith to reason which we previously saw to be untenable. If faith meant a belief that as a matter of fact Jesus died for our sins, the statement that our faith saves us would be really self-contradictory; it would mean that we were saved by a belief that something else than our belief saved us, namely, the death of Christ. But faith cannot be interpreted in this narrow fashion. A mere intellectual assertion or interpretation cannot save any one. To believe 'that Jesus died for me' is something more than an intellectual act, like the belief that Columbus discovered America or that the last of the Romanoffs was murdered by Bolsheviks. Its significance consists in the fact that it affects my conduct and my whole view of my life. If I think of Jesus as having died for my sins, I think of my own relation to my sins as different from what it was. And if I find in Jesus the means of reconciliation which God has set forth between Himself and me, I am bound to think differently, not only of God's action, but also of my own. If I am reconciled to God, He will act to me in a new way; but I shall also act to Him in a new way. Reconciliation must be expressed in terms of conduct on both sides, or it is nothing.

This is plain enough if we think of reconciliation between two human beings. Such a reconciliation means a difference of attitude. But that difference of attitude would be nothing apart from a difference of conduct. It would be absurd to talk about the putting away of hate and anger and suspicion if hate and the rest were still lurking behind every act; or of the ending of a quarrel if the self-seeking which roused the quarrel is still there to show itself in conduct. There is no reconciliation between me and

---

[1] Compare the constantly repeated words of Jesus, 'Thy faith hath saved thee.'

FAITH AND FORGIVENESS

another unless I am living the life of one who is reconciled to him. I am not reconciled to God unless I am living the life of one who is at peace with God—a life of freedom from anxiety and fear, of calm humility and cheerful goodwill, of resolute opposition to greed and force and lust, and of the constant subordination of my own interests to those of others.

In the light of such a doctrine of reconciliation the history of Christian society and of the Christian nations has been disheartening. Equally disheartening is a survey of Christianity to-day. We seem to look in vain for the results of the Atonement. The great movements of the last nineteen centuries give it the lie; the growth of the European nations after the conversion of the barbarian invaders to Christianity; the wild upheaval of the Crusades; the imperious activities of the mediaeval papacy; the fierce passions aroused by the Reformation, and the prostitution of religious convictions to political and dynastic ends; the exploitation of the races of the new world and the horrors perpetrated by the Christian slave-trading powers; the internecine wars of the seventeenth and eighteenth centuries; the brutal callousness of the industrial revolution; the vast organization of the modern world for the competitive production of wealth, and its tragic nemesis in the world war. All these force us to ask if the reconciliation of man to God has not been an empty dream. And yet the nations of Europe have been orthodox throughout all the miserable ages. Arianism and Socinianism have been stamped out. The doctrine of Christ's sacrifice has been practically unchallenged.

Has, then, the Atonement been a failure? To reach the answer we must return to the consideration of faith in the sacrifice of Christ. If that sacrifice, not confined to the great act upon Calvary, embraces Christ's whole life of obedience to God and devotion to man, how is it made available by faith? The answer is really simple yet far-reaching. Let us go back to first principles once more. Reconciliation is the removal of the barrier or sense of separation between two estranged parties—in this case between man and God. If this sense of separation is to continue, it must be because of the ignorance or unwillingness or inability of one of the parties—that is, of man—to secure its removal. In the case of the ethnic sacrifices, religious tradition and custom supplied all the knowledge that was deemed necessary by prescribing the offering and the method of their presentation; the need for divine blessing or communion ensured the willingness; and the sacrifices themselves did not exhaust human capacities, and in some instances made but moderate demands on them. But although these sacrifices did to some extent bring the results that were expected of them, their success was at most very imperfect. The reactions against the whole system which were considered in chapter v. have made this clear as regards the most thoughtful and earnest portion of mankind. Ignorance as to the true method of approach to God still lay heavy on man's mind; and, so far as that method was suspected, whether in India or Greece or Palestine, unwillingness and inability blocked the way to its use.

We can now see the effectiveness and uniqueness of the sacrifice of Christ. First, His life, from Nazareth to Calvary, showed that the one means of approach to God was the life of obedience and devotion. Between Himself and God there was no barrier at all. How could there be, when to Him it was food and drink, as He said, to do His Father's will, and when He never did or thought anything that could put Him 'in the wrong' with God, or that would enable any one to 'convince Him of sin'? But might not the revelation of this great truth still leave men unwilling to accept it? Such unwillingness might persist with the revelation of any other truth, but not of this. To understand such a conception of God is to fall in love with it, to see that it is the best possible, to long to enter into it. The love of Christ constrains men, puts pressure upon them. If Christ is lifted up, He draws all men unto Him. For the life of Christ was not one of mere rectitude, of justice and virtue; it went out in constant service to the needy, the weak, the helpless; and also to opponents, detractors, foes. Every day that He lived made this clearer; and even those who were unable to recognize it earlier were forced to see it when it was exhibited in the appalling simplicity of the horror and degradation of the cross. Such a revelation does not only instruct the intellect; it moves the will. To understand it is to set about reproducing it. To see is to admire; to admire is to love; to love is to imitate.

But if ignorance and unwillingness are thus both overcome, what of human inability and helplessness? What if we cannot do what we would? The will may seem fixed, yet the passions may rove as widely as before. But, once the old bad life is seen and hated for what it is, the sinner is conscious that a change has taken place. He is not looked on as a sinner, but as one who has been bidden to go and sin no more. He is forgiven. And here we pass to what is often called the doctrine of the mystical union with Christ, derived from the experience whose classical expression is given in the words of Paul. The acts and thoughts and ideals of the individual are replaced by others which he can only identify as belonging to Christ. Instead of his old desires for self-indulgence and self-assertion he now finds desires, hitherto unknown, for a life of service and self-renunciation. In other words, the mood that separated him from God has disappeared; in its place has come that union with the will of God which was the mainspring of all the activity of Christ. Instead of being unable to live as one who is reconciled to God, no other life is possible. Such a discovery was not peculiar to Paul. We find it again and again in the pages of religious biography; and what is more, the change on which it rests can be observed in numbers of simple yet strenuous and self-forgetting lives. To be conscious of it is to find in it something of the miraculous. But beneath the miracle lies a profound uniformity. Admiring affection lies very near to imitation. The inability to be meek, forgiving, confident, cheerful, kind, and generally, as we say, 'Christlike', is the inability to keep an ideal of this sort constantly before the mind, to concentrate upon it rather than upon its opposite. And most of us must sorrowfully confess that we cannot force ourselves to concentrate upon an ideal, however exalted or beautiful. But when that ideal has become incarnate in a person who, by his own devotion to us, wins ours to him, and who makes that appeal which can only be made by one personality upon another, the matter is different. Instead of forcing the mind to concentrate upon an ideal, we find ourselves forced by this devotion into a new life—a life in which the convictions and acts of the object of our devotion reproduce themselves. With the will to live the new life comes the power.

To find instances of this law we need not go beyond the experiences of friends or lovers. Affection is always building a bridge by which the life of the lover passes over to the beloved, and vice versa. And if this 'invasion,' as we may call it, of one life by another is specially striking when the invader is Christ, the great Lover of souls, the reason is that Christ is not to be thought of simply as a person distinct from ourselves; He is what every true man would wish to be. We find our real selves, as we are forced to express it, in Him. We grow up into Him. We become one with Him. What is partially true of all real and deep affection is completely true of Christ, and of the men and women who have found in Christ the secret of a new life.

We are, however, in danger of being drawn aside from the proper course of our argument; and the attempt to describe the experience of those with whom the reconciliation has been completed has perhaps exposed us to the danger of attributing to the majority the attainments of the few. It is more germane to our present purpose to point out how faith is involved in these three factors of the reconciling sacrifice of Christ—the removal of the ignorance, unwillingness, and inability that may bar the entrance into the new life. Faith, we agree, means more than the acceptance of certain statements as true. It means reliance on the authority and protection of the person who is its proper object. Hence to accept Christ's valuation and ideal of life is essentially a matter of faith. And this is equally true of its consequence—the desire to embrace the new ideal. And without this confidence in Christ the power to carry out the desire would be impossible. The sacrifice of Christ is made available for us by our faith, because without reliance on Him for our idea of the new life and its attainment that sacrifice would leave us precisely where we were. Faith, so understood, is indeed the entrance into the new life. Its possessor can say with truth that he is saved from sin and death, for he has escaped from all that kept up the barrier between him and God, the source of life; he is living and acting as a friend and

FAITH AND FORGIVENESS 281

not a foe of God; he has left behind the paralysing sense of estrangement, the slavery of the passions which he hated while he obeyed them. It is like ceasing to be Judas and becoming as Jesus, or like passing, as John puts it, from death to life.

Such an interpretation of salvation by faith will serve to make clear another point of great importance. The existence of a sinister gulf between faith and conduct has often been emphasized by critics of evangelical religion, and even suspected by its supporters. Action, we have often been told, does not matter in the eyes of the evangelical. Belief is everything. The apostle said that our faith was imputed to us for righteousness, meaning thereby, surely, that what others less instructed vainly hoped to attain by laborious self-discipline, we can achieve by a simple 'I believe.' Belief, indeed, it is often added, is what God desires; no amount of good or self-denying conduct can ever satisfy Him by itself. It is easy to see how such a doctrine would lead some to the inquisitorial zeal of a Torquemada, and others to the dangerous levels of antinomianism. Yet the position is not without its psychological justification. Faith is necessary, in the sense in which it has just been described—that is, reliance on an authoritative and beloved person for the establishment of a relation of friendship and fellowship with him, and the power to adopt the way of life to be learnt from him. The error lies, as so often, in the assumption of an ' either . . . or,' and in regarding faith and conduct as alternatives or rivals. Faith does not replace conduct or render it unnecessary. Faith makes conduct possible. To say ' Faith is everything, and therefore conduct does not matter,' is like saying ' Breathing is everything, therefore eating does not matter.' Faith is nothing if it is not the foundation of conduct. Reliance on Christ means the will and the power to live the life of fellowship or partnership with Christ. To say ' I believe in Christ,' and to exhibit conduct which Christ could never acknowledge as His, is to be guilty of a kind of contradiction in terms. Spite and envy, pride and quarrelsomeness, fear and anxiety, are not blemishes that can be overlooked, while they are deplored, because of the faith that more than condones them. They are signs that faith does not exist, save in some embryonic fashion. For if faith were really there, they would be impossible. Or, to put it in another way, saving faith is the faith that saves from these very things; and if we are not saved from them, where is our faith?

It thus appears that the Church has not been burdened with too much faith, but impoverished by too little. The so-called 'ages of faith' were not ages of faith at all. Of credulity, yes; and of unthinking acceptance of the confident formulation of mysteries that angels might desire to peer into. But faith is something very different from this. It has no more to do with an unhesitating repetition of the Athanasian or any other creed than with an untroubled acquiescence in the marvels of the Old Testament narratives. In the august tradition that stretches from the prophets to the apostles,[1] faith could never be anything that puts reason or argument to sleep. It is rather something to which all sound reason and argument point, and without which our whole experience of the world would be a contradiction. Such indeed is the Christian view of God and the world. Without confidence in Christ as the revealer of the true way of life, and the source of the power to follow it, life itself would be as futile as it would be unintelligible. We could understand neither its limitation nor its promise, its disappointed hopes, its thwarted ambitions, its sudden turning of pleasure into pain, its strange and mysterious satisfactions which dwell in the very midst of sorrow and anguish—in the valley, as it were, of the shadow of death— nor its irrepressible desires and longings, its marvellous tale of exultations and agonies, and love, and man's unconquerable mind.

We must confess that when we look for examples of such faith as this, even in the Christian Church, we are met by constant disappointments. It is true, indeed, that examples of it can be found in every age of Christendom, and in every religious community. Every organized endeavour to secure some new embodiment of justice or charity, freedom or social well-being among men has discovered that for the bulk of its reliable and steadfast support it must look to men and women whose Christianity is the most important

---

[1] 'Come let us think it out together' (Isa. i. 18); 'We must therefore conclude that' (Rom. iii. 28); 'What do you think about it?' (Matt. xviii. 12).

FAITH AND FORGIVENESS 283

thing in their lives. But this is not to say that the faith for which we are looking is identical with the authoritative doctrine of the Church. Experience of the chequered history of the Church as a whole, and of the life of any religious body as it is known to its pastors or leaders, as well as of any great movement for moral or social progress, shows that on the whole there is little to choose between those who make a scrupulous profession of faith in the ecclesiastical sense and those who refuse to do so; and that if the ranks of the helpers and friends of mankind include many whose faith the Church could not deny, they include many others whose orthodoxy would be recognized in no religious body. On the other hand, if we examine the vital and formative convictions of the great benefactors of men, the sources of their inspiring teaching and still more inspiring examples, whether we think of Socrates or Dante, Luther or Mazzini, Carlyle or J. S. Mill or Ruskin, Catharine of Siena or Elizabeth Fry, we are dealing with men and women who differed from one another in almost every article of their creed, but who were alike in their reliance on the worth and power of a life which esteemed sincerity, goodwill, and self-abnegation as of more value than great possessions, and set the service of mankind above every consideration of ease and comfort. If the Christian Church had ever showed itself as an assemblage of persons from whom such a spirit could be confidently expected, how different would have been the history of the world!

Such a contention as this will be deprecated in some quarters. It will be taken to suggest that the Christian Church has been a failure; that its teaching has had no result in the past, and may be neglected in the future. Rightly understood, however, it forms our only ground for confidence. For the Church has been a failure, if we consider what have been its high claims. Individual members of the Church, and little groups of people within her borders, have proved themselves to be the salt of the earth. But they have found in nearly every case the truth of the saying that a man's foes are they of his own household. If we think of an Athanasius, we must also think of the turbulent bishops and monks who turned the Council of Ephesus into an assembly of robbers; if we think of the Lollards, the reformers before the Reformation, we must think of the ecclesiastics who persecuted them and stamped them out ; if we think of a Melanchthon, we must also think of a Pope Alexander or a Pope Julius. If, to take a humbler but no less heroic example, we think of the Tolpuddle martyrs, we must also think of the supporters of Church and State who condemned them to penal servitude for daring to combine to demand a living wage.

Now, to identify the faith of Christianity with the doctrines that they all professed, persecutors and persecuted alike, would obviously be to reduce it to a meaningless abstraction. Such a faith could be no instrument of salvation. In the face of all the evils of pride and covetousness, love of power and self-indulgence, it would leave men, as it has left them, exactly where it found them. Nor can we gain anything from arguing that the less trustworthy exponents of religion did not really believe at all in any vital sense. Calvin had fewer doubts than Servetus ; the Dorsetshire magistrates would have been as horrified at the idea of denying the truth of the Atonement as were the simple-minded John Loveless[1] and his unfortunate friends. If faith in the reconciling work of Christ means merely the willingness to accept and repeat the statement that Christ died for our sins, we must admit that it has done nothing to make the world a better or happier place. But if it does not mean this, it must mean an identification with the spirit of Christ's reconciling work and life, and a definite attitude to God and man maintained by virtue of confidence in that life as the only life worth living. We shall then have no difficulty in seeing that such a faith, whether its possessors have been recognized as Christians or not, has been the only means of salvation, or, in the true sense of the word, goodness.

Simple goodness, as we have argued, is not enough. The heart of men demands something more than morality and the devotion to duty. We need those deep satisfactions that spring from friendship and intimacy. We live by admiration, hope, and love. We must reach out a hand to the unseen, and feel the unseen responding with a grip like our own. All this is involved in religion ; and we do little service to religion if we narrow either our needs or its powers. But to say that simple goodness is not enough is

[1] See *History of Trade Unionism*, by S. and B. Webb, 1920, pp. 145 f.

FAITH AND FORGIVENESS 285

not to say that it does not matter, or that it can be treated as a thing of minor importance. That is the error that has been solemnly proclaimed from a thousand evangelical pulpits. If proteids are not enough for a complete human diet, they are not therefore to be neglected as an element of food. Goodness, as the chemist would say, can only exist in composition. It is the accompaniment and flower of those harmonious relations between persons which it is the work of reconciliation to produce. But unless goodness is attained, it is vain to talk of reconciliation. The sacrifice for the sins of the whole world is useless apart from faith—the faith that carries out its reconciling virtues into holy tempers and unselfish ideals. A religion which can live contentedly in a world which contains gambling hells and brothels and acres of back-to-back houses, and the glaring contrasts of idle wealth and overworked penury, and the deep-seated suspicion with which labour and capital glare at each other, is a religion which has come to regard the blood of the covenant as an unclean thing. Is its world any better than the world of Amos? 'Bring no more vain oblations' or useless talk of sacrifice, 'but let judgement flow down as mountain streams.'

XII

SACRIFICE AND RECONCILIATION

IF our preceding argument can be considered successful, we are agreed that the sacrificial victim is understood by its offerers to be, before its actual immolation, in some definite relation with the deity ; it is also in some definite relation with the worshippers themselves. Hence the two sundered parties can by its means come at one another, and the end of sacrifice is attained.

It must be admitted that 'relation' is a vague and fluctuating term. But its vagueness corresponds to the vagueness that appears to underlie the thoughts of the worshippers. And if religious emotions and expectations are to be condemned because they are vague, those which survive will be painfully few. Similarly, we cannot assert that wherever sacrifice has been offered, this view of its efficacy has been in the mind of the persons who have brought it to the altar. What we do assert is that the existence of the sacrificial ritual, as we actually observe it, cannot be explained unless we regard this view—often, doubtless, obscured—as fundamental. And we have also seen that whatever we may think of the wisdom or folly of the countless generations who have built their shrines on hill-top or in jungle, the bridge they have longed for, perhaps in ignorance, has been set up by Christ. What they expected their victims to do He has really accomplished ; what they supposed their victims to be or to become He really was. Thus it comes about that we can see a new meaning and an unsuspected nobility in them when we find them 'fulfilled,' as we say, in Him. And we understand the abiding significance of His sacrificial work all the better when we look back from it to all the toil and travail of hope and faith, confident or trembling, that has built the temple and inspired the sacrificial prayer. Here, as so often, the complete achievement and the incomplete attempts illuminate one another.

SACRIFICE AND RECONCILIATION 287

What is left for us in this concluding chapter is to look at sacrifice, as we may put it, from the inside rather than the outside. We are now familiar with the close connexion between the aims of sacrifice and of reconciliation. The two sundered parties have to be brought together; the barrier between them has somehow to be removed. We have agreed that the victim on the altar was felt, more or less inadequately, to accomplish this; and that Christ really did so. How was the result brought about? If we could answer this question, we might possibly make a further discovery. For if Christ provides the explanation of all sacrificial rites by being the world's offering, it is not perhaps too bold to suppose that as the world's reconciliation He may lay bare to us the law of reconciliation. And in a world of suspicion, enmity, and hate, where men turn their backs and harden their hearts as resolutely and bitterly against God as against each other, this would be no small thing.

We have already raised the question whether this interpretation of Christ's work as reconciliation, and of His sacrifice as the result of His whole life, gives due weight to the powerful appeal of the passion and tragedy of His death, His agony in the garden, His suffering and torture on the cross. We may grant that the Gospels describe these with an extraordinarily majestic reticence, speaking as if the bitterest pangs could extort no more than the single cry ' I thirst,' or one deep groan when all was done, and suggesting that even in that moment of mortal weakness pain was utterly unable to break Him as it breaks the strongest and most heroic of men; that He was, as it were, upborne by some high resolve serving as an anodyne more powerful than any anæsthetic to nerves that otherwise would have been quivering. But can we, in spite of all this, forget the enormous appeal that has been made in every age and on the most diverse natures by that awful spectacle?[1] An instinctive reverence may lead us, as it led the evangelists, to avoid the expressions by which we might seek to do justice to a human martyrdom; but to the majority at least of Christians Christ is never more completely divine than when we contemplate all that His human

---

[1] 'Quaerens me sedisti lassus,' &c.

frame endured from the contemptuous cruelty of His executioners.

There is, however, a second question which rises quite as naturally in minds of an opposite cast. Can all this talk of reconciliation, and especially of reconciliation by the endurance of suffering and death, do justice to that sublime summing of all manhood—*virtus*—which we look for in Christ? Suffering, such persons will say, might arouse our pity and horror, and even, when we reflect that we might have acted like His torturers had we been there, our self-loathing and remorse. But admiration and worship, they will add, demand action in their object, and not merely endurance. ' To take arms against a sea of troubles,' ' to strive and thrive,' ' to set the face like a flint and draw the sword against oppression and tyranny and violence '—all this touches something in us which remains passive when we contemplate the cross. The patriot dies for his country, and the crusader for his faith; but they fall sword in hand, and not unavenged. It may be true that ' force is no remedy,' and that the meekness of the unresisting and uncomplaining sheep beneath the rough hands of the shearers is the type of the highest human excellence. But a career, and a death, that seem to have no place for the virtues of a Gideon or a David, an Alfred or a Garibaldi, a Wilberforce or an Abraham Lincoln, or even, we might add, a Judith or a Josephine Butler, will appear to many to be at least one-sided and imperfect.

We have put both these contentions strongly—so strongly, indeed, that some will suspect that they answer themselves. Yet is it possible to answer them both satisfactorily? Those who feel the force of the one will have no sympathy with the other. If Christ is the perfect example of suffering and endurance, He cannot be the embodiment of heroic activity. If He is, how can He be the type of all the world's great champions and men of action? The appeal of the passive endurance of the cross is at an end. Must we not surrender one great ideal if we are to preserve the other? Traditional Christian art and the whole succession of Christian praise leave us in no doubt as to the ideal which they would surrender. Yet such a surrender is not really inevitable. The difficulty, serious as it is, arises from an imperfect understanding of what we mean by reconciliation. It must

SACRIFICE AND RECONCILIATION

now be our object to discover whether, by examining the significance of this term, we can find a place in it for both these factors in human excellence, of which we can give up neither without a sense of impoverishment and loss that half destroys our satisfaction with the alternative we preserve.

Let us begin by considering a little more closely this matter of suffering. Suffering, we agree, makes a unique emotional appeal. Why? The answer does not lie on the surface. For one thing, the appeal is not always the same. There are different kinds of suffering, and their effect on the spectator is different. To take some humble instances. The rabbit caught in a trap, the poisonous snake writhing under repeated blows, or the lark helplessly fluttering with a broken wing, arouse quite different emotions. Again, we are conscious of one kind of feeling when we watch Fagin in the condemned cell, and another when we see Sidney Carton on the platform beneath the guillotine. As a matter of fact, suffering does not necessarily excite even pity, unless we feel that it is undeserved or at least that the punishment which causes it is greater than the crime. Even then, pity may lead one spectator to approach the sufferer and bind up his wounds, pouring in oil and wine, while another will simply be repelled by a situation with which he cannot grapple, and pass by on the other side.

But the pity of the good Samaritan, noble incentive as it was, is something quite different from the emotion of the Christian who gazes at the cross. To the Christian, Christ is not an innocent man set upon by scoundrels and horribly done to death. He is not like some helpless Prince Arthur, put out of the way because an obstacle to another's ambition and greed. With such as these, the emotion is roused by the sight of suffering and nothing else, or at all events, the sight of suffering along with indignation at the cruelty of those who inflict it. But there is another kind of suffering which is not the whole of the drama, but only an incident in it, as with Cordelia, dying through her devotion to a parent who is surrounded by unscrupulous and immoral enemies. Here what makes the difference is not the suffering by itself, but the end in whose service it is incurred. We pity the sufferer, but we admire the

T

resolute mind which refuses to be bent from its purpose by suffering or anything else. Endurance in itself is no object of admiration. Admiration we reserve for resolve and action ; it is the reward of the active, not of the passive virtues. We do not, even in our noblest moments, desire to emulate the sufferer ; the person we would emulate is the hero who can regard suffering as a thing of no moment compared with the prize which he has determined to win, for himself or for the world. Suffering, considered apart from the object for which it is borne, is a thing to be ended or got rid of as soon as possible. We do not expect the surgeon to spend time in sympathizing with us, but to restore us to health.

It must also be remembered that to estimate suffering quantitatively is impossible. Suffering cannot be reckoned up in units. The intensity of physical suffering depends on the sensitiveness of the nerves, which may be quite different in different individuals. To give way to pain, as we say, is to feel it more deeply. To turn the mind away from it is to be less conscious of it. In the excitement of rapid and vigorous action, the absorption of conflict or the exaltation produced by a great affection or an overmastering purpose, pain may be forgotten or unnoticed. Mental suffering is even harder to estimate. Is it caused by our own failure to reach some end we have put before us ? Then it may be transformed by the stern joy of the thought that a renewed effort will perhaps bring success. Is it caused by disappointment at the weakness and ingratitude and folly of others ? Then it may be swallowed up in the proud consciousness of a call to a larger sacrifice in their behalf and a completer self-abnegation, or by the mere pleasure which many natures can find in sheer endurance and the facing of repeated difficulties. Paradox as it seems, the nobler the character the less will it feel the suffering against which a mean or selfish nature has no protection. Who shall say which of two men suffers more from an attack of toothache or from a serious business loss, or decide whether the pain which one man may endure to save another from inconvenience or distress is greater or less than what the other, left to himself, would have been likely to experience ? One amount of suffering cannot be weighed against another ; nor can any one piece

SACRIFICE AND RECONCILIATION 291

of suffering be said to balance or to be an equivalent for some other for which it may be looked upon as a substitute.

The moral value and the emotional appeal of suffering, then, are both conditioned by the purpose for which the suffering is borne. Clearly, when we speak of one person suffering for another this is what we imply. The sufferer is bent on rendering a service to some one else, his pain being either the price he pays to confer the boon, or its inevitable accompaniment; in either case, it will be impossible for us to think of the suffering apart from the boon. The suffering of Christ was the suffering involved in the inestimable benefit He conferred on us in 'bringing us to God.' It produces in us not so much pity as gratitude. How was that suffering involved in Christ's work? As the payment of a price or as the inevitable accompaniment of His purpose? If the former, we are met by the question that perplexed the early theologians. To whom was the price paid? Three answers alone are possible: to the devil, to God, or to the demands made, we may suppose, by eternal justice. Each of these views, we need hardly point out, is unscriptural. If it is impossible now to think of the devil as having any right of ownership over us which would demand recognition by Christ, it is equally impossible for us to think of God the Father as holding us in a condition of servitude from which we could only be bought off by so much pain endured by the Son. The Bible at least is clear on that point when it uniformly represents Christ as sent or commanded by the Father to release us; and we might well ask, In what relation to God should we be left after the process of buying us off was completed? As to the demands of eternal justice, we really know too little about such an abstraction, considered apart from God, to be able to make any affirmation about such a transaction with it.

If, then, we cannot entertain this view of the sufferings of Christ as the payment of a price, a *quid pro quo*, we must think of them as something involved in the task set before Him. And if we bear in mind, as we must, the relativity of all suffering, whether of the body or the mind, we shall think more of the task itself than of what it might imply. We may be quite sure, at all events, that this is what Christ did. Every task that can attract a noble and heroic soul will involve suffering. But this suffering must be risked, and neglected. To do this is not Stoicism. There was nothing of the Stoic about Christ. Stoicism is essentially self-centred. The deeper heroism loses itself in its zeal and affection for others. Such was the heroism of Christ. But just because it lost itself in affection for others, it was best able to ignore and leave out of account the toil and peril of its steep ascent.

We come back, then, to the actual task of reconciliation which was set before Christ. What did this involve? And here we must beware of abstractions. The great temptation of the theologian in dealing with the Atonement has been to regard his problem as if it were a question of mathematics. On the one side is the human race, lost and ruined in sin; on the other is a perfect individual, Christ, over whom sin has no power. Christ voluntarily submits to death. What, then, is the effect of that death on the human race? Or, if we may assume that the race is thereby liberated, what does that liberation imply, and how is it brought about? It cannot be denied that the answers to this question have been unsatisfactory. Acute intellects in every age have devoted themselves to the subject, but the solutions show no sign of approaching each other. We can never expect them to do so while the terms employed are so far removed from actual experience. For what is meant by the race, which is thus lost and redeemed? To ask this suggests the old dispute between nominalist, realist, and conceptualist. Or, putting these technicalities aside, do we mean by the term all human individuals, dead, living, and to be born; or the great mass of persons who approximate to a general type, '*l'homme moyen sensuel*'; or have we in mind some metaphysical entity, which is greater than the sum of the individuals who may be taken to compose it? These are not simple problems even for the modern philosopher. They would not be simple for the Rabbinical thinkers from whom Paul learnt his phrases about the first and second man and the first and last Adam. Happily we need not spend time upon them here, for it will surely be agreed that Christ came to save individuals, men and women, and it is as individuals that we need salvation for ourselves. A transaction performed on behalf of the race can be nothing to

SACRIFICE AND RECONCILIATION

us, unless it is also performed for us as individuals. And when we consider the 'human race,' or any one section of it, in any one age or period, Babylon under Hammurabi, Athens under Pericles, Rome under Augustus, or London and Paris as they exist to-day, where persons of every level of moral exaltation and depravity are to be found, we cannot wonder at the absence of any agreement as to what the one work of Christ for such a bewildering diversity really is. The difficulties involved in thus discussing the race were not so obvious in an earlier age, when the race could be regarded as divided into the Church and the world, and when the differences between these two classes were felt to be so great that minor differences could be neglected. Membership in the, or a, visible Church cannot now be thought of as a guarantee of salvation; and the other differences between men refuse to be overlooked.

To protest against this reliance on an abstraction is not to forget the influences and similarities that bind us all together. No sooner do we think of differences than we are forced to think of likenesses. Society is made up of individuals who are like one another in certain respects and respond to their environment in a certain way. And each individual is influenced in a thousand ways for good or evil by the others who make up the various social groups to which he belongs. But while we allow this to the psychologist and the sociologist with caution, we must reluctantly deny it to the metaphysician. We cannot even refuse to listen to the biologist when he reminds us that the generations are bound together by ties of heredity, and that the unity of the race is longitudinal, so to speak, as well as latitudinal. The biologist has been claimed as an ally by the metaphysician, and the conception of a 'lost and ruined race' has been held to be proved by the conclusions of Darwin and Weismann. But this is surely to ask for more than we can justly demand. What is inherited is neither moral excellence nor immoral turpitude; it is that capacity to respond to certain influences, and the tendency to respond in a certain way, without which any society, even the most rudimentary, would be impossible. We have only to think of the individuals who have filled a large place in the history of any given period, or who have been conspicuous in public or

294 ALTAR, CROSS, AND COMMUNITY

social life in any one year through which we have lived, to recognize that heredity, when we have done our best to rate it high, does not denote any moral likeness between members of the same race or the same society ; and even less does it allow us to place humanity on one plane either of ruin or salvation.

The reconciling work of Christ, then, cannot be taken to mean that the race as such has been reconciled to God by any one act performed independently of it, any more than it can mean, if our previous argument is correct, that without it the race is in avowed hostility to God. We must put on one side the supposition that Christ's death, taken by itself, had some mysterious effect either on God or man, whether we understand by ' man ' the sum of individual men, or the ideal man, or the average man, or anything else. The difficulty of conceiving such an effect we have already sufficiently considered. To understand that work we must surely go back to the Gospels, and ask what was the effect which Jesus did actually produce on men, and how He produced it. And this is already clear to us. He impressed them first of all as going about doing good, and speaking as never man spoke. He shared their sorrows, felt the burden of their maladies and pains, put forth power to heal them in response to confidence on their part, entered into the shame of their sin, and, in answer to their faith, forgave them for it and broke its power over them. He faced contradiction and ingratitude, desertion and insult ; He refused to use for His own ends powers which He clearly possessed ; He chose to serve where He could have commanded, to let men alone where He might have punished, and pardon when He might have condemned. And into all this He flung an intensity of passion which caught men with sudden shocks of surprise—His stern set face as He travelled up to Jerusalem for the last time, His grief and distress as He looked at the city at the moment when it was opening its gates to receive His triumphant and jubilant followers ; His scathing attacks upon the religious leaders of society ; His yearning affection to His few unswerving companions ; the strange disturbance which swept through His spirit on the fatal night of His arrest, followed by His amazing calmness and austere dignity before both Jewish and Roman authorities ; and His unbroken

SACRIFICE AND RECONCILIATION 295

self-command throughout the long fierce torture on the cross. Indeed, for those who would lift the veil still farther from His inner life, and would ask what settled mood underlay those signs of ardour and dread, affection and scorn, we are irresistibly reminded of the Psalm which He Himself quoted just before the moment of His death, a Psalm which passes from the deepest consciousness of suffering and isolation to an equally buoyant confidence in God and the future over which God presides. Nor is this all. We can see Him impressing those who came nearest to Him with the sense that in Him was something divine. He made them understand what God was like; He showed them the Father; He made them feel that He was actually one thing with the Father. And when the miserable yet sublime tragedy of His death was over—a death to which no one could have forced Him to submit, and which was, therefore, like everything else He accomplished, undergone for them, for their sin and the sin of the whole evil world which had rejected Him—He appeared to them again. Not even death could end His love for them and His presence with them. Still more marvellous, that same presence was more than with them; it was in them. Even when they saw Him no more they possessed Him; His 'breath,' His spirit, had fallen upon them. What they had seen Him do they could, in His name, do themselves.

So much for the impression He made on them. But there was another impression they found they were making on themselves. As they saw and felt more of Him, they detected something fresh in themselves—a sense of harmony and peace with God; a fuller understanding of the new 'spirit' that was properly theirs; a readiness and ease in adopting the new way of life, at once gentle and adamantine, which had at first surprised them so much, but which they now knew was the one way to the Father. Though we have no record that Jesus ever spoke to the disciples like sinners whom He had forgiven, they were sure that in this new life which intercourse with Him had made possible their sins had been done away.

Naturally, His more intimate companions were the first to experience all this. But the experience was not confined to them. They were bound to communicate it. The discovery of the possibilities of the new peace and confidence and effectiveness could not be kept to themselves. It was offered to others, and it was accepted, first inside and then outside the Jewish circle in which Jesus and His disciples had lived. It was long before all that was implied by the message was understood. Perhaps that time has not arrived even yet. But that belief in Jesus which the disciples themselves had learnt through actual and personal friendship proved capable of bringing those who had never seen Him into the same relations of harmony with God, with themselves, and with each other. What held good for the disciples held good for those to whom their experience was communicated, in their own age and in every succeeding century.

If we look at this account again we shall see that it really describes the process of reconciliation, and thus, as we may say, the work of sacrifice at its best and fullest. Into a world where man dwells in perplexed estrangement from God there appears one who sets Himself at the side of all the men and women around Him, and is one with them in everything except their sin—that is, except the cause of their estrangement. At the same time He is one with God in His knowledge of God's demands, His devotion to God's will, and His enjoyment of God's full and unbroken love. As men yield themselves to Him, believe His promises, accept His offers, and follow His precepts, they find that they, too, are brought into touch with God ; and that the barriers which never existed for Christ now no longer exist for them. So far the elements in Christ's reconciliation are at least foreshadowed, as we have seen, in the ethnic sacrifices ; what He has done has been to translate these into terms of personal intercourse. But other elements in His work which we have observed are entirely new—eager, unwearied service, resolute endurance of ingratitude and misunderstanding, opposition and persecution, up to the limit of a violent and awful death ; the refusal to use supreme and irresistible power for any private advantage, and the voluntary and complete submission to all the dreadful consequences of others' sin.

Such was the mode of reconciliation that availed for all our race. Clearly it was no transaction in which we human beings were treated like things rather than persons ; nor was it anything done over our heads. It avails for us all because it makes offers which every man can accept and demands which every man can fulfil. It is universal because it neglects everything that is peculiar to any one age or belief or level of culture. It rests on what is common to human nature itself. Devotion and love, resolution and patience, courage and endurance, and the transforming effect of one nature on another—these are the means, carried to a height never known before, by which God chose to save mankind through Christ.[1]

Does this hold good of all mankind? Influenced by a small but very significant group of passages in Paul and John, Christian thought has held firmly to the pre-existence, and indeed the eternal pre-existence, of Christ. Arius has always been felt to have laid the axe to the root of the tree when he asserted that there was a time when Christ was not. Into the metaphysics of the question we must not allow ourselves to enter in this place; but we can at least observe that if such reconciliation as is here described is pre-eminently the work of Christ, it is not hard to think that whenever men have been reconciled to God we can see Christ. In every age and every religion men have experienced reconciliation with God, dim as their ideas both of God and of the essentials of reconciliation may have been. This will at once be recognized in the case of the Hebrew saints of the Old Covenant. Nor can it be denied of certain Greek philosophers, Roman Stoics, Oriental seers, or even of simpler souls reared in what we call paganism, without denying it to all save a small minority of Christians. It would then follow that if we must acknowledge the presence of Christ where we see His work being done, God has been from the beginning reconciling the world to Himself, and that the actual life of Christ on earth, as men saw it in

[1] Cf. Oman, *Grace and Personality* (1919), p. 140 : ' If it is the essential nature of God to have this personal relation to His children, He could be manifested only in a life perfectly lived among men, through a perfect relation to Himself. . . . The final triumph of this manifestation is the cross, the obedience unto death of the Prince of Peace in the service of God's Kingdom of Righteousness. When persecution for righteousness, even to shame and agony, stirs only pardon and supplication for His oppressors, it is turned from being an evidence of God's indifference into the triumph of His love; and by sharing in that triumph His children are made victorious over all evil.'

Jesus of Nazareth, was the supreme visible example of the great and secular operation of God in the Son of His love.

It was this, but it was something more. It was the supreme example of what we may call the law of reconciliation. We cannot reflect on human society as it presents itself to us to-day, or as we may study it in any previous age, without being convinced that reconciliation in its larger meaning is the most important condition of all prosperity and wellbeing. Human history is not simply the record of the waging of wars, but of the making of peace. The latter is not so dramatic as the former, but it is vastly more significant. If the matter had been studied more carefully, we should have learnt that peace, if it is not to be the transference of war to another and perhaps sterner sphere, is more than a nice adjustment of interests. It cannot be gained by throwing conflicting ideas or hopes into a balance weighted by the sword of the conqueror. Peace does not result from a balance of interests, but from an approximation of personalities.[1] Its basis is neither commercial nor material. We must confess that the examples of such a peace furnished by history are disappointingly few. But we can at least see that attempts to bring about peace by any other means have always resulted in failure. And if we turn from the struggles of nations to the reactions of smaller groups, families, or parties within a state, or single individuals with one another, we shall see that any reconciliation always contains the main elements in the process as we have described them—the union in the person of the reconciler or reconcilers of the true and permanent factors in both contentions, the eager and self-forgetful desire to bring both parties together, and the refusal to use force where persuasion, example, and goodwill are the appointed means.

In other words, the work of Christ is the norm of all reconciliation ; and this is true although any one who would bring about reconciliation among human beings has often to deal with parties, both of whom are unwilling to pass or lower the barrier, while Christ came as the emissary of one of the two sundered parties, and gave His life to the

[1] This is equally true of any peace or reunion between rival ecclesiastical bodies.

SACRIFICE AND RECONCILIATION

task of changing the mind and will of the other. And this conclusion will appear all the more important if we are willing to take the farther step to which our argument would seem to lead. If reconciliation with God is indeed more than a transaction performed for us, it means that we unite ourselves, when reconciled, with God's purpose and mind and will. Being is here impossible without doing. But reconciliation with God's mind and purpose is meaningless apart from reconciliation to a life of reconciling. For how do we know God's mind save through Christ ? And when we look at Christ to discover this, what do we find in Him but the reconciler? Hence the proper function of the Christian, who is himself reconciled to God in Christ, must be the reconciliation of opposing and sundered parties. For such work the world, in these distracted days after the war, is calling out piteously. Within the several nations of Europe the war, while it continued, brought a certain grim and unnatural reconciliation of its own. In our own country the problems of Ireland, of industry, and of the position of women were by common consent thrust, at least for a time, into the background. It was the same in Germany, in France, in Italy, among the Southern Slav peoples, and even, as we imagined at the time, in Russia. A common peril, or a common hope, makes strange bedfellows. But as the war dragged on these superficial harmonies disappeared ; and we are now left with a welter of suspicion, intrigue, and conflicting ambitions and interests within and without the old national boundaries, which, alike in their bitterness, their complexity, and their material resources, surpass anything known in previous ages, and which threaten to bring the whole fabric of civilization, tottering uneasily after the repeated shocks of war, to the ground.

Here, then, is an unavoidable task for the religion of reconciliation. The call has been uttered, but seldom clearly heard, and still more seldom responded to, in other ages. The mediaeval Church lifted her voice in the name of the Truce of God ; the Society of Friends has borne an unflinching witness for peace at all times and at all costs ; and it is safe to say that at the present time the only organized bodies from which the League of Nations receives any whole-hearted support are the Christian Churches.

The great majority of the convinced friends of international peace and goodwill have been Christian men and women ; but they have never been allowed to forget that they were in an all but hopeless minority among their co-religionists. The result made itself disastrously visible in the war and its consequences. In the tense days before the war, when we were being told, in tones of increasing assurance and authority, that a world conflict was inevitable, the Christian Church had no doctrine of reconciliation to preach to the nations ; when the cataclysm took place, few of her spokesmen could do anything save call on the God of battles to show the right and crush the oppressor and the tyrant, as if the Almighty Himself, twenty centuries after He had sent Jesus to commend His love to sinners, had no other alternative. Now that what we agree to call peace is sharpening old feuds and calling new ones into being, the Church seems condemned to look on helplessly at the desperate plight of the world and its statesmanship, or to pass by on the other side.

It is no wonder that thousands of intelligent people regard the Church as an amiable nonentity. What is the value, they ask, of its theology of the Atonement? It has a formal scheme of reconciliation, they agree, repeated with slight variations in a long succession of theological text-books, and based on an alleged proceeding which, if attempted in ordinary human society, would be either unjust or impossible. But, they urge, it knows no more than the rest of us about the real nature of reconciliation. The Church can neither reconcile men to God nor to one another. It would be difficult to maintain that this is unfair. ' By their fruits ye shall know them.' The reply may be made : ' You must not expect us (such is human weakness) to do what the Master did.' But this is to condemn ourselves for want of faith, or to condemn Him for want of power. The truth is that, in spite of all our theological treatises, the law of reconciliation through sacrifice, as it has been dimly foreshadowed even in the infancy of religion, and supremely exemplified for all time by Christ, is one of the things hidden from the wise and prudent, and never taught with either authority or knowledge by the society to whom He committed it once for all.

Another defence, however, may be attempted. ' It is

SACRIFICE AND RECONCILIATION 301

not the business of the Church, the company of the followers of Jesus, to make peace between the nations. It must leave them to go their own miserable and disastrous way. Its task lies with individuals.' Suppose we concede this despairing interpretation of the desire of all nations. We must then turn to the sphere of the life of individuals or, perhaps we shall be allowed to add, groups. How has the Church succeeded with the message of reconciliation there? The quarrels of other days between patrician and plebeian, freeman and serf, master and slave, rich and poor, have now organized themselves into the vast struggle between capital and labour which is being waged, it seems safe to say, in steadily increasing fierceness in three continents, and will soon perhaps be a dominating factor in the economic life of the other two. If the conflict could be solved by a redistribution of property or income, or of economic and industrial functions, the Church might find a reason for standing aside, reflecting that she had more important work to attend to, and that God had not made her a judge or divider among the sons of men. But no mere redistribution of commodities or functions will end the conflict. Its roots lie deep in human passions, suspicions, and jealousies—the memory of past wrongs, the love of power and authority, the thirst for vengeance and the fear of future oppression. To say that Christianity has nothing to do with these is to bid her turn from the holiest of her services to men, to condemn herself to inaction in the field where she should gain her noblest triumph. The unexpected success which has befallen some quite inexperienced ecclesiastic when he attempted to play the part of reconciler, and the widespread gratitude he has received, show how ready the world is to welcome the mediator.[1] The State may contrive the mechanism of mutual adjustment and *rapprochement*, in its Wages Boards and Whitley Councils; from whom should the spirit come more fitly than from those to whom has been committed the ministry of reconciliation?

Even on this ground, some will argue, the Church is an

---

[1] Compare, for example, the position of Cardinal Manning in the Dock Labourers' Strike in 1899 (see Webb, *History of Trade Unionism*, p. 404, also p. 332), and Bishop Westcott in relation to the Durham Miners' Strike in 1893.

intruder. She can do nothing in the sphere of economics. She is necessarily too ignorant. If she intervenes in such quarrels she will but receive the blows of both parties, and gain nothing for herself or for them. That she has generally been too ignorant to intervene in labour troubles with any success is painfully true. That such ignorance is necessary is a disastrous misunderstanding of the mind of the Prince of Peace. The knowledge that is needed is not simply the knowledge of what passes for economic law. It is the knowledge of the way in which men are actually brought together, of the spirit in which arguments can be used with any hope of success, and appeals made. But let us concede that she is to be denied even this knowledge, and all the results that would follow from its possession and use. Let us shut her out from dealing with societies, and admit that she must begin and end with individuals. The sphere to which she will then be confined is by no means insignificant. Human quarrelsomeness is not imprisoned in the political and industrial worlds. It lives and thrives in private life, between neighbours, acquaintances, members of the same family and adherents of the same Church. In these matters there are no diplomatic traditions, no ' iron laws of economics,' to impede her operations or distract her enthusiasms. A reflective observer from another world might well be surprised and perplexed that envy, hatred, and malice should abound even where the supremacy of the religion of Christ is professed and asserted. Another fact is even more serious—that in the face of such a defiance of her spirit the Church has no systematized teaching or method of treatment. She deplores the evil, she demands or begs for repentance and reformation. Few would suppose that she was wont to contemplate, as the most sacred thing she knew, the perfect and sufficient example of reconciliation once for all given to the world.

It is possible that some, while they are willing to admit that those who have been reconciled to God must themselves be reconcilers, will argue that such reconciliation consists only in bringing men to God, and that with the quarrels of men among themselves Christian people as such have nothing to do. It would seem to be enough to urge, in reply, that in the view of the New Testament reconciliation between men is the essential preliminary to

SACRIFICE AND RECONCILIATION

reconciliation with God.[1] It would indeed be asking for the self-contradictory to hope for peace with the God of harmony and goodwill and co-operation while nourishing pride and self-seeking towards men. Nor would it be more reasonable to imagine that the Christian himself could be at peace with God while he tolerated in his own neighbourhood, or in what might be a sphere of his own influence, the bitterness and evil-speaking, the bickering and malice which, if we may judge from Paul or from Jesus, are as hateful to God as the gross sins of the flesh. True, in the actual order of thought or conduct peace with God may precede peace with men. Zacchaeus' fourfold restoration may follow rather than precede the coming of Jesus to the sinner's house. And no one can blame religious teachers for urging reconciliation to God even upon the most selfish and quarrelsome. Only let it be remembered that such reconciliation, unless it involves the cessation of quarrels with men, amounts to nothing at all. And in most cases, in spite of theological schematism, obedience to the simple rule of Jesus will probably have the best results; we can best show men the entrance to peace with God by setting them in harmony with one another.

But this, viewed in the light of what has gone before, is no light task. 'Love to the loveless shown, that they might lovely be,' as it is the most Christlike thing that a man can set himself to do, so it is the hardest and the most heroic. And yet it is, of all tasks that we could set ourselves, that for which we can with most confidence demand all the resources of heaven. For if we can only enter into fellowship with God by sharing His passion for reconciliation and peace-making, that passion is what He is eager to share with us. Let a man start to desire it, and all heaven bends yearningly down to him. It is useless to talk about faith in the blood of Christ if we can heal no quarrels and disarm no enmities, if we cannot love the loveless or take the first step in some concession to the ungrateful or the hostile, or, worse still, if we pursue the heathen policy of sweeping out of our way the rivals who try to compete with us. But, once that faith is kindled,

[1] 1 John iv. 20 : ' He that loveth not his brother whom he hath seen,' &c. Cf. Matt. v. 24 (quoted p. 25), ' First be reconciled to thy brother,' &c.

the fire of God comes down to greet it. That is the time when we perceive how much of self-suppression, renunciation of ambitions, and bitterness of spirit is entailed by such a task and by such faith. We set forth to consecrate ourselves for their sake, and for His, and we find ourselves in contact with the ugliness and filth of the callousness and greed with which we have to identify ourselves as we try to bear it in His spirit. The prospect may easily appal. Even without the consciousness of making a definite refusal, the mind may turn away almost automatically to what seems a pleasanter and safer way of serving God. But if we can overcome this danger, we discover with surprising speed that to share the task of Christ means also to share His mind. We take up our cross as He took up His, we accept Him as our sacrifice, we lay our hand, so to speak, on His head, as the offerer laid his on the head of his victim; we acknowledge Him as our mediator, the revelation and guide into the presence of the Holiest, before whom no barrier can stand, and we find that the sacrifice which joins us to God joins God to us. In the reconciling life of Christ God has revealed to us the path that leads to Him.[1]

The law of reconciliation can and must be stated in terms of man as well as of God. All true reconciliation conforms to it. Reconciliation is one, whether both parties are human, or one is divine. 'To as many as received Him, to them gave He authority to become children of God, to those who believe on His name.' To-day the whole world is calling out for reconciliation. A new paganism of lust and greed (only another form of self-seeking) and of hatred is overflowing human society. The religion that cannot stay its advance is doomed. The religion that can defeat it has overcome the world. We talk vaguely about Christianity as the life of love—so vaguely that our half-hearted attempts at goodwill often evaporate and disappear in the mist. In the light of the

---

[1] Cf. Oman, *op. cit.*, p. 196: 'Only thus, in bearing and forbearing with one another, have we the fellowship of Christ's sufferings and enter into the sphere where Christ's blood, meaning His service and suffering, cleanses us from all sin. . . . In Christ's cross, therefore, above all else, we discern the gracious relation of our Father toward us, because there, as nowhere else, is the utter service of our brethren, unconditioned by their merit, shown to be the essential spirit of His family.'

SACRIFICE AND RECONCILIATION

Atonement, love means reconciliation, the ending of quarrels through Him who has brought us into fellowship or partnership with God, the creation of an atmosphere in which hostility and self-seeking wither and die. 'Blessed are the peacemakers, for they shall be called the children of God.' With their sacrifices God is well pleased.

Such a view of the reconciling sacrifice of Christ brings us back finally to a conception that has been very often misunderstood, and emphasized now too much and now too little, the priestly ministration of the servant of Christ. The sacrifice of Christ has reconciled us to God, and brought us into living and active harmony with His mind and will. That harmony was fundamental for Christ ; and to say that Christ's sacrifice has availed for us means that it has become equally fundamental for us. Thus the end to which Christ devotes Himself, reconciling men to God, will be the end to which we, once reconciled, devote ourselves.

But reconciliation to God, as we have seen, involves reconciliation to man. It thus follows that while from one point of view the sacrifice of Christ was unique, from another, sacrifice, as the Christlike work of reconciliation, is always needed, and must always be offered. What has been not very wisely called the priesthood of believers is something more than the right of direct access to God in prayer and worship and intercession. It is the sublime function of mediating, as Christ mediated, between those who are at variance. The priest stood to offer sacrifice, and the Christian's sacrifice is neither more nor less than reconciliation. He knows, indeed, that through the mediation of Christ he and all who come to Christ are reconciled to God. But this very experience shows him that in no spirit of rivalry to the Master, but in sheer harmony and union with Him, he too has his sacrifice to offer.

To attempt to translate this function of the Church, the redeemed and reconciled company of believers, into the terms of modern life raises at once the vision of a new world. But let us venture to imagine all those who confess the duty of a serious and genuine obedience to Christ, or, as we say, are conscious of any real access to God through Him, as resolutely concerned to knit up the ravelled sleeve of the political and industrial life of their time. Let us also imagine that they are more anxious to do this than to assist in securing any success or advantage for their own nation or class or party or church; and, further, that they are content to work according to the law of reconciliation revealed and carried out by Christ, identifying themselves both with the interests and hopes, and the disabilities and distresses, of the men who stand on the other side of the barrier, abjuring whatever endowments of wealth or position or power may be theirs, meeting even opposition with patience and injury with forgiveness. And let us imagine that all opposition between man and God is felt to call for the same sacrificial work—luxury and ostentation, pride and impurity, self-indulgence and tyranny. If all this could come about, a new and cleansing force would be found to be at work in the world. But it must be accomplished. Since everything which the Church calls sin and the moralist vice is the result and the sign of the barrier between man and God, the sacrifice of Christ, as long as that barrier exists, must be carried out by the Christ-like ministry of His followers. When such sacrifices are offered solemnly and regularly, and when they are looked upon as the natural and necessary function of the Christian, we may hope that the atoning work of Christ will be recognizable in a reconciled and renewed world.

NOTE ON PRIESTHOOD

In the history of religion the priest is of secondary importance as compared with the sacrifice. The priest exists for the sacrifice, and not the sacrifice for the priest. As regards the offerer, sacrifices can be divided into four classes—those offered by any one who wishes to approach a god or gods; those offered by the head of the social organization or group concerned, a king or tribal chief or the father of a family; those offered by any one of the above with the assistance of a specific functionary or priest; and those offered by a priest on behalf of the worshippers.

The priest has performed many functions. In the earlier stages of the priesthood he is often barely distinguishable from a king or a magician. He is chosen, or gains his position, as being a person of abnormal, or, as we might say, magical powers, and therefore fitter to deal with the mysterious and the unseen; or for his special holiness, which enables him to approach the god, when an ordinary man could not do so without danger; by means of his knowledge and training in the exact rites which are necessary to secure the success of the sacrifice; or because of a hereditary qualification. The position of the priest might be illustrated by that of the chaplain in a wealthy English family in the seventeenth or eighteenth century.

All these varieties of priesthood can be observed in the Old Testament. The first is rare; but even as regards the first, the 'man of god'—that is, the individual who, like Elijah, is specially 'in touch' with the supernatural—will be obviously marked out as one to offer sacrifices. The holiness of the priests, in a semi-material sense, is constantly insisted on in the Priests' Code, as well as in Ezekiel and the Law of Holiness. The story of Micah (Judges xvii.), who engages a professional priest, and is thus assured that his private chapel will be all that he hopes, and the hereditary position of the priests at Shiloh or Nob, as forming a close and influential caste, prepare us for the importance of the descendants of Zadok at Jerusalem and the house of Aaron in the Priests' Code.

But, until Deuteronomic times, the priest was not necessary for the sacrifice, though his presence would naturally be welcomed. When the monarchy was established the king acted as president at the sacrifice, as head alike of the nation and the Church, just as, when the kingship ceased in Athens and in Rome, the royal title was transferred to one of the official priests.

In the Old Testament, as elsewhere, the priests had other and older functions, both as to religious ceremonial and civil and social precedents.[1] As to the first, the priest's directions, at least in earlier times, were of more importance than his actual participation in the sacrificial ritual; as to the second, the priests, at least before the establishment of the monarchy, were constantly called in to act as judges or arbitrators (in Hebrew and other early societies the difference was not so great as to-day); as the guardian of the oracular ephod, the priest could also announce to inquirers what Jehovah wished or would allow them to do.[2] It is noteworthy that the Arabic *kahin*, from the same root as the Hebrew *kohen*, or priest, has sunk, in the Koran, to a diviner.[3]

When the sacrifices were interpreted spiritually, as in Ps. l. or Mic. vi. 8, the priest became unnecessary. The contrite heart and the humble life were a matter for the worshipper and his God alone. The same is true of the New Testament conception of worship. The Christian's 'reasonable service' needs no priest to render it valid. The first Epistle of Peter, indeed, twice speaks of the Christian community as a priesthood (ii. 5, 9), but the term is suggested by the metaphor of the spiritual sacrifices in the former of the two passages, and the context of the latter also forbids the pressing of any sacerdotal idea. Except in the Epistle to the Hebrews, Christ is not spoken of as a priest. His offering is thought of in terms of Isa. liii. and not of the Levitical altar. The argument of

---

[1] See Deut. xvii. 10, 11, xxiv. 8, xxxiii. 10; Jer. ii. 8, xvii. 18; Ezek. vii. 26; 2 Chron. xv. 3.

[2] 1 Sam. xiv. 18, xxiii. 6, xxx. 7 f; Hos. iii. 4.

[3] See the valuable note by S. R. Driver in *Priesthood and Sacrifice*, edited by Sanday, 1900, pp. 19 f.

NOTE ON PRIESTHOOD

Hebrews is that, for the Christian, priests are not needed.[1] Christ did more than all the priests could do, and far more effectively. To call Him a priest 'after the order of Melchizedek' is to say that in the Levitical sense He was not a priest at all. And the Christian's relation to Christ is in any case wholly different from that of the worshipper to any class of priest mentioned above.

In the early Church, as in the language of the New Testament, priests drop out of sight. The officers of the Church, both prophetic, teaching, charismatic, and administrative, have nothing priestly about them. The first Epistle of Clement, indeed, refers to priests and Levites as gifts of God and signs of His love of order (32, 40, 41); but this is only to show that there must be a corresponding orderliness, not a corresponding ministry, in the Christian Church. Tertullian is the first to speak of the bishop as a priest; the full sacerdotal dignity of the Christian ministry is first found in Cyprian and the Apostolical Constitutions. But the Western Church leaders knew little of the precise meaning of the Levitical terminology which they used so freely. They were concerned to claim the authority of the Old Testament for a conception of which the Old Testament knew nothing—a magisterial hierarchy which in the spirit of the officials of the Roman Empire was to rule the Church and dispense its blessings to men. The conception has remained in the Roman Church, strengthened by the increasing emphasis laid on the Eucharist as a sacrifice. Repudiated by Luther and the majority of Protestants, it has been adopted by large sections of the Anglican community, where, however, more stress is laid on the validity of its ministrations than on the authority in matters of administration of the bishop from whom its validity springs. Without a priest in the apostolic succession vouched for by episcopal ordination, one cannot be sure—such is the theory—that a sacrament will be a means of grace, and therefore to take part in such a sacrament is a sin.

The term 'the Priesthood of Believers' is often used in Protestant circles; but no sacerdotal duty, to be discharged by all Christian laymen, can be discovered either in the history or the theology of the Church. Sometimes the

[1] See p. 202.

phrase is used of the duty of intercession. But to a Christian intercession is not in any sense a priestly function. The Christian may be called a priest if priest is used in the quite unhistorical sense of 'any one who offers a sacrifice.' The Christian sacrifice, whether understood as one of praise and prayer, of a life devoted to God, or of the specific work of reconciliation in the spirit of Christ, is one which goes back to pre-Deuteronomic times, when every pious and honest man had free access to God, and could approach with boldness to the throne of grace. It is, as we have seen, the duty and privilege of every Christian to offer himself as a sacrifice of reconciliation. But priesthood has long suggested privilege and status, ideas entirely foreign to the disciple of Jesus; and it is wiser to drop the term altogether, as it is dropped in the Gospels, both as regards Jesus and His followers, and to fix our attention on the sacrifice to be offered.

INDEX OF NAMES AND SUBJECTS

A

Aaron, 203
Abbott, E. A., 168
Abel, 205
Abelard, 226 f, 232, 242
'Aboda Zara,' 247
Abrahams, L., 124
Admiration, 288, 290
Aeschylus, 270
Agape, 245, 249
Agni, 62 f
Alcestis, 183
Alexander, Pope, 284
Allen, A. V. G., 249
Altar Rites, relation of Jesus to, 178, 189, 191, 198, 243
American Indians, 44, 61, 268
Amos, on Sacrifice, 108, 141, 184, 285
Anahita, 83
Anglicanism, 257 f, 260 f
Anselm, on Atonement, 39, 223
Anthropomorphism, 39; in tribal gods, 41; Prophets and, 204
Antioch, 185
Antiphon, 254
Aphrodite, 69
Apocalypse, 148, 173, 193, 249
Apostolical Constitutions, 246
Apuleius, 85 f, 91
Aquinas, on Atonement, 224, 227 f; compared with Luther, 229
Arabia, 97, 104, 124
Arianism, 277, 297
Aristophanes, 75, 132
Aristotle, 132, 134, 154, 236, 238, 264
Arminianism, 230
Arnold, M., 75
Artemis, 69
Arval Brothers, 41
Asclepius, 22, 77, 134
Assouan, 122
Aswamedha, 59, 96
Athanasius, 241
Athena Polias, 83
Atonement, 30, 88, 98, 114, 116, 123, 151, 187, 198, 200, 217 f, 223 ff, 227 ff, 230, 237, 241 f. See *Ransom*

Atonement, Day of, 75, 98, 119 f, 151, 171, 198, 201
Attis, 83, 90, 92
Augustine, 125, 211, 223; Western thought and, 225; on Sacrifice, 230; on Eucharist, 252
Australians, native, 13, 32, 34, 39, 61, 97, 268
Azazel, 115

B

Baal, 105 f, 144
Babylon, 35, 59, 68, 87, 111, 124, 138, 145, 293
Badagas, sacrifice among, 35
Bantu, sacrifice among, 35, 51
Baptists, close, 261
Barnabas, Epistle of, 190, 210, 219, 245 f, 258
Bacon, Francis, 241
Barton, G. A., 84
Basden, 75
Bentham, J., 239
Bertholet, A., 124
Bethel, 141. See *Israel, Sacrifice*
Bethesda, Pool of, 270
'Bhakti,' 130
Bleek, 34
Blood, significance of, in sacrifice, 104, 117 f, 191 f, 204, 235, 240
Borneo, sacrifice in, 35, 52
Brahmanism, 126, 130 f, 183
Brāhmanas, 59, 62, 64
Buddha, the. See *Gotama*
Buddhism, 126 ff, 139
Bull, Jehovah figured as, 118
Buphonia, Rite of, 72
Burkitt, F. C., 104
Burney, C. F., 115
Burnt-offering, 27, 104
Bushman drawings, 34
Butler, Josephine, 288

C

Caiaphas, 186
Calvary, relation of sacrifice to, 188, 210, 212, 241, 278
Calvinist Theology, 23, 230, 284
Canaanite influence on Hebrew sacrifice, 102, 105, 140

311

INDEX OF

Canon of the Mass, 254
Carlyle, 283
Catholicism, 22 f, 27, 61, 115, 117, 121, 211, 230, 233, 240 f
Centralization of Worship, Hebrew, 109
Ceylon, 127
China, 127
Christian Science, 22, 89
Chronicles, Books of, 98
Church, 23, 225, 255, 282 f, 301
Cilicia, 89
Clapham Sect, the, 22
Clemen, 79, 91
Clement of Alexandria, 78; on Eucharist, 250
Clement of Rome, 64, 245 f, 254
Code, Priests', 99, 101 f
Common Meal, the, 38, 78, 89
Communion. See *Eucharist*
Community, 53, 266 f
Compitalia, 74
Conservatism, Religious, 18
Cooke, G. A., 105
Cordelia, 289
Corinth, Eucharistic abuses at, 141
Corn-spirit, the, 41, 71
Covenant, Book of, 99 f
Crete, 68, 80
Crooke, W., 36
Cross, the, 16 f, 26, 181, 192 ff, 212, 216, 240, 258, 278
Crucifixion. See *Cross, the*
Crusades, 277
Cumont, 27, 87, 89, 91, 137, 247
Cybele, 83
Cynics, 134
Cyprian, on Priesthood, 117; on Eucharist, 250
Cyril of Jerusalem, 250 f

D

Dale, R. W., 233
Dante, 90
Darwin, 132, 293
Davenport, 84
David, 120, 288
Death of Christ, 178, 180 ff, 191, 193, 210, 228 f, 236, 273, 277, 287, 294
Decalogue, 100, 265
Decius, 186, 188
Demeter, 69, 77 f
Democritus, 133
Desire, 37, 46
Deuteronomic Code, 100, 107 f, 110, 197; reformation, 100, 109 f, 144
Dhammapada, 128

Diaspora, 184, 198
Didache, 64, 245
Dieterich, A., 90, 92
Diodorus, 86
Diognetus, Epistle to, 219
Dionysus, 76, 78, 80, 89
Dispersion, Jews of, 185
Domestication of cattle, 118
Driver, S. R., 100, 102, 112, 116, 308; and Neubauer, 151
Du Bois, 37
Duchesne, Père, on Mass, 255
Durkheim, E., 28, 38, 56, 97

E

Egypt, 59, 83, 122
Eleusinian Mysteries, 68, 77 ff, 80, 86, 89
Elijah, 99, 105, 140, 207
Ellis, A. B., 36
Elohist Document, 99 f
Emotion, 27, 37, 192, 212, 289
'Eniautos Daimon,' 74
Epictetus, 137
Epicurus, 136
Epidauria, Festival of, 77
Epimenides, 75
Ethnic Rites, 27, 178, 215. See *Sacrifice*
Etruscans, 35
Eucharist, 13, 26 ff, 79, 155, 167, 168, 169, 199, 245 ff, 260, 271
Euripides, 69, 76, 80
Evangelical Revival, Theology of, 231; Eucharist in, 259
Evans, A. J., 68
Evolution, 11
Example of Christ, 278
Exile, 110 f, 197
Exorcism, 255
Expiation and Sacrifice, 45 f, 235
Ezekiel, 120, 145 ff, 197, 205
Ezra, 101

F

Faith, 179, 229, 274 ff, 281 ff
Farnell, L. R., 68, 70, 72, 78, 79, 83
Farquhar, 119, 132
Fasting and Sacrifice, 61
Fat, 104, 119
Faust, 240
Fear and guilt in Greek religion, 75
Feast of Tabernacles, 167
Fellowship and Sacrifice, 48, 271
Fertility Sacrifices, 71
Fijians, 43
Five thousand, feeding of, 168 f

NAMES AND SUBJECTS   313

Flood, the, 45
Follett, M. P., 268
Forgiveness, 159 ff, 273 ff
Foucart, 68, 78
Fourth Gospel. See *John, Gospel of*
Fowler, W. W., 35, 72 ff
Franks, R. S., 218, 223
Frazer, J. G., 12 f, 35 f, 75, 83, 97, 119, 204
Freemasonry, 84
Frere, W. H., 95
Friends, Society of, 23, 232, 299
Fry, Elizabeth, 283

G

Gardner, A., 249, 252
Gardner, P., 79, 87, 162
Gethsemane, 212
Gezer, 103
Gideon, 288
Gilgal, 141
Gilgamesh Epic, 45, 111
Glover, T. R., 70
Good Shepherd, 160, 168, 170 f
Gotama, 128 f, 133, 136, 143, 158
Gratitude, 212
Greece, 59 ff, 95 f, 148 f, 271
Greek Naturalism in Ethics, 137
Greek Philosophy, a preparation for Christ, 139
Greek Religion, 96, 133 f; Guilt in, 75
Greek Theology, Atonement in, 221
Gregory the Great, on Eucharist, 252
Guilt, 75, 112

H

Hall, Fielding, 128
Hammond, Liturgies, 251
Hammond, J. H. and B., 22
Haoma, 90
Harnack, A., 207
Harrison, J. E., 68, 74, 83
Headlam, A. C., 271
Healing, 22
Hebrews, Epistle to, 200 ff, 203 f, 206 f
Heraclitus, 132 f
Heredity, 293
Hermas, 210, 219
Herodotus, 33, 87, 104, 270
Hezekiah, reforms of, 100, 109
High-priestly Prayer. See *Intercessory*
Hinduism, 32, 59 ff, 66 f, 95 f, 108, 111, 130 f, 133, 271
Hippolytus, 78

Hobbes, 269
Holiness, Code, 110, 120, 163; ceremonial, 149; Hebrew conception of, 109, 113
Homer, 68 f, 91
Horace, 52
Horus, 83
Hose and McDougall, 35, 52
Hosea, 41, 141 f, 184
Hubert et Mauss, 62 f, 65

I

Ignatius, 219, 246
Imagination, 184
India, 59 ff. See *Hinduism*
Innocent III, 255
Instincts, primary, 37
Intercessory Prayer, 170 ff, 310
Interests, 39
Ionian Philosophers, 132
Iranian Religion, 87 f
Irenaeus, 219; on Eucharist, 249
Isaiah, on Hebrew Sacrifice, 141 f, 147, 150
Isis, 83, 85, 88, 91
Islam, Sacrifice in, 14, 15, 85, 127
Israel, 42, 46, 48, 97 ff, 103 f, 105 f, 109, 140

J

Jainism, 129
James, Epistle of, 197
Japan, 52, 127
Jehovah, 105 ff, 113, 118, 140, 143, 270
Jenness and Ballantyne, 41
Jeremiah, 143 ff
Jerusalem, 109, 144 f, 184
Jesus, as Deliverer, 181, 294 f; faith in, 179 f; and forgiveness 161; intercessory prayer, 171; Lamb of God, 172; and Sacrifice, 29, 155 f, 159 f, 165, 168, 177; Son of God, 176 f, 208, 297; Son of Man, 176 f; a revelation, 278; Ritschl on, 179
Jevons, F. B., 78
John, Gospel of, 157 f, 167 ff, 184
John the Baptist, 159, 172
Josiah, reforms of, 100, 109 f, 143 f
Joy, realized in society, 267
Judah, 141 f, 143, 219 f. See also *Israel*
Judaism, 121, 149, 165, 219 f
Judas Maccabeus. See *Maccabees*
Julius, Pope, 284
Junod, H. A., 36, 51
Justice, 137, 236 ff

INDEX OF

Justin Martyr, 89, 165, 210, 246 f, 258
Juvenal, 81, 188, 267

K

Kaaba, the, 14 f, 110
Kaffirs, 35 f, 39
Kali Sacrifice, 65
Kant, 266
Karma, 126, 128
Kennedy, H. A. A., 22, 91
Kennett, R. H., 100
Kent, C. F., 100
Kern, 73
Kings, Books of, 98
Kinship and Sacrifice, 48; in Arabia, 97
Kipper, significance of, 124
Knopf, R., 249

L

Lactantius, 256
Lambeth Conference, 261
Lares, 41, 74
Last Supper, 162 ff
Latin Festivals, 73 f
Law of Moses. See *Moses*
League of Nations, 299
Legalism, 146, 147
Leontopolis, 122
Levites, 104
Levitical Priesthood, 159, 173, 241
Levitical Sacrifices, 162, 174 f, 241
Leviticus, Book of, 100, 163
'Lex Talionis,' 237
Lidgett, J. S., 218
Lietzmann, on Mass, 255
Life, the object of Sacrifice, 46
Lightfoot, 190
Lincoln, A., 288
Livy, 33
Local Shrines, 110
Loisy, 78, 86
Lollards, 283
Loofs, F., 224, 252
Love, 108, 303
Loveless, 284
Lucius. See *Apuleius*
Lucretius, 84, 133
Luther, M., 184, 225, 228 ff, 256, 283
Lysis. See *Plato*

M

Ma Bellona, 83
Macalister, R. A. S., 103, 218
Maccabees, 122
Mackintosh, R., 218
Magic and Sacrifice, 41, 55 f, 106, 270 f, 307
Maimonides, 220
'Mana,' 39, 47, 74, 93
Manasseh, 109, 118
Manias, Religious, 84
Mannhardt, W., 41
Manning, Cardinal, 301
'Manuals of the Altar,' 163
Marcus Aurelius, 137
Masai, the, 43, 51
Mass, 16, 27, 64, 111, 117, 121, 123, 253 ff
Matriarchate, the, 51
Mazzini, 179, 283
McCurdy, J. F., 100
McDougall, W., 37, 52
Melanchthon, 284
Melchizedek, 203
Mercy and Justice, not antithetic, 238
Merker, H., 51, 58
Mesha, 118
Messianic Hope, 183, 193
Methodism, 23, 182, 231
Mexico, 32, 59
Micah, 143, 197
Mill, J. S., 179, 283
Milton, 139, 223
Minucius Felix, 249
Mithra, 84, 87 ff, 92, 247
Mithraism, 87 ff, 137, 251
Mohammed, 150, 179. See *Islam*
Molema, 35
Monarchy, Hebrew, 99
Moral effects, of Justice, 238; of Punishment, 239
Moral ideas in Priestly Code, 120 ff
Moses, Law of, 17, 101, 183, 202, 265
Moulton, J. H., 13, 262
Moulton, W. J., 100
Mozley, J. K., 218
Müller, F. Max, 62
Murray, G., 93
Mysteries, Dionysiac, 76; Eleusinian, 77, 80; Samothracian and Cretan, 80; Isiac, 85; Mithraic, 87; interrelation of, 90
Mystery Religions, 82, 83 ff, 91 ff
Myths, 33

N

Nairne, 94, 201, 203
Nassau, R. H., 51
Nemesis, 270
Neo-Paganism, 23, 304
New Covenant, in Jeremiah, 144, 146; in Ezekiel, 146; in Epistle to Hebrews, 204

NAMES AND SUBJECTS 315

Newman, J. H., on the Mass, 253
New Testament, 273 ff
Nirvana, 128

O

Oesterley and Box, 245
Old Testament, 27; atonement in prophecy, 151; ideas of sacrifice, 98, 197, 272
Olympians, the, 68, 74, 132
Oman, J., 297, 304
'Orenda,' 39
Origen, 221, 250
Osiris, 83, 88 f

P

Paganism, 80
Paget, F., on Sacramental Grace, 253
Palestine, Canaanite sanctuaries in, 109
Parilia, 74
Parker, T., 197
Passover, 14, 33, 116, 164, 167, 189
Paul, 20, 141, 183 f; and death of Jesus, 187, 192 f; ethical teaching, 188, 190, 195, 199; sacrifice, 185 ff, 189 f, 196; Mysticism in, 279, 292
Pausanias, 70, 72
Peace-offering, 27, 104 f, 111
Pelasgians, 67
Pentateuch, 98 f, 102. See *Leviticus, Deuteronomic Code, Priests' Code*
Peripatetics, 136. See *Aristotle*
Personality, 56, 298
Perugino, 182
Pharisees, 184 ff, 189, 265
Philo, 201
Philosophy, influence of, in Greece, 138; in India, 149
Pity, 289 f
Plato, 74 f, 134 ff, 148, 150, 154
Pliny, letter to Trajan, 245
Plutarch, 35, 132
Plymouth Brethren, 261
Political developments, affecting Roman religion, 81
Polycarp, 248
Polycrates, 270
Poplifugia, 72
Post-exilic age, 116
Prayer, 51, 93
Pre-existence, of Jesus, 297
Preparatio Evangelica, 17, 199-200
Priesthood, 30, 104, 140, 307 ff
Priests' Code, 53, 60, 99 ff, 111, 114, 116, 119 ff, 151, 159

Primitive man, 34
Primitive ideas, 35
Proksch, 99
Propitiation, 38, 46, 54, 112, 191, 223
Prophets, 98, 140, 143, 158. See *Amos, Isaiah, Ezekiel*
Protestantism, 16, 21 f, 27, 233, 240, 253, 256 ff, 276
Psalms, 97 f, 186, 295
'Psanyi,' 51, 55, 111, 123
Psychology, 30 f, 36 ff, 234
Punishment, 152, 236 ff, 240
Purgatory, 240

Q

'Q,' 158
Quakers. See *Friends, Society of*

R

Rabbinism, of Paul, 184, 188
Race, 292; relation to Christ, 294
Ransom, 162, 180, 219, 221 f, 223, 226, 235
Rashdall, H., 20, 161, 172, 191, 218; on R. W. Dale, 233
Reason and Faith, 274
Reconciliation, 20, 23 ff, 120; Science of, 24; in Eucharist, 28; in mystery religions, 93; in Hindu cults, 96; and Buddhism, 128; questions involved in, 233 ff; true meaning of, 240; relation to society, 269, 298; and faith, 276; in history, 277; bearing on Christ's manhood, 289; in life of Jesus, 294, 296; Christ's reconciliation and ethnic sacrifices, 296; through personality, 298; task of Christian discipleship, 299; Church's doctrine of, 302; with man, condition of salvation, 303; both human and divine, 304 f
Reformation, 261, 277, 283
Reformed churches, 261
Regifugium, 72
Reitzenstein, 90, 91, 93
Religion and Magic. See *Magic*
Religion, communal, 56
Religious Institutions, 59
Repentance, Jesus and, 159
Republic of Plato, 135, 137
Restoration of Temple, 100
Retributive Justice, 236
Reunion and Eucharist, 262
Riddance ceremonies, 96, 114 f

'Rites de Passage,' 66
Rites, similarity of, 32
Ritschl, 179; on Atonement, 232
Ritter and Preller, 133
Ritual Dances, 52, 71, 76
Ritual Laws in Old Testament, 99, 101, 102; importance of, 121
Rivers, W. H. R., 34, 36
Robinson, J. A., 246
Rogers, R. W., 45
Roman Gods, character of, 74
Rome, 32, 35, 62, 108, 183, 254
Routh, 219
Ruskin, 283

S

Sabazius, 83
Sacrifice, universality of, 14; and Christianity, 16, 21 f; alien to modern world, 18, 21; significance of, 28 ff, 103, 214; and unseen world, 39; and bribery and expiation, 43 ff; savage, 50, 52; Roman, 52; Hindu, 53 ff, 65 ff; Ritual of, 61; Greek, 68 ff, 137; Agriculture and, 71; in Israel, 98 ff; and morality, 54, 107, 213 ff; reaction against, 126 ff, 131 ff, 139 ff; and Atonement, 149; Jesus and, 174 f, 211, 215; Communion with God, 48, 175, 271; Magic and, 271; aim of, 272; Faith and, 274
Sacrifices, human, 47, 118, 169
Sallust, 93
Salvation Army, 23
Salvation, plan of, 18
Salvation, tribal view of, 43
Samothrace, 80, 86
Sanday, W., 161; and Headlam, A. C., 189
Sankhya Philosophy, 130
Saracens, sacrifice among, 50
Satapatha Brāhmana, 62, 64
Saunders, 128
Savage Society, conditions of, 40
Scapegoat, the, 75, 115, 151, 190
Schism, and Eucharist, 260 f
Schoolmen, on Atonement, 225
Scotists, 228
Secrecy in Greek ritual, 77
Seligman, 34
Serapis, 83
Servant of Jehovah, 150 ff, 162, 173, 181, 206, 242
Servetus, 284
Shaftesbury, Lord, 22
Shakespeare, 37, 288

Sin, 108, 112 f, 120, 230, 242
Sin-offering, 112, 114
Sinai, 204
Smith, W. Robertson, 38, 50, 97
Social service and Church, 23
Social evils in Israel, 148
Socinianism, 277
Socrates, 134 f; compared with Jesus, 154, 283
Soden, von, 201, 207
Soma, 62 f, 90
Somaj, Arya, and Brahmo, 131
Son of God, 176, 185, 187; of man, 176
Spencer and Gillen, 34, 38
Spencer, H., 12
Stengel, P., 69
Stoics, 134, 136 f, 156, 266, 292, 297
Suffering and manhood of Christ, 288, 291; its emotional appeal, 289; analysis of, 290; moral value of, 291
Synagogue, 122
Syncretism, 248; in Hebrew religion, 102
Synoptists, 156 f, 160 f, 163, 166, 168, 180

T

Tabernacle, 201, 205
Tabernacles, Feast of, 167
Taboos, 58, 101, 104, 108, 110, 117, 153, 192
'Tamid,' 201
Temple, abuses in, 145; central in Judaism, 149; of Ezekiel, 101, 147; Jerusalem, 183, 201; in Egypt, 122; Paganism in, 147; Sacrifice, 166
'Templum,' 53, 62
Tertullian, 222; on Eucharist, 250
Thargelia, 75
Theodosius, 93
Theosophy, 23
Thessalonika, 185
Thongas, 44, 52, 55, 274
Thucydides, 35
Tintoret, 182
Todas, 34, 36, 119
Torquemada, 281
Totemism, 28, 38, 97, 268
Tout, C. H., 58
Trajan, 245
Transubstantiation, 252
Trent, Council of, 252
Trespass-offering, 112
Tribal gods, 41
Tridentine doctrine of Mass, 252

Trisagion, 254
Truce of God, 299
Trumbull, H. C., 204
Tylor, E. B., 12

U

Uncleanness, 113 f
Unseen, belief in, 39
Urim and Thummim, 140
Utilitarianism, 43, 266

V

Vedas, 59, 64 f, 111, 130, 149
Veddahs, the, 32, 34
Vergil, 47, 84
Verrall, 80
Vicarious Punishment, 230
Victim, function of, 177; death of, 178; at Passover, 189
Vincent, Père, 103
Virtue, 264, 266, 288

W

Webb, S. and B., 284, 301
Weismann, 293
Wellhausen, 97, 204
Wesley, C., 231, 259
Wesley, J., 22, 85, 228, 231, 233
Westcott, B. F., 167, 172, 301
Westermarck, 36, 47
Wieland, 246
Wilberforce, 22, 288
Woman of Samaria, 167
Works, salvation by, 180
Wundt, 43

X

Xenophanes, 39, 133

Y

'Yoma,' 62, 98, 116, 123, 124, 171

Z

Zahn, 207
Zarathustra, 87
Zeus, 72 f, 78, 136
Zionism, 14
Zwemer, 14
Zwingli, 27; on Eucharist, 257

INDEX OF SCRIPTURE REFERENCES

	PAGE
Gen. iv. 10	117
,, viii. 21	45, 111
,, xxii.	118
,, xxviii. 18	114
,, xxxi. 13	114
,, xxxii. 30	46
Exod. xx. 1-17	100
,, xxi. 1	99
,, xxiii. 19	99
,, xxxiv. 17-26	100
,, xxxiv. 26	119
,, xxxv.	102
Lev. i. ff	163
,, i. 9	196
,, iv. 1	112
,, v. 1	112
,, vi. 1	113
,, vi. 6	112
,, vi. 7	163
,, vi. 8 ff	163
,, vii. 38	163
,, x. 17	151
,, xiv.	156
,, xiv. 4	114
,, xvi.	115, 116
,, xvii. 11	124
Num. v. 15 ff	114
,, xiv. 33	151
,, xv. 24 ff	119
,, xv. 30	119
,, xix. 1-22	114
,, xxx. 15	151
Deut. iv. 24	207
,, xii.-xxvi.	100
,, xii. 15	104
,, xvii. 10	308
,, xvii. 12	119
,, xxi. 23	190
,, xxiv. 8	308
,, xxxiii. 10	308
Joshua viii. 3	221
Judges vi. 18	272
,, xvii. 13	104
1 Sam. ii. 13 ff	105
,, xiv. 18	308
,, xv. 22	140
,, xxi. 4 ff	43
,, xxiii. 6	308
,, xxvi. 19	110
,, xxx. 8	308
2 Sam. iv. 4	105
,, xxiv.	142
1 Kings xviii.	48
2 Kings iii. 27	118
,, xvi. 3	119
,, xvii. 17	119
,, xxi. 6	119
,, xxii.	100
,, xxiii.	100
1 Chron. viii. 33	105
2 Chron. xv. 3	308
Ps. xxvi. 6	123
,, xxvii. 6	123
,, xxxiv. 18	145
,, xl. 5	123, 145
,, xl. 6-8	202
,, l. 9	123, 145
,, l. 10	44
,, li.	119, 197
,, li. 16-27	145
,, lxvi. 13-15	123
,, lxxii.	106
,, lxxxiv.	117
,, xci.	114
,, cxxii.	117
,, cxxxvii. 4	110
,, cxlvi.	106
Isa. i. 16, 25	143
,, i. 18	282
,, vi. 5	46
,, xxxvii.	142
,, liii.	151-2, 173, 238
,, lvii. 15	145
,, lviii. 6	197
,, lxvi. 2	145
Jer. ii. 8	308
,, vii. 22	144
,, viii. 8	144
,, x. 12-25	144
,, xi. 1-8	144
,, xi. 15-23	144
,, xvii. 18	308
,, xxxi. 31	144, 202
,, xxxii. 35	119
,, xliv. 15 ff	145
Ezek. iv. 14 ff	145
,, vii. 26	308
,, viii. 6	145
,, xviii. 5	145
,, xviii. 6	112
,, xviii. 21	143
,, xxi. 21	35
,, xxxvi.	238
,, xxxvi. 22 ff	146
,, xxxvi. 26	143
,, xliii. 7	145
,, xliv. 9 ff	148
,, xlvi. 16	148
Hos. ii. 16	105
,, iii. 4	308
,, vi. 6	155
Mic. iv. 10	143
,, v. 12	143
,, vi.	119
,, vi. 7	118
,, vi. 8	197, 308
,, vii. 18	143
Mal. i. 11	246
Matt. v. 23-24	246
,, v. 24	123, 303
,, vi. 2-18	156
,, ix. 2	159
,, ix. 6	160
,, ix. 13	155
,, xii. 7	155
,, xii. 31	159
,, xiii. 19	240
,, xiv. 33	176
,, xvi. 8	221

SCRIPTURE REFERENCES

Matt. xvi. 16 176	John xvii. 168	Eph. i. 7 191
,, xvi. 18–19....157		,, ii. 6 194
,, xvi. 19 160	Acts ii. 42 244	,, ii. 13 191
,, xvii. 22 160	,, ii. 45–46 244	,, ii. 16 193
,, xviii.........159	,, x. 35 179	,, v. 2 189
,, xviii. 12 282	,, xiv. 13........ 96	
,, xviii. 18 160	,, xv. 20, 29 192	Phil. ii. 8 ......193, 196
,, xx. 19 160	,, xvii. 23 112	,, ii. 17 ....189, 196
,, xx. 28 ..160 f, 165	,, xix. 23 ff 96	,, ii. 25 196
,, xxi. 19 157		,, iii. 18 193
,, xxvi. 244	Rom. iii. 25 191	,, iv. 18 ....189, 196
,, xxvi. 2 160	,, iii. 28 282	
,, xxvi. 28..161, 162	,, iv. 7 221	Col. i. 20 ..191, 193, 194
	,, v. 6 187	,, ii. 14 ....193, 194
Mark i. 44 156	,, v. 9 191	
,, ii. 10 160	,, vii. 23–24 238	1 Thess. iv. 14 187
,, vi. 52 176	,, viii. 3........189	,, v. 10 187
,, vii. 4 159	,, viii. 32 196	
,, viii. 29 176	,, viii. 34 187	Heb. ii. 15 203
,, ix. 31 160	,, xii. 1 189	,, v. 4 202
,, x. 33 160	,, xiii. 6........196	,, vii. 27 201
,, x. 45....160, 161, 165	,, xv. 16 ..189, 196	,, viii. 8........202
		,, ix. 204
,, xiv. 24 ..161, 162	1 Cor. i. 13 193	,, ix. 15 205
,, xv. 39 176	,, i. 17 193	,, ix. 24 201
	,, i. 23 193	,, ix. 28 206
Luke i. 68 160	,, ii. 2 193	,, x. 4 204
,, ii. 38 160	,, ii. 8 193	,, x. 5 202
,, iii. 3 159	,, v. 7 189	,, x. 16 202
,, v. 14 156	,, viii. 1........192	,, xii. 2 193
,, v. 24 160	,, ix. 22 188	,, xii. 24 204
,, ix. 20 176	,, x. 16 191	,, xiii. 11 201
,, ix. 44 160	,, x. 18 189	,, xiii. 20 204
,, xi. 42....123, 157	,, x. 20 189	
,, xviii. 32 160	,, xi. 244	Jas. i. 27 197
,, xxii. 244	,, xi. 25 191	
,, xxii. 19 165	,, xi. 24 162	1 Pet. i. 2, 19 191
,, xxii. 20 ..161, 162	,, xv. 3–4 187	
,, xxiii. 47 176		1 John i. 7 191
,, xxiv. 21 160	2 Cor. ii. 15 196	,, iv. 20 303
	,, v. 14–15 187	
John ii. 21 168	,, v. 21 190	Rev. v. 6 ......170, 173
,, iii. 13 157	,, ix. 12 196	,, xi. 8 193
,, iii. 14 169	,, xiii. 4........193	
,, iv. 10, 13 f...167		Ecclus. xxxv. 123
,, vi. 168	Gal. i. 16 194	
,, vii. 37 167	,, iii. 1 193	2 Macc. ii. 10 207
,, vii. 39 168	,, iii. 13 190	4 Macc. vi. 28, 29 ..123
,, x. 15 168	,, v. 11 193	,, xvii. 22 123
,, xi. 50 186	,, v. 24 193	
,, xii. 32 165	,, vi. 12 ff 193	

www.ingramcontent.com/pod-product-compliance
Lightning Source LLC
Chambersburg PA
CBHW050622300426
44112CB00012B/1611